T0248805

Information Technology: Theory and Practice

Information Technology:
Theory and Practice

Edited by
Roberts Goddings

WILLFORD **P**RESS

www.willfordpress.com

Published by Willford Press,
118-35 Queens Blvd., Suite 400,
Forest Hills, NY 11375, USA

Copyright © 2018 Willford Press

This book contains information obtained from authentic and highly regarded sources. Copyright for all individual chapters remain with the respective authors as indicated. All chapters are published with permission under the Creative Commons Attribution License or equivalent. A wide variety of references are listed. Permission and sources are indicated; for detailed attributions, please refer to the permissions page and list of contributors. Reasonable efforts have been made to publish reliable data and information, but the authors, editors and publisher cannot assume any responsibility for the validity of all materials or the consequences of their use.

Trademark Notice: Registered trademark of products or corporate names are used only for explanation and identification without intent to infringe.

ISBN: 978-1-68285-477-8

Cataloging-in-Publication Data

Information technology : theory and practice / edited by Roberts Goddings.
p. cm.
Includes bibliographical references and index.
ISBN 978-1-68285-477-8
1. Information technology. I. Goddings, Roberts.
T58.5 .I54 2018
004--dc23

For information on all Willford Press publications
visit our website at www.willfordpress.com

Contents

Permissions

List of Contributors

Index

Preface

The process of using computers for studying, transmitting and manipulating data falls under the field of information technology. Some of its allied fields include computer hardware and software, e-commerce, internet, telecommunications, etc. Data storage, data retrieval and database management are the key aspects of information technology. This book is a valuable compilation of topics, ranging from the basic to the most complex advancements in this field. This book, with its detailed analyses and data, will prove immensely beneficial to professionals and students involved in this area at various levels.

This book is a result of research of several months to collate the most relevant data in the field.

When I was approached with the idea of this book and the proposal to edit it, I was overwhelmed. It gave me an opportunity to reach out to all those who share a common interest with me in this field. I had 3 main parameters for editing this text:

1. Accuracy – The data and information provided in this book should be up-to-date and valuable to the readers.

2. Structure – The data must be presented in a structured format for easy understanding and better grasping of the readers.

3. Universal Approach – This book not only targets students but also experts and innovators in the field, thus my aim was to present topics which are of use to all.

Thus, it took me a couple of months to finish the editing of this book.

I would like to make a special mention of my publisher who considered me worthy of this opportunity and also supported me throughout the editing process. I would also like to thank the editing team at the back-end who extended their help whenever required.

Editor

Hierarchy and the Nature of Information

Ron Cottam [1,*], Willy Ranson [2,†] and Roger Vounckx [1,†]

Academic Editors: Mark Burgin and Wolfgang Hofkirchner

[1] The Living Systems Project, Department of Electronics and Informatics, Vrije Universiteit Brussel (VUB), Pleinlaan 2, Brussels B-1050, Belgium; rvounckx@etro.vub.ac.be

[2] Interuniversity Micro Electronics Center (IMEC) vzw, Kapeldreef 75, Leuven B-8001, Belgium; wranson@etro.vub.ac.be

* Correspondence: ricottam@etro.vub.ac.be
† These authors contributed equally to this work.

Abstract: We address the nature of information from a systemic structural point of view. Starting from the Natural hierarchy of living systems, we elucidate its decomposition into two partial hierarchies associated with its extant levels and inter-level regions, respectively. External observation of a hierarchical system involves the generation of approximate hyperscalar representations of these two partials, which then reintegrate to give a singular metascalar result. We relate Havel's categories of reality and Peirce's categories of experience to this result, and indicate that the ultimate result of the reintegration of hyperscalar data and context is a sign which is information.

Keywords: hierarchy; hyperscale; metascale; Ivan Havel; Charles Peirce; information

1. Introduction

Nature tends towards hierarchical relationships. Unfortunately, conventional views of hierarchy do not provide an all-inclusive representation of the properties of a hierarchical system. Either we are restricted to a representation in which differently sized entities are nested within each other (e.g., atoms, molecules, cells ... called a scalar or compositional hierarchy by Salthe [1]), or one in which there is no simple extant link between the different descriptive levels of the system (e.g., physics, chemistry, biology ... called a specification or subsumption hierarchy by Salthe [1]). The situation is complicated by the pragmatic tendency of evolution to scavenge prior existing features in creating new ones, and consequently biology does not uniquely exhibit hierarchical configurations. For example, "What serves for thermoregulation is re-adapted for gliding; what was part of the jaw becomes a sound receiver; guts are used as lungs and fins turn into shovels. Whatever happens to be at hand is made use of" [2]. Consequently, although we believe that the Nature tends towards the hierarchical relationships we describe, this may not always be apparent in the results of evolution. Gilaie-Dotan *et al.* [3], for example, have demonstrated non-hierarchical functioning in the human cortex. A second aspect is that massive information processing, as in the brain, is faster in paralleled structures. This leads to the heterarchical character of neural networks, although the compression of parallel processing to the serial output required for muscle action takes place through hierarchical structures. Dodig-Crnkovic and Giovagnoli [4] have described Nature as a hierarchically organized network of networks, which corresponds to our own viewpoint.

Salthe has published extensively on the concept of hierarchy (see, for example, [1]). While he has before now expressed to the authors that hierarchy is a human mental construct, devoid of any other reality, we note that in [5] with Eldredge, for example, he takes a more ontological position (in reference to Salthe's 1975 book, among other references, they state that "The several concrete proposals of this kind ... have for the most part been constructed only from an epistemological perspective").

Hierarchy permits the generation of simple representations of complex informational domains, thus supporting faster survival-promoting reactions to environmental stimuli, and as such it is a primary cognitive mechanism used by all living systems, not just humans. This, of course, raises the question of the validity of representation in information theory. Our own position is clearly that representation is a necessary "computational" device for survival and therefore for evolution itself. Any other position would negate the importance of hierarchy in Nature. As Dodig-Crnkovic and Giovagnoli [4] comment in their discussion of connectionist approaches, " . . . it is correct that there is 'no computation without representation'".

We present a radically different representation of hierarchy from Salthe's two variants—a *model hierarchy*—which is on a higher organizational plane when compared to the two preceding representations, and which is in fact the parent of both of them [6]. It is worth noting that this formulation of a model hierarchy automatically includes heterarchy in its purview, as individual model layers can be formulated as neural networks, for example.

Current approaches to the definition of information lack attention to *this particular* model-hierarchical character of Nature. Information is most often defined on the basis of order or entropy, but it is questionable whether this approach is valid for living systems, where a duality of order or entropy is prevalent [6]. We find it parsimonious to first define information with respect to the Natural (living) hierarchy—where the greatest complications and complexity are found—and then to reduce this formulation where necessary to correspond to a simpler specific context: we will address this aspect later in the paper.

We will first look at the general properties of a model hierarchy in its context of representing a living system, and then tackle the thorny problem of external access to hierarchical scales, leading to the definition of hyperscale and the reintegrative character of metascale. Next we will look at the relationships between this formulation and the work of Ivan Havel [7] and Charles Peirce [8], which will lead us to a derivation of information in Natural hierarchies.

2. Hierarchical Systems

Figure 1 illustrates our general representational form of a *model hierarchy*. It is vital to note that this kind of representation *is not* consistent with, most particularly, a composition hierarchy. A model hierarchy is an entirely new kind of representation, which is generic to other hierarchical schemes. We cannot emphasize this enough: understanding of the way a model hierarchy "operates" requires complete disconnection from other more conventional and, at first sight, similar arrangements. We make the bold move of proposing that this representation is primarily ontological in character, as we will describe later in the paper. The different levels of such a hierarchy are NOT nested within each other, as are those of a composition hierarchy, while individual levels refer to different specifications of the described system, in a manner similar to those of a subsumption hierarchy (Salthe himself has referred to a model hierarchy as "a subsumption hierarchy constructed in terms of scale"!).

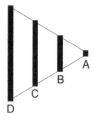

Figure 1. The simple representation of a model hierarchy. Vertical line length indicates how much information is necessary to set up the local model.

Other hierarchical relationships for information have been previously published (e.g., recently [9,10]), but none of these are related to the present exposition, in that the published proposals do not have the generality of character of a model hierarchy. Most particularly, the work of Floridi (e.g., [11]) on Levels of Abstraction is not directly relatable to the hierarchical scheme described in this paper, as he is solely referring to views of a system from outside—his Levels of Abstraction are a guide to epistemological experience rather than references to ontology, unlike the levels in a model hierarchy. A second point of disagreement, although Floridi would describe a model hierarchy as a *gradient of abstractions*, is that in our representation all of the levels of the scheme are coupled together to create a self-consistent whole, and local events or structures (*i.e.*, generally, models and transits between them) are specifically controlled by global properties (and, of course, *vice versa*). It is worth noting here Havel's [7] insistence that things and events are only distinguished by differences in time scale: "In the world of all scales there is no essential difference: things are just long-lasting events and events are just short-lived things, where -long- and -short- are relative with respect to our temporal scale perspective".

Figure 2 illustrates the basic nature of a model hierarchy. It is important to note that complexity is engendered as soon as modeling is attempted; consequently, a modeled system always exists within a more-or-less complex phase space, as indicated in the figure. We do not address here the way in which a model hierarchy is instantiated or evolves, merely the form which it ultimately exhibits (the startup problem is one which besets analysis and synthesis of all kinds of scientific endeavors). We have portrayed the system in terms of a graph in Figure 3; the most difficult aspect of this is that the graph axes are uncommon in that they are automatically nonlinear and possibly discontinuous—thus the simplification which we make in our habitual representations of a model hierarchy (e.g., as in Figure 1). The vertical axis describes the degree of Rosennean complexity [12] at particular locations in the phase space, while the horizontal axis is more problematic in terms of its definition (Rosen's definition of complexity is in terms of representational incompleteness: he defines complexity as a situation which is not simulable except by application of an infinite number of different representations). Havel [7] has characterized investigative endeavors in terms of three descriptions: he refers to *absolute*, *subjective* and *objective* representations. We will meet all of these three later in the paper, but for the moment we will retain solely the *absolute*, which, for Havel, is a purely ontological description. A further significant aspect of Havel's work [7] is the development of his idea of *scale*. This is a purely *relative* concept, which refers to the "distance" in terms of the size of a feature or event from the location in terms of "size" which is the focus of interest. We believe that the best characterization of the horizontal axis in Figure 1 is as a combination of these two parts of Havel's work: it is an *absolute* (ontological) formulation of Havel's *scale*. It is, therefore, easy to see how a model hierarchy could be unfortunately mistaken for a composition hierarchy. Figure 2 indicates how a survivalist tendency to promote "computational ease" creates islands of simplicity within the co-generated complex phase space of a system. These islands appear as Newtonian potential wells, and the evolution of their depth results in local complexity being "dumped" out of them and into the local phase space. The net result of evolution, therefore, is of a pair of identifiable local features: one which is a comparatively easy-to-compute simplified model, and the other which is the consequent "ecosystem" from which it has apparently "emerged". It is clear in this scheme that the resulting extant "scales" are *not* nested within each other—they are local individual emergences from the global systemic phase space. Habitually in hierarchical representation, there is a clear distinction between the hierarchy of control and the hierarchy of organization. This, however, is not the case for a model hierarchy, such as is discussed here: different hierarchical levels consist of systemic models, which can imply either control, or organization (information systems or matter-and-energy exchange), or any one of these. We believe that this model-hierarchical representation of Nature is more ontologically correct than that implied by other lower-level representations, such as a composition hierarchy, which implies the necessity for a completely new look at our presuppositions about the emergence of Nature from the big bang, and of its consequent evolution.

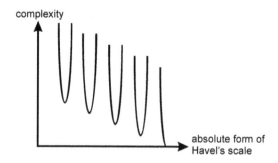

Figure 2. The representation of a system in terms of a complex phase space with localized extant levels or scales which appear as Newtonian potential wells that present a simplified route to effective survivalist "computation".

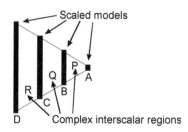

Figure 3. A model hierarchy, indicating the different model levels A, B, C, D and the inter-scalar complex regions P, Q, R.

We will always portray a hierarchy lying on its side, as in Figure 1, because we do not believe that in a Natural hierarchy the conventionally indicated "top" of the hierarchy has precedence or overall control. The length of the vertical lines indicates the amount of *information* required to circumscribe the associated model: more complicated models require more information, and in the figure the simplest, or highest, level of the hierarchy is on the right-hand side (labeled "A") as indicated by the line lengths. The word "information" appears somewhat awkwardly here, as we will later define information as appearing at a completely different location in a hierarchy; it is tempting to use "data" instead, but this would give a wrong impression—we will later address this question of "information" or "data" appearing in different guises in different functional locations. With the aim of consolidating this approach, it is easy to see how this representation could describe a business organization, for example, where A would be the chief executive, B the vice-executives, C the middle management and D the workforce. We must again insist that we are here talking about a *model* hierarchy and *not* a composition hierarchy!

Regions in between the extant models (e.g., between B and C) are complex in character. This mirrors the unexpected difficulty with an "equation" such as 1 + 1 = 2. There is no way that we can independently and logically derive the 2 from 1 + 1—fortunately, it is a result defined in number theory so we never have to! Such an "equation" is, in fact, both hierarchical and partially irreversible: given that we have moved from left to right, we then lack sufficient information to say what was initially on the left-hand side (it could well have been 1 + 1, but equally well 4 − 2 or 8/4!). The complex regions between levels of a model hierarchy are similar in character: not only is it impossible to purely logically carry out the transit between, for example, C and B in the figure, but having done so we lack sufficient information to logically return to C. This seems, at first sight, to be a trivial property, but it controls everything that takes place in a Natural hierarchy.

The complex inter-model regions have yet another important characteristic. If we consider, for example, model C in the figure, then it is clear that it is just a reduced representation of the entire system itself. The model, however, invisibly "contains" a large amount of information which is absent from its formulation (in our example of a business structure, the model C of middle management misses out most of the characteristics of the work force D which it represents). This missing (or "contained") information is itself represented in the complex region leading up to C (by way of the globality of communications linking the work force D to and from middle management C). Figure 3 illustrates the complicated character of a Natural hierarchy. Transit from model D to model C passes through complex region R where there is an absence of simple logical relationships. This indicates the biggest problem when dealing with a Natural hierarchy: if the inter-scalar regions are so complex (in fact, they are multiply fractal in character [6]), then how on earth can we deal with relations between adjacent models? Possibly the most important aspect of Natural hierarchy is that knowledge of the entire system's global properties is required to deal with local inter-scalar transit [6].

In Figure 3, model A is very limited, and, consequently, its "contained" information appearing in region P is very extensive. Model B is more complicated, so its "contained" information in region Q is more constrained, and so on. Figure 4 illustrates this situation. The black lines, as before, represent the local system models; the gray regions represent the associated "contained" or "hidden" information (it is tempting to associate this "contained" or "hidden" information with the "hidden variables" found in, for example, David Bohm's formulation of quantum theory; we believe that this association is justified). Intuitively, this set of gray regions forms a second partial hierarchy in opposition to the first one. This provides us with the general form of a Natural hierarchy [13]. The gray complex regions in Figure 4 (e.g., Q in Figure 3) operate as locally constructed scaled representations of the system's environment—regions from which their associated models (e.g., B in Figure 3) have emerged.

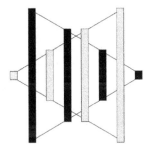

Figure 4. The relationship between the two contra-oriented hierarchies. Black lines indicate the local models; gray regions indicate their associated "contained" information.

3. The Generation of Hyperscale

As we have indicated in Figure 4, the two (partial) hierarchies are interleaved in a single structure. It will be convenient in this context, however, for us to draw them out separately as shown in Figure 5. From here on in we will retain this convenient fictitious separation.

Figure 5. The two partial hierarchies drawn out separately for convenience.

We have pointed out already the difficulty of transiting between the adjacent model levels of a Natural hierarchy. The problem, however, is much more serious than that. At some point in our argument we must take into account the location from which we are observing the hierarchy. If it represents ourselves, we must define from which scale we are observing the structure. If, however, it represents a living system different from ourselves, we must be looking in from the outside. In conjunction with the problem of inter-scalar transit, this makes it virtually impossible to know what is happening inside the hierarchy, and, in particular, it is impossible to access the different models themselves to any degree of accuracy. This is surprising, as we are apparently mentally capable of systematically addressing all the different scales of a living entity.

Nature has come up with a neat solution to this problem. We generate, from outside a Natural hierarchy, a high-level approximate representation of all of the internal scales, which we can then make use of as if it were the hierarchy itself [14]. This representation, illustrated in Figure 6, is called *hyperscale*. Not only is this representation generated in terms of observation from outside a living entity, it is a property of the living entity itself—automatically generated internally as a step towards being able to represent itself to its environment in a chosen manner (e.g., through evolution, biological cells have been shut off from their environment by their lipid layer, which then permits advantageous channels of communication between them and their environments).

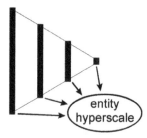

Figure 6. The establishment of a hyperscalar representation of the internal scales of a Natural hierarchy.

We must not forget that our derivation resulted in *two* partial hierarchies. Consequently, we will have two hyperscalar representations (Figure 7), one for the entity itself and one for its context or environment.

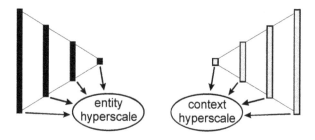

Figure 7. The generation of a hyperscalar representation for *both* of the partial hierarchies in a Natural hierarchy.

4. Hyperscale Reintegration and Metascale

As we intimated earlier, the two separate hierarchies are only partially independent—they are both part of the same system description. It turns out to be a major characteristic, most particularly of living systems but also marginally of non-biological systems, that all aspects of a complete system are partially independent, partially coupled. Living systems exhibit this partiality more strongly than non-biological systems for two reasons: firstly because their scalar character is more complex, and secondly because their inter-scalar transits are more difficult as these regions are more complexly fractal. Specifically for living systems, we find that the two hierarchies are partially coupled, the two hyperscales are partially independent, and those hyperscales are ultimately reintegrated to give a singular system unification in the form of *metascale* (see Figure 8).

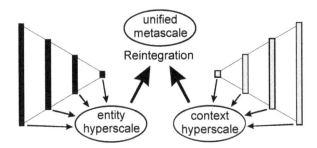

Figure 8. Reintegration of the two hyperscales to give a singular unified *metascalar* representation.

We have here described these processes as a temporal sequence, but more realistically they are temporally unified, and consequently the overall character of a Natural hierarchy is one of unification, and the dual nature of its internal processes is not necessarily evident from outside. So, hyperscale is itself a dual concept: living entities generate it internally themselves, and it is also constructed in the mind of an observing cognitive agent. For an external cognitive agent, the processes of hyperscale generation and metascalar reintegration are part of an epistemological experience.

5. Havel's Categories of Reality

Ivan Havel [7] has circumscribed the ontological character of Nature by three levels of "reality". He characterizes the underlying ontological character of Nature as absolute: a level of reality which is fundamental but inaccessible to direct investigation. He accepts the conventional "subjective" character as that pertaining to a single cognitive being.

However, his take on "objective" is very different (see Figure 9). Havel points out that what we call "objective" is the common acceptance by a majority of human agents of the results of their epistemological experiences: he re-formulates "objective" as a group subjective. In our present context of hierarchy we can find all of these three levels of description. The two partial hierarchies—whose internal properties are directly inaccessible—correspond to Havel's absolute. A version of his objective corresponds to the integration of the different systemic scales into an externally accessible hyperscalar representation, and the unified metascalar representation corresponds to his (or conventional) subjective.

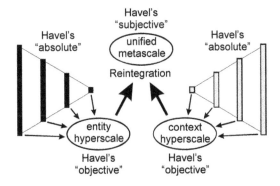

Figure 9. The correspondence between parts of the hierarchical system description and Havel's absolute, objective and subjective descriptions.

6. Peirce's Categories of Experience

Charles Peirce's [8] semiotic approach to Nature categorizes the character of experience into three levels—firstness, secondness and thirdness:

firstness, as a quality of feeling (referenced to an abstraction);
secondness, as an actuality (referenced to a correlate);
thirdness, as a forming of habits (referenced to an interpretant).

In his semiotics, everything is a sign. Nothing "exists" except as a sign. "Redness" is a sign:

- the quality or feeling of redness...where you are aware of it as "something existent" but not conscious of it as distinct and "red"...is *firstness*;
- when you are aware that "there's a distinct and unique experience of 'redness' in my vision"...that is *secondness*. It is distinct; you can define it as unique in itself in that time and space;
- when you are talking about that experience in the abstract or generality, for example, "when it's going to be a nice day tomorrow, there is always a redness in the sky at sunset" . . . that is *thirdness* (we are indebted to Edwina Taborsky for this succinct comparison of firstness, secondness and thirdness).

If we associate Peirce's three levels with our description of Natural hierarchy, we get Figure 10. The process leading to the formulation of hyperscale (referenced to an abstraction) corresponds to firstness; hyperscalar representation itself (referenced to a correlate) corresponds to secondness; the reintegration process leading to the unification of metascale (referenced to an interpretant) corresponds to thirdness; the metascalar representation itself is a *sign*, where the interpretant is the cognitive organism in its subjectivity.

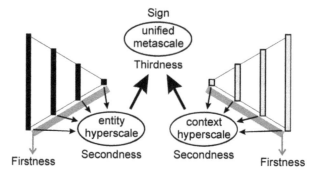

Figure 10. The correspondence of Peirce's three levels of experience with regions of the dual-to-singular hierarchical representation.

7. The Derivation of Information

It is unfortunate that the English language is relatively poor in words which relate to different levels of completeness of epistemological content, and in the precise characterization of meaning of such words as exist. This aspect relates also to our earlier comment on the common use of the word "information" in different epistemological settings. At the lowest level of definition, in this work we take data to be elements of epistemological observation which are devoid of contextual clarification, for example an abstract number or a word isolated from its sentence. On the other hand, at the highest level of definition we take *information* to be a *complete* epistemological experience, so far as we are able to define it. This means that information effectively constitutes *data* in its *most complete available context*. However, given the impossibility we have described to unequivocally observe from outside the internal scalar levels of a hierarchical system, the nature of the content of those levels will be less well defined externally than internally.

Consequently, although when viewed from outside the scalar content of a hyperscalar representation may appear to be complete, its approximated origin precludes completeness either of content or context. This suggests that we would need other words to relate to content which is intermediate between data and information. However, far more scientific attention to hierarchy will need to exist before such words are automatically forthcoming. Suffice it to say that when viewed from its own level, the content of a hierarchical scale is correctly described as information, while its appearance from outside the model of partial hierarchy is less correctly described as such.

The dissociation of scalar model levels from the complex inter-scalar regions in a hierarchy, and the recognition that a specific scalar level is derived from its local complex layer, means that this is a (partial) separation of data from context, as indicated in Figure 11. Reintegration of these two (partial) characters then gives a unified metascale, as shown in the figure. Conventionally, cognition is only associated with neural processing, but a wider view is beginning to prevail, where the activity of non-neural organisms is included in the definition. For example, amoebas can hunt their prey and orient themselves with respect to infrared light, although they have no neurons; plant roots are related to neural cells, and in the related domain of study their actions are associated with the concept of cognition (see, for example [15]).

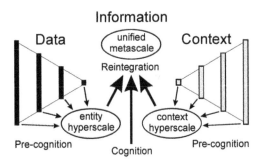

Figure 11. The derivation of information from the two partial hierarchies via the two (partial) hyperscales pertaining to data and context.

We hypothesize that the reality of a singular metascale corresponds to information *per se*: as Schroeder [16] points out, " . . . information has been formulated as identification of a variety, where identification is understood as that which either selects, distinguishes one out of many, or that which makes the many into one (a whole)". This high-level metascalar formulation incorporates the properties of all of a living system's scalar properties in such a unified form that individual selection is also possible: it combines Schroeder's [17] "two complementary manifestations of information".

In Peircian terms (Figure 10), information is a *sign* which exists as the *content* of an *interpretant*.

8. Information in Less-than-Hierarchical Systems

It is a moot point whether a non-hierarchical arrangement can be called a system. Systems always include life at some level of their reality [18], and life is always multi-scalar. Be that as it may, we should look at the derivation of information in non-hierarchical situations. Surprisingly, there is no difference from the hierarchical case. Even a single-leveled "system" must be examined from outside (which is an apparent scalar difference), leading to the generation, in our mind, of an approximate hyperscalar representation of the single level. After that, things progress in much the same way as for the hierarchical case to the mental creation of a metascalar representation.

But what about Shannon's [19] single-level definition of information, for example? Surely this will be different, precise and accurate as it appears to be? Well, no. Order and entropy are external representations of internal properties. The difference here is that if we are in a clearly non-living situation, the "inter-scalar" difference between inside and outside views is negligible, and Shannon's formula gives good correspondence with other theoretical derivations or measurements. Consequently, the primary criterion for information definition is whether we are addressing a living setting or not. Our own context in doing so is clearly a living one, and this is the basic aspect of the entire scale-to-hyperscale-to-metascale sequence we have described.

Acknowledgments: The authors gratefully acknowledge the support of the Vrije Universiteit Brussel and the Interuniversity Micro Electronics Center vzw in carrying out the research upon which this paper is based.

Author Contributions: All three authors contributed equally in developing the concepts involved in this work. The paper itself was written by Ron Cottam and Willy Ranson.

Conflicts of Interest: The authors declare no conflict of interest.

References

1. Salthe, S.N. Hierarchical structures. *Axiomathes* **2012**, *22*, 355–383. [CrossRef]
2. Sigmund, K. *Games of Life: Explorations in Ecology, Evolution, and Behavior*; Oxford University Press: New York, NY, USA, 1993.
3. Gilaie-Dotan, S.; Perry, A.; Bonneh, Y.; Malach, R.; Bentin, S. Seeing with profoundly deactivated mid-level visual areas: Non-hierarchical functioning in the human visual cortex. *Cereb. Cortex* **2009**, *19*, 1687–1703. [CrossRef] [PubMed]
4. Dodig-Crnkovic, G.; Giovagnoli, R. Computing nature—A network of networks of concurrent information processes. In *Computing Nature*; SAPERE Series; Dodig-Crnkovic, G., Giovagnoli, R., Eds.; Springer: Berlin/Heidelberg, Germany, 2013; pp. 1–22.
5. Eldredge, N.; Salthe, S.N. Hierarchy and Evolution. In *Oxford Surveys in Evolutionary Biology—Volume 1*; Oxford University Press: Oxford, UK, 1984; pp. 184–208.
6. Cottam, R.; Ranson, W.; Vounckx, R. A framework for computing like Nature. In *Computing Nature*; SAPERE Series; Dodig-Crnkovic, G., Giovagnoli, R., Eds.; Springer: Berlin/Heidelberg, Germany, 2013; pp. 23–60.
7. Havel, I.M. Scale dimensions in nature. *Int. J. Gen. Syst.* **1995**, *23*, 303–332. [CrossRef]
8. Peirce, C.S. *Collected Papers of Charles Sanders Peirce*; Hartshorne, C., Weiss, P., Burks, A., Eds.; Belknap Press: Cambridge, MA, USA, 1932.
9. Casini, L.; Illari, P.M.; Russo, F.; Williamson, J. Models for prediction, explanation and control: Recursive bayesian networks. *Theoria* **2011**, *70*, 5–33.
10. Clarke, B.; Gillies, D.; Illari, P.; Russo, F.; Williamson, J. Mechanisms and the evidence hierarchy. *Topoi* **2014**, *33*, 339–360. [CrossRef]
11. Floridi, L. The Method of Levels of Abstraction. *Minds Mach.* **2008**, *18*, 303–329. [CrossRef]
12. Rosen, R. *Life Itself*; Columbia UP: New York, NY, USA, 1991.
13. Cottam, R.; Ranson, W.; Vounckx, R. Autocreative hierarchy I: Structure—Ecosystemic dependence and autonomy. *SEED J.* **2004**, *4*, 24–41.
14. Cottam, R.; Ranson, W.; Vounckx, R. Living in hyperscale: Internalization as a search for reunification. In Proceedings of the 50th Annual Conference of the International Society for the Systems Sciences, Rohnert Park, CA, USA, 9–14 July 2006; Wilby, J., Allen, J.K., Loureiro-Koechlin, C., Eds.; Curran Associates, Inc.: North Miami Beach, FL, USA, 2013; pp. 1–22.
15. Garzón, P.C. Plants: Adaptive behavior, root-brains, and minimal cognition. *Adapt. Behav.* **2011**, *19*, 155–171. [CrossRef]
16. Schroeder, M.J. Foundations for science of information: Reflection on the method of inquiry. *Triplec* **2011**, *9*, 377–384.
17. Schroeder, M.J. From philosophy to theory of information. *Inf. Theor. Appl.* **2011**, *18*, 56–68.
18. Cottam, R.; Ranson, W.; Vounckx, R. Life and simple systems. *Syst. Res. Behav. Sci.* **2005**, *22*, 413–430. [CrossRef]
19. Shannon, C.E. A mathematical theory of communication. *Bell Syst. Tech. J.* **1948**, *27*, 379–423 & 623–656. [CrossRef]

2

The Treewidth of Induced Graphs of Conditional Preference Networks Is Small

Jie Liu and Jinglei Liu *

School of Computer and Control Engineering, Yantai University, Yantai 264005, China; 1634034956@qq.com
* Correspondence: jinglei_liu@sina.com

Academic Editor: Willy Susilo

Abstract: Conditional preference networks (CP-nets) are recently an emerging topic as a graphical model for compactly representing ordinal conditional preference relations on multi-attribute domains. As we know, the treewidth, which can decrease the solving complexity for many intractability problems, is exactly a fundamental property of a graph. Therefore, we can utilize treewidth to solve some reasoning tasks on induced graphs, such as the dominance queries on the CP-nets in the future. In this paper, we present an efficient algorithm for computing the treewidth of induced graphs of CP-nets; what we need is to make an assumption that the induced graph of a CP-net has been given. Then, we can leverage the *Bucket Elimination* technique to solve treewidth within polynomial time. At last, it is revealed that by our experiment, the treewidth of induced graphs of CP-nets is much smaller with regard to the number of vertices. For example, for an induced graph of CP-net with 1024 vertices, its treewidth is only 10. As far as we know, this is the first time, using the *Bucket Elimination*, to compute the treewidth of an induced graph of a CP-net. This approach for solving the treewidth may lay a good foundation for efficiently solving dominance queries on CP-nets in the future.

Keywords: conditional preference networks; induced graph; treewidth; bucket elimination; dominance queries

1. Introduction

Conditional preference networks (CP-nets) [1,2] have permeated our daily life as a specific graphical model. As a novel graphical tool, it has been used for representation and reasoning preference by the intuitive and compact preference statements since 1999. Recently, CP-nets have also played a crucial role in the areas of decision theory [3,4], recommender systems [5], and databases [6]. Many graph problems, however, are NP-hard [7]; the induced graphs of CP-nets are no exception. Parameter calculation theory [8,9] has provided strong support to solve NP-hard problems in recent years. Treewidth was coined by Robertson and Seymour on graph minors [10], which provides some new ideas for researching graphical models, such as probabilistic reasoning, constraint satisfaction, and knowledge representation and reasoning. CP-nets are a graphical model for compactly representing conditional qualitative preference relations [1,11]. Therefore, various queries and operations have been carried out on the induced graphs of CP-nets. It is well known that most combinatorial optimization problems are NP-complete problems. Luckily, however, these NP-complete problems will be solved in polynomial time if the treewidth of the input graph is bounded by a constant. Namely, ordering queries and dominance queries with respect to acyclic CP-nets will be answered efficiently in the number of variables if the treewidth of induced graphs of CP-nets have been obtained.

In this paper, we investigate how to compute the treewidth of induced graphs of CP-nets in Section 4.2. When the treewidth of induced graphs of CP-nets is computed by our algorithm, some reasoning tasks will become rather simple. For example, let us consider the evening dress case [1]—CP-nets express a user's preference for evening dress, we then work out the treewidth of its induced graph. Obviously, some operations, such as dominance queries [1], can be solved quickly. We apply a heuristic search method, *Bucket Elimination* [12], to find the treewidth of induced graphs of CP-nets. Though our algorithm seems to be applicable to undirected induced graphs of CP-nets, in Darwiche's textbook [13], the authors introduce the process of how to *moralize* a directed graph into a undirected graph. This method can be used in the induced graphs for CP-nets. The goal of our research, as well as the focus of this paper, is to apply heuristic search techniques to the problem of finding the treewidth of induced graphs of CP-nets of real world interest.

The main contributions of this work are threefold.

1   We explore the treewidth problem about the induced graphs of CP-nets— as far as we know, there is no literature availlable to study the treewidth characterization of induced graphs of CP-nets.
2   We design a more efficient algorithm to solve the treewidth of induced graphs of CP-nets utilizing a *Bucket Elimination* approach; this approach uses the randomness characteristics of input order to speed search.
3   We find that the treewidth of induced graphs of CP-nets is very small; this interesting discovery may lay the foundation for designing an algorithm for solving tractable reasoning tasks, such as dominance queries, in the future.

The remainder of this paper is organized as follows: Section 2 provides background on treewidth and some important notions—tree decomposition of a graph, CP-nets, and induced graphs of CP-nets. In Section 3, we introduce related work of treewidth and CP-nets. In Section 4, we present an algorithm to compute the treewidth of induced graphs of CP-nets, in the meantime providing a detailed example to illustrate the performing procedure of the algorithm. In Section 5, we explain our experimental setup and metrics, and give our experimental results in simulated data. Finally, we discuss a number of interesting directions for future theoretical research and applications in Section 6.

2. Background on Treewidth and CP-nets

Below, we first give a more detailed introduction of the necessary concepts, such as treewidth, CP-nets, and its induced graph.

2.1. Treewidth

The notion of treewidth was introduced by Robertson and Seymour in their work on graph minors [10].

Definition 1. *A tree decomposition of a graph $G = (V, E)$ is a pair (X, T), where $\{X_i \in X \mid i = 1, \cdots, n\}$ is a set of subsets of V, and T is a tree. Also, each node of T is exactly equal to an arbitrary subset of X. The (X, T) possess the following properties:*

(i) $\bigcup_{i \in T} X_i = V$. *That is, each graph vertex is contained in at least one tree node.*
(ii)   *If vertices v and w both are connected in a graph G, then v and w are contained in at least one subset X_i.*
(iii) *Considering the three nodes i, j, k in the tree, when j exists in the path of i and $k, X_i \cap X_k \subseteq X_j$, that is, common vertices of i and k must appear in the j.*

Definition 2. *The width of tree decomposition $D = (X, T)$ equals $max_{X_i \in X} \mid X_i \mid -1$, and the minimum width of a tree decomposition of G is the treewidth of the graph G.*

Figure 1 shows a graph G and one of its tree decompositions; from it, we can draw the result that the width of the tree decomposition is two.

In fact, treewidth has a close relationship with chordal graphs [14], and they have a special tree decomposition called a clique tree. So, we can further give an equivalent definition of treewidth: the treewidth of G is one less than the size of the largest clique in the chordal graph containing G with the smallest clique number. A chordal graph with this clique size may be obtained by adding an edge between every two vertices that both belong to at least one of the sets X_i.

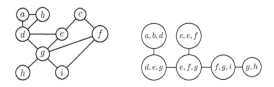

Figure 1. Graph G and its tree decomposition.

Actually, the treewidth of some graphs is determinate, and the graphs for which treewidth is easier to compute are those with a known constant treewidth. For example, tree structure is a special kind of graph, and its treewidth is 1. A complete graph, or a clique with n vertices, is the least tree-like type of graph; it has a treewidth of $n - 1$ [15]. Moreover, series-parallel graphs (SPG) have a treewidth of 2, and a treewidth of $m-grid$ is m [16]. There are other types of graphs that do not have constant treewidth, but for which the treewidth can be found in polynomial time. One example is the chordal graph, or triangulated graph. Although determining the treewidth of an arbitrary graph is NP-complete [17], in practical application, we can use heuristic algorithms to construct tree decomposition, thus obtaining its approximate optimal treewidth. In past research, *Bucket Elimination* and *Separator* techniques [18] have often been used in these heuristic algorithms. In this paper, we will concentrate on computing the treewidth of induced graphs of CP-nets, and illustrate in detail how to use *Bucket Elimination* to obtain treewidth in the next section.

2.2. CP-nets

We assume that readers are familiar with standard notions of CP-nets; next, we review the basics of CP-nets briefly.

Let $V = \{X_1, \cdots, X_n\}$ be a set of variables. $Dom(X_i)$ indicates the sets of variables of X_i, and $|Dom(X_i)|$ denotes its size. $\Omega = \times_{i=1}^{n} Dom(X_i)$ denotes all combinations of variables. The size $|\Omega| = \prod_{i=1}^{n} Dom(X_i)$ denotes the total number of outcomes. Any two outcomes $o, o' \in \Omega$ are regarded as swap outcomes if and only if they have only one different attribute value. If X_i is preferred over X_j then, X_j is a parent node of X_i. We define $Pa(X_i)$ as the parents set of X_i.

Definition 3. *A CP-net* $N =< V, E >$ *is a directed graph over variables* $V = \{X_1, \cdots, X_n\}$, *whose nodes are annotated with conditional preference tables* $CPT(X_i)$ *for each* $X_i \in V$. *Each conditional preference table* $CPT(X_i)$ *express the preference on* $Dom(X_i)$ *with respect to different assignments on the variable set* $Pa(X_i)$.

Definition 4. *Let* $N =< V, E >$ *be a CP-net, then the corresponding directed graph* $N' =< \Omega, IE >$ *is called the induced graph of N, where IE is the directed edges set indicating all the swapping relations. The induced graph* N' *has* $|\Omega|$ *nodes, considering the antisymmetry of the preference relation; there also are at most* $n|\Omega|/2$ *edges in the induced graph of N.*

Here we use a group of examples to illustrate the semantics of CP-net and its induced graph.

Example 1. *Consider the simple CP-net in Figure 2 that expresses my preference of weekend activities. This network consists of two variables, W and P, standing for the weather and plan, respectively. Now, I strictly prefer sunny* (W_s) *to rainy* (W_r), *while my preference between film* (P_f) *and ball* (P_b) *is conditioned on the weather to be served: I prefer playing basketball if served a sunny day, and seeing a film if served a rainy day.*

Figure 2 shows the preference graph over outcomes induced by this CP-net. An arrow in this graph directed from outcome o_i *to* o_j *indicates that a preference for* o_i *over* o_j *can be determined directly from one of the CPTs in the CP-net. For example, the fact that* $W_s P_b$ *is preferred to* $W_s P_f$ *(as indicated by the direct arrow between them) is a direct consequence of the semantics of* $CPT(P)$. *The top-left element* (W_sP_b) *is the best outcome, while the bottom-left element* (W_rP_b) *is the worst.*

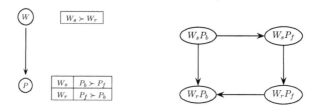

Figure 2. An example of CP-net named "My Weekend".

Next, we will give a complicated example of a CP-net.

Example 2. *Figure 3 illustrates another CP-net that expresses my preferences for the weekend. It consists of four variables, M, W, P, and R, standing for mood, weather, plan, and rest, respectively. With the underlying assumption that I always prefer a good mood to a bad mood, and good weather is preferred to bad weather. While my preference between the film and ball is conditioned on the combination of mood and weather, if I am happy and the weather is sunny, or I am not happy and the weather is rain, then playing basketball is my choice rather than film. Otherwise, I will go to a film. Finally, if I choose to play basketball, then I will take a bath to relax. On the contrary, I might have a big meal. Figure 4 shows the corresponding induced graph of the CP-net shown in Figure 3.*

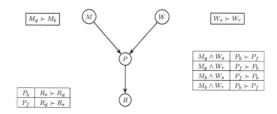

Figure 3. An example of a CP-net named "My Weekend 1 ".

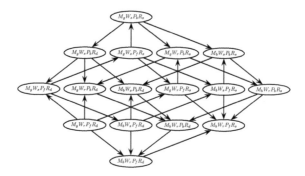

Figure 4. The induced graph of the CP-net "My Weekend 1".

Through the example above, we can see that the structure of the induced graph becomes more complex with the increase in the number of variables of CP-nets. At this moment, treewidth, as an important property, can naturally be used in the induced graphs of CP-nets.

3. Related Work

Given a set of attributes, CP-nets can not only express users' preferences, but also indicate the relationships between them. Pervious work has mainly focused on learning and reasoning CP-nets. For example, how to express a user's preferences in database queries [19], how to solve the expressive power on two kinds of specific CP-nets [2]. Guerin [20] presented an online heuristic algorithm for learning CP-nets from user queries, however, their algorithm does not always converge to the original CP-nets. Bigot *et al.* [21] studied how probabilistic conditional preference networks can be learnt, both in off-line and on-line settings. It is interesting to learn not a single model, but a probabilistic model that can compactly represent the preferences of a group of users. Liu *et al.* [22] studied conditional preference in recommender systems. Goldsmith *et al.* [23] researched the computational complexity of testing dominance and consistency in CP-nets, and proved that both dominance and consistency for general CP-nets are PSPACE-complete. Up to now, there has been little research investigating the structural properties of the induced graph of CP-nets, because its structure is rather complicated. As we know, the treewidth is interpreted as a significant property of arbitrary graphs in the study of Graph Minor. If the treewidth of a graph is obtained, we can perform some efficient reasoning over the induced graphs of CP-nets.

There are some papers working on determining treewidth and finding the optimal tree-decompositions. Given a graph G and an integer k, it is NP-complete to decide whether the treewidth of G is at most k or not [17]. Bodlaender *et al.* [24] proved that the treewidth problem is NP-complete for graphs with small maximum degree. The paper [25] gave a linear time algorithm that either outputs a tree-decomposition of G with treewidth at most k or determines that the treewidth of G is larger than k, for all constant k. For the Minimum Spanning Caterpillar Problem for bounded treewidth graphs, Dinneen and Khosravani [26] gave a linear time algorithm to solve it, but they assume that an approximate tree-decomposition of width bounded by a constant is given. Moreover, the treewidth problem of cographs [27], circular arc graphs [28], and chordal bipartite graphs [29], are polynomial solvable. However, so far, there are no papers to research the character of treewidth of the induced graphs of CP-nets.

As we all know, treewidth always has a parameterized complexity result on graphical models. Koster *et al.* [30] studied how to use tree decomposition to solve combinatorial optimization problems. In addition, Zhao *et al.* [31,32] published two papers that exploit tree decomposition to solve some problems about computational biology. In the area of graphical models, including knowledge representation and reasoning, probabilistic reasoning, and constraint satisfaction [33,34], all these studies focused on some graphs to represent abundant information about the real world. Since CP-nets can represent and reason users' preference represented by graphical model, treewidth can be applied in CP-nets naturally. In this paper, we study the treewidth problem on the induced graphs of CP-nets. Through the experiment in Section 5.2, we believe that any treewidth of the induced graph of a CP-net is small.

From Boutilier *et al.*'s paper [1], we know that there are four different paths from the outcome $\bar{a}\bar{b}c$ to the outcome abc in the induced graph. Our purpose is to find an optimal flipping sequence for $abc \succ \bar{a}\bar{b}c$; that is, to find the shortest path from these four paths. Fortunately, we can compute all-pairs shortest paths in induced graphs by leveraging low treewidth [35]. Since we have found that the treewidth of the induced graphs of CP-nets is small, we can quickly find the shortest path (optimal flipping sequence) in the induced graph. Therefore, solving dominance queries on the CP-nets is efficient.

4. Treewidth of the Induced Graphs of CP-nets

In this section, we mainly introduce the process of *Bucket Elimination* to solve treewidth, and a detailed algorithm pseudo-code.

4.1. Bucket Elimination Technique

The so-called elimination means that the vertices in a undirected graph are continuously eliminated, and how to get the *vertex elimination order* over the vertices is crucial in solving the treewidth. The notion of finding optimal vertex elimination orders is based on Bertele and Brioschi's [36] work on non-serial dynamic programming. This idea plays a role in a variety of algorithms in graphical models.

We begin with a series of definitions to explain the notion of *Bucket Elimination* in detail. First of all, we define the operation of eliminating a vertex from a graph as the process of adding an age between every pair of a vertex's neighbours that are not already adjacent, then removing the vertex and all edges incident to it.

A *vertex elimination order* over the vertices in a graph is a total order. When we eliminate some vertices, a group of graphs come into being. Clearly, the vertex elimination order is an total order on the given graph with n vertices. We would count an elimination order by its width, with the underlying assumption that we gain the elimination order $\pi = (C, A, B, D, E)$. The width of an elimination order is defined as the maximum degree of any vertex when it is eliminated from the graph. For example, the width of π is the maximal of these values in Figure 5; namely, $width(\pi) = \max(4, 2, 2, 1, 0) = 4$. An elimination order can determine only one width, the number of total vertex elimination orders of a graph with n vertices is $n!$.

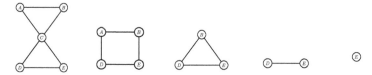

Figure 5. A five vertices graph for finding treewidth by eliminating vertices with the vertex elimination order $\pi = (C, A, B, D, E)$.

Importantly, the treewidth of a graph is the minimum width over all elimination orders, or, in other words, we must find an optimal vertex elimination order so that we can accurately conclude the treewidth of a graph. In Figure 6, the elimination order $\pi_{opt} = (A, B, C, D, E)$ is optimal. Notice that there is more than one optimal vertex elimination order. Finally, we have the following equation: $treewidth(G) = width(\pi_{opt}) = \max(2, 1, 2, 1, 0) = 2$.

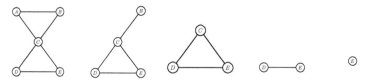

Figure 6. Finding the treewidth of a five vertices graph by eliminating vertices with the vertex elimination order $\pi_{opt} = (A, B, C, D, E)$.

We give the quantitative characterization of the number of attributes of CP-nets, the number of vertices of the induced graph, and the number of elimination orders in Figure 7. In fact, the elimination orders selected by our algorithm is a certain constant but exponential. Due to the fact that the induced graph of a CP-net is a special kind graph, and when the variable number is only 7, the number of total elimination orders is extremely large. So, we can not compute the width of all elimination orders to gain the treewidth of a graph in a practical application. According to the characteristics of randomness, we randomly select a certain number of vertex elimination orders to compute the treewidth of induced graphs. A simple example computing the treewidth of an induced graph with 4 vertices, is shown in Section 4.3.

$|V|$	$|N|$	$|\pi|$
1	2	2
2	4	24
3	8	40320
4	16	20922789888000
5	32	263130836933693530167218012160000000
6	64	126886932185884164103433389335161480802865516174545192198801894375214704230400000000000000
7	128	3856204823625804217356770659234636406174931095902235902788284032763734025751655435606861685885073615340300518330589163475921729322624988577661149552450393577600346447092792476924955852800000000000000000000000000000000000

Figure 7. $|V|$, $|N|$ and $|\pi|$ are the number of variables of CP-nets, vertices of induced graphs, and elimination orders, respectively.

While the number of vertices is large enough, the consumption of time and resources are also huge. However, there exists many specific graphs whose treewidth are constants or small [37]. Therefore, in practical application, we only need to solve the approximate optimal treewidth of graphs by some specific heuristic approach. Next, an example solving the treewidth of an induced graph will be given. Notice that, for the graph with five vertices in Figure 8, the number of total elimination orders is 120, Figure 9 only give one fifth of these 120 elimination order.

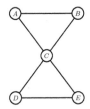

Figure 8. A graph on which we find the treewidth.

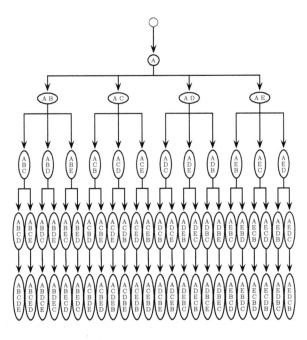

Figure 9. Fractional vertex elimination orders of Figure 8.

Given the number of elimination orders, we randomly select the vertices orders to solve the treewidth of this graph. In the next section, we describe this algorithm.

4.2. Algorithm for the Treewidth of an Induced Graph

Here we focus on our thought of the algorithm. First, Liu and Liao [2] gave the definition of induced graphs of CP-nets, which is derived from the CP-nets based on *ceteris paribus* semantics. So, it is assumed that, the induced graphs of CP-nets have not only been solved by the approach of literature [2] in advance, but has also been converted into an adjacency matrix of the corresponding underlying graph, so the adjacency matrix is the parameters of our algorithm. Since its vertex elimination orders are $n!$, in the program, we do not calculate the width of total vertex elimination orders. This reason has been explained in Section 4.1. Next, a certain amount of random vertex elimination orders are obtained. Then, this algorithm works by iterating through all sets of vertex elimination orders in order to find the approximate optimal treewidth. For instance, we in turn compute the degree of each vertex from the elimination order $\pi = (B, A, C, D, E)$. The function for solving the degree of the vertex is named $Deg()$. The adjacency matrix will be changed every time the degree of one vertex has been obtained, which will be accomplished in the $ChangeMatrix()$ function. At the same time, we take the maximum degree in the set of vertex elimination order as the width of this order. Finally, the minimum selected from all widths of vertex elimination orders is the treewidth of a graph. The pseudo-code of the proposed algorithm is summarized in Algorithm 1.

Algorithm 1: solving treewidth of included graphs of CP-nets N'.

Input: An adjacency matrix $A[i, j]$ of induced graph
Output: The treewidth of N'

```
1  treewidth ← 0;
2  Mdec ← 0;
3  mdec ← 0;
   // Calculate the total number of vertex elimination order sum.
4  foreach m ← 1 to sum do
       // Calculate the width of vertex elimination order in turn in term of the
          order produced randomly.
5      foreach i ← 1 to N do
6          mdec = Deg(i);
7          if mdec > Mdec then
8          |   Mdec ← mdec;
9          end
10         ChangeMatrix(i);
11     end
       // Find minimum width of all orders.
12     return Treewidth ;
13 end
```

4.3. A Motivate Example

Now, we give a motivate example to demonstrate the solving procedure for Algorithm 1 in detail. In Figure 2, there are two binary-valued variables, and its induced graph has four vertices. For simplicity, let A, B, C, and D stand for these outcomes ($W_s P_b$, $W_s P_f$, $W_r P_f$, and $W_r P_b$), respectively. Initially, the induced graph was converted into a undirected graph stored in the 4 by 4 adjacency matrix. If there is a relationship between two vertices, the corresponding value in the adjacency matrix is set to 1. Otherwise, the value is set to 0, and the number of total elimination orders is 24. The program randomly selects half of the total amounts; namely, the practical number of elimination orders is 12. For example, $\pi_1 = (D, B, A, C)$ and $width(\pi_1) = \max(2, 2, 1, 0) = 2$, $\pi_4 = (B, A, D, C)$ and $width(\pi_4) = \max(2, 2, 1, 0) = 2$, and $\pi_{10} = (D, A, B, C)$, and $width(\pi_{10}) = \max(2, 2, 1, 0) = 2$, etc. Finally, the smallest value we work out as above is the treewidth of this induced graph. Table 1 shows the results with different elimination orders. Obviously, the treewidth is 2 in terms of our algorithm.

Table 1. The width in different elimination orders.

	π	width
π_1	$DBAC$	$\max(2, 2, 1, 0) = 2$
π_2	$ACDB$	$\max(2, 2, 1, 0) = 2$
π_3	$CDAB$	$\max(2, 2, 1, 0) = 2$
π_4	$BADC$	$\max(2, 2, 1, 0) = 2$
π_5	$DABC$	$\max(2, 2, 1, 0) = 2$
π_6	$CABD$	$\max(2, 2, 1, 0) = 2$
π_7	$CDAB$	$\max(2, 1, 1, 0) = 2$
π_8	$DACB$	$\max(2, 1, 1, 0) = 2$
π_9	$CBDA$	$\max(2, 1, 1, 0) = 2$
π_{10}	$DABC$	$\max(2, 1, 1, 0) = 2$
π_{11}	$BCAD$	$\max(2, 1, 1, 0) = 2$
π_{12}	$BACD$	$\max(2, 1, 1, 0) = 2$

In addition, the treewidth of induced graph of given CP-net is 5 in Figure 4 by Algorithm 1.

4.4. Time Complexity Analysis

Theorem 1. *The time complexity of Algorithm 1 is $O(c_1 n^2 + c_1 c_2 n)$.*

The variable n is the number of vertices of the induced graphs of CP-nets, c_1 is a certain constant of randomly generated but exponential elimination orders (please refer to Section 4.1 on how to choose c_1), and c_2 is the maximal in-degree of the induced graph.

Proof. In Algorithm 1, firstly, we arbitrary select some vertex elimination orders from c_1 orders. this has $\binom{c_1}{1} = c_1$ kinds of selection methods. Secondly, to compute the treewidth of the induced graph, we need to iterate through all the vertices set n. Then, we compute the degree of this vertex when eliminating each vertex, its time complexity is $O(n)$. At the same time, the change of adjacency matrix includes two parts. One iterates through all the vertices to judge whether there is a relationship between arbitrary vertex, the other forms a clique which consists of all the vertices having a relationship with the deleted vertex. The time complexity of this process is $O(n + c_2)$. Finally, the minimum selected from all widths of vertex elimination orders is the treewidth of the induced graph. Therefore, combined with the three steps, the execution time in Algorithm 1 is:

$$O(c_1) \times [O(n) \times [O(n) + O(n + c_2)]]$$
$$= O(c_1) \times [O(n) \times [O(2n) + O(c_2)]]$$
$$= O(c_1)] \times [O(2n^2) + O(c_2 n)]$$
$$= O(c_1 n^2) + O(c_1 c_2 n)$$
$$= O(c_1 n^2 + c_1 c_2 n).$$

According to the above analysis, the time complexity of Algorithm 1 is $O(c_1 n^2 + c_1 c_2 n)$.

$\square$

5. Experimental Evaluation

5.1. Experimental Environment

Our algorithm was implemented in C++ and went through an intensive profiling phase. The experiments were run using Microsoft Visual Studio 2008, on a Lenovo V480 running 64-bit Windows 8 equipped with 4GB DDR3 memory and dominant frequency of 2.4GHz i5-Intel CPU. The run times are averaged over 10 runs for each unique problem instance. Moreover, we generated several different instances for each given induced graph model. Finally, each induced graph instances was ensured to compute the accurate treewidth.

5.2. Experimental Results on Simulated Data

In this section, we comment on the experiments we have carried out for the *Bucket Elimination* algorithm for computing the treewidth of the given induced graph in Table 2. Firstly, we define the size $|E_1|$ of a induced graph N' as the total number of edges in N', and we already know that $|E_1| = n|\Omega|/2$ by Definition 4. Moreover, we also define the size $|E_2|$ of a graph with n vertices as the total number of edges.

$$|E_2| = n(n-1)/2 \tag{1}$$

Table 3 shows the relationship between V, n, $|E_1|$, and $|E_2|$, where V and n denote the size of the variables of CP-nets and of the vertices of the induced graph, respectively. The size of $|E_2|$ is much more than $|E_1|$'s; thus, when computing the treewidth of the induced graphs of CP-nets, we need not consider too many edges. Apparently, it improves the running efficiency of the program.

Table 2. Experimental results of the induced graphs of CP-nets.

n	8	16	32	64	128	256	512	1024
$|E|$	12	32	80	192	448	1024	2304	5120
tw	1	2	6	7	8	9	9	10
$time(s)$	0.016	0.031	0.094	0.313	1.103	4.064	15.102	61.057

Table 3. The relationship between V, n, $|E_1|$, and $|E_2|$.

V	n	$|E_1|$	$|E_2|$
2	4	4	6
3	8	12	28
4	16	32	128
5	32	80	496
6	64	192	2016
7	128	448	8128

Table 2 lists the number of test cases, the range of the number of vertices n, edges $|E|$, *time*, as well as induced graphs with treewidth tw produced by Algorithm 1. More details on the different sets can be found below, but one thing that stands out immediately is that when the number of edges is different in the same induced graph, treewidth is not necessarily equal, and with an increase in the number of edges, treewidth gradually becomes larger. In Figure 10, it is more intuitive to express the relationship between the treewidth of an induced graph and the number of edges in the induced graph with 16 vertices and different edges.

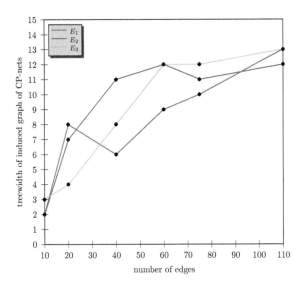

Figure 10. Treewidth corresponding to different edges in a given induced graph with 16 vertices.

For the induced graph of a CP-net with 1024 vertices, though we have randomly generated ten thousand elimination orders to solve treewidth, it is far less than the total elimination orders. Therefore, in this situation, the treewidth of the induced graph of a CP-net calculated by our algorithm could not be regarded as the accurate value, but it can be regarded as the upper bound of treewidth. It also comes to the conclusion that the treewidth of the induced graphs of CP-nets is still small when it has too many vertices.

6. Conclusions and Future Work

We know that some search algorithms can be used to traverse the improving search tree to find an improving sequence that supports dominance queries [1]— it means that we should find an optimal path over the induced graph. However, when the treewidth of a graph is small, an optimal path will be easier to find. Just as we have shown that the treewidth of induced graphs of CP-nets is much smaller in Section 5.2, so, dominance queries may be solved efficiently.

In this paper, we use a *Bucket Elimination* to compute the treewidth of the induced graphs of CP-nets. Although the time complexity of a *Bucket Elimination* is exponential in the treewidth of the given induced graphs of CP-nets, we randomly select a certain number of vertex elimination orders according to the characteristics of randomness, and the number of edges of the induced graphs of CP-nets is finite, which not only improves running time but also computes accurate treewidth of the induced graphs of CP-nets. Also, our research will make some operations over the induced graphs of CP-nets more feasible.

As everyone knows, program parallelization is getting more and more attention in recent years. Running on a multi-core computer is obviously much faster than on a single core. Then, we would implement the algorithm in parallel to improve the efficiency of computing the treewidth of the induced graphs of CP-nets in the near future.

Recently, a dynamic programming of the style of the classic Held-Karp algorithm has been given for the *Traveling Salesman Problem* [18], and Shoikhet and Geiger [38] have suggested that an algorithm of Arnborg *et al.* [38] can be used to compute treewidth. This algorithm builds a tree decomposition, and also leverages the dynamic programming idea. We would also like to compare our algorithms to the above dynamic algorithms experimentally in future work. Furthermore, in this paper, the induced graph of CP-net has been converted to undirected graph to compute its treewidth.

Our research would pay attention to how to compute the treewidth of directed induced graphs of CP-net—this will also be an interesting question in the future.

Acknowledgments: We gratefully acknowledge the detailed and helpful comments of the anonymous reviewers, who have enabled us to considerably improve this paper. This work was supported by Natural Science Foundation of China (61572419, 61403328, 61403329), and Shandong Province Natural Science Foundation (ZR2013FM011, 2015GSF115009, ZR2014FQ016, ZR2014FQ026).

Author Contributions: Jinglei Liu was the leader of this work and proposed the idea to solve the treewidth of induced graph of CP-nets. Jie Liu assisted with the data preprocessing, conducted the experiments, and prepared the manuscript.

Conflicts of Interest: The authors declare no conflict of interest.

References

1.   Boutilier, C.; Brafman, R.; Domshlak, C.; Hoos, H.; Poole, D. CP-nets: A tool for representing and reasoning with conditional ceteris paribus preference statements. *J. Artif. Intell. Res.* **2004**, *21*, 135–191.

2.   Liu, J.L.; Liao, S.Z. Expressive efficiency of two kinds of specific CP-nets. *Inf. Sci.* **2015**, *295*, 379–394.

3.   Majid, Z.A.L.; Emrouznejad, A.; Mustafa, A.; Al-Eraqi, A.S. Aggregating preference ranking with fuzzy Data Envelopment Analysis. *Knowl. Based Syst.* **2010**, *23*, 512–519.

4.   Chen, H.; Zhou, L.; Han, B. On compatibility of uncertain additive linguistic preference relations and its application in the group decision making. *Knowl. Based Syst.* **2011**, *24*, 816–823.

5.   Ha, V.; Haddawy, P. Toward Case-Based Preference Elicitation: Similarity Measures on Preference Structures. In Proceedings of the 14th Conference on Uncertainty in Artificial Intelligence, Madison, WI, USA, 24–26 July 1998; pp. 193–201.

6.   Mindolin, D.; Chomicki, J. Contracting preference relations for database applications. *Artif. Intell.* **2009**, *175*, 1092–1121.

7.   Garey, M.R.; Johnson, D.S. *Computers and Intractability: A Guide to the Theory of NP-Completeness*; W.H. Freeman: San Francisco, CA, USA, 1979.

8.   Downey, R.G.; Fellows, M.R. *Parameterized Complexity*; Springer: Berlin/Heidelberg, Germany, 2012.

9.   Chen, J.E. Parameterized computation and complexity: A new approach dealing with NP-hardness. *J. Comput. Sci. Technol.* **2005**, *20*, 18–37.

10. Robertson, N.; Seymour, P.D. Graph minors. II. Algorithmic aspects of tree-width. *J. Algorithms* **1986**, *7*, 309–322.

11. Mattei, N.; Pini, M.S.; Rossi, F.; Venable, K.B. Bribery in voting with CP-nets. *Ann. Math. Artif. Intell.* **2013**, *68*, 135–160.

12. Dechter, R. Bucket elimination: A unifying framework for probabilistic inference. In *Learning in Graphical Models*; Springer: Berlin/Heidelberg, Germany, 1998; pp. 75–104.

13. Darwiche, A. *Modeling and Reasoning With Bayesian Networks*; Cambridge University Press: Cambridge, UK, 2009.

14. Kosowski, A.; Li, B.; Nisse, N.; Suchan, K. k-chordal graphs: From cops and robber to compact routing via treewidth. In *Automata, Languages, and Programming*; Springer: Berlin/Heidelberg, Germany, 2012; pp. 610–622.

15. Dow, P.A. Search Algorithms for Exact Treewidth. Ph.D. Thesis, University of California Los Angeles, Los Angeles, CA, USA, 2010.

16. Gao, W.Y.; Li, S.H. Tree decomposition and its Application in Algorithm: Survey. *Comput. Sci.* **2012**, *39*, 14–18.

17. Arnborg, S.; Corneil, D.G.; Proskurowski, A. Complexity of finding embeddings in ak-tree. *SIAM J. Algebraic Discret. Methods* **1987**, *8*, 277–284.

18. Bodlaender, H.L.; Fomin, F.V.; Koster, A.M.; Kratsch, D.; Thilikos, D.M. *On Exact Algorithms for Treewidth*; Springer: Berlin/Heidelberg, Germany, 2006.

19. Kießling, W. Foundations of preferences in database systems. In Proceedings of the 28th International Conference on Very Large Data Bases, Hong Kong, China, 20–23 August 2002; pp. 311–322.

20. Guerin, J.T.; Allen, T.E.; Goldsmith, J. Learning CP-net Preferences online from user queries. In *Algorithmic Decision Theory*; Springer: Berlin/Heidelberg, Germany, 2013; pp. 208–220.

21. Bigot, D.; Mengin, J.; Zanuttini, B. Learning probabilistic CP-nets from observations of optimal items. In Proceedings of the 7th European Starting AI Researcher Symposium, Prague, Czech Republic, 18–19 August 2014; IOS Press: Amsterdam, The Netherlands, 2014; pp. 81–90.

22. Liu, W.Y.; Wu, C.H.; Feng, B.; Liu, J.T. Conditional preference in recommender systems. *Expert Syst. Appl.* **2015**, *42*, 774–788.

23. Goldsmith, J.; Lang, J.; Truszczynski, M.; Wilson, N. The computational complexity of dominance and consistency in CP-nets. *J. Artif. Intell. Res.* **2008**, *33*, 403–432.

24. Bodlaender, H.L.; Thilikos, D.M. Treewidth for graphs with small chordality. *Discret. Appl. Math.* **1997**, *79*, 45–61.

25. Bodlaender, H.L. A linear time algorithm for finding tree-decompositions of small treewidth. In Proceedings of the 25th Annual ACM Symposium on Theory of Computing, San Diego, CA, USA, 16–18 May 1993; ACM: New York, NY, USA, 1993; pp. 226–234.

26. Dinneen, M.J.; Khosravani, M. A linear time algorithm for the minimum spanning caterpillar problem for bounded treewidth graphs. In *Structural Information and Communication Complexity*; Springer: Berlin/Heidelberg, Germany, 2010; pp. 237–246.

27. Bodlaender, H.L.; Möhring, R.H. The pathwidth and treewidth of cographs. *SIAM J. Discret. Math.* **1993**, *6*, 181–188.

28. Sundaram, R.; Singh, K.S.; Rangan, C.P. Treewidth of circular-arc graphs. *SIAM J. Discret. Math.* **1994**, *7*, 647–655.

29. Kloks, T.; Kratsch, D. Treewidth of chordal bipartite graphs. *J. Algorithms* **1995**, *19*, 266–281.

30. Koster, A.M.; van Hoesel, S.P.; Kolen, A.W. Solving partial constraint satisfaction problems with tree decomposition. *Networks* **2002**, *40*, 170–180.

31. Zhao, J.; Che, D.; Cai, L. Comparative pathway annotation with protein-DNA interaction and operon information via graph tree decomposition. *Pac. Symp. Biocomput.* **2007**, *12*, 496–507.

32. Zhao, J.; Malmberg, R.L.; Cai, L. Rapid ab initio prediction of RNA pseudoknots via graph tree decomposition. *J. Math. Biol.* **2008**, *56*, 145–159.

33. De Givry, S.; Schiex, T.; Verfaillie, G. Exploiting tree decomposition and soft local consistency in weighted CSP. In Proceedings of the 21st National Conference on Artificial Intelligence, Boston, MA, USA, 16–20 July 2006; Volume 6, pp. 1–6.

34. Jégou, P.; Ndiaye, S.; Terrioux, C. Dynamic Heuristics for Backtrack Search on Tree-Decomposition of CSPs. In Proceedings of the 20th International Joint Conference on Artificial Intelligence, Hyderabad, India, 6–12 January 2007; pp. 112–117.

35. Planken, L.; de Weerdt, M.; van der Krogt, R. Computing All-Pairs Shortest Paths by Leveraging Low Treewidth. *J. Artif. Intell. Res.* **2012**, *43*, 353–388.

36. Bertele, U.; Brioschi, F. *Nonserial Dynamic Programming*; Elsevier: Amsterdam, The Netherlands, 1972.

37. Zhang, C.; Naughton, J.; DeWitt, D.; Luo, Q.; Lohman, G. On supporting containment queries in relational database management systems. In Proceedings of the 2001 ACM SIGMOD International Conference on Management of Data, Santa Barbara, CA, USA, 21–24 May 2001; Volume 30, pp. 425–436.

38. Shoikhet, K.; Geiger, D. A practical algorithm for finding optimal triangulations. In Proceedings of the Fourteenth National Conference on Artificial Intelligence and Ninth Innovative Applications of Artificial Intelligence Conference, Providence, RI, USA, 27–31 July 1997; pp. 185–190.

3

A Minimum-Entropy Based Residual Range Cell Migration Correction for Bistatic Forward-Looking SAR

Yuebo Zha [†,*], **Wei Pu** [†], **Gao Chen** [†], **Yulin Huang** [†] and **Jianyu Yang** [†]

School of Electronic Engineering, University of Electronic Science and Technology of China, 2006 Xiyuan Road, Gaoxin Western District, Chengdu 611731, China; pwuestc@163.com (W.P.); jzchenriver@163.com (G.C.); yulinhuang@uestc.edu.cn (Y.H.); jyyang@uestc.edu.cn (J.Y.)
* Correspondence: zhayuebo@163.com
† These authors contributed equally to this work.

Academic Editor: Willy Susilo

Abstract: For bistatic forward-looking synthetic aperture radar (BFSAR), motion errors induce two adverse effects on the echo, namely, azimuth phase error and residual range cell migration (RCM). Under the presumption that residual RCM is within a range resolution cell, residual RCM can be neglected, and azimuth phase error can be compensated utilizing autofocus methods. However, in the case that residual RCM exceeds the range resolution, two-dimensional defocus would emerge in the final image. Generally speaking, residual RCM is relatively small and can be neglected in monostatic SAR, while the unique characteristics of BFSAR makes the residual RCM exceeding range resolution cell inevitable. Furthermore, the excessive residual migration is increasingly encountered as resolutions become finer. To cope with such a problem, minimum-entropy based residual RCM correction method is developed in this paper. The proposed method eliminates the necessity of the parametric model when estimating the residual RCM. Moreover, it meets the practical needs of BFSAR owing to no requirement of exhaustive computation. Simulations validate the effectiveness of the proposed method.

Keywords: bistatic forward-looking SAR; residual RCM; minimal-entropy

1. Introduction

Synthetic aperture radar (SAR) has been used in many civilian and military fields with its all-weather and day/night ability [1]. However, the azimuth resolution is greatly limited in the forward-looking terrain for monostatic SAR, which restricts the application in airplane navigation, landing, *etc.* Then, bistatic forward-looking SAR (BFSAR) arouses researchers' concern, and the radar platform configuration mode, resolution theory, field test, and imaging algorithms are studied [2–6].

In order to obtain the desired azimuth resolution, relative motion between platforms and the desired scene is the key point. Nevertheless, it introduces range cell migration (RCM), which induces a strong azimuth-range coupling [7] in BFSAR, at the same time. RCM correction is essential to compensate the RCM and eliminate the azimuth-range coupling in frequency domain imaging algorithms. However, due to the motion errors and approximations in imaging algorithms, RCM cannot be compensated completely. When the residual RCM is within a range resolution cell, residual RCM can be neglected. This is the general presumption for almost all the existing autofocus algorithms, such as phase gradient autofocus (PGA) [8], Mapdrift (MD) [9], phase difference (PD) [10] and metric-based autofocus [11–14].

Generally speaking, residual RCM is relatively small and can be neglected in monostatic SAR, while the unique characteristics of BFSAR makes the residual RCM exceeding range resolution cell inevitable. On one hand, the separated platforms of BFSAR induce motion errors much larger than the errors in monostatic SAR raw data. On the other hand, range walk, the linear component of RCM, is only taken into consideration in the imaging algorithms of BFSAR, while the range curvature and the higher order terms are neglected. However, the impacts of these higher order terms become serious when the squint angle gets larger [15,16] and the resolution gets higher. In this situation, residual RCM correction becomes a necessary procedure for BFSAR imaging.

In principle, it is possible to compute the excessive residual RCM from orbit and altitude data provided by an ancillary instrument such as inertial measurement units (IMU) and global positioning system (GPS). Nevertheless, measurement uncertainties on the data would limit the accuracy, and the data remain unknown for some unmanned aerial vehicles without ancillary instruments. Thus, signal-based residual RCM correction is indispensable.

To correct residual RCM, two alternative strategies are available. One is to estimate the azimuth phase errors firstly, and then calculate the residual RCM from the estimated azimuth phase errors by exploiting their analytical relationship. In [17], the range compressed data is processed to a new coarser range resolution so that the presumption for autofocus is met. Therefore, the azimuth phase errors can be obtained using autofocus from the new range compressed data and then the residual RCM can be calculated and compensated. However, as the azimuth phase errors are estimated in coarse resolution, the estimation precision of azimuth phase errors and residual RCM can not satisfy the demands of high resolution BFSAR. Furthermore, range curvature and the higher order terms, which are neglected in the imaging algorithms, cannot be compensated.

The other one is to estimate the residual RCM independently. The residual RCM correction method proposed in [18] is based on the image quality metrics in [19]. The residual RCM of the echoes is modeled as a polynomial, and the coefficients of this polynomial are chosen to optimize a global quantity by minimizing the image entropy or maximizing the image contrast. However, the parametric model of the residual RCM restricts the estimation accuracy.

In this paper, based on the entropy metric, we present a relatively simple non-parametric correction algorithm for BFSAR to estimate the residual RCM. In this algorithm, a coordinate descent scheme is employed, where we minimize the entropy by sequentially updating the residual RCM parameters one at a time. From the derivation, the optimal single entropy-minimizing residual RCM parameter can be obtained in analytical form as the solution of a polynomial equation, thus enabling a fast focusing of the range focusing procedure with no computation exhaustive steps such as line-search.

The remainder of this paper is organized as follows: Section 2 establishes the signal model of BFSAR in the presence of motion errors. Based on the signal model, the migration property of BFSAR is analyzed and a range focusing procedure is conducted in order to obtain the coarse range focusing echo. Section 3 analyzes the influence of residual RCM, verifies the necessity of residual RCM correction, and proposes a residual RCM estimation method based on minimal entropy. Numerical simulations are given in Section 4. Section 5 concludes this paper.

2. Problem Formulation

Signal Model of BFSAR

The emphasis of this section lies in eliminating the range migration and realizing coarse range focusing in the presence of motion errors.

The geometric model in Figure 1 provides the basis for BFSAR imaging. In an ideal condition, the transmitter and receiver are moving along parallel tracks with equal velocity. The squint angles

ϕ_T, ϕ_R and initial ranges R_{Tcen}, R_{Rcen} shown in Figure 1 are measured at the composite beam center crossing time of target P.

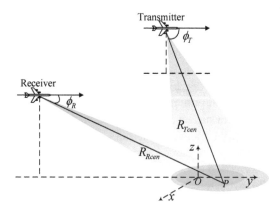

Figure 1. Geometric model of BFSAR.

Assume that Linear Frequency Modulated (LFM) pulses are transmitted by the radar. The demodulated signal from the reference target in the presence of motion errors can be adequately described by

$$s(\tau, t) = rect[\frac{\tau - \bar{R}(t)/c}{T_r}]rect(\frac{t}{T_a}) \exp\left\{ -j\pi K_r[\tau - \frac{\bar{R}(t)}{c}]^2 \right\} \exp\left\{ -j2\pi\frac{\bar{R}(t)}{\lambda} \right\} \qquad (1)$$

where K_r is the transmitted chirp rate, T_r is the timewidth of the LFM pulse, and T_a is the synthetic aperture time. The range time is given by τ, and t denotes the cross-range time, λ is the wave-length, c is the speed of propagation.

In Equation (1), $\bar{R}(t)$ is the instantaneous two-way range of reference target P in the presence of motion errors. $\bar{R}(t)$ can be formulated as

$$\bar{R}(t) = R(t) + \delta R(t), \qquad (2)$$

where $\delta R(t)$ denotes the instantaneous range displacement induced by motion errors, and $R(t)$ represents the nominal instantaneous two-way range,

$$R(t) = \sqrt{R_{Tcen}^2 + (Vt)^2 - 2R_{Tcen}Vt\cos\phi_T} + \sqrt{R_{Rcen}^2 + (Vt)^2 - 2R_{Rcen}Vt\cos\phi_R}. \qquad (3)$$

Expand (3) at $t = 0$ to its Taylor series and $R(t)$ can be rewritten as

$$R(t) = R_{Tcen} + R_{Rcen} - (V\cos\phi_R + V\cos\phi_R)t + (\frac{V^2\sin^2\phi_R}{2R_{Rcen}} + \frac{V^2\sin^2\phi_T}{2R_{Tcen}})t^2 + o(t). \qquad (4)$$

The linear and quadratic terms in Equation (4) are called the range walk and range curvature, respectively. Using the Doppler centroid estimation method in [20], range walk migration can be estimated. After range compression and range walk compensation, a coarse range focusing signal $s'(\tau, t)$ is obtained.

$$s'(\tau, t) = \sin c[\tau - \frac{R_{Tcen} + R_{Rcen} + \Delta R(t)}{c}]rect(\frac{t}{T_a}) \exp[-j\frac{2\pi}{\lambda}\bar{R}(t)] \qquad (5)$$

where $\Delta R(t)$ in the range profile is residual range cell migration (RCM)

$$\Delta R(t) = \delta R(t) + (\frac{V^2 \sin^2 \phi_R}{2R_{Rcen}} + \frac{V^2 \sin^2 \phi_T}{2R_{Tcen}})t^2 + o(t). \tag{6}$$

Residual RCM introduces a 2D defocus in the final image. In order to obtain high resolution BFSAR image, residual RCM correction is essential before the azimuth procedures such as autofocus, nonlinear chirp scaling (NLCS) [21] and azimuth compression. In the following section, a residual RCM correction method based on minimum entropy is proposed.

3. Residual RCM Correction

In this section, dominant scatterers are selected from the BFSAR image as the input of the proposed residual RCM correction method. The reason for the adoption of dominant scatterers is that the signal-noise ratio (SNR) in the area of dominant scatters is high, which can directly cause high residual RCM estimation accuracy. At first, quality range cells are picked out based on the contrast measurement because high contrast indicates a range cell containing more prominent scatterers than a cell with low contrast. M means the number of range cells picked out based on the based on the contrast measurement. Then, the brightest scatterers of the M range cells are selected. In order to consider the computation burden and the generalizability, M is always set to be quarter of the range cell numbers. For the sake of convenience in subsequent processing, these scatterers are shifted to the image center. The next important step is windowing these shifted scatterers in order to preserve the width of the dominant blur and meanwhile suppress the noise and interference from the neighboring clutter. The size of the window can be determined by the average response of these shifted scatterers. The Gaussian window is adopted in the whole processing. Finally, quality scatterers are chosen from these windowed scatterers based on the criteria that the main lobe energy is much higher than the background noise and the interference is negligible for both the main lobe and sidelobes [1].

The specific implement steps are performed as follows. (1) Estimate the main lobe width utilizing the average response of selected scatterers. (2) Calculate the proportion of the main lobe energy to the total signal energy for each selected scatterer. (3) Set a threshold, and select dominant scatterers. The threshold should ensure that selected scatterers are prominent and not influenced by neighboring clutter interference. In the actual situation, the threshold is set to be half of the amplitude of the brightest scatterers. Then, these selected dominant scatterers will be utilized to estimate phase errors.

In addition, the residual RCM is assumed to be identical for all the selected dominant scatterers in the BFSAR data. Strictly, residual RCMs of scatterers located at different ranges are not the same. However, this space variance can be solved by dividing the BFSAR data into several blocks along the range, whereby residual RCMs in each block are similar. After the segmenting operation, the problem of residual RCM correction can be formulated as [19]

$$z(m, n) = \sum_{k=0}^{M-1} s'(k, n) \exp(j\frac{2\pi}{M}mk) \exp(j2\pi k \Delta R_n) \tag{7}$$

where m, n and k are the indices of range, azimuth bins, and range frequency, respectively, and M, N are the numbers of range and azimuth samples, respectively. $s'(k, n)$ denotes the fast Fourier transformation (FFT) results of $s'(\tau, t)$ with respect to range yields, and ΔR_n is the residual RCM in the nth azimuth bin. An entropy-based residual RCM estimation method is proposed to estimate the $\Delta R_n (n = 1, 2, \cdots, N)$ in Equation (7).

3.1. Minimum-Entropy Estimation

In the minimum-entropy residual RCM correction algorithm, ΔR_n is designed to minimize the entropy of $z(m, n)$.

$$E = \ln S - \frac{1}{S} \sum_{m=0}^{M-1} \sum_{n=0}^{N-1} |z(m,n)|^2 \ln |z(m,n)|^2 \tag{8}$$

where

$$S = \sum_{m=0}^{M-1} \sum_{n=0}^{N-1} |z(m,n)|^2. \tag{9}$$

Entropy can be used to measure the smoothness of a distribution function. It is generally acknowledged that the BFSAR images with better range focusing quality have smaller entropy. Owing to this property, BFSAR residual RCM correction is performed by satisfying the global minimum-entropy criterion to find $\Delta R_n (n = 1, 2, \cdots, N)$. The minimum-entropy residual RCM estimate can be obtained by

$$\Delta R = \underset{\Delta R}{\arg\min} \, E(\Delta R) \tag{10}$$

where $\Delta R = [\Delta R_1, \Delta R_2, \cdots, \Delta R_N]$ is a vector of residual RCM correction parameter. Since there is no closed-form solution for Equation (10), an iterative numerical minimization procedure is needed to solve the optimal range displacement parameters.

3.2. Coordinate Descent

In this subsection, an iterative method based on coordinate descent to solve for the optimal residual RCM parameters in Equation (10) is discussed. In the coordinate descent optimization, each parameter is optimized in turn, while holding the remaining parameters constant. For our application, coordinate descent is applied to maximize the objective function in Equation (10).

Suppose that the residual RCM at the qth iteration for the nth parameter is estimated. In coordinate descent scheme, an iteration is defined as a complete cycle through all N range displacement parameters. All the other residual RCM variables are fixed at constants, where the first $(n-1)$ parameters have already been updated in the qth iteration. Now, the objective function reduces to a function of a single variable ΔR_n,

$$\Delta R_n^q = \underset{\Delta R_n}{\arg\min} \left[E(\Delta R_1^q, \cdots, \Delta R_{n-1}^q, \Delta R_n, \Delta R_{n+1}^{q-1}, \cdots, \Delta R_N^{q-1}) \right]. \tag{11}$$

3.3. Analytical Solution

Function (11) is a typical scalar minimization problem, and a computationally expensive numerical line-search can be utilized. Here, the optimal single minimum-entropy parameter can be obtained in analytical form, thus enabling a fast procedure with no line-search steps.

Expand $E(\Delta R_n)$ in (11) at ΔR_n^q to its Taylor series as follows and the cubic and higher order items are ignored:

$$E(\Delta R_n) = E \Big|_{\Delta R_n = \Delta R_n^q} + E' \Big|_{\Delta R_n = \Delta R_n^q} (\Delta R_n - \Delta R_n^q) + E'' \Big|_{\Delta R_n = \Delta R_n^q} (\Delta R_n - \Delta R_n^q)^2 \tag{12}$$

The first and second order derivatives of entropy with respect to ΔR_n are obtained in the following:

$$E' = -\sum_{m=0}^{M-1}\sum_{n=0}^{N-1}[1 + \ln|z(m,n)|^2]\frac{d|z(m,n)|^2}{d\Delta R_n} \tag{13}$$

$$E'' = -\sum_{m=0}^{M-1}\sum_{n=0}^{N-1}\frac{1}{|z(m,n)|^2}\frac{d^2|z(m,n)|^2}{d\Delta R_n^2}. \tag{14}$$

Since $|z(m,n)|^2 = z(m,n)z^*(m,n)$,

$$\frac{d|z(m,n)|^2}{d\Delta R_n} = 2\operatorname{Re}[z^*(m,n)\frac{dz(m,n)}{d\Delta R_n}]$$

$$= -\frac{4\pi}{Mc}\operatorname{Im}\left\{\left[\sum_{k=0}^{M-1}ks'(k,n)\exp(j\frac{2\pi}{M}km)\exp(j2\pi k\Delta R_n)\right]z^*(m,n)\right\} \tag{15}$$

$$\frac{d^2|z(m,n)|^2}{d\Delta R_n^2} = -\frac{8\pi^2}{M^2c^2}\operatorname{Re}\left\{\left[\sum_{k=0}^{M-1}k^2s'(k,n)\exp(j\frac{2\pi}{M}km)\exp(j2\pi k\Delta R_n)\right]z^*(m,n)\right\}$$
$$+\frac{8\pi^2}{M^2c^2}\left|\sum_{k=0}^{M-1}k^2s'(k,n)\exp(j\frac{2\pi}{M}km)\exp(j2\pi k\Delta R_n)\right|^2. \tag{16}$$

By solving for $E'(\Delta R_n) = 0$, a closed-form solution for (11) is obtained, which results in the following update equation.

$$\Delta R_n^{q+1} = \Delta R_n^q - \frac{E'\big|_{\Delta R_n = \Delta R_n^q}}{E''\big|_{\Delta R_n = \Delta R_n^q}}. \tag{17}$$

The proposed iterative method constructs a local quadratic curve to gradually approach the extremum of the objective function (11). Moreover, in order to make the iteration converge towards a minimum point, these quadratic curves should be convex and namely satisfy (18)

$$E''\big|_{\Delta R_n = \Delta R_n^q} > 0. \tag{18}$$

At this stage, residual RCM can be estimated and corrected precisely. Then, azimuth procedures, such as autofocus, NLCS, and azimuth compression, should be performed to get the well-focused BFSAR images.

4. Numerical Results

Simulation experiment is performed to verify the theoretical analysis and proposed residual RCM correction method. Table 1 lists the main parameters used in the simulation.

Table 1. Simulation parameters.

Parameter	Value
Carrier frequency	10 GHz
Band width	40 MHz
Synthetic aperture time	0.75 s
Nominal Radar platform velocity	120 m/s
Pulse repetition frequency	600 Hz
Coordinates of transmitter	(-6000,0,8000) m
Coordinates of receiver	(0,-6000,8000) m
Coordinates of scene center	(0,0,0) m

Two nominal parallel linear flight paths are assumed for BFSAR imaging. However, in reality, deviations from these nominal linear trajectories of transmitter and receiver are introduced in X, Y and Z direction. The deviation in the X-direction accounts for along-track nominal velocity changes that are generally compensated via an on-board adjustment of the pulse repetition frequency or, via azimuth re-sampling of SAR raw data. Therefore the forward velocity errors are assumed to be negligible, and we focus on how the deviations of the other two directions affect the residual RCM. The motion errors in Y and Z direction are shown in Figure 2. A ground point target is assumed to be located in the scene center and the coordinates of the other two target are (100,0,0) m and (−100,0,0) m, respectively. Therefore, all the targets in the echo signal are related to range displacements induced by the radars' maneuver.

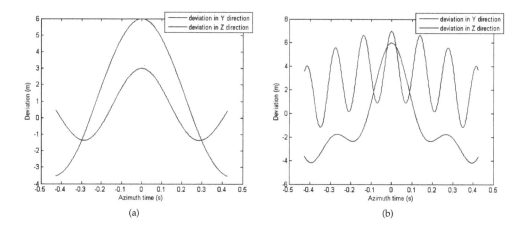

(a)   (b)

Figure 2. (a) Deviations of transmitter from the nominal flight path. (b) Deviations of receiver from the nominal flight path.

The simulation results are shown in Figure 3a,b. Figure 3a is the data after range compression and RCM correction while Figure 3b denotes the residual RCM corrected data. The figures suggest that the residual RCM is corrected well for the case of multiple point targets.

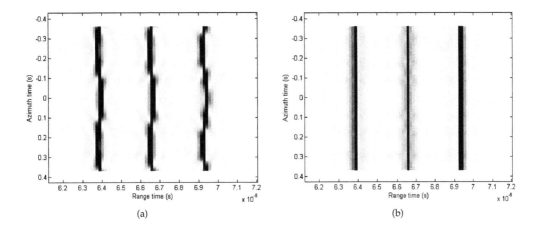

(a)   (b)

Figure 3.   (a) Data after range compression and RCM correction.   (b) Data after residual RCM correction.

The true range displacement and the estimated range displacement are shown in Figure 4a. It can be clearly seen that the estimated range displacement matches quite well with the true range displacement. In terms of estimation performance, the estimation error is shown in Figure 4b, and the variation of the root mean square (RMS) of an overall estimation error is smaller than 0.04 m with the default estimation accuracy Δr = 0.004 m. The nondefocus validity constraint of the estimation error is $\lambda/16$ = 0.01875 m, and the maximum estimation error is 0.004 m. Hence, the nondefocus validity constraint is satisfied, and, therefore, the range displacement estimated can be utilized to compensate for the azimuth phase errors (APE).

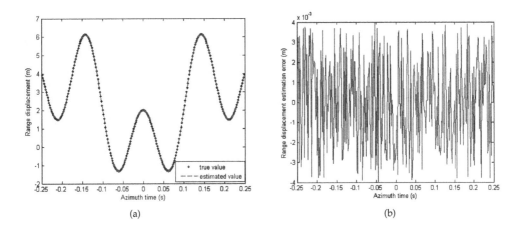

(a)   (b)

Figure 4. (a) Range displacement. (b) Range displacement estimation errors.

Then, the effect of noise on estimation accuracy is evaluated. White Gaussian noise with different signal-to-noise ratios (SNR) is added to the range-compressed data. A Monte Carlo simulation is conducted and the RMS of estimation error is shown in Figure 5 with SNR ranging from 10 to 30 dB. It is obvious that the proposed algorithm is insensitive to noise and can provide reliable estimation even for the data with low SNR.

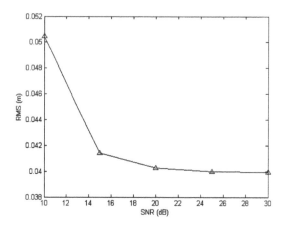

Figure 5. RMS of estimated range displacement error *versus* SNR.

5. Conclusions

This paper proposes the signal model of BFSAR in the presence of motion errors and analyzes in detail the influence of excessive residual RCM on the full compressed image. A minimal-entropy based residual RCM correction method is presented in this paper. By utilizing the coordinate decent scheme, we minimize the entropy by sequentially updating the residual RCM parameters one at a time. In the coordinate decent scheme, the optimal single entropy-minimizing residual RCM parameter can be obtained in analytical form. The proposed method eliminates the necessity of the parametric model and improves the estimation accuracy. Moreover, it meets the practical needs of BFSAR owing to no requirement of exhaustive computation. This method can be used in other SAR configuration modes with excessive residual RCM. Simulations and experiments using real BFSAR data are carried out to confirm the effectiveness of the algorithm.

Acknowledgments: This work is supported by the National Nature Science Foundation (61201272), the Research Fund for Doctoral Program of Ministry of Education (20130185120012), and the Fundamental Research Funds for the Central Universities (ZYGX2013J018).

Author Contributions: Yuebo Zha: Field data acquisitions, algorithm developing, data processing and writing of the paper; Wei Pu: Field data acquisitions, algorithm developing, data processing and writing of the paper; Gao Chen: Field data acquisitions, algorithm developing, data processing and writing of the paper; Yulin Huang: Field data acquisitions, project managing and managing; Jianyu Yang: Field data acquisitions, project managing and managing.

Conflicts of Interest: The authors declare no conflict of interest.

References

1. Cumming, I.G.; Wong, F.H. *Digital Processing of Synthetic Aperture Radar Data: Algorithms and Implementation*; Artech House: Norwood, MA, USA, 2005.
2. Wu, J.; Yang, J.; Yang, H.; Huang, Y. Optimal geometry configuration of bistatic forward-looking SAR. In Proceedings of the IEEE International Conference on Acoustics, Speech and Signal Processing (ICASSP 2009), Taipei, Taiwan, 19–24 April 2009; pp. 1117–1120.
3. Balke, J. Field test of bistatic forward-looking synthetic aperture radar. In Proceedings of the 2005 IEEE International Radar Conference, Arlington, VA, USA, 9–12 May 2005; pp. 424–429.
4. Shin, H.-S.; Lim, J.-T. Omega-k algorithm for airborne spatial invariant bistatic spotlight SAR imaging. *IEEE Trans. Geosci. Remote Sens.* **2009**, *47*, 238–250.
5. Wu, J.; Yang, J.; Huang, Y.; Yang, H.; Wang, H. Bistatic forward-looking SAR: Theory and challenges. In Proceedings of the 2009 IEEE Radar Conference, Pasadena, CA, USA, 4–8 May 2009; pp. 1–4.
6. Qiu, X.; Hu, D.; Ding, C. Some reflections on bistatic SAR of forward-looking configuration. *Geosci. Remote Sens. Lett. IEEE* **2008**, *5*, 735–739.

7. Shin, H.S.; Lim, J.T. Omega-k algorithm for airborne forward-looking bistatic spotlight SAR imaging. *IEEE Geosci. Remote Sens. Lett.* **2009**, *6*, 312–316.

8. Wahl, D.E.; Eichel, P.H.; Ghiglia, D.C.; Jakowatz, C.V., Jr. Phase gradient autofocus-a robust tool for high resolution SAR phase correction. *IEEE Trans. Aerosp. Electron. Syst.* **1994**, *30*, 827–835.

9. Lu, Y.; Ng, W.; Yeo, T.; Zhang, C. Autoregressive spectral estimation for SAR map-drift autofocusing. In Proceedings of the APMC '97, 1997 Asia-Pacific Microwave Conference Proceedings, Hong Kong, China, 2–5 December 1997; Volume 1, pp. 61–64.

10. Calloway, T.M.; Donohoe, G.W. Subaperture autofocus for synthetic aperture radar. *IEEE Trans. Aerosp. Electron. Syst.* **1994**, *30*, 617–621.

11. Kragh, T.J. Monotonic iterative algorithm for minimum-entropy autofocus. In Proceedings of the Adaptive Sensor Array Processing (ASAP) Workshop, Lexington, MA, USA, 6–7 June 2006.

12. Morrison, R.L.; Do, M.N.; Munson, D.C. SAR image autofocus by sharpness optimization: A theoretical study. *IEEE Trans. Image Process.* **2007**, *16*, 2309–2321.

13. Wang, J.; Liu, X. SAR minimum-entropy autofocus using an adaptive-order polynomial model. *IEEE Geosci. Remote Sens. Lett.* **2006**, *3*, 512–516.

14. Zeng, T.; Wang, R.; Li, F. SAR image autofocus utilizing minimum-entropy criterion. *IEEE Geosci. Remote Sens. Lett.* **2013**, *10*, 1552–1556.

15. Wu, J.; Yang, J.; Huang, Y.; Yang, H.; Kong, L. Spatial variance of bistatic sar with one fixed station. *IEICE Trans.* **2012**, *95*, 3270–3278.

16. Garza, G.; Qiao, Z. Resolution analysis of bistatic SAR. *Proc. SPIE* **2011**, *8021*, 361–372.

17. Doerry, A.W. *Autofocus Correction of Excessive Migration in Synthetic Aperture Radar Images*; United States Department of Energy: Washington, DC, USA, 2004.

18. González-Partida, J.-T.; Almorox-González, P.; Burgos-García, M.; Dorta-Naranjo, B.-P. SAR system for UAV operation with motion error compensation beyond the resolution cell. *Sensors* **2008**, *8*, 3384–3405.

19. Wang, J.; Kasilingam, D. Global range alignment for ISAR. *IEEE Trans. Aerosp. Electron. Syst.* **2003**, *39*, 351–357.

20. Li, W.; Yang, J.; Huang, Y.; Kong, L.; Wu, J. An improved radon-transform-based scheme of doppler centroid estimation for bistatic forward-looking SAR. *IEEE Geosci. Remote Sens. Lett.* **2011**, *8*, 379–383.

21. Wu, J.; Li, Z.; Huang, Y.; Yang, J.; Yang, H.; Liu, Q.H. Focusing bistatic forward-looking SAR with stationary transmitter based on keystone transform and nonlinear chirp scaling. *IEEE Geosci. Remote Sens. Lett.* **2014**, *11*, 148–152.

4

Invariance as a Tool for Ontology of Information

Marcin J. Schroeder

Akita International University, Akita, Japan/193-2 Okutsubakidai, Yuwa, Akita-shi, 010-1211 Akita, Japan; mjs@aiu.ac.jp

Academic Editors: Mark Burgin and Wolfgang Hofkirchner

Abstract: Attempts to answer questions regarding the ontological status of information are frequently based on the assumption that information should be placed within an already existing framework of concepts of established ontological statuses related to science, in particular to physics. However, many concepts of physics have undetermined or questionable ontological foundations. We can look for a solution in the recognition of the fundamental role of invariance with respect to a change of reference frame and to other transformations as a criterion for objective existence. The importance of invariance (symmetry) as a criterion for a primary ontological status can be identified in the methodology of physics from its beginnings in the work of Galileo, to modern classifications of elementary particles. Thus, the study of the invariance of the theoretical description of information is proposed as the first step towards ontology of information. With the exception of only a few works among publications which set the paradigm of information studies, the issues of invariance were neglected. Orthodox analysis of information lacks conceptual framework for the study of invariance. The present paper shows how invariance can be formalized for the definition of information and, accompanying it, mathematical formalism proposed by the author in his earlier publications.

Keywords: information; ontology of information; invariance of information

1. Introduction

The main goal of this article is to examine invariance of information with respect to transformations and to use the concept of invariance as a tool for the study of its structure and its modes of existence. It is a legitimate question why we can expect any relationship between invariance and existence of information. Before the answer is given, let us consider a more general problem of the way the ontological status of concepts can be established. The questions about what actually exists and how this existence is dependent on the existence of something else are as old as philosophical inquiry and were given a multitude of answers. Several of these answers fell into oblivion due to very clear deficiencies, but some are repeated in spite of their questionable merit. Quite often the only justification is in the common sense view of reality.

The modern common sense understanding of existence is highly eclectic and frequently inconsistent. Thus, in many discussions, with a pretense to being philosophical, we can find statements mixing Aristotelian substance understood as the composition of matter formed together with the Democritean materialistic distinction of matter and void, and with the curious combination of "matter and energy" as substrata of every objectively existent entity that is "physical, not mental" (an echo of Cartesian dualism). Expressions such as "physical reality", "physical space", "physical entity", or statements such as "information is physical", are used as if they were self-explanatory.

Mixing equivocal concepts of inconsistent philosophical systems is just a matter of ignorance and does not deserve critical analysis. A more complicated issue is the use of epistemic concepts for ontological qualification, such as in the expression "physical reality". When James Frederick Ferrier, in his 1854 *Institutes of Methaphysic the Theory of Knowing and Being*, introduced his division of philosophy into epistemology and ontology, the distinction was much simpler and his division could be sharp. Quantum mechanics blurred the division, as the fact of performing a measurement or observation became essentially inseparable from the issue of existence and identity of the object of inquiry.

Of course, this type of philosophical problem born within theories of modern physics is not related to the most frequent errors of the confusion of epistemic and ontological concepts and criteria. Thus, qualification of something (space, reality, entity, *etc.*) as "physical", because some or many physicists studied it, is meaningless and using this qualification as an ontological criterion is obvious nonsense. After all, physicists studied caloric or aether, not to mention notorious N-rays of René Blondlot. It makes sense to qualify an object of inquiry as physical if it has an empirically testable theory formulated according to the methodology of physics, but such qualification has limited ontological importance. The majority of concepts in physics have multiple, inconsistent theories with very different consequences for ontological interpretation.

Physics, as well as other disciplines of science, such as biology, requires continued revisions of the ontological status of its concepts. Revolutions of relativity and quantum mechanics took place a century ago, but still there is no consensus on their consequences for ontology. On the other hand, developments in modern physics can, and actually do, drive and guide development of ontology or philosophy in general. What can we learn from physics in the matters of ontology without being exposed to the danger that some near future scientific development could falsify it? More extensive discussion of this issue can be found in an earlier publication of the author [1]. For the purpose of the present article, it will be sufficient to consider only one lesson, and this lesson comes not from the content of physical theories, but from the methodology of mathematics and physics. For this reason we do not have to worry about its vulnerability to scientific progress. This lesson came out of the relatively recent developments in mathematics and physics, but its teaching applies to the entire evolution of physics starting from Galileo and, in a more general context, of knowledge from pre-Socratic philosophy.

Pre-Socratic philosophers recognized the role of that which is invariant in the changing world. Even Heraclitus, who believed that everything is changing, sought knowledge in the invariant patterns of changes. This epistemological assumption that the knowable must be invariant was sometimes appended by the ontological claims going much farther, that only that which does not change can exist, but this was just one of many possible positions. The interest in what is not changing was accompanied by the interest in the cosmos, *i.e.*, a harmonious whole and, therefore, in harmony understood as a regular structure. For many centuries these methodological principles stimulated interest in numbers and geometry, but the next essential step required a major revolution in the methods of inquiry. The earliest explicit statement by Galileo of the principle that the description of objective reality has to be invariant with respect to the change of observer (reference frame), who can be in a different place, can measure time differently, or who can move with constant speed, marks the beginning of physics as a scientific discipline.

Newton's formalization of this rule in his principles of mechanics remained within epistemological considerations. However, both Galileo and Newton contributed to the transition in ontological foundations of physics by revitalization of the atomistic ideas of Democritus, although more in the Epicurean spirit. The Aristotelian concept of ubiquitous matter was replaced by the opposition of matter (existence) and void (nonexistence). This qualitative character of matter was soon replaced by a new quantitative concept. Newton was using the expression "bulk of matter", but soon the concept of mass appeared. The recognition of the equivalence of the inertial and gravitational mass seemed a good confirmation of its primary ontological status. In the next century, the ancient idea of the qualitative conservation of matter was replaced by the quantitative principle of conservation of mass. Mass gained not only ontic character, but also became eternal.

It took much longer to explicitly formulate the principle of energy conservation, but by the middle of the 19th century the principles of mass, energy, and momentum conservation in isolated systems were ready. Simplicity of the division into materialistic opposition entity—matter characterized quantitatively by mass *vs.* non-existence—the void was disturbed by the wave theory of light and later by the more general theory of electromagnetic waves. The idea of aether as an exotic form of matter was an attempt to maintain uniformity of entities, which failed when special relativity theory eliminated it. However, the same theory brought the equivalence of mass and energy and the possibility that the entities characterized by mass and energy (particles) can be transformed into entities characterized exclusively by energy (waves of fields) and *vice versa*.

Quantum mechanics and, following it, theories of elementary particles and quantum fields destroyed once again the clarity of the picture. Wave-particle duality became a universal feature of whatever exists giving all entities characteristics of both types, but while some entities are associated with waves of fields which have ontic (*i.e.*, primary) status (e.g., photons as quanta of the electromagnetic field), while some others (e.g., electrons) are associated with the waves of epistemological character (waves of probability distribution or, alternatively, wave functions). Even more disturbing consequence of these developments is the possibility that the void can have non-vanishing energy states. Thus, the void is no more equivalent to non-existence and has to be considered an entity, although of an exotic type.

It is clear that modern physics calls for a new philosophical framework in which the division into epistemology and ontology has to be reconsidered. However, together with the destruction of the traditional framework of philosophical reflection, modern physics brought some new methods of analysis of the high value for philosophy. Probably the most important is the recognition and understanding of the role of invariants of transformations.

A theorem proved by Emmy Noether [2] associates the invariance of the description of motion with respect to transformations with the conservation laws for some magnitudes. Thus, the description (law) of motion is invariant with respect to continuous translations of space (transition between observers in space) or time (change of time coordinate between observers), making momentum, respectively, energy, conserved magnitudes. Symmetry (*i.e.*, invariance) of the law of motion with respect to rotation (orientation of the observer) will result in the conservation of angular momentum. This has extraordinary importance both for physics and for philosophical interpretation. Conservation of energy turns out not to be a discovery of something that already existed independently of our inquiry, but is simply a logical consequence of our requirement that the selection of a starting point of time measuring should not influence the description of motion. Thus, we have an implication: if we want to have descriptions of reality independent from the choice of the observer (reference frame), we should consider energy, momentum, angular momentum, *etc.*, because they will be conserved in this description. This is a theoretical counterpart of the empirical rule of replicability of observations or measurements.

Noether's theorem has some limiting conditions regarding the application to mechanical systems of particular types and to the way they are described (e.g., continuity of transformations), but its role in physics transcends these limits. Additionally, the importance of the study of groups of transformations was not new. The transition from classical mechanics to relativity was already recognized as a change of the group of transformations which preserves dynamical laws.

The recognition of the role of symmetries in mathematics goes back to Felix Klein and his 1872 Erlangen Program [3]. Klein proposed to study geometries through analysis of groups of transformations preserving their fundamental structure. This geometric context was the reason why invariants of transformations became called symmetric and the groups of transformations preserving some structures are called "groups of symmetries".

The program influenced not only mathematics and physics, but became, in the second half of the 20th century, the main source of inspiration for the influential direction of philosophical structuralism. The association of invariance with respect to transformations became the most important tool for the structural analysis in scientific disciplines, in the humanities, and in philosophy. Symmetries of chemical molecules (*i.e.*, groups of spatial transformations preserving their identity as given molecule) became the main tool for physical chemistry, as they turned out to be determinants of chemical properties of compounds. Thus, we have the following correspondence: group of symmetries—internal structure of molecules—macroscopic chemical properties of substances.

In the study of artificial and natural intelligence, the invariants of the groups of transformations of the configuration of sensory mechanisms were identified with what we humans experience as objects of perception [4]. This last example is of special importance to the subject of the present paper, as the identification of objects of sensory perception is obviously related to the recognition of what actually exists in the phenomenological perspective.

The philosophy of physics is very far from the resolution of many problems in the assessment of the ontological status of the concepts used in theories of modern physics. However, there is no doubt that the most important tool for this task is in the analysis of, and the reflection on, the invariance with respect to groups of transformations which makes the description of physical reality objective.

There is another lesson that we can learn from physics, in particular from its modern developments. The invariance with respect to transformations associated with the changes of observer or, more formally, the changes of the reference frame corresponds to the preservation of the structural characteristics of the objects of inquiry. This suggests that ontological analysis corresponds to structural analysis of the objects of study. This is not a surprise, as existence of an entity is inseparable from its identity and this identity is established by structural characteristics. Thus, when we ask questions about the mode of existence, we have to focus on the structural characteristics. Both mathematics and physics give us extensive methodological knowledge of these matters.

The purpose of this article is to initiate a similar approach in the philosophy of information. The ultimate goal is to develop a tool for the study of its ontology, but also for the study of the structural analysis of information. The literature of the subject of the modes of existence of information is very broad, so the present paper will not attempt to review the large variety of earlier publications addressing the issues related to ontology of information. It would be a formidable, but pointless task, because of many different ways information is defined and understood. The diversity of the ways in which information is defined or understood leads to a large multiplicity of ramifications in its description and study. Moreover, discussions of the ontological status of information are not always carried out with clearly and correctly defined concepts. Thus, it is obvious that the large variety of definitions of information must result in differences in the views on the modes of its existence. Instead, the focus will be on the issue of invariance, with very selective literature references to most important contributions to the discussion of ontology of information, especially those which set paradigms for popular views on information existence. For analysis of the ways in which information studies considered invariance these differences between the ways information is understood or interpreted do not constitute an obstacle. Moreover, the task becomes quite easy as very little was published on information in the context of invariance or symmetry.

The constructive (as opposed to critical) part of the paper, which follows the historical remarks on invariance of information will use the concept of information introduced and elaborated by the author in his earlier publications. Although it is quite different from the variety of concepts used by other authors, its high level of generality justifies identification of virtually every other well-defined concept of information in the literature as its special case. Finally, the invariance of information will be formalized within mathematical formalism developed by the author for his concept of information. It has to be emphasized that this formalism is a result of the choice of particular mathematical foundations in general algebra. The choice is a matter of judgment which mathematical theory can be useful, but not of necessity. The author is aware that another mathematical framework, for instance, category theory, could be used as well.

2. Sources of Problems in Ontology of Information

The term "information" is one of the most recent additions to the catalog of scientific and philosophical vocabulary, but one that generates never ending discussions over its conceptualization and ontological status. Of course, the former issue is epitomized in the question "What is information?"

should be resolved before the latter. However, it is a natural course of the intellectual inquiry that every attempt to define information is first tested against the use of this term in more restricted contexts of specialized disciplines of science where the term "information" already acquired certain meaning, usually informal or intuitive. In these contexts the use of the term suggested some forms of existence of information, although typically without much care for the precise and consistent statement regarding its ontological status.

For instance, Claude Shannon, whose 1948 article on a mathematical theory of communication, republished the next year with the commentary by Warren Weaver in book format to become a paradigm for information theory, uses in the introduction the terms "information" and "message" interchangeably: "In the present paper we will extend the theory to include a number of new factors, in particular the effect of noise in the channel, and the savings possible due to the statistical structure of the original message and due to the nature of the final destination of the information. The fundamental problem of communication is that of reproducing at one point either exactly or approximately a message selected at another point" [5]. A few pages further he writes about quantities of the form of entropy that "play a central role in information theory as measures of information, choice and uncertainty" [6].

Shannon did not write explicitly that the terms "information", "message", "choice", and "uncertainty" are equivalent. Actually, he did not use much the term "information" in his paper and the latter of the statements quoted above where the word "information" has its very infrequent appearance was in the section with the title "Choice, Uncertainty and Entropy" which shows that information was of secondary importance to him. It is clear that whether he considered the concept of information important or not, and whatever he understood by this term, did not have primary ontological status. The association of his entropy as a measure of "information, choice and uncertainty" with physical entropy seemed to be, for him and the early commentators of his work, rather accidental. The loose and indefinite association of information with uncertainty (whatever the choice out of the many possible ways to understand this word) suggested by Shannon was used by interpreters and popularizers of his work (Warren Weaver, Colin Cherry, and others) as a justification for their own interpretation of information as a reduction or resolution of uncertainty. However, in this case, information becomes an epistemological concept.

At first sight, the evolution of the view on the ontological status of information seems straightforward and parallel to the evolution of its epistemological status towards an increasingly fundamental, general, scientific concept. The rediscovery of the 1926 work of Leo Szilard on the solution of Maxwell's Demon paradox by the association of the increase of physical entropy with cognitive functions of the demon [7], and the book of Erwin Schrödinger "What is Life?" in which life, with its genetic information transmission in reproduction and metabolism, was presented as generated by negative entropy of sunlight, directed attention to the more fundamental relationship between information, physics, and life [8].

The instances of information in biology, in particular, genetics, justified the necessity for disambiguation of the concepts of information and knowledge. Technological advances in computer science directed interests towards the "physics of information". Computers as physical devices (most likely understood as technological artifacts designed with the use of physics) do not communicate information, but process it through physical operations, which stimulated interest in studying information as a subject of physical inquiry. The most prominent propagator of the idea that "information is physical" was Rolf Landauer, who wrote a series of influential articles on this subject [9–12].

The phrase, which he repeated in some variants in several titles of his papers, became an epitome of the entire direction of the study of information as a physical phenomenon. However, Landauer did not go much farther than others in his views on the ontological status of information in spite of calling it a "physical entity" in the title of his 1999 article, where he writes "Information is inevitably inscribed in a physical medium. It is not an abstract entity. It can be denoted by a hole in a punched card, by the orientation of a nuclear spin, or by the pulses transmitted by a neuron" [11]. The association with physical phenomena in his opinion is through the necessity to represent (sic!) information in a physical medium. Representation in the physical medium does not entail existence as an object with the ontological status identical with the status of objects considered in physics. It is basically the same view as that of Donald MacKey, elaborated in his 1969 book *Information, Mechanism and Meaning,* expressed in the popular slogan "there is no information without representation" [13]. There is a close resemblance of such a representation to the concept of channels in the original paper of Shannon "The *channel* is merely the medium used to transmit the signal from transmitter to receiver" [5]. The use of the term "representation" is betraying underlying hidden assumptions of a certain "receiver" or "destination" to whom something is presented. In any case, information has, in all these views, only secondary existence dependent on the primary existence of a physical medium.

The actual revolution came with the view expressed by John Archibald Wheeler in his famous epitome "it from bit" [14]. Wheeler not only gave information independent, primary existence, but relegated everything else to the status of secondary one: "Now I am in the grip of a new vision, that everything is Information" [15].

As it can be expected, "it from bit" is not the most popular view on the ontological status of information. Quite frequently it is presented as a mere curiosity, but there are many enthusiasts of this view among physicists. However, the objections to Landauer's "information is physical" are rare. Unfortunately, the approval of this view is too frequently followed by the question formulated in the anachronistic language of the 19th century popularization of physics: "How is information related to matter and energy"?

This is an expression of the popular conviction that the scientific view of "physical reality" is a safe platform for the ontological analysis of the new concept of information and, in the common sense view of reality, matter and energy are two ontological categories of undeniable primary existence. After all, the entirety of social life is organized around "material goods or resources" and "energy".

This type of naive escape from the challenges encountered in the study of information to the apparently scientifically-sanctioned common sense view of reality is a stumbling block in attempts to develop a philosophy and science of information. Of course, Wheeler's "Everything is Information" is not a solution to the question about the ontological status of information, either. After all, "everything" is not an ontological concept and there is no clear presentation in his works of the definition of information. However, Wheeler explicitly addressed the issue of the ontological status of information without sweeping it under the carpet of "physicality". What is missing in his view of the status of information as a more fundamental entity than traditionally recognized substances is missing also in more restrained views of Landauer and his followers. It is lack of the answer to the question of how to determine and distinguish the ontological status of concepts, such as information, fields, particles, *etc.*

In the introduction to this paper, presenting the problem in the general context, pointed at the analysis of invariance with respect to transformations as a tool for establishing the criteria for ontological status and, for the development of following it, structural analysis. Justification was in the lesson from the methodology of physics. In the following, this line of thinking will be applied to the study of information.

3. Invariance and Structure

In the popular view of physics and other "hard sciences", the main characteristic of science is its use of quantitative methods. Information theory, as the discipline born in the work of Shannon's famous article of 1948 [5], became so popular because it introduced a wide range of quantitative methods into the study of communication within many contexts which, earlier, were dominated by qualitative methodology. The best example is psychology. In the popular reception of information theory, its subject is a measure of information, entropy, and its use for a wide range of applications. Apparently, there is no need for qualitative methods of information, as those quantitative methods are superior, more precise, and more useful in applications. This explains why, in the course of dozens of years, so little attention was paid to structural and, therefore, qualitative characteristics of information. At least this lack of interest was common among followers of Shannon's approach.

There was another, independent direction of the study of information, which programmatically rejected Shannon's approach and formulated its own approach in terms of structural analysis. The most explicit rejection was in the work of Rene Thom in his *Structural Stability and Morphogenesis* [16].

We will start from the question of whether qualitative and quantitative methods of inquiry are necessarily mutually exclusive. Since the category of qualitative methods is frequently defined as "all, which is not quantitative" (the typical view presented in textbooks in statistics), which of course is a gross oversimplification and overgeneralization, we have to specify what the meaning of "qualitative" characteristics of the subject of inquiry are. Otherwise we risk multiple misunderstandings.

In this paper "qualitative" is understood as equivalent to "structural". This means that an object (whatever is its ontological status—"physical", "real", mental, or other entity) has to be considered as a structure built of components in some relationship to each other, and that this structure determines its qualities, understood as modes of external manifestation of the internal structure. Thus, we eliminate from our consideration the issue of qualia and their status. Qualities are expressions of inherent characteristics of the subject of study and they are not dependent on the way of their apprehension. This does not preclude the influence of the qualities on the mutual interactions of objects, or interactions between the object and observer, the latter interaction producing perception of qualities. It is clear that this position is related to the attempts of objectification of the study, which can be identified as the main tenet of the scientific methodology.

The popular view that physics is a purely quantitative discipline comes from its identification with its pre-relativistic and pre-quantum mechanical theories (classical physics) to which typical secondary education is limited. These theories were built around the concept of physical magnitudes which have numerical values in real numbers. These magnitudes represent observables (the numerical values obtained directly from measuring devices) or the results of arithmetic operations of actions of functions on these values. The choice of physical dimension assigned to observables depends on the type of measuring device in experiments. The state of a physical system was described by a complex of the values of observables. In some cases instead of numbers (scalars), the values of observables are vectors or matrices which, in particular, coordinatization have the form of sequences or arrays of real numbers.

Modern physics destroyed this simple vision of physics as a study of physical magnitudes. The state of a physical system is not described as a collection of values of observables anymore. Structural characteristics replaced numerical values. Very different algebraic structures replaced the algebra of real numbers. The governing rule in the choice of the structures was their invariance with respect to the group of transformations; in classical cases the transformations are those already considered by Galileo (Galileo's relativity), in relativistic cases it is a different group (Lorentz group). Traditional separation of quantitative methods and structural (qualitative) methods lost its meaning.

There are many reasons, such as insufficiency of the conceptual framework of physics for biology or for the studies of other complex systems, for more radical changes in theoretical methods of science [1,17,18]. The direction of these changes is away from the traditional quantitative methodology even in higher degrees, and it is pointing at a structural analysis of a new type.

In the following sections, the methodological concept of invariance will be used to analyze the historical relationship between the quantitative and qualitative (structural) characterizations of information in the past research and to attempt setting a bridge between them for further work.

4. Historical Perspective: Hartley

Many historical accounts of information theory consider, as its original source, the paper published by Claude E. Shannon in 1948 or, alternatively, the book published one year later where this paper was followed by explanatory remarks from Warren Weaver [5]. Although the impact of Shannon's paper, and especially of the book, was so great that they were being compared to "a bomb, and something of a delayed-action bomb" [19], if we want to trace the origins of some conceptions and misconceptions regarding information, we have to go twenty years back to the paper "Transmission of Information" by Ralph V. L. Hartley [20]. Even earlier, Harry Nyquist published two papers of great importance for telegraph transmission problems (both quoted by Shannon together with Hartley's article), but they were not addressing directly the conceptual aspects of general information theory. However, Hartley's contribution in this respect was much more influential for the further direction of the study of information, than it is usually recognized. Some ideas appearing in Hartley's paper had clear resonance in the literature of the subject in several decades. It is very unlikely that it is just a matter of coincidence.

Shannon gave credit to Hartley, but not in the full extent: "I started with information theory, inspired by Hartley's paper, which was a good paper, but it did not take account of things like noise and best encoding and probabilistic aspects" [21]. Definitely, Hartley did not address the issue of noise, explicitly, although he considered distortions. However, he was concerned about the matters of encoding and of probabilistic issues, although his decisions about how to deal with these matters, in each case accompanied with careful explanations, were different from those of Shannon. However, in some cases, he did exactly what Shannon did in his famous book.

He focused, for instance, on the "engineering problem" as can be seen in his statement "In order then for a measure of information to be of practical engineering value it should be of such a nature that the information is proportional to the number of selections" [20]. It is very likely (although it is a pure speculation) that Shannon was influenced by Hartley in writing his famous declaration of disinterest in the matters of info-semantics: "Frequently the messages have *meaning*; that is they refer to or are correlated according to some system with certain physical or conceptual entities. These semantic aspects of communication are irrelevant to the engineering problem. The significant aspect is that the actual message is one *selected from a set* of possible messages" [5].

Hartley formulated his view in a much more reserved and more elaborated way and was looking for a solution to more general problems (admittedly of less practical value). First, we can see in the first sentence of the abstract of his paper "A quantitative measure of 'information' is developed which is based on physical as contrasted with psychological considerations" [20]. The use of quotation marks for the word "information" seems significant. Then, in the introduction, he presents the purpose of his preoccupation with such a measure: "When we speak of the capacity of a system to transmit information we imply some sort of quantitative measure of information. S commonly used, information is a very elastic term, and it will first be necessary to set up for it a more specific meaning as applied to the present discussion. As a starting place for this let us consider what factors are involved in communication; [...] In the first place, there must be a group of physical symbols, such as words, dots and dashes or the like, which by general agreement convey certain meanings to the parties communicating. In any given communication the sender mentally selects a particular symbol and by some bodily motion [...] causes the attention of the receiver to be directed to that particular symbol. By successive selections a sequence of symbols is brought to the listener's attention. At each selection there are eliminated all of the other symbols which might have been chosen. [...] Inasmuch as the precision of the information depends upon what other symbol sequences might have been chosen it would seem reasonable to hope to find in the number of those sequences the desired quantitative measure of information. The number of symbols available at any one selection obviously varies widely with the type of symbols used, with the particular communicators and with the degree of previous understanding existing between them. [...] It is desirable therefore to eliminate the psychological factors involved and to establish a measure of information in terms of purely physical quantities" [20].

In the following section "Elimination of Psychological Factors" Hartley observes that the sequence of symbols can be generated by conscious selection, or by an automatic mechanism as a result of chance operations. On the other hand, the receiver may be either unfamiliar with the code or its parts, or less skilled in distinguishing distorted signals (in the earlier section and in the following one he refers also to communicators using different languages). For this reason, he wants to eliminate from consideration any specific assumptions regarding the generation of symbols.

He writes: "Thus, the number of symbols available to the sending operator at certain of his selections is here limited by psychological rather than physical considerations. Other operators using other codes might make other selections. Hence in estimating the capacity of the physical system to transmit information we should ignore the question of interpretation, make each selection perfectly arbitrary, and base our result on the possibility of the receiver's distinguishing the result of selecting any one symbol from that of selecting any other. By this means the psychological factors and their variations are eliminated and it becomes possible to set up a definite quantitative measure of information based on physical considerations alone" [20].

Hartley's strong emphasis on the physical considerations was probably motivated by the fact that he wanted to consider that communication means a very wide range of physical phenomena allowing transmission of sounds or pictures. For this purpose he involved in his study the matters of discretization of continuous magnitudes. However, these aspects of his paper will not concern us in the present paper.

It is important to observe that his derivation of the formula for the quantitative measure of information $H = n \times log_m(s)$, where s is the number of symbols available in all selections and n is a number of selections, m is arbitrarily chosen according to the preferable choice of the unit of information, involved the assumption of invariance. In this particular case, the invariance is with respect to the grouping of the "primary symbols" (here associated with physically distinct states of the physical system) into "secondary symbols" representing psychologically determined and, therefore, subjective symbols carrying meaning. The choice of the formula makes values of H independent from grouping.

For historical reasons, we should notice that Hartley refers to the situation when "non-uniform codes" are used. In this context he observes that the choice of secondary symbols may be restricted, "Such a restriction is imposed when, in computing the average number of dots per character for a non-uniform code, we take account of the average frequency of occurrence of the various characters in telegraph messages" [20]. We can understand it in the post-Shannon perspective, and with some dose of guessing, as the text at this point is not very clear, that he postulates to use the encoding (we know now that it is optimal) by grouping primary symbols in such a way that the differences between frequencies of different characters are compensated and the direct correspondence to the equally likely primary level symbols is restored. Then the difference in the number of selections will not influence our measure of information.

Additionally, Hartley considers the issue of reduction in the number of consecutive choices related to words rather than characters in the context of speech communication: "In speech, for example, we might assume the primary selections to represent the choice of successive words. On that basis s would represent the number of available words. For the first word of a conversation this would correspond to the number of words in the language. For subsequent selections the number would ordinarily be reduced because subsequent words would have to combine in intelligible fashion with those preceding. Such limitations, however, are limitations of interpretation only [...]" [20].

Summarizing, we can find in Hartley's article several aspects of the study of information which can be identified with the orthodox approach:

- Information is associated with the selection from a predefined list of choices, and its measure with the number of selections, in each selection with the number of eliminated choices by actual selection (Weaver writes in his contribution to the book with Shannon "To be sure, this word information in communication theory relates not so much to what you *do* say, as to what you *could* say" [22]).
- Information is a subject of engineering, in particular with engineering of communication.
- Information is considered in the context of selections made by a sending operator and by a receiver.
- The meaning of information (necessary for Hartley, but only "frequent" for Shannon) belongs to psychological aspects of information which, because of its variability, has to be eliminated from consideration.
- The measure of information involves a logarithm of the size of a variety of symbols, from which selection (for Hartley) ensures invariance between different ways to encode information.

- Encoding (understood as grouping primary symbols to represent secondary symbols used by communicators) is arbitrary as long as we have equal probability of secondary symbols, but requires some restrictions, otherwise.
- The measure of information is invariant with respect to the permutation of symbols or words as long as we do not change the number of choices in consecutive selections.

Hartley made one important methodological assumption which did not attract much attention in the orthodox approach. It was the use of the concept of invariance, which he applied in the context of the transition to a different encoding understood as grouping of primary symbols into secondary ones. However, his preoccupation with the engineering aspects and emphasis on the elimination of psychological aspects of information prevented him from asking the fundamental question regarding a relationship between the structure of information at the primary level, its transformations, and invariants of these transformations.

5. Historical Perspective: Shannon

Popular perception, amplified by the statements expressed by people involved in the early development of information theory, even by Shannon (as we could see above in his interview), is that Hartley did not consider differences in frequencies of characters in messages. It is clearly a false view. He considered those differences but, right or wrong, as psychological aspects of communication which should be eliminated from consideration.

He wanted to have a measure of information invariant with respect to the change of language. Of course, it made more difficult the discovery of the association between his measure and physical entropy (although, for instance on Boltzmann's grave, the formula for entropy is in its simplified form, corresponding to Hartley's measure). However, Shannon did not recognize the association with physical entropy as significant, either. For him and for many others at that time it was mere curiosity.

John R. Pierce, who co-authored with Shannon and B. Oliver one of the earliest papers on information theory [23], the paper which sometimes is considered more important for the explosion of the new discipline than Shannon's book, even in the 1980 edition of his book popularizing the subject "An Introduction to Information Theory: Symbols, Signals and Noise" reiterated his view from the earlier editions "Here I will merely say that the efforts to marry communication theory and physics have been more interesting than fruitful. Certainly, such attempts have not produced important new results or understanding, as communication theory has in its own right. Communication theory has its origins in the study of electrical communication, not in statistical mechanics, and some of the ideas important to communication theory go back to the very origins of electrical communication" [24].

Someone can defend Pierce's statement, that it is about communication theory, not about information theory, but this statement is in the chapter about the origins of information theory and it follows the paragraph where he writes explicitly about information and explains its meaning "Thus, *information* is sometimes associated with the idea of *knowledge* through its popular use rather than *uncertainty* and the resolution of uncertainty, as it is in communication theory" [24].

Hartley's decision to disregard different frequencies of characters depending on the choice of the language and their order (*i.e.*, structural characteristics of messages) was purely rational, conscious, and can be understood as an expression of his concern to maintain invariance of the measure of information appropriate for the scientific study free from psychological factors. However, this concern cannot defend his position.

While the particular choice of grouping of primary symbols can be considered an arbitrary psychological factor, the fact that his measure of information is an invariant of permutations of selections makes his measure of a questionable value for analysis of information outside of the question of the rate of transmission. After all, is it important to know the value of the measure for a message, if the measure does not change when we list first all a's from the message, then all b's, and so on?

Hartley's error was in the confusion of two different matters. On one side we have the reasons for a particular choice of frequencies of characters controlled by cultural aspects of language development and evolution, and also the reasons why characters in the strings of characters are ordered in this, or another, way. These are "psychological factors". However, the fact that characters appear with non-uniform probability, and that the order of the characters matters, are as objective as the fall of an apple from the tree. Thus, they cannot be relegated to irrelevant characteristics of information. Hartley addressed both issues, but focused on the ways how to eliminate them from consideration.

The first error was corrected by Shannon in his revolutionary paper. We do not have to inquire why it happens or what the reasons are for differences between particular instances of languages, but we have to recognize that symbols of natural or artificial languages are subject of some probabilistic distribution which, frequently, is not uniform. For uniform distribution, Hartley's formula is sufficient. If the distribution is not uniform (and finite) we can generalize it to Shannon's entropy, which describes the contribution to the measure of information carried by each of the symbols:

$$H(n,p) = -\sum p_i log_2(p_i), \sum p_i = 1, with\, i = 1, \ldots, n \qquad (1)$$

However, it does not mean that this is the ultimate solution of the problem. We can see that the measure of information proposed by Shannon is reducing invariance. It is not invariant with respect to replacements of characters by other characters of different probability. Thus, the measure of information becomes dependent on the probability distribution. We have to clarify the role of probability distribution in the formula. Does it describe the information, message, or the language?

The question is less trivial than it may seem at first. Pierce reports the information received from William F. Friedman about curious facts related to the frequency of the use of letters: "Gottlob Burmann, a German poet who lived from 1737 to 1805, wrote 130 poems, including a total of 20,000 words, without once using the letter R. Further, during the last seventeen years of his life, Burmann even omitted the letter from his daily conversation. In each of five stories published by Alonso Alcala y Herrera in Lisbon in 1641 a different vowel was suppressed. Francisco Navarrete y Ribera (1659), Fernando Jacinto de Zurita y Haro (1654), and Manuel Lorenzo de Lizarazu y Berbuizana (1654) provided other examples. In 1939, Ernest Vincent Wright published a 267-page novel, *Gadsby*, in which no use is made of the letter E" [25].

How much information is being carried by each letter of Wright's novel? Should we use the probability distribution with no character of probability 0, or that transformed by the exclusion of the letter "e"? Hartley's concerns seem vindicated.

The process of text generation is governed by the probability distribution which reflects the structural aspects of the text and which reflects much more than just the probability distribution of characters used in statistical research for the English language. Even taking into account idiosyncratic features of someone's way of expression, such as suppression of some letters, or simple preference, may not be enough.

Shannon was aware of the influence of the structural aspects of language. He recognized the problem of the lack of invariance with respect to the order of generation of symbols (letters or words), but his attempt to solve the problem through the use of conditional probabilities and frequencies of groups of characters of increasing size, or even frequencies of word sequences was inconclusive. His comments on the randomly generated examples of "approximations to English" are disarming in their naiveté: "The particular sequence of ten words 'attack on an English writer that the character of this' is not at all unreasonable. It appears then that a sufficiently complex stochastic process will give a satisfactory representation of a discrete source" [26]. It is not satisfactory at all. At least, Shannon did not provide any criterion for his satisfaction and the sequence is just gibberish. That we have parts of it that follow grammatical rules is an obvious result of the fact that probability distribution gives precedence to typical combinations of words, and their typicality comes from being in agreement with the rules of grammar. Non-grammatical sequences have probability close to zero in actual texts. However, this does not change the fact that the sequence in the example does not make any sense.

It is not clear why later on the next page he claimed that we have any reason to believe that the generation of texts should be described as a discrete Markoff process. Grammatical rules of inflection allow, in some languages, almost unlimited structural permutations. The errors in writing made by dyslexics and everyone's way of reading show that words in a natural language do not function as sequences created letter after letter, where the latter is selected based on the choice of the former or even several preceding ones.

To avoid misunderstanding, there is possibility that, in the human language acquisition, the frequencies of the patterns of words play an important role, as supporters of the Distributional Hypothesis claim. This idea goes back a long time to the studies of Zelig Harris [27] and to more influential, but slightly more general views of John Rupert Firth [28]. However, it is completely unlikely that the actual process of language production has the form which can be associated with a stochastic process, either directly or as a heuristic method of study.

In the general study of information as a concept independent from the specific, "engineering" issues of the theory of communication, Shannon must be given credit for going beyond Hartley's initial insight in developing a powerful tool of probabilistic methods of inquiry. Hartley tried, intentionally, to eliminate the need for taking into account various probability distributions and postulated the use of the uniform distribution. He was aware of the difficulties in the choice of particular distributions, due to their dependence on structural characteristics, which for him belonged to psychological factors. Due to this, he accepted the invariance of the measure of information to allow unlimited structural transformations.

Shannon, twenty years later and with the knowledge of more recent developments in logic and computation theory was aware that the authentic theory of information must take into account its structural characteristics. He disregarded the importance of semantics of information, but in his time this attitude was not unusual. Of course, the assumption that the meaning of information is irrelevant for its study is against our intuition, especially because in the common use of the word information, "information without any meaning", *i.e.*, one which cannot generate knowledge, seems to be an oxymoron.

We have to remember that, in many other disciplines, semantics was relegated to the study of the matters on the mind side of the mind-body problem. Meaning was still associated with intention or "aboutness" which, by Brentano's Thesis, was the main characteristic of the mental, as opposed to the material, and only the latter could be a subject of scientific inquiry in the popular view of the time. Furthermore, the focus of theoretical studies in the related disciplines (for instance logic or linguistic) in the period between the two World Wars was on the syntactic studies.

To avoid philosophical problems with the concept of meaning, various substitute concepts were explored (sense or model). There was no commonly accepted methodology of semantics. Therefore, Shannon's declaration of his disinterest in the meaning, "These semantic aspects of communication are irrelevant to the engineering problem" [5], may seem little bit arrogant, but was in the spirit of the times. Finally, although the criticism of this declaration from the side of those who tried in the next few years to develop semantics for information, such as Yehoshua Bar-Hillel and Rudolf Carnap [29,30] and who, for the reason of the negligence of the semantic issues disqualified Shannon's approach from the status of a theory of information was, in the opinion of the present author, well justified, their attempts had similar weakness. The proposed semantics of information was formulated in purely syntactic terms, as it was pointed out by the present author elsewhere [31].

Shannon's approach in this respect was in the full agreement with logic and, with the recently born new discipline, studying computation. These disciplines were also mainly interested in the structural issues of information. The problem was that the methods he proposed were not very effective, at least outside of the quite specific "ergodic sources" of information and even, in this particular case, he did not propose anything regarding the nature of information beyond the calculation of entropy. This, of course, does not depreciate his tremendous contributions to the study of communication, where these type of issues are irrelevant.

Here, someone can question the phrase "anything regarding the nature of information beyond the calculation of entropy." Why is it not sufficient? Entropy can be calculated for every finite probability distribution, and whenever it is finite for the continuous distributions. Thus, there is nothing in entropy which was not already in the probability distribution. Moreover, different probability distributions may produce the same entropy. It can be easily verified that very different instances of information, characterized by different probability distributions, have the same quantitative expressions in entropy. Thus, the invariance of entropy here is going beyond significant distinctions of information. We can avoid this problem by making the assumption that information is actually characterized by a probability distribution, entropy is just one of the possible quantitative characteristics of probability distributions and, therefore, also of information. However, in this case, we reduce unwanted invariance only slightly and definitely not sufficiently, and at the same we eliminate information theory. Information theory becomes indistinguishable from the probability theory.

It does not help much if we reformulate probability theory in terms of random variables and refer to entropy as a characteristic of random variables. We can say that a random variable is carrying information and its measure is entropy, but it is just assigning the name "information" to a nebulous concept without any specific meaning. Moreover, in this approach shortcomings of entropy start to be even more visible. In an earlier article, the author advocated the use of a better, alternative, but closely-related measure of information [32]:

$$Inf(n,p) = \sum p_i log_2 (np_i), \sum p_i = 1, with\, i = 1, \dots, n. \qquad (2)$$

It can be easily recognized that this measure can be associated with an instance of the Kullback-Leibler measure (but here there is present an important issue why this particular instance), or that it comes from the difference between Hartley's measure (maximum information irrespective to actual probability distribution) and Shannon's entropy: $Inf(n,p) = H_{Hartley} - H_{Shannon}$.

Equivalently, Shannon's entropy is the difference between the maximum of the alternative measure $Inf(n,max)$, which is the case when the probability measure of one particular choice is 1, and other choices have probability of all other choices is 0 (which happens to be equal to $H_{Hartley}$) and the alternative measure for a given probability distribution $Inf(n,p)$.

Shannon's entropy tells us how much of unknown and potential information we can have in a system, if we already know that the information has some specific form, for instance, enforced by the use of a particular language or particular encoding. Thus, *if* information has some structure going beyond the use of particular letters with the frequency corresponding to that of the English language, this structural information will be accounted for in entropy. *If not*, then entropy is not telling us anything. The problem is that we know only the probability distribution for letters in the particular language of the message. Thus, entropy tells us only about the "space" for information in the system, not how much information is actually there.

This is in complete agreement with Weaver's statement "To be sure, this word information in communication theory relates not so much to what you *do* say, as to what you *could* say" [22]. It is significant that Shannon referred to redundancy, not entropy, in his rediscovery of the characterization of the languages through their frequencies of characters used by al-Khindi already more than a thousand years earlier for cryptographic purposes.

The author's earlier articles provided an extensive argumentation for the advantages of the use of the alternative measure, which will be not repeated here [31,32]. It is enough to say that it eliminates problems in the use of the concept of information in physics (where the curious concept of "negentropy" had to be introduced, as a positive magnitude which has the opposite value to the positive entropy, in order to save consistency with observed reality), and eliminates several deficiencies of entropy when applied to random variables, such as its divergence in the limit for transition into continuous distributions, its lack of invariance with respect to linear transformations of coordinates, *etc.*

Unfortunately, but not unexpectedly due to the close relationship with entropy, the alternative measure, itself, does not resolve the problems related to the invariance of either of the measures, which, in both cases, goes way beyond the invariance with respect to structural transformations of information. After all, both measures are for one choice of the character, which is only a small component of the whole, and usually singular characters do not carry meaning, nor can reflect the structure of entire information. This fact has a natural consequence that the class of transformations determined by the properties of these small components is too large and does not reflect the invariant properties of entire structure. However, when focusing on the information which actually is in the system, not on the available "space" for this information within the variety of possible choices, we can try to find a better description of the relationship between the quantitative and structural characteristics of information.

6. Historical Perspective: From Turing to Kolmogorov and Chaitin

The 1936 paper of Alan Turing opens the new era of computation [33]. This epoch-making paper, together with the paper of Alonzo Church [34] refining his own earlier work, and the slightly earlier published paper of Emil Post [35], opened new ways of thinking about information, although in this time nobody used the term "information" in the context of computation. The expression "information processing" became popular much later.

Turing and Post directly referred to the processes performed by a machine involving manipulation of symbols and, therefore, put their work in the context similar to some extent to that of the work of Hartley. However, the subject of their work was understood in the key terms of logic, numbers, or calculation.

The leading theme of these, and many other works, was Kurt Gödel's Theorem [36]. While Gödel's result by ruining Hilbert's hopes, in hindsight, may seem a "black swan" of Nassim Taleb [37]. It was surprising in its apparent predictability (after all, Peano's arithmetic involves the Axiom of Choice, and the furious resistance against this axiom at the turn of the century intended to prevent involvement of any concepts which are not results of the finitary, well defined constructions). For the subject of the present paper, Gödel's Theorem is not so important, although it motivated Turing and Church in their work (the formal objective of their papers was a reproduction of Gödel's Theorem in different terms), but the method of Gödel numbers which he used in his proof.

Here we can see what was missing in the work of Hartley and what will be soon missing in the work of Shannon. Gödel managed to harness the apparently variable, elusive, and psychologically-determined aspects of the language into arithmetical description. Every expression, no matter how long, if finite, and no matter how complicated of any linearly structured language can be encoded in a unique way by the natural (Gödel) numbers [38]. Moreover, the concepts belonging to the analysis of these expressions (such as being well defined, being in logical relations of inference) can be encoded exactly the same way. Gödel used this encoding to show the existence of some sentences for which neither verification, nor refutation, is possible if, in the theory, we can reconstruct the arithmetic of natural numbers.

Of course, the numbers here do not measure or count anything. However, the structural relations within the text are expressed in the form which can be analyzed the same way as any other arithmetical formulas. This stimulated Church, Turing, and Post to describe processes of arithmetic in as simple a way as possible, and then the latter two authors described these fundamental processes in terms of the work of a simple machine which gets some input number and is producing an output number. Of course numbers can represent arbitrary text encoded, for example, in the form of Gödel's number, or in some other way. Turing showed that it is possible to design not only an a-machine (automatic machine) for every particular process, but also a unique simple machine, such that its work can be controlled by the input to produce output of any other a-machine applied to the part of the input, a Universal Turing Machine.

This is not only an earlier, but also a much deeper, revolution in the analysis of information, but nobody used in 1936 the word "information", and the theory of information has its popularly recognized date of birth 12 years later, if we forget or marginalize, as most people today do, the little known contribution of Hartley.

Turing (as well as Church, Post, and others) showed that the structural aspects of information can be examined not necessarily through statistical analysis, and that they are accessible to direct logical and mathematical studies. We can see here not only a methodology for dealing with the structural aspects of information, but also an approach where invariance plays the main role. Turing's universal machine is an excellent tool for this purpose. For instance, we can replace the question about the existence of an a-machine achieving some task, by the question whether a universal Turing machine can achieve it. Additionally, to compare two instances of information (if in the format acceptable to the machine) we can compare the inputs, which produce these instances as the machine's output.

Andrey Kolmogorov [39] and Gregory Chaitin [40], published independently and only after earlier publications of Ray Solomonoff [41,42] regarding related ideas, the description of an approach to the measuring of information in a string of symbols (its algorithmic complexity) by the length of the shortest program (input) for a universal Turing machine that produces this string. The standard terminology—algorithmic complexity—is referring to the fact that this measure depends on the structure of information, while Shannon's entropy does not.

We have here a measure of information which is invariant with respect to transformations performed by a universal Turing machine, but these transformations form a structure significantly different from those usually considered in the context of invariance. Instead of the group of transformations (each transformation has its inverse) we have, in this case, only a semigroup. There are many issues regarding the assessment of the meaning of computability (the necessary condition for measurability and application of the method) for some instances of information, which cannot be presented in the form of a finite string of symbols (e.g., irrational numbers). Turing, himself, considered a number computable if its arbitrary finite substring can be produced by a universal machine which gets in its input the number of required digits to be printed (more precisely, in his original 1936 paper he writes about the production of the number's n-th digit).

With this assumption, or without, we have some fundamental problems which are crucial for the domain of artificial intelligence, for the questions about implementation of the work of the brain, *etc.* Since the resistance to the claims of adequate interpretation of the work of brain is well known from works of John R. Searle [43,44], e.g., his Chinese Room Argument, and the arguments given by him and others do not address exactly the issues considered in this paper, I will omit the discussion of these matters. However, it is interesting that Searle uses as an argument against the possibility of consciousness in a device of the type of Turing machine its "multiple realizability", *i.e.*, the fact that a Turing machine can be implemented in many different physical systems. Thus, the invariance of the outcomes of the work of the machine (information) with respect to the changes of physical implementation is an argument against any authentic artificial intelligence.

In earlier papers of the author [45,46] these problems were addressed in the context of the autonomy of a Turing machine, which is relevant here. Can we say that a Turing machine without any involvement of human beings actually performs calculations of the values of functions defined on the set of natural numbers and with their values in the set of natural numbers?

My negative answer to this question was based on the claim that there is nothing in the machine which can put together the sequence of symbols (for instance of 0 s and 1 s) into a whole which is interpreted as a natural number. Moreover, someone who can see only the outcome of the work of the Turing machine cannot say what exactly is the number supposedly produced by the machine (100 can be a binary representation of the number 4 as represented in the decimal system, or can be itself a decimal representation, or can be a Gödel's number standing for some expression from an unknown language). Of course, we are coming back to the issue of meaning which was already a significant concern of Hartley. Yes, we can say that it is not an "engineering problem" or that it is "psychological factor", but it does not solve it, whether it is or is not. This is not the only problem of this type.

The issue can be addressed without any reference to the involvement of human consciousness. In such an approach, we can ask about the integration of information. Physics, more exactly quantum mechanics, provides examples of integrated information in the instances of superposition of states necessary to describe particles which cannot be considered as having definite properties or of states describing entangled particles. However, we do not need quantum physics and we can find more intuitive examples. We have in our human experience many other instances of objects that lose their identity when we separate them into parts.

This calls for the methodology which considers an additional characteristic of information: its level of integration.

7. Duality of Structural and Selective Manifestations of Information

Integration of information was considered the author's earlier publications in the context of two aspects or manifestations of information [47,48]. These two manifestations are always associated with each other in the coexisting dual characteristics of the same concept of information, but in two different, although related, information carriers. Information carrier is a variety or multiplicity standing in the opposition to the one (selected or constructed) for which some mode of transformation into unity (selection or construction) is considered. The original formulation of this definition was that information is an identification of a variety, where this identification can be made by the selection of "one" out of "many" (selective manifestation), or making "one" out of "many" by binding the "many" into a whole "one". The selective manifestation can be characterized in a quantitative manner, for instance through the probability distribution function describing the choice (transition from many to one) and, consequently, by functional magnitude; for instance, of the type of entropy, quantifying ("measuring") this distribution in some respects, or as explained in an earlier section of this article, by the preferred alternative measure [32]. Structural manifestation can be characterized by the level of information integration understood as a degree in which a binding structure can be decomposed into its components (in the mathematical formalism developed earlier by the author it was factorization into the direct product of component structures [48,49]).

The duality can be understood as a consequence of the definition of information introduced above. The only possibility for making the specific selection of an element from the information carrier is that each of the elements of the carrier has some structure consisting of some lower level variety bound into a whole. This structure gives each of the elements an identity (typically described in terms of "properties") allowing directed selection. On the other hand, when we construct a structure from some set of elements, there is a variety of ways how this structure as a whole can be built. The variety of potential structures from which one particular structure is selected forms the upper level information carrier.

In the special, but limited, context of information systems described in the form of a tape for Turing machine, the dual character of these two aspects, structural and dynamic, was utilized in algorithmic complexity measures. It is worth noticing the shift of attention from the length of the computation understood as a number of selections of the values for the current cell or square of the tape (traditional focus of algorithmic complexity) to the length of the input necessary to produce the measured information item expressing the minimal size of the structured input.

Finally, we can formulate what we mean by an information system. It is an information carrier in which the mode of transformation into unity is defined.

This conceptual framework for information is very general. The concept which is used in the definition is a categorical opposition of one and many. This means that this opposition cannot be defined and has to be considered a primitive concept for the theory of information. The high level of abstraction may generate doubts whether it is possible to develop a sufficiently-rich theory of information. The following section will disprove such concerns. The positive aspect of the approach presented in this section is the fact that virtually all clearly-defined concepts of information in the literature can be considered special cases of the concept defined above.

This is quite obvious when we compare the selective manifestation of information described above with all approaches inspired by the work of Shannon. The selection of the one out of many can be described by a probability distribution, or by an instruction within the head of a Turing machine. Similarly, Rene Thon's approach to study information through the structures defined on manifolds can be associated with the structural manifestation of information.

Thus, if we find methods to analyze information in terms of invariance in the conceptual framework presented here, we can extend the study to a wide range of particular instances of information in the literature.

8. Formalism for the Theory of Information

The concept of information defined as identification of a variety can be formalized with the use of concepts of general algebra. More extensive presentation of the formalization of information theory can be found in several of my earlier publications [49,50]. The point of departure in formalization of the duality of information manifestation can be found in the way we are associating information, understood in the linguistic way, with the relation between sets and their elements formally expressed by "$x \in A$". The informational aspect of the set theory can be identified in the separation axiom schema, which allows interpretation of $x \in A$ as a statement of some formula $\varphi(x)$ formulated in the predicate logic which is true whenever $x \in A$. The set A consists then of all elements which possess the property expressed by $\varphi(x)$.

If we are interested in a more general concept of information, not necessarily based in any formal language, we can consider a more general relationship than $x \in A$ described by a binary relation R built between the set S and its power set 2^S by the membership of elements of S in the closures f(A) of subsets A of S for some closure operator f. If this closure operator is trivial (for every subset A its closure f(A) = A) we get the usual set-theoretical relation of belonging to a set. In a more general case, only closed subsets correspond to properties.

The concept of information requires a variety (many), which can be understood as an arbitrary set S (called a carrier of information). Information system is this set S equipped with the family of subsets $\Im$ satisfying conditions: entire S is in $\Im$ and, together with every subfamily of $\Im$, its intersection belongs to $\Im$; *i.e.*, $\Im$ is a Moore family. Of course, this means that we have a closure operator defined on S (*i.e.*, a function f on the power set 2^S of a set S such that [51]:

(1)   For every subset A of S, $A \subseteq f(A)$;
(2)   For all subsets A, B of S, $A \subseteq B \Rightarrow f(A) \subseteq f(B)$; and
(3)   For every subset A of S, $f(f(A)) = f(A)$.

The set S with a closure operator f defined on it is usually called a closure space and is represented by the symbol $<S, f>$.

The Moore family $\Im$ of subsets is simply the family f-Cl of all closed subsets, *i.e.*, subsets A of S such that A = f(A). The family of closed subsets $\Im$ = f-Cl is equipped with the structure of a complete lattice L_f by the set theoretical inclusion. L_f can play a role of the generalization of logic for information systems that are not necessarily linguistic, although it does not have to be a Boolean algebra. In many cases it maintains all fundamental characteristics of a logical system [31].

Information itself is a distinction of a subset $\Im_0$ of $\Im$, such that it is closed with respect to (pair-wise) intersection and is dually-hereditary, *i.e.*, with each subset belonging to $\Im_0$, all subsets of S including it belong to $\Im_0$ (*i.e.*, $\Im_0$ is a filter in L_f).

The Moore family $\Im$ can represent a variety of structures of a particular type (e.g., geometric, topological, algebraic, logical, *etc.*) defined on the subsets of S. This corresponds to the structural manifestation of information. Filter $\Im_0$ in turn, in many mathematical theories associated with localization, can be used as a tool for identification, *i.e.*, selection of an element within the family $\Im$, and, under some conditions, in the set S. For instance, in the context of Shannon's selective information based on a probability distribution of the choice of an element in S, $\Im_0$ consists of elements in S which have probability measure 1, while $\Im$ is simply the set of all subsets of S.

Now, when we have mathematical formalism for information, we can proceed to formalization of the theory of invariants. For this purpose we can use the well-developed theory of functions between closure spaces preserving their structures, *i.e.*, homomorphisms of closure spaces.

If we have two closure spaces <S, f> and <T, g>, then a function φ from closure space <S, f> to <T, g> is called a homomorphism of closure spaces if it satisfies the condition:

$\forall A \subseteq S: \phi(f(A)) \subseteq g(\phi(A))$.

This condition defines continuous functions in the case of topological spaces and, as in topology, for general transitive closure spaces it is equivalent to the requirement that the inverse image of every g-closed subset is f-closed.

Now, when we add a condition that the function φ is bijective, we get an isomorphism of closure spaces. Finally, isomorphisms from <S, f> on itself (*i.e.*, when S = T) are called automorphisms or transformations of closure spaces. It can be easily shown that the class of all automorphisms on a closure space <S, f> forms a group with respect to composition of functions.

Now, with the accumulated knowledge of mathematical theory developed for the study of closure spaces [51] we have a complete conceptual toolkit for the study of the invariants of the transformations of information systems.

It is not a surprise that, in addition to the extensive study of topological invariants, the entire Erlangen Program of Felix Klein can be formulated in this mathematical formalism.

9. Conclusions

A closure operator defining an information system is a very general concept, which can be used to define geometric, topological, logical, and algebraic structures. This gives us an opportunity to formalize a very broad class of different types of information associated with geometry, topology, logic, *etc.* The invariance of the description of information is here identical with the invariance of the closure space with respect to transformations preserving its structure. For instance, for topological information, such transformations are continuous functions.

Now, when the toolkit for the study of the transformations of information systems and their invariants is ready, the next task is to apply it to the analysis of more specific instances of information. This task is going beyond the scope of the present paper and will be attempted in future publications.

Conflicts of Interest: The author declares no conflict of interest.

References

1. Schroeder, M.J. Crisis in Science: In Search for New Theoretical Foundations. *Prog. Biophys. Mol. Biol.* **2013**, *113*, 25–32. [CrossRef] [PubMed]
2. Noether, E. Invariante Variationsprobleme. *Nachrichten von der Gesellschaft der Wissenschaften zu Göttingen, Mathematisch-Physikalische Klasse* **1918**, *1918*, 235–257. (In German)
3. Klein, F.C. A comparative review of recent researches in geometry. **2008**, arXiv: 0807.3161v1. [CrossRef]
4. Pitts, W.; McCulloch, W.S. How we know universals; the perception of auditory and visual forms. *Bull. Math. Biophys.* **1947**, *9*, 127–147. [CrossRef] [PubMed]
5. Shannon, E.C. A mathematical theory of communication. In *The Mathematical Theory of Communication*; University of Illinois Press: Urbana, IL, USA, 1949; p. 3.
6. Shannon, E.C. A mathematical theory of communication. In *The Mathematical Theory of Communication*; University of Illinois Press: Urbana, IL, USA, 1949; p. 20.
7. On the Decrease of Entropy in a Thermodynamic System by the Intervention of Intelligent Beings. In *Quantum Theory and Measurement*; Wheeler, J.A., Zurek, W.H., Eds.; Princeton University Press: Princeton, NJ, USA, 1983; pp. 539–548 (*Engl. Transl.*); Szilard, L. Uber die Entropieverminderung in einem thermodynamischen System bei Eingriffen intelligenter Wesen. *Zeitschrift für Physik* **1929**, *53*, 840–856.
8. Schrödinger, E. *What is Life?*; Cambridge University Press: Cambridge, UK, 1945.
9. Landauer, R. Information is Physical. *Phys. Today* **1991**, *44*, 23–29. [CrossRef]
10. Landauer, R. The Physical Nature of Information. *Phys. Lett. A* **1996**, *217*, 188–193. [CrossRef]
11. Landauer, R. Information is a Physical Entity. *Phys. A* **1999**, *263*, 63–67. [CrossRef]
12. Landauer, R. Information is Inevitably Physical. In *Feynman and Computation: Exploring the Limits of Computers*; Hey, A.J.G., Ed.; Perseus: Reading, MA, USA, 1999; pp. 77–92.

13. MacKay, D.M. *Information, Mechanism and Meaning*; MIT Press: Cambridge, MA, USA, 1969.
14. Wheeler, J.A. Information, Physics, Quantum: The Search for Links. In *Complexity, Entropy, and the Physics of Information*; Zurek, W.H., Ed.; Addison-Wesley: Redwood City, CA, USA, 1990; pp. 3–28.
15. Wheeler, J.A.; Ford, K. *Geons, Black Holes, and Quantum Foam: A Life in Physics*; W. W. Norton: New York, NY, USA; 1998.
16. Thom, R. *Structural Stability and Morphogenesis*; Benjamin: Reading, MA, USA, 1975.
17. Schroeder, M.J. The Role of Information Integration in Demystification of Holistic Methodology. In *Integral Biomathics: Tracing the Road to Reality*; Simeonov, P.L., Smith, L.S., Ehresmann, A.C., Eds.; Springer: Berlin, Germany, 2012; pp. 283–296.
18. Simeonov, P.L.; Brezina, E.H.; Cottam, R.; Ehresmann, A.C.; Gare, A.; Goranson, T.; Gomez-Ramirez, J.; Josephson, B.D.; Marchal, B.; Matsuno, K. Stepping Beyond the Newtonian Paradigm in Biology: Towards an Integrable Model of Life—Accelerating Discovery in the Biological Foundations of Science INBIOSA White Paper. In *Integral Biomathics: Tracing the Road to Reality*; Simeonov, P.L., Smith, L.S., Ehresmann, A.C., Eds.; Springer: Berlin, Germany, 2012; pp. 319–418.
19. Pierce, J.R. The early days of information theory. *IEEE Trans. Inf. Theory* **1973**, *19*, 3–8. [CrossRef]
20. Hartley, R.V.L. Transmission of Information. *Bell Syst. Tech. J.* **1928**, *7*, 535–563. [CrossRef]
21. Ellersick, F.W. A conversation with Claude Shannon. *IEEE Commun. Mag.* **1984**, *22*, 123–126. [CrossRef]
22. Shannon, E.C.; Weaver, W. *The Mathematical Theory of Communication*; University of Illinois Press: Urbana, IL, USA, 1949; p. 100.
23. Oliver, B.; Pierce, J.; Shannon, C.E. The Philosophy of PCM. *Proc. Inst. Radio Eng.* **1948**, *36*, 1324–1331. [CrossRef]
24. Pierce, J.R. *An Introduction to Information Theory: Symbols, Signals and Noise*; Dover: New York, NY, USA, 1980; p. 24.
25. Pierce, J.R. *An Introduction to Information Theory: Symbols, Signals and Noise*; Dover: New York, NY, USA, 1980; p. 48.
26. Shannon, E.C.; Weaver, W. *The Mathematical Theory of Communication*; University of Illinois Press: Urbana, IL, USA, 1949; p. 14.
27. Harris, Z. Distributional structure. *Word* **1954**, *10*, 146–162. [CrossRef]
28. Firth, J.R. A synopsis of linguistic theory 1930–1955. In *Studies in Linguistic Analysis*; Philological Society: Oxford, UK, 1957; pp. 1–32. Reprinted: *Selected Papers of J. R. Firth 1952–1959*; Palmer, F.R., Ed.; Longman: London, UK, 1968.
29. Bar-Hillel, Y.; Carnap, R. *An Outline of a Theory of Semantic Information*; Technical Report No. 247; Research Laboratory of Electronics, MIT: Cambridge, MA, USA, 1952. Reprinted: In *Language and Information: Selected Essays on Their Theory and Application*; Addison-Wesley: Reading, MA, USA, 1964; pp. 221–274.
30. Bar-Hillel, Y. Semantic Information and Its Measures. In *Transactions of the Tenth Conference on Cybernetics*; Foundation: New York, NY, USA, 1952; pp. 33–48. Reprinted: In *Language and Information: Selected Essays on Their Theory and Application*; Addison-Wesley: Reading, MA, USA, 1964; pp. 298–310.
31. Schroeder, M.J. Search for Syllogistic Structure of Semantic Information. *J. Appl. Non-Class. Logic* **2012**, *22*, 83–103. [CrossRef]
32. Schroeder, M.J. An Alternative to Entropy in the Measurement of Information. *Entropy* **2004**, *6*, 388–412. [CrossRef]
33. Turing, A.M. On computable numbers, with an application to the Entscheidungsproblem. *Proc. Lond. Math. Soc. Ser. 2* **1936**, *42*, 230–265, cor. *43*, 544–546.
34. Church, A. An unsolvable problem of elementary number theory. *Am. J. Math.* **1936**, *58*, 345–363. [CrossRef]
35. Post, E.L. Finite Combinatory Processes—Formulation 1. *J. Symb. Logic* **1936**, *1*, 103–105. [CrossRef]
36. Gödel, K. *On Formally Undecidable Propositions of Principia Mathematica and Related Systems*; Dover: New York, NY, USA, 1992; (*Engl. Transl.*); Gödel, K. Über formal unentscheidbare Sätze der Principia Mathematica und verwandter Systeme I. *Monatshefte für Mathematik und Physik* **1931**, *38*, 173–198.
37. Taleb, N.N. *The Black Swan: The Impact of the Highly Improbable*; Random House: New York, NY, USA, 2007.
38. Gödel, K. *On Formally Undecidable Propositions of Principia Mathematica and Related Systems*; Dover: New York, NY, USA, 1992; p. 40 (*Engl. Transl.*); Gödel, K. Über formal unentscheidbare Sätze der Principia Mathematica und verwandter Systeme I. *Monatshefte für Mathematik und Physik* **1931**, *38*, 173–198.
39. Kolmogorov, A.N. Three approaches to the definition of the "quantity of information". *Problemy Peredachi Informatsii* **1965**, *1*, 3–11.
40. Chaitin, G.J. On the Length of Programs for Computing Finite Binary Sequences. *JACM* **1966**, *13*, 547–569. [CrossRef]

41. Solomonoff, R. *A Preliminary Report on a General Theory of Inductive Inference*; Technical Report ZTB-138; Zator Co.: Cambridge, MA, USA, 1960.

42. Solomonoff, R. A Formal Theory of Inductive Inference. *Inf. Control* **1964**, *7*, 1–22. [CrossRef]

43. Searle, J.R. *The Rediscovery of the Mind*; MIT Press: Cambridge, MA, USA, 1992.

44. Searle, J.R. *The Mystery of Consciousness*; NYREV: New York, NY, USA, 1997.

45. Schroeder, M.J. From Proactive to Interactive Theory of Computation. In Proceedings of the 6th AISB Symposium on Computing and Philosophy: The Scandal of Computation—What is Computation, Exeter, UK, 2–5 April 2013; pp. 47–51.

46. Schroeder, M.J. Autonomy of Computation and Observer Dependence. In Proceedings of the 7th AISB Symposium on Computing and Philosophy: Is Computation Observer Dependent Bishop, Goldsmiths, UK, 1–4 April 2014. Available online: http://doc.gold.ac.uk/aisb50/AISB50-S03/AISB50-S3-Schroeder-paper.pdf (accessed on 26 February 2016).

47. Schroeder, M.J. Philosophical Foundations for the Concept of Information: Selective and Structural Information. In Proceedings of the Third International Conference on the Foundations of Information Science, Paris, France, 4–7 July 2005. Available online: http://mdpi.org/fis2005/F.58.paper (accessed on 26 February 2016).

48. Schroeder, M.J. Quantum Coherence without Quantum Mechanics in Modeling the Unity of Consciousness. In *Quantum Interaction*, Proceedings of the Third International Symposium, QI 2009, Saarbrücken, Germany, 25–27 March 2009; Bruza, P., Sofge, D., Lawless, W., van Rijsbergen, K., Klusch, M., Eds.; Springer: Heidelberg, Germany, 2009; Volume 5494, pp. 97–112.

49. Schroeder, M.J. From Philosophy to Theory of Information. *Int. J. Inf. Theor. Appl.* **2011**, *18*, 56–68.

50. Schroeder, M.J. Algebraic Model for the Dualism of Selective and Structural Manifestations of Information. In *RIMS Kokyuroku*; No. 1915; Kondo, M., Ed.; Research Institute for Mathematical Sciences, Kyoto University: Kyoto, Japan, 2014; pp. 44–52.

51. Birkhoff, G. *Lattice Theory*, 3rd ed.; American Mathematical Society Colloquium Publications: Providence, RI, USA, 1967; Volume XXV.

5

On Solving the Fuzzy Customer Information Problem in Multicommodity Multimodal Routing with Schedule-Based Services

Yan Sun [1,2], **Maoxiang Lang** [1,2,*] **and Jiaxi Wang** [1]

[1] School of Traffic and Transportation, Beijing Jiaotong University, Beijing 100044, China; sunyanbjtu@163.com (Y.S.); wangjiaxi@bjtu.edu.cn (J.W.)

[2] MOE Key Laboratory for Urban Transportation Complex Systems Theory and Technology, Beijing Jiaotong University, Beijing 100044, China

* Correspondence: mxlang@bjtu.edu.cn

Academic Editor: Willy Susilo

Abstract: In this study, we combine the fuzzy customer information problem with the multicommodity multimodal routing with schedule-based services which was explored in our previous study [1]. The fuzzy characteristics of the customer information are embodied in the demanded volumes of the multiple commodities and the time windows of their due dates. When the schedule-based services are considered in the routing, schedule constraints emerge because the operations of block container trains should follow their predetermined schedules. This will restrict the routes selection from space-time feasibility. To solve this combinatorial optimization problem, we first build a fuzzy chance-constrained nonlinear programming model based on fuzzy possibility theory. We then use a crisp equivalent method and a linearization method to transform the proposed model into the classical linear programming model that can be effectively solved by the standard mathematical programming software. Finally, a numerical case is presented to demonstrate the feasibility of the proposed method. The sensitivity of the best solution with respect to the values of the confidence levels is also examined.

Keywords: multicommodity; multimodal routing; fuzzy demanded volume; fuzzy soft time window; fuzzy chance-constrained programming

1. Introduction

The routing problem has always been a highlight in combinatorial optimizations. Great importance has been attached to it, not only in the transportation field, but also in many other industries such as telecommunications, manufacturing and the Internet [2]. The routing problem aims at improving the performance of a system by reasonably distributing the flow of the object (data, signal or products) in it. As for the multimodal routing problem, it is defined as selecting the best routes to move commodities from their origins to their destinations through a multimodal service network. The multimodal routing problem arises under the following conditions.

The remarkable growth of international trade in recent years stimulates the worldwide commodity circulation, which significantly expands the geographical scale of the transportation network, extends the freight transportation distance, and leads to a more complex transportation environment. All these tendencies present great challenges for decision makers from various aspects including transportation cost, efficiency, reliability and so on. Meanwhile, because of the integrative combination of the respective advantages of different transportation service modes, multimodal transportation has been proved to be a more cost-efficient [3] and environment-friendly [4] means compared with the traditional uni-modal transportation in a long-haul transportation setting. Therefore, large numbers of enterprises decide to adopt multimodal transportation schemes to transport their products or materials. According to the relevant statistics, the volume fulfilled by the multimodal transportation accounts for 80% of the total freight volume in North America [5]. However, the logistics cost is still high, and accounts for approximately 30%–50% of the total production cost of enterprises [6]. Consequently, lowering transportation costs by advanced multimodal routing becomes an effective approach for enterprises to raise profits and maintain competitiveness in the global market [2].

By considering the practical demand of lowering the transportation costs by selecting the best multimodal routes, many researchers have devoted themselves to the multimodal routing problem (or intermodal routing problem) in recent decades. Barnhart and Ratliff [7] developed a foundational framework on modeling intermodal routing, and introduced a solution procedure with matching to solve the routing problem from Cincinnati to Atlanta/Chattanooga. Boardman *et al.* [8] designed a real-time intermodal routing decision support system by incorporating the k-shortest path double-swap method with database and user interface. Lozano and Storchi [9], Lam and Srikanthan [10] and Boussedjra *et al.* [11] highlighted the intermodal/multimodal shortest path problem. They separately developed an *ad hoc* modified chronological algorithm, clustering technique accelerated k-shortest algorithm and multi-label label correcting shortest path algorithm, to identify the shortest path in the intermodal/multimodal service network. Zhang and Guo [12] described the physical structure of the multimodal service network, and proposed a foundational network assignment model for the multimodal routing problem. Zhang *et al.* [13] formulated the multimodal routing problem as a generalized shortest path problem, built a 0–1 integer programming model based on Reddy and Kasilingam's work [14], and adopted Dijkstra algorithm to obtain the optimal solution of the model. Winebrake *et al.* [15] developed a geospatial model to find optimal routes with different objectives in the intermodal transportation network. The construction and solution of the model were implemented by ArcGIS software. Kim *et al.* [16] and Chang *et al.* [17] both analyzed the intermodal sea–truck routing problem for container transportation in South Korea, and formulated classical programming models to solve the empirical cases in South Korea. The proposed models were solved by standard mathematical programming software. Liu *et al.* [18] explored the dynamic path optimization for multimodal service network. The network deformation method was used in their study to transform the initial network into a directed simple graph. This enabled the problem to be effectively solved by a modified Dijkstra algorithm. Cho *et al.* [19] presented a weighted constrained shortest path model and a label setting algorithm to draw the optimal international intermodal routing. They applied the proposed method to a real-world routing case from Busan to Rotterdam. Sun and Lang [20] as well as Xiong and Wang [21] separately discussed the bi-objective optimization for the multimodal routing problem that aims at minimizing transportation costs and transportation time. The normalized normal constraint method and Taguchi genetic algorithm were utilized to generate the Pareto frontier of the problem. The former also conducted a sensitivity analysis of the Pareto frontier with respect to demand and supply.

Above all, substantial accomplishments have been achieved in the multimodal routing problem. However, some research potential still exists.

(1) The majority of the current studies concentrated on the single commodity flow routing problem. In practice, decision makers usually need to plan routes for multiple commodities in their planning horizons. In addition, the best routing for multiple commodities is not the simple set of the respective independent best routes for all commodities, because the multimodal service network is usually capacitated. Therefore, it is necessary to combine the multicommodity flow with the multimodal routing.

(2) In the current studies, rail schedules are rarely considered in the model formulation. Many studies, especially the domestic ones, formulated the rail service as a time-flexible pattern that is similar to the road service, and hence simplified the connection between different transportation services in the terminals as a continuous "arrival-transshipment-departure" procedure. Actually, rail services are organized by predetermined schedules, especially in China, and train schedules will restrict the routing because of space-time feasibility. If the transportation of a commodity along a route cannot match the schedules of the rail services on it, the planned route is infeasible in the practice. Consequently, consideration of schedules in routing modeling is quite worthwhile.

(3) Multimodal routing in most current studies was oriented on the certain customer information, which means all customer information is determined and known when making routing decisions. However, as has been claimed in many studies as well as indicated in the practice, customer information, especially their demands, is difficult to determine during the planning period. Many studies on other transportation problems, e.g., the vehicle routing problem [22–24] and service network design problem [25,26], have all paid great attention to the uncertain issues from the fuzzy or stochastic viewpoint. Hence uncertain customer information is also a characteristic that should not be neglected in the multimodal routing problem.

The first two issues above have already been explored in our previous study (see Reference [1]). In this study, we will focus on integrating the fuzzy customer information problem into this previous study in order to develop the initial problem into its extended version: schedule-constrained multicommodity multimodal routing problem with fuzzy customer information.

Similar to the transportation scenario constructed in Reference [1], the rail service (the schedule-based service) in the multimodal service network specifically refers to the "point-to-point" block container train service. This kind of service is operated directly and periodically from its loading organization station to its unloading organization station. For the convenience of modeling, the same block container train in different periods is treated as a different one. The road service is formulated as an uncapacitated time-flexible service, which matches the superiority of the road service (container trucks) in its organization flexibility. Transshipment is not necessary when the commodity arrives at and then departs from a terminal by road service, and a road service route can be covered entirely or partly in the routing. For the convenience of modeling, a road service can be divided into several segments, e.g., a directed road service route (g, h, i, j) is divided into sub segments (g, h), (g, i), (g, j), (h, i), (h, j), and (i, j).

For the convenience of readability, we briefly introduce the schedule Constraints (1)–(4) resulting from the actual transportation practice that the operation of block container trains should follow their predetermined schedules. For detailed relative information, we can refer to Reference [1].

(1) If the commodity plans to be moved by rail service from the current terminal (loading organization station) to the successor terminal (unloading organization station), its arrival time at the current terminal should not be later than the upper bound of the loading operation time window of the block container train at the same terminal.

(2) In the above situation, if the arrival time of the commodity at the terminal is earlier than the lower bound of the operation time window of the block container train at the same terminal, it should wait until the lower bound of the time window.

(3) After being loaded on the train, the commodity should wait until the departure time of the train. Then it departs from the current terminal to the successor terminal, and arrives at the successor terminal at the arrival time of the train.

(4) The commodity should wait until the lower bound of the unloading operation time window of the train at the successor terminal, and then gets unloaded from it.

For the uncertain customer information problem, we will explain it in detail by using a whole section. After defining the symbols that will be used in the model formulation (Section 2), we organize the remaining sections of this study as follows. In Section 3, we analyze the uncertain characteristics of the customer information from the fuzzy viewpoint, and propose fuzzy demands and fuzzy soft due date time windows to define the uncertainty. In Section 4, a fuzzy chance-constrained nonlinear programming model for the routing problem is established based on fuzzy possibility theory. In Section 5, we introduce a crisp equivalent method and a linearization method to transform the proposed model into its equivalent linear programming form, after which the routing problem can be effectively solved by the standard mathematical programming software. In Section 6, a numerical case is presented to demonstrate the feasibility of the proposed model, and the sensitivity of the best solution with respect to the values of the confidence levels is also examined. Finally, conclusions of this study are drawn in Section 7.

2. Notations

N: terminal set in the multimodal service network, h, i, and j are the terminal indexes;

A: directed transportation arc set in the multimodal service network, and $A = \{(i, j)| i \in N, j \in N\}$;

K: commodity set, and k is the commodity index;

Γ_{ij}: set of rail services on (i, j);

Ω_{ij}: set of road services on (i, j);

S: transportation service set in the multimodal service network, s and r are the service indexes, $S = \cup_{(i,j) \in A} \{S_{ij}\}$ where S_{ij} is transportation service set on (i, j), and $S_{ij} = \Gamma_{ij} \cup \Omega_{ij}$;

$\delta^-(i)$: predecessor terminal set to terminal i, and $\delta^-(i) \subseteq N$;

$\delta^+(i)$: successor terminal set to terminal i, and $\delta^+(i) \subseteq N$;

o_k: origin terminal of commodity k;

d_k: destination terminal of commodity k;

$t^k_{release}$: release time of commodity k from its origin terminal;

$[l^s_i, u^s_i]$: loading/unloading operation time window of rail service s at terminal i;

SD^s_i, SA^s_j: scheduled departure time and scheduled arrival time of service s from terminal i and at terminal j on (i, j);

Q^s_{ij}: available carrying capacity of rail service s at terminal i, unit: TEU;

t_{ijs}: transportation time of service s on (i, j), especially for $s \in \Gamma_{ij}$, the effective transportation time $t_{ijs} = l^s_i - SD^s_i$, unit: h;

c^s_{ij}: unit transportation costs of by service s on (i, j), unit: ¥/TEU;

c_s: unit loading/unloading operation costs of service s, unit: ¥/TEU;

c_{store}: unit inventory costs of rail service s, unit: ¥/TEU-h;

c_{pick}: additional charges for picking up the unit commodity from shipper at a rail terminal by rail service at origin, unit: ¥/TEU;

ϕ_k: a 0-1 indicating parameter, if the above service is demanded, $\phi_k = 1$, otherwise $\phi_k = 0$;

$c_{delivery}$: additional charges for delivering the unit commodity from rail terminal to receiver by rail service at destination, unit: ¥/TEU;

μ_k: a 0-1 indicating parameter, if the above service is demanded, $\mu_k = 1$, otherwise $\mu_k = 0$;

π: inventory period free of charge, unit: h;

M: a large enough positive number;

X^k_{ijs}: 0-1 variable, If commodity k is moved on (i, j) by service s, $X^k_{ijs} = 1$, otherwise $X^k_{ijs} = 0$ (decision variable);

Y^k_i: arrival time of commodity k at terminal i (decision variable);

Z^k_{ijs}: charged inventory time at terminal i before being moved on (i, j) by rail service s, unit: h (decision variable).

3. Fuzzy Characteristics of the Customer Information

3.1. Fuzzy Demanded Volume

It is difficult to master the accurate demand information of the customers when planning the best multimodal routes in advance. On the one hand, the planning is earlier than the actual transportation; and, on the other hand, due to the impact of many uncertain factors in production and consumption, the demands (measured by demanded volumes of the commodities) negotiated by shippers and receivers are difficult to be determined during the planning period. Consequently, there is a great challenge for the decision makers in that the demands are uncertain before the actual transportation starts. The advance routing should deal with this uncertainty. Generally, there is not enough historical data that can be utilized to fit the probability distributions for all the uncertain demands, but the decision makers can effectively estimate the demands according to their expertise. Therefore, when the stochastic demands are unattainable, it is worthwhile to adopt fuzzy logic to estimate the uncertainty of the demands.

In this study, we use a triangular fuzzy number to represent the demanded volume of a commodity flow. For commodity k, its fuzzy volume is defined as:

$$\tilde{q}_k = \left(q_k^L, q_k^M, q_k^U \right) \forall k \in K$$

where $q_k^L < q_k^M < q_k^U$, and q_k^M is the most likely volume of commodity k.

Consequently, the total volume of commodities loaded on a block container train is:

$$V_{ijs} = \sum_{k \in K} \tilde{q}_k \cdot X_{ijs}^k \forall (i,j) \in A, \forall s \in \Gamma_{ij}$$

V_{ijs} is also a triangular fuzzy number according to the fuzzy arithmetic rules, and can be rewritten as:

$$\widetilde{V_{ijs}} = \left(\sum_{k \in K} q_k^L \cdot X_{ijs}^k, \sum_{k \in K} q_k^M \cdot X_{ijs}^k, \sum_{k \in K} q_k^U \cdot X_{ijs}^k \right) = \left(V_{ijs}^L, V_{ijs}^M, V_{ijs}^U \right) \forall (i,j) \in A, \forall s \in \Gamma_{ij}$$

3.2. Fuzzy Soft Time Window

Due date is closely related to the customer satisfaction level. It can be a time point or a time window. In general, a customer considers that the transportation service is satisfactory when the arrival time of the commodity at the destination is neither too early nor too late. Therefore, time windows are more suitable than time points to represent the due dates of moving commodities. Moreover, in practice, customers also accept violation of the time windows to some degree. In that case, the satisfaction level of the customer will decrease when the violation degree increases. Therefore, the time windows in this study are soft ones instead of hard ones that stress the arrival time of a commodity at its destination must be within the time window.

The customers may consider "good" if the arrival time at the destination is within the time window, while "all right" or "bad" or other personal human feelings if the arrival time is out of the range of the time window [24]. Hence, we can use trapezoidal fuzzy numbers to represent the due date, and further measure the customer satisfaction quantitatively using the fuzzy membership function [27,28]. For commodity k, its due date is defined as:

$$\tilde{T}_k = \left(T_k^{min}, T_k^L, T_k^U, T_k^{max} \right) \forall k \in K$$

where $T_k^{min} < T_k^L < T_k^U < T_k^{max}$, and $[T_k^L, T_k^U]$ is the time window that the customer considers the arrival time of the commodity at the destination to be neither too early nor too late. The corresponding satisfaction level in the fuzzy soft time window is shown in Figure 1.

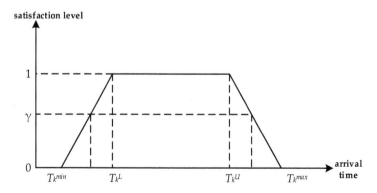

Figure 1. Satisfaction level in the fuzzy soft time window.

The membership function of the time window is as Equation (1), where $\mu_k\left(Y_{d_k}^k\right)$ is also the customer satisfaction level when commodity k arrives at its destination d_k at $Y_{d_k}^k$.

$$\mu_k\left(Y_{d_k}^k\right) = \begin{cases} \dfrac{Y_{d_k}^k - T_k^{min}}{T_k^L - T_k^{min}}, T_k^{min} \leq Y_{d_k}^k < T_k^L \\ 1, T_k^L \leq Y_{d_k}^k \leq T_k^U \\ \dfrac{Y_{d_k}^k - T_k^{max}}{T_k^U - T_k^{max}}, T_k^U < Y_{d_k}^k \leq Y_k^{max} \\ 0, otherwise \end{cases} \quad \forall k \in K \tag{1}$$

Assuming that the customer satisfaction level should not be lower than the confidence level γ ($\gamma \in [0, 1]$), the acceptable arrival time at the destination ranges from $\left[\left(T_k^L - T_k^{min}\right) \cdot \gamma + T_k^{min}\right]$ to $\left[\left(T_k^U - T_k^{max}\right) \cdot \gamma + T_k^{max}\right]$.

4. Model Formulation

The schedule-constrained multicommodity multimodal routing problem aims to select the best time-feasible routes for all commodity flows through the multimodal service network. Oriented on the customers' practical demand of lowering the total transportation costs, minimizing the generalized costs of all commodities is therefore set as the optimization objective. The generalized costs include transportation costs en route, loading/unloading operation costs and inventory costs at terminals, as well as the customer-specific additional rail origin-pickup/destination-delivery service costs. First, we formulate this problem as a nonlinear programming model with fuzzy parameters (M1). The framework of M1 derives from the model in Reference [1].

- Objective Function:

$$minimize \sum_{k \in K} \tilde{q}_k \cdot \sum_{(i,j) \in A} \sum_{s \in S_{ij}} c_{ij}^s \cdot X_{ijs}^k \tag{2}$$

$$+ \sum_{k \in K} \tilde{q}_k \cdot \sum_{i \in N} \left(\sum_{h \in \delta^-(i)} \sum_{r \in S_{hi}} c_r \cdot X_{hir}^k + \sum_{j \in \delta^+(i)} \sum_{s \in S_{ij}} c_s \cdot X_{ijs}^k \right) \tag{3}$$

$$+ \sum_{k \in K} \tilde{q}_k \cdot \sum_{(i,j) \in A} \sum_{s \in \Gamma_{ij}} c_{store} \cdot Z_{o_kjs}^k \tag{4}$$

$$+ \sum_{k \in K} \tilde{q}_k \cdot \phi_k \cdot \sum_{j \in \delta^+(o_k)} \sum_{s \in \Gamma_{o_kj}} c_{pick} \cdot X_{o_kjs}^k + \sum_{k \in K} \tilde{q}_k \cdot \mu_k \cdot \sum_{j \in \delta^-(d_k)} \sum_{s \in \Gamma_{id_k}} c_{delivery} \cdot X_{id_ks}^k \tag{5}$$

- Subject to:

$$\sum_{j \in \delta^+(i)} \sum_{s \in S_{ij}} X_{ijs}^k - \sum_{h \in \delta^-(i)} \sum_{r \in S_{hi}} X_{hir}^k = \begin{cases} 1, i = o_k \\ 0, \forall i \in N \setminus \{o_k, d_k\} \quad \forall k \in K, \forall i \in N \\ -1, i = d_k \end{cases} \tag{6}$$

$$\sum_{s \in S_{ij}} X_{ijs}^k \leq 1 \ \forall k \in K, \forall (i,j) \in A \tag{7}$$

$$\widetilde{V_{ijs}} \leq Q_{ij}^s \ \forall (i,j) \in A, \forall s \in \Gamma_{ij} \tag{8}$$

$$Y_{o_k}^k = t_{release}^k \forall k \in K \tag{9}$$

$$\left(max\left\{Y_i^k, SD_i^s\right\} + t_{ijs} - Y_j^k\right) \cdot X_{ijs}^k = 0 \forall k \in K, \forall (i,j) \in A, \forall s \in S_{ij} \tag{10}$$

$$Y_i^k \leq u_i^s \cdot X_{ijs}^k + M\left(1 - X_{ijs}^k\right) \forall k \in K, \forall (i,j) \in A, \forall s \in \Gamma_{ij} \tag{11}$$

$$\mu_k \left(Y_{d_k}^k \right) \geqslant \gamma \; \forall k \in K \tag{12}$$

$$\left(max \left\{ 0, l_i^s - Y_i^k - \pi \right\} - Z_{ijs}^k \right) \cdot X_{ijs}^k = 0 \; \forall k \in K, \forall (i,j) \in A, \forall s \in \Gamma_{ij} \tag{13}$$

$$X_{ijs}^k \in \{0,1\} \; \forall k \in K, \forall (i,j) \in A, \forall s \in S_{ij} \tag{14}$$

$$Y_i^k \geqslant 0 \; \forall k \in K, \forall i \in N \tag{15}$$

$$Z_{ijs}^k \geqslant 0 \; \forall k \in K, \forall (i,j) \in A, \forall s \in \Gamma_{ij} \tag{16}$$

Equations (2)–(5) are the transportation costs en route, loading and unloading costs at terminals, inventory costs at terminal as well as the rail origin-pickup and destination-delivery service costs, respectively. Their summation is the generalized costs that the decision maker plans to minimize.

Constraint Set (6) are the commodity flow conservation equation. Constraint Sets (6) and (7) ensure the integrity of each commodity flow that one and only one route can be selected to move the commodity through the multimodal service network. Constraint Set (8) is the capacity constraint resulting from the limited available carrying capacity of a block container train. Constraint Set (9) assumes the arrival time of the commodity at its origin equals its release time. Constraint Set (10) ensures the compatibility requirements between decision variables X_{ijs}^k and Y_j^k. Constraint Set (11) ensures the arrival time of the commodity at a terminal will not exceed the upper bound of the operation time window of the utilized block container train at the same terminal. Constraint Set (12) is the customer satisfaction level constraint. Constraint Set (13) is similar to Constraint Set (10), and ensures the compatibility requirements among decision variables X_{ijs}^k, Y_i^k and Z_{ijs}^k. Constraint Sets (14)–(16) are variable domain constraints.

In M1, the Objective Function (2)–(5) and Constraint Set (8) are involved with fuzzy parameters, the mathematical meaning of minimizing the objective and of the constraint are hence not clear, consequently M1 is not a well-defined model. In order to obtain a well-defined model, we need to transform the fuzzy objective and the fuzzy constraint set into their respective crisp equivalents. Based on Liu and Iwamura's theoretical framework on chance-constrained programming in a fuzzy environment [29], we can obtain M1's crisp equivalent fuzzy chance-constrained programming model (M2) as follows. (M2 is a well-defined model.)

- Objective Function:

$$minimize \overline{f} \tag{17}$$

- Subject to:

$$Pos \left\{ f(X,Y,Z,\tilde{q}) \leqslant \overline{f} \right\} \geqslant \alpha \tag{18}$$

$$Pos \left\{ \widetilde{V_{ijs}} \leqslant Q_{ij}^s \right\} \geqslant \beta \; \forall (i,j) \in A, \forall s \in \Gamma_{ij} \tag{19}$$

Constraint Sets (6), (7), and (9)–(16).

In M2, $Pos\{\cdot\}$ denotes the possibility of the event in $\{\cdot\}$ [29]. α and β are predetermined confidence levels that indicate the decision maker's subjective preference for the corresponding issues, and $\alpha, \beta \in [0, 1]$. $f(X,Y,Z,\tilde{q})$ is the objective value of M1 where $X = \cup_{k \in K, (i,j) \in A, s \in S_{ij}} \left\{ X_{ijs}^k \right\}$, $Y = \cup_{k \in K, i \in N} \left\{ Y_i^k \right\}$, $Z = \cup_{k \in K, (i,j) \in A, s \in \Gamma_{ij}} \left\{ Z_{ijs}^k \right\}$ and $\tilde{q} = \cup_{k \in K} \{\tilde{q}_k\}$. For $\forall (X,Y,Z)$, $f(X,Y,Z,\tilde{q})$ is also a triangular fuzzy number based on the fuzzy arithmetic rules. When confidence level α is given, there possibly exist several potential $\overline{f}$ that satisfy Constraint Set (18). Minimizing $\overline{f}$ as the objective of M2 will find the minimal value (min$\overline{f}$) of $f(X,Y,Z,\tilde{q})$ with confidence level α. Constraint Set (19) means the possibility that the total volume of commodities loaded on a block container train do not exceed its available carrying capacity should not be lower than the given confidence level β.

5. Solution Strategy

M2 is a fuzzy chance-constrained nonlinear programming model. Because of the restrictions of the fuzzy chance constraint sets and the nonlinear constraint sets, it is difficult to solve this by the exact solution algorithm that can be effectively implemented by the standard mathematical software. Therefore, it is necessary to conduct some transformations to M2. It is obvious that the problem will be effectively solvable if M2 can be transformed into a linear programming model. For this purpose, we conduct the following transformations to M2 successively.

5.1. Crisp Equivalent of the Fuzzy Chance Constraint Sets

We consider a general triangular fuzzy number $\tilde{a} = (a^L, a^M, a^U)$ where $a^L > a^M > a^U > 0$, let $\mu_{\tilde{a}}(x)$ denote its membership function whose expression is as Equation (20).

$$\mu_{\tilde{a}}(x) = \begin{cases} \dfrac{x - a^L}{a^M - a^L}, & a^L \leqslant x \leqslant a^M \\ \dfrac{a^U - x}{a^U - a^M}, & a^M \leqslant x \leqslant a^U \\ 0, & otherwise \end{cases} \tag{20}$$

The definition of $Pos\{\tilde{a} \leqslant b\}$ is as [29]: $Pos\{\tilde{a} \leqslant b\} = sup\{\mu_{\tilde{a}}(x) | x \in R, x \leqslant b\}$. **Lemma:** $\forall \tilde{a} = (a^L, a^M, a^U)$, for any predetermined confidence level $\lambda \in [0, 1]$, $Pos\{\tilde{a} \leqslant b\} \geqslant \lambda$ if and only if $b \geqslant (1 - \lambda) \cdot a^L + \lambda \cdot a^M$.

Proof: First we prove $Pos\{\tilde{a} \leqslant b\} \geqslant \lambda \Rightarrow b \geqslant (1 - \lambda) \cdot a^L + \lambda \cdot a^M$ (sufficiency), and the proof is also illustrated by Figure 2.

$$\left. \begin{array}{c} Pos\{\tilde{a} \leqslant b\} \geqslant \lambda \Rightarrow sup\{\mu_{\tilde{a}}(x) | x \in R, x \leqslant b\} \geqslant \lambda \Rightarrow b \geqslant x^* \\ \dfrac{x^* - a^L}{a^M - a^L} = \lambda \Rightarrow x^* = (a^M - a^L) \cdot \lambda + a^L \\ \Rightarrow b \geqslant (1 - \lambda) \cdot a^L + \lambda \cdot a^M. \end{array} \right\} \Rightarrow b \geqslant (a^M - a^L) \cdot \lambda + a^L$$

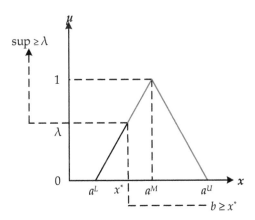

Figure 2. Diagram of the sufficiency proof.

Then we prove $b \geqslant (1 - \lambda) \cdot a^L + \lambda \cdot a^M \Rightarrow Pos\{\tilde{a} \leqslant b\} \geqslant \lambda$ (necessity), and the proof is also illustrated by Figure 3.

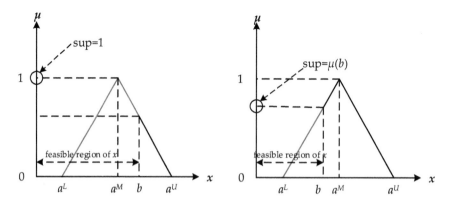

Figure 3. Diagram of the necessity proof.

If $a^M \leqslant b$, $sup\{\mu_{\tilde{a}}(x)|x \in R, x \leqslant b\} = 1 \Rightarrow Pos\{\tilde{a} \leqslant b\} = 1 \Rightarrow Pos\{\tilde{a} \leqslant b\} \geqslant \lambda$.

If $a^M > b$,
$$\left.\begin{array}{c} sup\{\mu_{\tilde{a}}(x)|x \in R, x \leqslant b\} = \mu_{\tilde{a}}(b) = \dfrac{b - a^L}{a^M - a^L} \Rightarrow Pos\{\tilde{a} \leqslant b\} = \dfrac{b - a^L}{a^M - a^L} \\[3mm] b \geqslant (1 - \lambda) \cdot a^L + \lambda \cdot a^M \Rightarrow \dfrac{b - a^L}{a^M - a^L} \geqslant \lambda \end{array}\right\} \Rightarrow Pos\{\tilde{a} \leqslant b\} \geqslant \lambda.$$

Above all, the proposed lemma is proven.

According to the lemma above, the crisp equivalent of fuzzy chance Constraint Set (18) is:

$$\bar{f} \geqslant (1 - \alpha) \cdot \sum_{k \in K} q_k^L \cdot \omega_k + \alpha \cdot \sum_{k \in K} q_k^M \cdot \omega_k \tag{21}$$

where ω_k represents the following function.

$$\sum_{(i,j) \in A} \sum_{s \in S_{ij}} c_{ij}^s \cdot X_{ijs}^k + \sum_{i \in N} \left(\sum_{h \in \delta^-(i)} \sum_{r \in S_{hi}} c_r \cdot X_{hir}^k + \sum_{j \in \delta^+(i)} \sum_{s \in S_{ij}} c_s \cdot X_{ijs}^k \right) + \sum_{(i,j) \in A} \sum_{s \in \Gamma_{ij}} c_{store} \cdot Z_{o_k js}^k$$
$$+ \varphi_k \cdot \sum_{j \in \delta^+(o_k)} \sum_{s \in \Gamma_{o_k j}} c_{pick} \cdot X_{o_k js}^k + \mu_k \cdot \sum_{j \in \delta^-(d_k)} \sum_{s \in \Gamma_{id_k}} c_{delivery} \cdot X_{id_k s}^k$$

Similarly, the crisp equivalent of fuzzy chance Constraint (19) set is:

$$Q_{ij}^s \geqslant (1 - \beta) \cdot V_{ij s}^L + \beta \cdot V_{ij s}^M \forall (i,j) \in A, \forall s \in \Gamma_{ij} \tag{22}$$

where $V_{ij s}^L = \sum_{k \in K} q_k^L \cdot X_{ij s}^k$ and $V_{ij s}^M = \sum_{k \in K} q_k^M \cdot X_{ij s}^k$.

5.2. Linearization of the Nonlinear Constraint Sets

Proposition 1: Nonlinear Constraint Set (10) is equivalent to the following linear Constraint Sets (23)–(26).

$$SD_i^s + t_{ijs} - Y_j^k \geqslant M \cdot \left(X_{ijs}^k - 1 \right) \quad \forall k \in K, \forall (i,j) \in A, \forall s \in \Gamma_{ij} \tag{23}$$

$$SD_i^s + t_{ijs} - Y_j^k \leqslant M \cdot \left(1 - X_{ijs}^k \right) \quad \forall k \in K, \forall (i,j) \in A, \forall s \in \Gamma_{ij} \tag{24}$$

$$Y_i^k + t_{ijs} - Y_j^k \geqslant M \cdot \left(X_{ijs}^k - 1 \right) \forall k \in K, \forall (i,j) \in A, \forall s \in \Omega_{ij} \tag{25}$$

$$Y_i^k + t_{ijs} - Y_j^k \geqslant M \cdot \left(1 - X_{ijs}^k \right) \forall k \in K, \forall (i,j) \in A, \forall s \in \Omega_{ij} \tag{26}$$

Proposition 2: Nonlinear Constraint Set (13) is equivalent to the following linear Constraint Sets (27) and (28).

$$Z_{ijs}^k \geq M \cdot \left(X_{ijs}^k - 1\right) + \left(l_i^s - Y_i^k - \pi\right) \quad \forall k \in K, \forall (i,j) \in A, \forall s \in \Gamma_{ij} \tag{27}$$

$$Z_{ijs}^k \leq M \cdot X_{ijs}^k \quad \forall k \in K, \forall (i,j) \in A, \forall s \in \Gamma_{ij} \tag{28}$$

The two propositions above have been proved in our previous study. For the detailed proof processes, we can refer to Section 4.4 in Reference [1].

5.3. Final Formulation of the Problem (M3)

- Objective Function:

$$minimize \bar{f}$$

- Subject to:

$$\sum_{j \in \delta^+(i)} \sum_{s \in S_{ij}} X_{ijs}^k - \sum_{h \in \delta^-(i)} \sum_{r \in S_{hi}} X_{hir}^k = \begin{cases} 1, i = o_k \\ 0, \forall i \in N\{o_k, d_k\} \quad \forall k \in K, \forall i \in N \\ -1, i = d_k \end{cases}$$

$$\sum_{s \in S_{ij}} X_{ijs}^k \leq 1 \, \forall k \in K, \forall (i,j) \in A$$

$$\bar{f} \geq (1-\alpha) \cdot \sum_{k \in K} q_k^L \cdot \omega_k + \alpha \cdot \sum_{k \in K} q_k^M \cdot \omega_k$$

$$Q_{ij}^s \geq (1-\beta) \cdot V_{ijs}^L + \beta \cdot V_{ijs}^M \forall (i,j) \in A, \forall s \in \Gamma_{ij}$$

$$Y_{o_k}^k = t_{release}^k \forall k \in K$$

$$SD_i^s + t_{ijs} - Y_j^k \geq M \cdot \left(X_{ijs}^k - 1\right) \quad \forall k \in K, \forall (i,j) \in A, \forall s \in \Gamma_{ij}$$

$$SD_i^s + t_{ijs} - Y_j^k \leq M \cdot \left(1 - X_{ijs}^k\right) \quad \forall k \in K, \forall (i,j) \in A, \forall s \in \Gamma_{ij}$$

$$Y_i^k + t_{ijs} - Y_j^k \geq M \cdot \left(X_{ijs}^k - 1\right) \, \forall k \in K, \forall (i,j) \in A, \forall s \in \Omega_{ij}$$

$$Y_i^k + t_{ijs} - Y_j^k \geq M \cdot \left(1 - X_{ijs}^k\right) \, \forall k \in K, \forall (i,j) \in A, \forall s \in \Omega_{ij}$$

$$Y_i^k \leq u_i^s \cdot X_{ijs}^k + M\left(1 - X_{ijs}^k\right) \forall k \in K, \forall (i,j) \in A, \forall s \in \Gamma_{ij}$$

$$\mu_k\left(Y_{d_k}^k\right) \geq \gamma \forall k \in K$$

$$Z_{ijs}^k \geq M \cdot \left(X_{ijs}^k - 1\right) + \left(l_i^s - Y_i^k - \pi\right) \quad \forall k \in K, \forall (i,j) \in A, \forall s \in \Gamma_{ij}$$

$$Z_{ijs}^k \leq M \cdot X_{ijs}^k \, \forall k \in K, \forall (i,j) \in A, \forall s \in \Gamma_{ij}$$

$$X_{ijs}^k \in \{0,1\} \forall k \in K, \forall (i,j) \in A, \forall s \in S_{ij}$$

$$Y_i^k \geq 0 \forall k \in K, \forall i \in N$$

$$Z_{ijs}^k \geq 0 \, \forall k \in K, \forall (i,j) \in A, \forall s \in \Gamma_{ij}$$

Currently, M3 is composed of a linear objective function and linear constraint sets, and is hence a **mixed integer linear programming model** with three kinds of decision variables including $X = \cup_{k \in K, (i,j) \in A, s \in S_{ij}} \left\{X_{ijs}^k\right\}$, $Y = \cup_{k \in K, i \in N} \left\{Y_i^k\right\}$ and $Z = \cup_{k \in K, (i,j) \in A, s \in \Gamma_{ij}} \left\{Z_{ijs}^k\right\}$. Because it belongs to the linear programming, M3 is effectively solvable by many exact solution algorithms (e.g., Branch-and-Bound algorithm and Simplex Algorithm) that can be performed on much standard mathematical programming software (e.g., Lingo and Cplex). We can then obtain the global optimal solution of M3 by using this method.

6. Numerical Case Study and Sensitivity Analysis

In this section, we design a numerical case to demonstrate the feasibility of the proposed method in solving the multicommodity multimodal routing problem with fuzzy customer information. The multimodal service network in this case is shown in Figure 4. Before solving the problem, all the values regarding the schedules, release times and due dates of the multiple commodities are all discretized into real numbers.

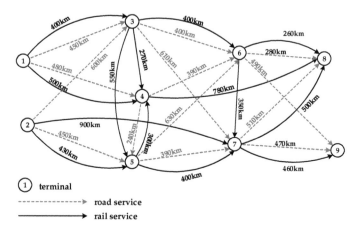

Figure 4. A multimodal service network.

The schedules of the block container trains operated in the multimodal transportation are presented in Table 1.

Table 1. Schedules of the container block trains.

Rail service No.	1	2	3	4	5	6	7
origin	1	1	2	2	3	3	3
loading start time	9	13	15	21	23	1	17
loading cutoff time	10.5	13.5	16	24	25	1.5	20
departure time	11	14	16.5	24.5	25.5	4	21
destination	3	4	5	7	4	5	6
arrival time	15	19	22	31	27	9.5	26
unloading start time	15.5	20	22.5	31.5	27.5	10	26.5
operation period(unit: day/train)	1	1	1	1	1	1	1
available capacity(unit: TEU)	20	30	15	30	40	35	20
Rail service No.	8	9	10	11	12	13	14
origin	4	5	5	6	6	7	7
loading start time	3	1	6	11	1	14	21
loading cutoff time	6	2	8	14	3	17	22
departure time	7	2.5	9	15	4	18	22.5
destination	8	4	7	7	8	8	9
arrival time	17	6	13	18.5	7	23	28
unloading start time	18	7	13.5	19	7.5	24	28.5
operation period(unit: day/train)	1	1	1	1	1	1	1
available capacity(unit: TEU)	40	35	45	25	20	30	20

Transportation costs (unit: ¥/TEU) and times (unit: h) en route of the services in the multimodal service network are given in Table 2.

Table 2. Transportation service costs and times en route.

Arc	Costs		Time		Arc	Costs		Time	
	Rail	Road	Rail	Road		Rail	Road	Rail	Road
(1, 3)	1310	2700	4.5	5.5	(4, 6)	-	2340	-	5.5
(1, 4)	1513	2880	6	6	(4, 8)	2080	-	11	-
(2, 3)	-	3600	-	10	(5, 4)	1108	-	4.5	-
(2, 5)	1371	2700	6	7.5	(5, 6)	-	3780	-	9
(2, 7)	2323	-	7	-	(5, 7)	1310	2340	4.5	5.5
(3, 4)	1047	-	2	-	(6, 7)	1209	-	4	-
(3, 5)	1614	-	6	-	(6, 8)	1027	1680	3.5	4.5
(3, 6)	1310	2400	5.5	6	(6, 9)	-	2940	-	8.5
(3, 7)	-	3660	-	10	(7, 8)	1513	3060	6	8.5
(4, 5)	-	1440	-	3.5	(7, 9)	1432	2820	6	8

The loading/unloading costs of rail services and of road services are 195 ¥/TEU and 25 ¥/TEU, respectively. The inventory costs of rail services are 3.125 ¥/TEU-h, and the inventory period free of charge is 48 h. The additional rail service origin-pickup and destination-delivery costs are 225 ¥/TEU and 337.5 ¥/TEU, respectively.

In the numerical case, there are six commodity flows that need to be moved through the multimodal service network, and their information is presented in Table 3.

Table 3. Customer information of the commodity flows.

No.	O	D	Pickup	Delivery	Release Time	Volume	Due Date
1	1	8	√	×	8	(16, 24, 33)	[35, 55, 68, 80]
2	1	9	√	√	15	(8, 17, 25)	[40, 50, 55, 61]
3	1	9	×	√	5	(17, 26, 32)	[33, 40, 50, 70]
4	2	8	√	√	0	(22, 30, 38)	[45, 60, 75, 90]
5	2	8	×	√	13	(14, 20, 27)	[50, 65, 77, 89]
6	2	9	√	×	19	(13, 20, 28)	[60, 75, 80, 95]

Let $\alpha = 0.9$, $\beta = 0.9$ and $\gamma = 0.9$, and by using the Branch-and-Bound algorithm implemented by Lingo 12 on a Lenovo Laptop with Intel Core i5 3235 M 2.60 GHz CPU and 4 GB RAM, we can obtain the best routes for the six commodity flows (see in Table 4). The computation lasts 1 s. Note that there is no transshipment at the terminal with an asterisk.

Table 4. Best multimodal routes under $\alpha = \beta = \gamma = 0.9$.

No.	Best Multimodal Routes
1	(1)—Train 2—(4)—Train 8—(8)
2	(1)—Train 1—(3)—Road Service—(6*)—Road Service—(9)
3	(1)—Train 2—(4)—Road Service—(5)—Train 10—(7)—Road Service—(9)
4	(2)—Train 4—(7)—Train 13—(8)
5	(2)—Train 4—(7)—Road Service—(8)
6	(2)—Road Service—(5)—Train 10—(7)—Train 14—(9)

To further discuss the numerical case, we will analyze the sensitivity of the best solution of M3 with respect to the values of the three confidence levels. First we examine how the confidence level α and β influence the multicommodity multimodal routing. In order to explain the performance of the routing by comparing the planned costs (best solution of M3), the actual minimal costs, and actual costs, we should first simulate the actual multimodal transportation case by randomly generating deterministic volumes of the commodity flows according to their triangular fuzzy volumes. The fuzzy simulation is as follows.

For $k=1:|K|$
  Generate a random number $q_k^* \in [q_k^L, q_k^U]$;
  Calculate its membership $\mu_{\tilde{q}_k}(q_k^*)$ according to Equation (20);
  Generate a random number $\tau \in [0, 1]$;
   If $\mu_{\tilde{q}_k}(q_k^*) \geqslant \tau$;
    $q_k^* \rightarrow$the actual volume of commodity k;
   End
 End

After T fuzzy simulations (in this study, $T = 30$), we can obtain T deterministic volume sets for the commodity set. The explored problem is hence transformed into a routing problem in a certain environment. For the T deterministic volume sets, first we calculate their actual best routes and corresponding actual minimal costs by solving M1 with Constraint Sets (10) and (13) linearized, and then get their average actual minimal costs. Second, we calculate their respective actual costs when moving the commodities along the planned routes, and then obtain their average actual costs.

In this sensitivity analysis, we keep $\gamma = 0.9$, and let α vary from 0.3 to 0.6 with step size of 0.1, and β from 0.1 to 1.0 with step size of 0.1, the sensitivity of the three kinds of costs with respect to the values of α and β is shown in Figure 5.

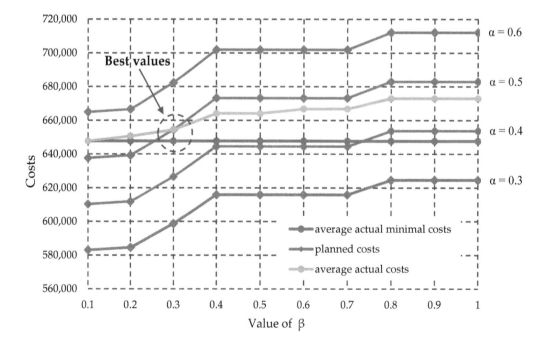

Figure 5. Sensitivity of the three kinds of costs with respect to the values of α and β.

As we can see from Figure 5: (1) when confidence level α is given, larger values of confidence level β will lead to larger planned costs, and the increase of the planned costs is stepwise. Similarly, when confidence level β is given, larger values of confidence level α will also lead to larger planned costs, and the increase of the planned costs in this situation is linear; (2) The actual costs are only related to confidence level β. The values of confidence level α do not influence the actual costs. Similar to the variation of the planned costs, larger values of confidence level β will lead to larger planned costs, and the increase of the actual costs is stepwise; (3) The actual minimal costs is not related to confidence level α and confidence level β.

It should be noted that too large or too small values of α and of β will increase the gaps among the planned costs, the actual costs and the actual minimal costs. In this numerical case, the best value of confidence level α is 0.5, and the best value of confidence level β is 0.3. Therefore, in the practical fuzzy multicommodity multimodal routing, in order to make better fuzzy multicommodity multimodal routing decision to meet the practice, the values of the two confidence levels should be moderate, to which great importance ought to be attached.

Then, to examine how customer satisfaction level γ influences the multicommodity multimodal routing, we conduct the sensitivity of the best solution of M3 with respect to the value of γ. Let γ vary from 0.4 to 1.0 with step size of 0.05, and keeping $\alpha = \beta = 0.9$, we can obtain Figure 6 that illustrates the result of the sensitivity analysis.

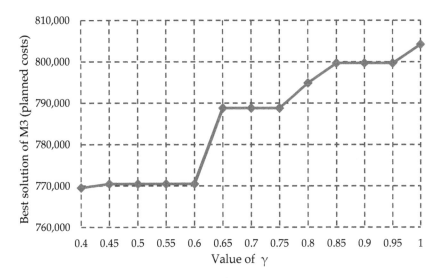

Figure 6. Sensitivity of the best solution with respect to the value of γ.

As we can see from Figure 6, considering a reasonable customer satisfaction level range, when the customer satisfaction level is lower than 0.6 ($\gamma < 0.6$), its variation has only a slight influence on the multicommodity multimodal routing. However, when $\gamma \geqslant 0.6$, Figure 6 shows that larger values of confidence level γ will result in a larger value of the total generalized costs of the routing, and the increase of the total generalized costs is stepwise. The sensitivity analysis above clearly indicates that restricting the multicommodity multimodal routing to meet stricter customer satisfaction levels will increase the costs of the multimodal service network system to some degree, which is logical according to practical experience.

7. Conclusions

In this study, we apply the fuzzy customer information problem to multicommodity multimodal routing with schedule-based services. The main contribution of this study is that it comprehensively considers the following characteristics in modeling the multimodal routing: (1) multicommodity flows as an optimization object; (2) schedule constraints existing in practice; and (3) fuzzy customer information as the formulation environment. All the formulation characteristics enhance the feasibility of the multimodal routing in dealing with the practical problems. In addition, this study proposes a crisp equivalent method and a linearization method to enable this problem to be formulated by a linear programming model that can be effectively solved by exact solution algorithms (e.g., Branch-and-Bound algorithm). This solving strategy can provide an exact benchmark for systematically testing various heuristic algorithms that will be developed in our future study.

Although several advances have been made by this study, weaknesses still exist. The most significant one is that this study still considers the multimodal service network as a deterministic system. Actually, due to the man–facility–environment impact, operation delays of the container block trains are common, and the travel time of container trucks on the road cannot remain deterministic. Therefore, the multimodal service network is a kind of fuzzy system. Accordingly, our future study will focus on integrating the fuzzy multimodal service network into our current study.

Acknowledgments: This study was supported by the National Natural Science Foundation Project (No. 71390332-3) of the People's Republic of China. The authors would also like to thank Cyril Bernard Lucas from United Kingdom, author of the book *"Atomic and Molecular Beams: Production and Collimation"* (Emails: C.B.Lucas@physics.org, cb.lucas@hotmail.co.uk), for his great contributions to helping us edit and polish the language of this paper.

Author Contributions: Yan Sun wrote this paper, and proposed the mathematical model together with Maoxiang Lang. Yan Sun and Jiaxi Wang conducted the numerical experiment and sensitivity analysis. Maoxiang Lang checked this paper in detail before submitting it to the journal. All authors have discussed and contributed to the manuscript. All authors have read and approved the final manuscript.

Conflicts of Interest: The authors declare no conflict of interest.

References

1. Sun, Y.; Lang, M. Modeling the Multicommodity Multimodal Routing Problem with Schedule-Based Services and Carbon Dioxide Emission Costs. *Math. Probl. Eng.* **2015**, *2015*, 406218. [CrossRef]
2. Sun, Y.; Lang, M.; Wang, D. Optimization Models and Solution Algorithms for Freight Routing Planning Problem in the Multi-modal Transportation Networks: A Review of the State-of-the-Art. *Open Civ. Eng. J.* **2015**, *9*, 714–723. [CrossRef]
3. Janic, M. Modelling the full costs of an intermodal and road freight transport network. *Transp. Res. Part D Transp. Environ.* **2007**, *12*, 33–44. [CrossRef]
4. Liao, C.H.; Tseng, P.-H.; Lu, C.-S. Comparing carbon dioxide emissions of trucking and intermodal container transport in Taiwan. *Transp. Res. Part D Transp. Environ.* **2009**, *14*, 493–496. [CrossRef]
5. Zhang, S. Introduction to multimodal transport in America and Canada. *Containerization* **2009**, *20*, 6–9. [CrossRef]
6. Min, H. International intermodal choices via chance-constrained goal programming. *Transp. Res. Part A Gen.* **1991**, *25*, 351–362. [CrossRef]
7. Barnhart, C.; Ratliff, H.D. Modeling intermodal routing. *J. Bus. Logist.* **1993**, *14*, 205–223.
8. Boardman, B.S.; Malstrom, E.M.; Butler, D.P.; Cole, M.H. Computer assisted routing of intermodal shipments. *Comput. Ind. Eng.* **1997**, *33*, 311–314. [CrossRef]
9. Lozano, A.; Storchi, G. Shortest viable path algorithm in multimodal networks. *Transp. Res. Part A Policy Pract.* **1997**, *35*, 225–241. [CrossRef]
10. Lam, S.K.; Srikanthan, T. Accelerating the K-Shortest Paths Computation in Multimodal Transportation Networks. In Proceedings of the IEEE 5th International Conference on Intelligent Transportation Systems, Singapore, Singapore, 3–6 September 2002; pp. 491–495.
11. Boussedjra, M.; Bloch, C.; Moudni, A.E.I. An exact method to find the intermodal shortest path (ISP). In Proceedings of the 2004 IEEE International Conference on Networking, Sensing and Control, Taipei, Taiwan, 21–23 March 2004; pp. 1075–1080.
12. Zhang, J.Y.; Guo, Y.H. A multimode transportation network assignment model. *J. China Railw. Soc.* **2004**, *24*, 114–116.
13. Zhang, Y.H.; Lin, B.L.; Liang, D.; Gao, H.Y. Research on a Generalized Shortest Path Method of Optimizing Intermodal Transportation Problems. *J. China Railw. Soc.* **2006**, *28*, 22–26.
14. Reddy, V.R.; Kasilingam, R.G. Intermodal transportation considering transfer costs. Available online: http://d.wanfangdata.com.cn/ExternalResource/tdxb201110001%5E1 (accessed on 3 March 2016).

15. Winebrake, J.J.; Corbett, J.J.; Falzarano, A.; Hawker, J.S.; Korfmacher, K.; Ketha, S.; Zilora, S. Assessing energy, environmental, and economic tradeoffs in intermodal freight transportation. *J. Air Waste Manag. Assoc.* **2008**, *58*, 1004–1013. [CrossRef]

16. Kim, H.J.; Chang, Y.T.; Lee, P.T.W.; Shin, S.H.; Kim, M.J. Optimizing the transportation of international container cargoes in Korea. *Marit. Pol. Mgmt. Flagship J. Int. Ship. Port Res.* **2008**, *35*, 103–122. [CrossRef]

17. Chang, Y.T.; Lee, P.; Kim, H.J.; Shin, S.H. Optimization model for transportation of container cargoes considering short sea shipping and external cost: South Korean case. *Transp. Res. Rec. J. Transp. Res. Board* **2010**, *2166*, 99–108. [CrossRef]

18. Liu, J.; He, S.W.; Song, R.; Li, H.D. Study on optimization of dynamic paths of intermodal transportation network based on alternative set of transport modes. *J. China Railw. Soc.* **2011**, *33*, 1–6.

19. Cho, J.H.; Kim, H.S.; Choi, H.R. An intermodal transport network planning algorithm using dynamic programming-a case study: from Busan to Rotterdam in intermodal freight routing. *Appl. Intell.* **2012**, *36*, 529–541. [CrossRef]

20. Sun, Y.; Lang, M.X. Bi-objective optimization for multi-modal transportation routing planning problem based on Pareto optimality. *J. Ind. Eng. Manag.* **2015**, *8*, 1195–1217. [CrossRef]

21. Xiong, G.W.; Wang, Y. Best routes selection in multimodal networks using multi-objective genetic algorithm. *J. Combin. Optim.* **2014**, *28*, 655–673. [CrossRef]

22. Teodorović, D.; Pavković, G. The fuzzy set theory approach to the vehicle routing problem when demand at nodes is uncertain. *Fuzzy Sets Syst.* **1996**, *82*, 307–317. [CrossRef]

23. Erbao, C.; Mingyong, L. A hybrid differential evolution algorithm to vehicle routing problem with fuzzy demands. *J. Comput. Appl. Math.* **2009**, *231*, 302–310. [CrossRef]

24. López-Castro, L.F.; Montoya-Torres, J.R. Vehicle routing with fuzzy time windows using a genetic algorithm. In Proceedings of the 2011 IEEE Workshop on Computational Intelligence in Production And Logistics Systems, Paris, France, 11–15 April 2011; pp. 1–8.

25. Lium, A.G.; Crainic, T.G.; Wallace, S.W. A study of demand stochasticity in service network design. *Transp. Sci.* **2009**, *43*, 144–157. [CrossRef]

26. Bai, R.; Wallace, S.W.; Li, J.; Chong, A.Y.L. Stochastic service network design with rerouting. *Transp. Res. Part B Methodol.* **2014**, *60*, 50–65. [CrossRef]

27. Ji, X.; Iwamura, K.; Shao, Z. New models for shortest path problem with fuzzy arc lengths. *Appl. Math. Model.* **2007**, *31*, 259–269. [CrossRef]

28. Ghannadpour, S.F.; Noori, S.; Tavakkoli-Moghaddam, R.; Ghoseiri, K. A multi-objective dynamic vehicle routing problem with fuzzy time windows: Model, solution and application. *Appl. Soft Comput.* **2014**, *14*, 504–527. [CrossRef]

29. Liu, B.; Iwamura, K. Chance constrained programming with fuzzy parameters. *Fuzzy Sets Syst.* **1998**, *94*, 227–237. [CrossRef]

6

Information Extraction Under Privacy Constraints [†]

Shahab Asoodeh *, Mario Diaz, Fady Alajaji and Tamás Linder

Department of Mathematics and Statistics, Queen's University, Kingston, Canada; 13madt@queensu.ca (M.D.);
fady@mast.queensu.ca (F.A.); linder@mast.queensu.ca (T.L.)
* Correspondence: s.asoodeh@queensu.ca

† Parts of the results in this paper were presented at the 52nd Allerton Conference on Communications,
Control and Computing [1] and the 14th Canadian Workshop on Information Theory [2].

Academic Editors: Mikael Skoglund, Lars K. Rasmussen and Tobias Oechtering

Abstract: A privacy-constrained information extraction problem is considered where for a pair of correlated discrete random variables (X, Y) governed by a given joint distribution, an agent observes Y and wants to convey to a potentially public user as much information about Y as possible while limiting the amount of information revealed about X. To this end, the so-called *rate-privacy function* is investigated to quantify the maximal amount of information (measured in terms of mutual information) that can be extracted from Y under a privacy constraint between X and the extracted information, where privacy is measured using either mutual information or maximal correlation. Properties of the rate-privacy function are analyzed and its information-theoretic and estimation-theoretic interpretations are presented for both the mutual information and maximal correlation privacy measures. It is also shown that the rate-privacy function admits a closed-form expression for a large family of joint distributions of (X, Y). Finally, the rate-privacy function under the mutual information privacy measure is considered for the case where (X, Y) has a joint probability density function by studying the problem where the extracted information is a uniform quantization of Y corrupted by additive Gaussian noise. The asymptotic behavior of the rate-privacy function is studied as the quantization resolution grows without bound and it is observed that not all of the properties of the rate-privacy function carry over from the discrete to the continuous case.

Keywords: data privacy; equivocation; rate-privacy function; information theory; minimum mean-squared error estimation; additive channels; mutual information; maximal correlation

---

1. Introduction

With the emergence of user-customized services, there is an increasing desire to balance between the need to share data and the need to protect sensitive and private information. For example, individuals who join a social network are asked to provide information about themselves which might compromise their privacy. However, they agree to do so, to some extent, in order to benefit from the customized services such as recommendations and personalized searches. As another example, a participatory technology for estimating road traffic requires each individual to provide her start and destination points as well as the travel time. However, most participating individuals prefer to provide somewhat distorted or false information to protect their privacy. Furthermore, suppose a software company wants to gather statistical information on how people use its software. Since many users might have used the software to handle some personal or sensitive information -for example, a browser for anonymous web surfing or a financial management software- they may not want to share their data with the company. On the other hand, the company cannot legally collect the raw data either, so it needs to entice its users. In all these situations, a tradeoff in a conflict between utility advantage and privacy breach is required and the question is how to achieve this tradeoff. For example, how can a company collect high-quality aggregate information about users while strongly guaranteeing to its users that it is not storing user-specific information?

To deal with such privacy considerations, Warner [3] proposed the *randomized response model* in which each individual user randomizes her own data using a local randomizer (*i.e.*, a noisy channel) before sharing the data to an untrusted data collector to be aggregated. As opposed to *conditional security*, see, e.g., [4–6], the randomized response model assumes that the adversary can have unlimited computational power and thus it provides *unconditional* privacy. This model, in which the control of private data remains in the users' hands, has been extensively studied since Warner. As a special case of the randomized response model, Duchi *et al.* [7], inspired by the well-known privacy guarantee called differential privacy introduced by Dwork *et al.* [8–10], introduced locally differential privacy (LDP). Given a random variable $X \in \mathcal{X}$, another random variable $Z \in \mathcal{Z}$ is said to be the ε-LDP version of X if there exists a channel $Q : X \to Z$ such that $\frac{Q(B|x)}{Q(B|x')} \leq \exp(\varepsilon)$ for all measurable $B \subset \mathcal{Z}$ and all $x, x' \in \mathcal{X}$. The channel Q is then called as the ε-LDP mechanism. Using Jensen's inequality, it is straightforward to see that any ε-LDP mechanism leaks at most ε bits of private information, *i.e.*, the mutual information between X and Z satisfies $I(X, Z) \leq \varepsilon$.

There have been numerous studies on the tradeoff between privacy and utility for different examples of randomized response models with different choices of utility and privacy measures. For instance, Duchi *et al.* [7] studied the optimal ε-LDP mechanism $\mathcal{M} : X \to Z$ which minimizes the risk of estimation of a parameter θ related to P_X. Kairouz *et al.* [11] studied an optimal ε-LDP mechanism in the sense of mutual information, where an individual would like to release an ε-LDP version Z of X that preserves as much information about X as possible. Calmon *et al.* [12] proposed a novel privacy measure (which includes maximal correlation and chi-square correlation) between X and Z and studied the optimal privacy mechanism (according to their privacy measure) which minimizes the error probability $\Pr(\hat{X}(Z) \neq X)$ for any estimator $\hat{X} : Z \to X$.

In all above examples of randomized response models, given a private source, denoted by X, the mechanism generates Z which can be publicly displayed without breaching the desired privacy level. However, in a more realistic model of privacy, we can assume that for any given private data X, nature generates Y, via a fixed channel $P_{Y|X}$. Now we aim to release a public display Z of Y such that the amount of information in Y is preserved as much as possible while Z satisfies a privacy constraint with respect to X. Consider two communicating agents Alice and Bob. Alice collects all her measurements from an observation into a random variable Y and ultimately wants to reveal this information to Bob in order to receive a payoff. However, she is worried about her private data, represented by X, which is correlated with Y. For instance, X might represent her precise location and Y represents measurement of traffic load of a route she has taken. She wants to reveal these measurements to an online road monitoring system to received some utility. However, she does not want to reveal too much information about her exact location. In such situations, the utility is measured with respect to Y and privacy is measured with respect to X. The question raised in this situation then concerns the maximum payoff Alice can get from Bob (by revealing Z to him) without compromising her privacy. Hence, it is of interest to characterize such competing objectives in the form of a quantitative tradeoff. Such a characterization provides a controllable balance between utility and privacy.

This model of privacy first appears in Yamamoto's work [13] in which the rate-distortion-equivocation function is defined as the tradeoff between a distortion-based utility and privacy. Recently, Sankar *et al.* [14], using the quantize-and-bin scheme [15], generalized Yamamoto's model to study privacy in databases from an information-theoretic point of view. Calmon and Fawaz [16] and Monedero *et al.* [17] also independently used distortion and mutual information for utility and privacy, respectively, to define a privacy-distortion function which resembles the classical rate-distortion function. More recently, Makhdoumi *et al.* [18] proposed to use mutual information for both utility and privacy measures and defined the *privacy funnel* as the corresponding privacy-utility tradeoff, given by

$$t_R(X;Y) := \min_{\substack{P_{Z|Y}:X \multimap Y \multimap Z \\ I(Y;Z) \geq R}} I(X;Z) \tag{1}$$

where $X \multimap Y \multimap Z$ denotes that X, Y and Z form a Markov chain in this order. Leveraging well-known algorithms for the information bottleneck problem [19], they provided a locally optimal greedy algorithm to evaluate $t_R(X;Y)$. Asoodeh *et al.* [1], independently, defined the *rate-privacy function*, $g_\varepsilon(X;Y)$, as the maximum achievable $I(Y;Z)$ such that Z satisfies $I(X;Z) \leq \varepsilon$, which is a dual representation of the privacy funnel (1), and showed that for discrete X and Y, $g_0(X;Y) > 0$ if and only if X is *weakly independent* of Y (cf, Definition 9). Recently, Calmon *et al.* [20] proved an equivalent result for $t_R(X;Y)$ using a different approach. They also obtained lower and upper bounds for $t_R(X;Y)$ which can be easily translated to bounds for $g_\varepsilon(X;Y)$ (cf. Lemma 1). In this paper, we develop further properties of $g_\varepsilon(X;Y)$ and also determine necessary and sufficient conditions on P_{XY}, satisfying some symmetry conditions, for $g_\varepsilon(X;Y)$ to achieve its upper and lower bounds.

The problem treated in this paper can also be contrasted with the better-studied concept of *secrecy* following the pioneering work of Wyner [21]. While in secrecy problems the aim is to keep information secret only from wiretappers, in privacy problems the aim is to keep the private information (not necessarily all the information) secret from everyone including the intended receiver.

1.1. Our Model and Main Contributions

Using mutual information as measure of both utility and privacy, we formulate the corresponding privacy-utility tradeoff for discrete random variables X and Y via the rate-privacy function, $g_\varepsilon(X;Y)$, in which the mutual information between Y and displayed data (*i.e.*, the mechanism's output), Z, is maximized over all channels $P_{Z|Y}$ such that the mutual information between Z and X is no larger than a given ε. We also formulate a similar rate-privacy function $\hat{g}_\varepsilon(X;Y)$ where the privacy is measured in terms of the squared maximal correlation, ρ_m^2, between, X and Z. In studying $g_\varepsilon(X;Y)$ and $\hat{g}_\varepsilon(X;Y)$, any channel $Q : Y \to Z$ that satisfies $I(X;Z) \le \varepsilon$ and $\rho_m^2(X;Z) \le \varepsilon$, preserves the desired level of privacy and is hence called a *privacy filter*. Interpreting $I(Y;Z)$ as the number of bits that a privacy filter can reveal about Y without compromising privacy, we present the rate-privacy function as a formulation of the problem of maximal *privacy-constrained information extraction* from Y.

We remark that using maximal correlation as a privacy measure is by no means new as it appears in other works, see, e.g., [22,23] and [12] for different utility functions. We do not put any likelihood constraints on the privacy filters as opposed to the definition of LDP. In fact, the optimal privacy filters that we obtain in this work induce channels $P_{Z|X}$ that do not satisfy the LDP property.

The quantity $g_\varepsilon(X;Y)$ is related to a notion of the *reverse* strong data processing inequality as follows. Given a joint distribution P_{XY}, the strong data processing coefficient was introduced in [24,25], as the smallest $s(X;Y) \le 1$ such that $I(X;Z) \le s(X;Y)I(Y;Z)$ for all $P_{Z|Y}$ satisfying the Markov condition $X \multimap Y \multimap Z$. In the rate-privacy function, we instead seek an upper bound on the maximum achievable rate at which Y can display information, $I(Y;Z)$, while meeting the privacy constraint $I(X;Z) \le \varepsilon$. The connection between the rate-privacy function and the strong data processing inequality is further studied in [20] to mirror all the results of [25] in the context of privacy.

The contributions of this work are as follows:

- We study lower and upper bounds of $g_\varepsilon(X;Y)$. The lower bound, in particular, establishes a multiplicative bound on $I(Y;Z)$ for any optimal privacy filter. Specifically, we show that for a given (X,Y) and $\varepsilon > 0$ there exists a channel $Q : Y \to Z$ such that $I(X;Z) \le \varepsilon$ and

$$I(Y;Z) \ge \lambda(X;Y)\varepsilon \tag{2}$$

  where $\lambda(X;Y) \ge 1$ is a constant depending on the joint distribution P_{XY}. We then give conditions on P_{XY} such that the upper and lower bounds are tight. For example, we show that the lower bound is achieved when Y is binary and the channel from Y to X is symmetric. We show that this corresponds to the fact that both $Y = 0$ and $Y = 1$ induce distributions $P_{X|Y}(\cdot|0)$ and $P_{X|Y}(\cdot|1)$ which are equidistant from P_X in the sense of Kullback-Leibler divergence. We then show that the upper bound is achieved when Y is an erased version of X, or equivalently, $P_{Y|X}$ is an erasure channel.

- We propose an information-theoretic setting in which $g_\varepsilon(X;Y)$ appears as a natural upper-bound for the achievable rate in the so-called "dependence dilution" coding problem. Specifically, we examine the joint-encoder version of an *amplification-masking tradeoff*, a setting recently introduced by Courtade [26] and we show that the dual of $g_\varepsilon(X;Y)$ upper bounds the masking rate. We also present an estimation-theoretic motivation for the privacy measure $\rho_m^2(X;Z) \le \varepsilon$. In fact, by imposing $\rho_m^2(X;Y) \le \varepsilon$, we require that an adversary who observes Z cannot efficiently estimate $f(X)$, for any function f. This is reminiscent of *semantic security* [27] in the cryptography community. An encryption mechanism is said to be semantically secure if the adversary's advantage for correctly guessing *any function* of the privata data given an observation of the mechanism's output (*i.e.*, the ciphertext) is required to be negligible. This, in fact, justifies the use of maximal correlation as a measure of privacy. The use of mutual information as privacy measure can also be justified using Fano's inequality. Note that

$I(X;Z) \leq \varepsilon$ can be shown to imply that $\Pr(\hat{X}(Z) \neq X) \geq \frac{H(X)-1-\varepsilon}{\log(|\mathcal{X}|)}$ and hence the probability of adversary correctly guessing X is lower-bounded.

- We also study the rate of increase $g_0'(X;Y)$ of $g_\varepsilon(X;Y)$ at $\varepsilon = 0$ and show that this rate can characterize the behavior of $g_\varepsilon(X;Y)$ for any $\varepsilon \geq 0$ provided that $g_0(X;Y) = 0$. This again has connections with the results of [25]. Letting

$$\Gamma(R) := \max_{\substack{P_{Z|Y}:X-\!\circ\!-Y-\!\circ\!-Z \\ I(Y;Z) \leq R}} I(X;Z)$$

one can easily show that $\Gamma'(0) = \lim_{R \to 0} \frac{\Gamma(R)}{R} = s(X;Y)$, and hence the rate of increase of $\Gamma(R)$ at $R = 0$ characterizes the strong data processing coefficient. Note that here we have $\Gamma(0) = 0$.

- Finally, we generalize the rate-privacy function to the continuous case where X and Y are both continuous and show that some of the properties of $g_\varepsilon(X;Y)$ in the discrete case do not carry over to the continuous case. In particular, we assume that the privacy filter belongs to a family of additive noise channels followed by an M-level uniform scalar quantizer and give asymptotic bounds as $M \to \infty$ for the rate-privacy function.

1.2. Organization

The rest of the paper is organized as follows. In Section 2, we define and study the rate-privacy function for discrete random variables for two different privacy measures, which, respectively, lead to the information-theoretic and estimation-theoretic interpretations of the rate-privacy function. In Section 3, we provide such interpretations for the rate-privacy function in terms of quantities from information and estimation theory. Having obtained lower and upper bounds of the rate-privacy function, in Section 4 we determine the conditions on P_{XY} such that these bounds are tight. The rate-privacy function is then generalized and studied in Section 5 for continuous random variables.

2. Utility-Privacy Measures: Definitions and Properties

Consider two random variables X and Y, defined over *finite* alphabets $\mathcal{X}$ and $\mathcal{Y}$, respectively, with a fixed joint distribution P_{XY}. Let X represent the *private data* and let Y be the *observable data*, correlated with X and generated by the channel $P_{Y|X}$ predefined by nature, which we call the *observation channel*. Suppose there exists a channel $P_{Z|Y}$ such that Z, the *displayed data* made available to public users, has limited dependence with X. Such a channel is called the *privacy filter*. This setup is shown in Figure 1. The objective is then to find a privacy filter which gives rise to the highest dependence between Y and Z. To make this goal precise, one needs to specify a measure for both utility (dependence between Y and Z) and also privacy (dependence between X and Z).

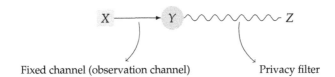

Fixed channel (observation channel)   Privacy filter

Figure 1. Information-theoretic privacy.

2.1. Mutual Information as Privacy Measure

Adopting mutual information as a measure of both privacy and utility, we are interested in characterizing the following quantity, which we call the *rate-privacy function* (since mutual information is adopted for utility, the privacy-utility tradeoff characterizes the optimal *rate* for a given privacy level, where rate indicates the precision of the displayed data Z with respect to the observable data Y for a privacy filter, which suggests the name),

$$g_\varepsilon(X;Y) := \sup_{P_{Z|Y} \in \mathscr{D}_\varepsilon(P)} I(Y;Z) \tag{3}$$

where (X, Y) has fixed distribution $P_{XY} = P$ and

$$\mathscr{D}_\varepsilon(P) := \{P_{Z|Y} :\ X\!-\!\circ\!-Y\!-\!\circ\!-Z,\ I(X; Z) \le \varepsilon\}$$

(here $X\!-\!\circ\!-Y\!-\!\circ\!-Z$ means that X, Y, and Z form a Markov chain in this order). Equivalently, we call $g_\varepsilon(X; Y)$ the *privacy-constrained information extraction function*, as Z can be thought of as the extracted information from Y under privacy constraint $I(X; Z) \le \varepsilon$.

Note that since $I(Y; Z)$ is a convex function of $P_{Z|Y}$ and furthermore the constraint set $\mathscr{D}_\varepsilon(P)$ is convex, [28, Theorem 32.2] implies that we can restrict $\mathscr{D}_\varepsilon(P)$ in (3) to $\{P_{Z|Y} :\ X\!-\!\circ\!-Y\!-\!\circ\!-Z,\ I(X; Z) = \varepsilon\}$ whenever $\varepsilon \le I(X; Y)$. Note also that since for finite $\mathscr{X}$ and $\mathscr{Y}$, $P_{Z|Y} \to I(Y; Z)$ is a continuous map, therefore $\mathscr{D}_\varepsilon(P)$ is compact and the supremum in (3) is indeed a maximum. In this case, using the Support Lemma [29], one can readily show that it suffices that the random variable Z is supported on an alphabet $\mathscr{Z}$ with cardinality $|\mathscr{Z}| \le |\mathscr{Y}| + 1$. Note further that by the Markov condition $X\!-\!\circ\!-Y\!-\!\circ\!-Z$, we can always restrict $\varepsilon \ge 0$ to only $0 \le \varepsilon < I(X; Y)$, because $I(X; Z) \le I(X; Y)$ and hence for $\varepsilon \ge I(X; Y)$ the privacy constraint is removed and thus by setting $Z = Y$, we obtain $g_\varepsilon(X; Y) = H(Y)$.

As mentioned earlier, a dual representation of $g_\varepsilon(X; Y)$, the so called *privacy funnel*, is introduced in [18,20], defined in (1), as the least information leakage about X such that the communication rate is greater than a positive constant; $I(Y; Z) \ge R$ for some $R > 0$. Note that if $t_R(X; Y) = \varepsilon$ then $g_\varepsilon(X; Y) = R$.

Given $\varepsilon_1 < \varepsilon_2$ and a joint distribution $P = P_X \times P_{Y|X}$, we have $\mathscr{D}_{\varepsilon_1}(P) \subset \mathscr{D}_{\varepsilon_2}(P)$ and hence $\varepsilon \to g_\varepsilon(X; Y)$ is non-decreasing, i.e., $g_{\varepsilon_1}(X; Y) \le g_{\varepsilon_2}(X; Y)$. Using a similar technique as in [30, Lemma 1], Calmon *et al.* [20] showed that the mapping $R \mapsto \frac{t_R(X;Y)}{R}$ is non-decreasing for $R > 0$. This, in fact, implies that $\varepsilon \mapsto \frac{g_\varepsilon(X;Y)}{\varepsilon}$ is non-increasing for $\varepsilon > 0$. This observation leads to a lower bound for the rate privacy function $g_\varepsilon(X; Y)$ as described in the following lemma.

Lemma 1 ([20]). *For a given joint distribution P defined over $\mathscr{X} \times \mathscr{Y}$, the mapping $\varepsilon \mapsto \frac{g_\varepsilon(X;Y)}{\varepsilon}$ is non-increasing on $\varepsilon \in (0, \infty)$ and $g_\varepsilon(X; Y)$ lies between two straight lines as follows:*

$$\varepsilon \frac{H(Y)}{I(X; Y)} \le g_\varepsilon(X; Y) \le H(Y|X) + \varepsilon \tag{4}$$

for $\varepsilon \in (0, I(X; Y))$.

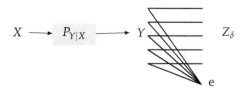

Figure 2. Privacy filter that achieves the lower bound in (4) where Z_δ is the output of an erasure privacy filter with erasure probability specified in (5).

Using a simple calculation, the lower bound in (4) can be shown to be achieved by the privacy filter depicted in Figure 2 with the erasure probability

$$\delta = 1 - \frac{\varepsilon}{I(X; Y)} \tag{5}$$

In light of Lemma 1, the possible range of the map $\varepsilon \mapsto g_\varepsilon(X; Y)$ is as depicted in Figure 3.

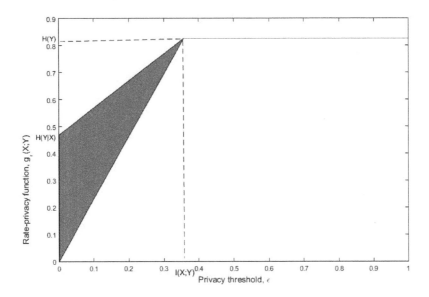

Figure 3. The region of $g_\varepsilon(X;Y)$ in terms of ε specified by (4).

We next show that $\varepsilon \mapsto g_\varepsilon(X;Y)$ is concave and continuous.

Lemma 2. *For any given pair of random variables (X,Y) over $\mathcal{X} \times \mathcal{Y}$, the mapping $\varepsilon \mapsto g_\varepsilon(X;Y)$ is concave for $\varepsilon \geq 0$.*

Proof. It suffices to show that for any $0 \leq \varepsilon_1 < \varepsilon_2 < \varepsilon_3 \leq I(X;Y)$, we have

$$\frac{g_{\varepsilon_3}(X;Y) - g_{\varepsilon_1}(X;Y)}{\varepsilon_3 - \varepsilon_1} \leq \frac{g_{\varepsilon_2}(X;Y) - g_{\varepsilon_1}(X;Y)}{\varepsilon_2 - \varepsilon_1} \tag{6}$$

which, in turn, is equivalent to

$$\left(\frac{\varepsilon_2 - \varepsilon_1}{\varepsilon_3 - \varepsilon_1}\right) g_{\varepsilon_3}(X;Y) + \left(\frac{\varepsilon_3 - \varepsilon_2}{\varepsilon_3 - \varepsilon_1}\right) g_{\varepsilon_1}(X;Y) \leq g_{\varepsilon_2}(X;Y) \tag{7}$$

Let $P_{Z_1|Y} : Y \to Z_1$ and $P_{Z_3|Y} : Y \to Z_3$ be two optimal privacy filters in $\mathscr{D}_{\varepsilon_1}(P)$ and $\mathscr{D}_{\varepsilon_3}(P)$ with disjoint output alphabets $\mathcal{Z}_1$ and $\mathcal{Z}_3$, respectively.

We introduce an auxiliary binary random variable $U \sim$ Bernoulli(λ), independent of (X,Y), where $\lambda := \frac{\varepsilon_2 - \varepsilon_1}{\varepsilon_3 - \varepsilon_1}$ and define the following random privacy filter $P_{Z_\lambda|Y}$: We pick $P_{Z_3|Y}$ if $U = 1$ and $P_{Z_1|Y}$ if $U = 0$, and let Z_λ be the output of this random channel which takes values in $\mathcal{Z}_1 \cup \mathcal{Z}_3$. Note that $(X,Y) \multimap Z \multimap U$. Then we have

$$\begin{aligned} I(X;Z_\lambda) &= I(X;Z_\lambda, U) = I(X;Z_\lambda|U) = \lambda I(X;Z_3) + (1-\lambda)I(X;Z_1), \\ &\leq \varepsilon_2 \end{aligned}$$

which implies that $P_{Z_\lambda|Y} \in \mathscr{D}_{\varepsilon_2}(P)$. On the other hand, we have

$$\begin{aligned} g_{\varepsilon_2}(X;Y) \geq I(Y;Z_\lambda) &= I(Y;Z_\lambda, U) = I(Y;Z_\lambda|U) = \lambda I(Y;Z_3) + (1-\lambda)I(Y;Z_1) \\ &= \left(\frac{\varepsilon_2 - \varepsilon_1}{\varepsilon_3 - \varepsilon_1}\right) g_{\varepsilon_3}(X;Y) + \left(\frac{\varepsilon_3 - \varepsilon_2}{\varepsilon_3 - \varepsilon_1}\right) g_{\varepsilon_1}(X;Y) \end{aligned}$$

which, according to (7), completes the proof. □

Remark 1. By the concavity of $\varepsilon \mapsto g_\varepsilon(X;Y)$, we can show that $g_\varepsilon(X;Y)$ is a *strictly* increasing function of $\varepsilon \leq I(X;Y)$. To see this, assume there exists $\varepsilon_1 < \varepsilon_2 \leq I(X;Y)$ such that $g_{\varepsilon_1}(X;Y) = g_{\varepsilon_2}(X;Y)$.

Since $\varepsilon \mapsto g_\varepsilon(X;Y)$ is concave, then it follows that for all $\varepsilon \geq \varepsilon_2$, $g_\varepsilon(X;Y) = g_{\varepsilon_2}(X;Y)$ and since for $\varepsilon = I(X;Y)$, $g_{I(X;Y)}(X;Y) = H(Y)$, implying that for any $\varepsilon \geq \varepsilon_2$, we must have $g_\varepsilon(X;Y) = H(Y)$ which contradicts the upper bound shown in (4).

Corollary 3. *For any given pair of random variables* (X,Y) *over* $\mathcal{X} \times \mathcal{Y}$, *the mapping* $\varepsilon \mapsto g_\varepsilon(X;Y)$ *is continuous for* $\varepsilon \geq 0$.

Proof. Concavity directly implies that the mapping $\varepsilon \mapsto g_\varepsilon(X;Y)$ is continuous on $(0,\infty)$ (see for example [31, Theorem 3.2]). Continuity at zero follows from the continuity of mutual information. $\square$

Remark 2. Using the concavity of the map $\varepsilon \mapsto g_\varepsilon(X;Y)$, we can provide an alternative proof for the lower bound in (4). Note that point $(I(X;Y), H(Y))$ is always on the curve $g_\varepsilon(X;Y)$, and hence by concavity, the straight line $\varepsilon \mapsto \varepsilon \frac{H(Y)}{I(X;Y)}$ is always below the lower convex envelop of $g_\varepsilon(X;Y)$, i.e., the chord connecting $(0, g_0(X;Y))$ to $(I(X;Y), H(Y))$, and hence $g_\varepsilon(X;Y) \geq \varepsilon \frac{H(Y)}{I(X;Y)}$. In fact, this chord yields a better lower bound for $g_\varepsilon(X;Y)$ on $\varepsilon \in [0, I(X;Y]$ as

$$g_\varepsilon(X;Y) \geq \varepsilon \frac{H(Y)}{I(X;Y)} + g_0(X;Y) \left[1 - \frac{\varepsilon}{I(X;Y)} \right] \tag{8}$$

which reduces to the lower bound in (4) only if $g_0(X;Y) = 0$.

2.2. Maximal Correlation as Privacy Measure

By adopting the mutual information as the privacy measure between the private and the displayed data, we make sure that only limited bits of private information is revealed during the process of transferring Y. In order to have an estimation theoretic guarantee of privacy, we propose alternatively to measure privacy using a *measure of correlation*, the so-called maximal correlation.

Given the collection $\mathcal{C}$ of all pairs of random variables $(U,V) \in \mathcal{U} \times \mathcal{V}$ where $\mathcal{U}$ and $\mathcal{V}$ are general alphabets, a mapping $T : \mathcal{C} \to [0,1]$ defines a measure of correlation [32] if $T(U,V) = 0$ if and only if U and V are independent (in short, $U \perp\!\!\!\perp V$) and $T(U,V)$ attains its maximum value if $X = f(Y)$ or $Y = g(X)$ almost surely for some measurable real-valued functions f and g. There are many different examples of measures of correlation including the Hirschfeld-Gebelein-Rényi maximal correlation [32–34], the information measure [35], mutual information and f-divergence [36].

Definition 4 ([34]). Given random variables X and Y, the maximal correlation $\rho_m(X;Y)$ is defined as follows (recall that the correlation coefficient between U and V, is defined as $\rho(U;V) := \frac{\text{cov}(U;V)}{\sigma_U \sigma_V}$, where $\text{cov}(U;V), \sigma_U$ and σ_V are the covariance between U and V, the standard deviations of U and V, respectively):

$$\rho_m(X;Y) := \sup_{f,g} \rho(f(X), g(Y)) = \sup_{(f(X),g(Y)) \in \mathcal{S}} \mathbb{E}[f(X)g(Y)]$$

where $\mathcal{S}$ is the collection of pairs of real-valued random variables $f(X)$ and $g(Y)$ such that $\mathbb{E}f(X) = \mathbb{E}g(Y) = 0$ and $\mathbb{E}f^2(X) = \mathbb{E}g^2(Y) = 1$. If $\mathcal{S}$ is empty (which happens precisely when at least one of X and Y is constant almost surely) then one defines $\rho_m(X;Y)$ to be 0. Rényi [34] derived an equivalent characterization of maximal correlation as follows:

$$\rho_m^2(X;Y) = \sup_{f:\mathbb{E}f(X)=0,\mathbb{E}f^2(X)=1} \mathbb{E}\left[\mathbb{E}^2[f(X)|Y] \right]. \tag{9}$$

Measuring privacy in terms of maximal correlation, we propose

$$\hat{g}_\varepsilon(X;Y) := \sup_{P_{Z|Y} \in \hat{\mathcal{D}}_\varepsilon(P)} I(Y;Z)$$

as the corresponding rate-privacy tradeoff, where

$$\hat{\mathcal{D}}_\varepsilon(P) := \{P_{Z|Y} : X \!-\!\!\circ\!\!-\! Y \!-\!\!\circ\!\!-\! Z, \rho_m^2(X;Z) \leq \varepsilon, P_{XY} = P\}$$

Again, we equivalently call $\hat{g}_\varepsilon(X;Y)$ as the privacy-constrained information extraction function, where here the privacy is guaranteed by $\rho_m^2(X;Z) \leq \varepsilon$.

Setting $\varepsilon = 0$ corresponds to the case where X and Z are required to be statistically independent, i.e., absolutely no information leakage about the private source X is allowed. This is called *perfect privacy*. Since the independence of X and Z is equivalent to $I(X;Z) = \rho_m(X;Z) = 0$, we have $\hat{g}_0(X;Y) = g_0(X;Y)$. However, for $\varepsilon > 0$, both $g_\varepsilon(X;Y) \leq \hat{g}_\varepsilon(X;Y)$ and $g_\varepsilon(X;Y) \geq \hat{g}_\varepsilon(X;Y)$ might happen in general. For general $\varepsilon \geq 0$, it directly follows using [23, Proposition 1] that

$$\hat{g}_\varepsilon(X;Y) \leq g_{\varepsilon'}(X;Y)$$

where $\varepsilon' := \log(k\varepsilon + 1)$ and $k := |\mathcal{X}| - 1$

Similar to $g_\varepsilon(X;Y)$, we see that for $\varepsilon_1 \leq \varepsilon_2$, $\hat{\mathcal{D}}_{\varepsilon_1}(P) \subset \hat{\mathcal{D}}_{\varepsilon_2}(P)$ and hence $\varepsilon \to \hat{g}_\varepsilon(X;Y)$ is non-decreasing. The following lemma is a counterpart of Lemma 1 for $\hat{g}_\varepsilon(X;Y)$.

Lemma 5. *For a given joint distribution P_{XY} defined over $\mathcal{X} \times \mathcal{Y}$, $\varepsilon \mapsto \frac{\hat{g}_\varepsilon(X;Y)}{\varepsilon}$ is non-increasing on $(0, \infty)$.*

Proof. Like Lemma 1, the proof is similar to the proof of [30, Lemma 1]. We, however, give a brief proof for the sake of completeness.

For a given channel $P_{Z|Y} \in \hat{\mathcal{D}}_\varepsilon(P)$ and $\delta \geq 0$, we can define a new channel with an additional symbol e as follows

$$P_{Z'|Y}(z'|y) = \begin{cases} (1-\delta)P_{Z|Y}(z'|y) & \text{if } z' \neq e \\ \delta & \text{if } z' = e \end{cases} \tag{10}$$

It is easy to check that $I(Y;Z') = (1-\delta)I(Y;Z)$ and also $\rho_m^2(X;Z') = (1-\delta)\rho_m^2(X;Z)$; see [37, Page 8], which implies that $P_{Z'|Y} \in \hat{\mathcal{D}}_{\varepsilon'}(P)$ where $\varepsilon' = (1-\delta)\varepsilon$. Now suppose that $P_{Z|Y}$ achieves $\hat{g}_\varepsilon(X;Y)$, that is, $\hat{g}_\varepsilon(X;Y) = I(Y;Z)$ and $\rho_m^2(X;Z) = \varepsilon$. We can then write

$$\frac{\hat{g}_\varepsilon(X;Y)}{\varepsilon} = \frac{I(Y;Z)}{\varepsilon} = \frac{I(Y;Z')}{\varepsilon'} \leq \frac{g_{\varepsilon'}(X;Y)}{\varepsilon'}$$

Therefore, for $\varepsilon' \leq \varepsilon$ we have $\frac{g_{\varepsilon'}(X;Y)}{\varepsilon'} \geq \frac{\hat{g}_\varepsilon(X;Y)}{\varepsilon}$. $\square$

Similar to the lower bound for $g_\varepsilon(X;Y)$ obtained from Lemma 1, we can obtain a lower bound for $\hat{g}_\varepsilon(X;Y)$ using Lemma 5. Before we get to the lower bound, we need a data processing lemma for maximal correlation. The following lemma proves a version of *strong* data processing inequality for maximal correlation from which the typical data processing inequality follows, namely, $\rho_m(X;Z) \leq \min\{\rho_m(Y;Z), \rho_m(X;Y)\}$ for X, Y and Z satisfying $X \multimap Y \multimap Z$.

Lemma 6. *For random variables X and Y with a joint distribution P_{XY}, we have*

$$\sup_{\substack{X \multimap Y \multimap Z \\ \rho_m(Y;Z) \neq 0}} \frac{\rho_m(X;Z)}{\rho_m(Y;Z)} = \rho_m(X;Y)$$

Proof. For arbitrary zero-mean and unit variance measurable functions $f \in \mathcal{L}^2(\mathcal{X})$ and $g \in \mathcal{L}^2(\mathcal{Z})$ and $X \multimap Y \multimap Z$, we have

$$\mathbb{E}[f(X)g(Z)] = \mathbb{E}\left[\mathbb{E}[f(X)|Y]\mathbb{E}[g(Z)|Y]\right] \leq \rho_m(X;Y)\rho_m(Y;Z)$$

where the inequality follows from the Cauchy-Schwartz inequality and (9). Thus we obtain $\rho_m(X;Z) \leq \rho_m(X;Y)\rho_m(Y;Z)$.

This bound is tight for the special case of $X \to Y \to X'$, where $P_{X'|Y}$ is the backward channel associated with $P_{Y|X}$. In the following, we shall show that $\rho_m(X;Y)\rho_m(Y;X') = \rho_m(X;X')$.

To this end, first note that the above implies that $\rho_m(X;Y)\rho_m(Y;X') \geq \rho_m(X;X')$. Since $P_{XY} = P_{X'Y}$, it follows that $\rho_m(X;Y) = \rho_m(Y;X')$ and hence the above implies that $\rho_m^2(X;Y) \geq \rho_m(X;X')$. One the other hand, we have

$$\mathbb{E}[[\mathbb{E}[f(X)|Y]]^2] = \mathbb{E}[\mathbb{E}[f(X)|Y]\mathbb{E}[f(X')|Y]] = \mathbb{E}[\mathbb{E}[f(X)f(X')|Y]] = \mathbb{E}[f(X)f(X')]$$

which together with (9) implies that

$$\rho_m^2(X;Y) \leq \sup_{f:\mathbb{E}f(X)=0,\mathbb{E}f^2(X)=1} \mathbb{E}[f(X)f(X')] \leq \rho_m(X;X')$$

Thus, $\rho_m^2(X;Y) = \rho_m(X;X')$ which completes the proof. $\square$

Now a lower bound of $\hat{g}_\varepsilon(X;Y)$ can be readily obtained.

Corollary 7. *For a given joint distribution P_{XY} defined over $\mathcal{X} \times \mathcal{Y}$, we have for any $\varepsilon > 0$*

$$\hat{g}_\varepsilon(X;Y) \geq \frac{H(Y)}{\rho_m^2(X;Y)} \min\{\varepsilon, \rho_m^2(X;Y)\}$$

Proof. By Lemma 6, we know that for any Markov chain $X\!-\!\circ\!-\!Y\!-\!\circ\!-\!Z$, we have $\rho_m(X;Z) \leq \rho_m(X;Y)$ and hence for $\varepsilon \geq \rho_m^2(X;Y)$, the privacy constraint $\rho_m^2(X;Z) \leq \varepsilon$ is not restrictive and hence $\hat{g}_\varepsilon(X;Y) = H(Y)$ by setting $Y = Z$. For $0 < \varepsilon \leq \rho_m^2(X;Y)$, Lemma 5 implies that

$$\frac{\hat{g}_\varepsilon(X;Y)}{\varepsilon} \geq \frac{H(Y)}{\rho_m^2(X;Y)}$$

from which the result follows. $\square$

A loose upper bound of $\hat{g}_\varepsilon(X;Y)$ can be obtained using an argument similar to the one used for $g_\varepsilon(X;Y)$. For the Markov chain $X\!-\!\circ\!-\!Y\!-\!\circ\!-\!Z$, we have

$$
\begin{aligned}
I(Y;Z) &= I(X;Z) + I(Y;Z|X) \leq I(X;Z) + H(Y|X)\\
&\overset{(a)}{\leq} \log\left(k\rho_m^2(X;Z)+1\right) + H(Y|X)
\end{aligned}
\tag{11}
$$

where $k := |\mathcal{X}| - 1$ and (a) comes from [23, Proposition 1]. We can, therefore, conclude from (11) and Corollary 7 that

$$\varepsilon\frac{H(Y)}{\rho_m^2(X;Y)} \leq \hat{g}_\varepsilon(X;Y) \leq \log(k\varepsilon+1) + H(Y|X) \tag{12}$$

Similar to Lemma 2, the following lemma shows that the $\hat{g}_\varepsilon(X;Y)$ is a concave function of ε.

Lemma 8. *For any given pair of random variables (X,Y) with distribution P over $\mathcal{X} \times \mathcal{Y}$, the mapping $\varepsilon \mapsto \hat{g}_\varepsilon(X;Y)$ is concave for $\varepsilon \geq 0$.*

Proof. The proof is similar to that of Lemma 2 except that here for two optimal filters $P_{Z_1|Y} : Y \to Z_1$ and $P_{Z_3|Y} : Y \to Z_3$ in $\hat{\mathcal{D}}_{\varepsilon_1}(P)$ and $\hat{\mathcal{D}}_{\varepsilon_3}(P)$, respectively, and the random channel $P_{Z_\lambda|Y} : Y \to Z$ with output alphabet $\mathcal{Z}_1 \cup \mathcal{Z}_3$ constructed using a coin flip with probability γ, we need to show that $P_{Z_\lambda|Y} \in \hat{\mathcal{D}}_{\varepsilon_2}(P)$, where $0 \leq \varepsilon_1 < \varepsilon_2 < \varepsilon_3 \leq \rho_m^2(X;Y)$. To show this, consider $f : \mathcal{X} \to \mathbb{R}$ such that $\mathbb{E}[f(X)] = 0$ and $\mathbb{E}[f^2(X)] = 1$ and let U be a binary random variable as in the proof of Lemma 2. We then have

$$
\begin{aligned}
\mathbb{E}[\mathbb{E}^2[f(X)|Z_\lambda]] &= \mathbb{E}\left[\mathbb{E}[\mathbb{E}^2[f(X)|Z_\lambda]|U]\right]\\
&\overset{(a)}{=} \gamma\mathbb{E}[\mathbb{E}^2[f(X)|Z_3]] + (1-\gamma)\mathbb{E}[\mathbb{E}^2[f(X)|Z_1]]
\end{aligned}
\tag{13}
$$

where (a) comes from the fact that U is independent of X. We can then conclude from (13) and the alternative characterization of maximal correlation (9) that

$$
\begin{aligned}
\rho_m^2(X; Z_\lambda) &= \sup_{f:\mathbb{E}[f(X)]=0,\mathbb{E}[f^2(X)]=1} \mathbb{E}[\mathbb{E}^2[f(X)|Z_\lambda]] \\
&= \sup_{f:\mathbb{E}[f(X)]=0,\mathbb{E}[f^2(X)]=1} \left[\gamma\mathbb{E}[\mathbb{E}^2[f(X)|Z_3]] + (1-\gamma)\mathbb{E}[\mathbb{E}^2[f(X)|Z_1]]\right] \\
&\leq \gamma\rho_m^2(X; Z_3) + (1-\gamma)\rho_m^2(X; Z_1) \leq \gamma\varepsilon_3 + (1-\gamma)\varepsilon_1
\end{aligned}
$$

from which we can conclude that $P_{Z_\lambda|Y} \in \hat{\mathscr{D}}_{\varepsilon_2}(P)$. $\square$

2.3. Non-Trivial Filters For Perfect Privacy

As it becomes clear later, requiring that $g_0(X; Y) = 0$ is a useful assumption for the analysis of $g_\varepsilon(X; Y)$. Thus, it is interesting to find a necessary and sufficient condition on the joint distribution P_{XY} which results in $g_0(X; Y) = 0$.

Definition 9 ([38]). The random variable X is said to be *weakly* independent of Y if the rows of the transition matrix $P_{X|Y}$, i.e., the set of vectors $\{P_{X|Y}(\cdot|y), y \in \mathscr{Y}\}$, are linearly dependent.

The following lemma provides a necessary and sufficient condition for $g_0(X; Y) > 0$.

Lemma 10. For a given (X, Y) with a given joint distribution $P_{XY} = P_Y \times P_{X|Y}$, $g_0(X; Y) > 0$ (and equivalently $\hat{g}_0(X; Y) > 0$) if and only if X is weakly independent of Y.

Proof. $\Rightarrow$ direction:

Assuming that $g_0(X; Y) > 0$ implies that there exists a random variable Z over an alphabet $\mathscr{Z}$ such that the Markov condition $X \!-\!\circ\!- Y \!-\!\circ\!- Z$ is satisfied and $Z \perp\!\!\!\perp X$ while $I(Y; Z) > 0$. Hence, for any z_1 and z_2 in $\mathscr{Z}$, we must have $P_{X|Z}(x|z_1) = P_{X|Z}(x|z_2)$ for all $x \in \mathscr{X}$, which implies that

$$
\sum_{y\in\mathscr{Y}} P_{X|Y}(x|y)P_{Y|Z}(y|z_1) = \sum_{y\in\mathscr{Y}} P_{X|Y}(x|y)P_{Y|Z}(y|z_2)
$$

and hence

$$
\sum_{y\in\mathscr{Y}} P_{X|Y}(x|y)\left[P_{Y|Z}(y|z_1) - P_{Y|Z}(y|z_2)\right] = 0
$$

Since Y is not independent of Z, there exist z_1 and z_2 such that $P_{Y|Z}(y|z_1) \neq P_{Y|Z}(y|z_2)$ and hence the above shows that the set of vectors $P_{X|Y}(\cdot|y)$, $y \in \mathscr{Y}$ is linearly dependent.

$\Leftarrow$ direction:

Berger and Yeung [38, Appendix II], in a completely different context, showed that if X being weakly independent of Y, one can always construct a binary random variable Z correlated with Y which satisfies $X \!-\!\circ\!- Y \!-\!\circ\!- Z$ and $X \perp\!\!\!\perp Z$, and hence $g_0(X; Y) > 0$. $\square$

Remark 3. Lemma 10 first appeared in [1]. However, Calmon *et al.* [20] studied (1), the dual version of $g_\varepsilon(X; Y)$, and showed an equivalent result for $t_R(X; Y)$. In fact, they showed that for a given P_{XY}, one can always generate Z such that $I(X; Z) = 0$, $I(Y; Z) > 0$ and $X \!-\!\circ\!- Y \!-\!\circ\!- Z$, or equivalently $g_0(X; Y) > 0$, if and only if the smallest singular value of the conditional expectation operator $f \mapsto \mathbb{E}[f(X)|Y]$ is zero. This condition can, in fact, be shown to be equivalent to the condition in Lemma 10.

Remark 4. It is clear that, according to Definition 9, X is weakly independent of Y if $|\mathscr{Y}| > |\mathscr{X}|$. Hence, Lemma 10 implies that $g_0(X; Y) > 0$ if Y has strictly larger alphabet than X.

In light of the above remark, in the most common case of $|\mathscr{Y}| = |\mathscr{X}|$, one might have $g_0(X; Y) = 0$, which corresponds to the most conservative scenario as no privacy leakage implies no broadcasting of observable data. In such cases, the rate of increase of $g_\varepsilon(X; Y)$ at $\varepsilon = 0$, that is $g_0'(X; Y) := \frac{d}{d\varepsilon}g_\varepsilon(X; Y)|_{\varepsilon=0}$, which corresponds to the initial efficiency of privacy-constrained information extraction, proves to be very important in characterizing the behavior of $g_\varepsilon(X;Y)$ for all $\varepsilon \geq 0$. This is because, for example, by concavity of $\varepsilon \mapsto g_\varepsilon(X;Y)$, the slope of $g_\varepsilon(X;Y)$ is maximized at $\varepsilon = 0$ and so

$$g_0'(X;Y) = \lim_{\varepsilon \to 0} \frac{g_\varepsilon(X;Y)}{\varepsilon} = \sup_{\varepsilon > 0} \frac{g_\varepsilon(X;Y)}{\varepsilon}$$

and hence $g_\varepsilon(X;Y) \leq \varepsilon g_0'(X;Y)$ for all $\varepsilon \leq I(X;Y)$ which, together with (4), implies that $g_\varepsilon(X;Y) = \varepsilon \frac{H(Y)}{I(X;Y)}$ if $g_0'(X;Y) \leq \frac{H(Y)}{I(X;Y)}$. In the sequel, we always assume that X is not weakly independent of Y, or equivalently $g_0(X;Y) = 0$. For example, in light of Lemma 10 and Remark 4, we can assume that $|\mathcal{Y}| \leq |\mathcal{X}|$.

It is easy to show that, X is weakly independent of binary Y if and only if X and Y are independent (see, e.g., [38, Remark 2]). The following corollary, therefore, immediately follows from Lemma 10.

Corollary 11. *Let Y be a non-degenerate binary random variable correlated with X. Then $g_0(X;Y) = 0$.*

3. Operational Interpretations of the Rate-Privacy Function

In this section, we provide a scenario in which $g_\varepsilon(X;Y)$ appears as a boundary point of an achievable rate region and thus giving an information-theoretic operational interpretation for $g_\varepsilon(X;Y)$. We then proceed to present an estimation-theoretic motivation for $\hat{g}_\varepsilon(X;Y)$.

3.1. Dependence Dilution

Inspired by the problems of information amplification [39] and state masking [40], Courtade [26] proposed the *information-masking tradeoff* problem as follows. The tuple $(R_u, R_v, \Delta_A, \Delta_M) \in \mathbb{R}^4$ is said to be achievable if for two given separated sources $U \in \mathcal{U}$ and $V \in \mathcal{V}$ and any $\varepsilon > 0$ there exist mappings $f : \mathcal{U}^n \to \{1, 2, \ldots, 2^{nR_u}\}$ and $g : \mathcal{V}^n \to \{1, 2, \ldots, 2^{nR_v}\}$ such that $I(U^n; f(U^n), g(V^n)) \leq n(\Delta_M + \varepsilon)$ and $I(V^n; f(U^n), g(V^n)) \geq n(\Delta_A - \varepsilon)$. In other words, $(R_u, R_v, \Delta_A, \Delta_M)$ is achievable if there exist indices K and J of rates R_u and R_v given U^n and V^n, respectively, such that the receiver in possession of (K, J) can recover at most $n\Delta_M$ bits about U^n and at least $n\Delta_A$ about V^n. The closure of the set of all achievable tuple $(R_u, R_v, \Delta_A, \Delta_M)$ is characterized in [26]. Here, we look at a similar problem but for a joint encoder. In fact, we want to examine the achievable rate of an encoder observing both X^n and Y^n which masks X^n and amplifies Y^n at the same time, by rates Δ_M and Δ_A, respectively.

We define a $(2^{nR}, n)$ *dependence dilution* code by an encoder

$$f_n : \mathcal{X}^n \times \mathcal{Y}^n \to \{1, 2, \ldots, 2^{nR}\}$$

and a list decoder

$$g_n : \{1, 2, \ldots, 2^{nR}\} \to 2^{\mathcal{Y}^n}$$

where $2^{\mathcal{Y}^n}$ denotes the power set of $\mathcal{Y}^n$. A *dependence dilution triple* $(R, \Delta_A, \Delta_M) \in \mathbb{R}^3_+$ is said to be achievable if, for any $\delta > 0$, there exists a $(2^{nR}, n)$ dependence dilution code that for sufficiently large n satisfies the utility constraint:

$$\Pr\left(Y^n \notin g_n(J)\right) < \delta \tag{14}$$

having a fixed list size

$$|g_n(J)| = 2^{n(H(Y) - \Delta_A)}, \qquad \forall J \in \{1, 2, \ldots, 2^{nR}\} \tag{15}$$

where $J := f_n(X^n, Y^n)$ is the encoder's output, and satisfies the privacy constraint:

$$\frac{1}{n} I(X^n; J) \leq \Delta_M + \delta \tag{16}$$

Intuitively speaking, upon receiving J, the decoder is required to construct list $g_n(J) \subset \mathcal{Y}^n$ of fixed size which contains likely candidates of the actual sequence Y^n. Without any observation, the decoder can only construct a list of size $2^{nH(Y)}$ which contains Y^n with probability close to one. However, after J is observed and the list $g_n(J)$ is formed, the decoder's list size can be reduced to

$2^{n(H(Y)-\Delta_A)}$ and thus reducing the uncertainty about Y^n by $0 \leq n\Delta_A \leq nH(Y)$. This observation led Kim *et al.* [39] to show that the utility constraint (14) is equivalent to the amplification requirement

$$\frac{1}{n}I(Y^n;J) \geq \Delta_A - \delta \tag{17}$$

which lower bounds the amount of information J carries about Y^n. The following lemma gives an outer bound for the achievable dependence dilution region.

Theorem 12. *Any achievable dependence dilution triple (R, Δ_A, Δ_M) satisfies*

$$\begin{cases} R \geq \Delta_A \\ \Delta_A \leq I(Y;U) \\ \Delta_M \geq I(X;U) - I(Y;U) + \Delta_A \end{cases}$$

for some auxiliary random variable $U \in \mathcal{U}$ with a finite alphabet and jointly distributed with X and Y.

Before we prove this theorem, we need two preliminary lemmas. The first lemma is an extension of Fano's inequality for list decoders and the second one makes use of a single-letterization technique to express $I(X^n;J) - I(Y^n;J)$ in a single-letter form in the sense of Csiszár and Körner [29].

Lemma 13 ([39,41]). *Given a pair of random variables (U, V) defined over $\mathcal{U} \times \mathcal{V}$ for finite $\mathcal{V}$ and arbitrary $\mathcal{U}$, any list decoder $g : \mathcal{U} \to 2^{\mathcal{V}}$, $U \mapsto g(U)$ of fixed list size m (i.e., $|g(u)| = m$, $\forall u \in \mathcal{U}$), satisfies*

$$H(V|U) \leq h_b(p_e) + p_e \log |\mathcal{V}| + (1 - p_e) \log m$$

where $p_e := \Pr(V \notin g(U))$ and $h_b : [0,1] \to [0,1]$ is the binary entropy function.

This lemma, applied to J and Y^n in place of U and V, respectively, implies that for any list decoder with the property (14), we have

$$H(Y^n|J) \leq \log |g_n(J)| + n\varepsilon_n \tag{18}$$

where $\varepsilon_n := \frac{1}{n} + (\log |\mathcal{Y}| - \frac{1}{n} \log |g_n(J)|)p_e$ and hence $\varepsilon_n \to 0$ as $n \to \infty$.

Lemma 14. *Let (X^n, Y^n) be n i.i.d. copies of a pair of random variables (X, Y). Then for a random variable J jointly distributed with (X^n, Y^n), we have*

$$I(X^n;J) - I(Y^n;J) = \sum_{i=1}^{n}[I(X_i;U_i) - I(Y_i;U_i)]$$

where $U_i := (J, X_{i+1}^n, Y^{i-1})$.

Proof. Using the chain rule for the mutual information, we can express $I(X^n;J)$ as follows

$$\begin{aligned} I(X^n;J) &= \sum_{i=1}^{n} I(X_i;J|X_{i+1}^n) = \sum_{i=1}^{n} I(X_i;J,X_{i+1}^n) \\ &= \sum_{i=1}^{n}[I(X_i;J,X_{i+1}^n,Y^{i-1}) - I(X_i;Y^{i-1}|J,X_{i+1}^n)] \\ &= \sum_{i=1}^{n} I(X_i;U_i) - \sum_{i=1}^{n} I(X_i;Y^{i-1}|J,X_{i+1}^n) \end{aligned} \tag{19}$$

Similarly, we can expand $I(Y^n; J)$ as

$$
\begin{aligned}
I(Y^n; J) &= \sum_{i=1}^{n} I(Y_i; J|Y^{i-1}) = \sum_{i=1}^{n} I(Y_i; J, Y^{i-1}) \\
&= \sum_{i=1}^{n} [I(Y_i; J, X_{i+1}^n, Y^{i-1}) - I(Y_i; X_{i+1}^n|J, Y^{i-1})] \\
&= \sum_{i=1}^{n} I(Y_i; U_i) - \sum_{i=1}^{n} I(Y_i; X_{i+1}^n|J, Y^{i-1})
\end{aligned} \tag{20}
$$

Subtracting (20) from (19), we get

$$
\begin{aligned}
I(X^n; J) - I(Y^n; J) &= \sum_{i=1}^{n} [I(X_i; U_i) - I(Y_i; U_i)] - \sum_{i=1}^{n} [I(X_i; Y^{i-1}|J, X_{i+1}^n) - I(X_{i+1}^n; Y_i|J, Y^{i-1})] \\
&\overset{(a)}{=} \sum_{i=1}^{n} [I(X_i; U_i) - I(Y_i; U_i)]
\end{aligned}
$$

where (a) follows from the Csiszár sum identity [42]. □

Proof of Theorem 12. The rate R can be bounded as

$$
\begin{aligned}
nR &\geq H(J) \geq I(Y^n; J) \tag{21} \\
&= nH(Y) - H(Y^n|J) \\
&\overset{(a)}{\geq} nH(Y) - \log|g_n(J)| - n\varepsilon_n \\
&\overset{(b)}{=} n\Delta_A - n\varepsilon_n \tag{22}
\end{aligned}
$$

where (a) follows from Fano's inequality (18) with $\varepsilon_n \to 0$ as $n \to \infty$ and (b) is due to (15). We can also upper bound Δ_A as

$$
\begin{aligned}
\Delta_A &\overset{(a)}{=} H(Y^n) - \log|g_n(J)| \\
&\overset{(b)}{\leq} H(Y^n) - H(Y^n|J) + n\varepsilon_n \\
&= \sum_{i=1}^{n} H(Y_i) - H(Y_i|Y^{i-1}, J) + n\varepsilon_n \\
&\leq \sum_{i=1}^{n} H(Y_i) - H(Y_i|Y^{i-1}, X_{i+1}^n, J) + n\varepsilon_n \\
&= \sum_{i=1}^{n} I(Y_i; U_i) + n\varepsilon_n \tag{23}
\end{aligned}
$$

where (a) follows from (15), (b) follows from (18), and in the last equality the auxiliary random variable $U_i := (Y^{i-1}, X_{i+1}^n, J)$ is introduced.

We shall now lower bound $I(X^n; J)$:

$$
\begin{aligned}
n(\Delta_M + \delta) &\geq I(X^n; J) \\
&\overset{(a)}{=} I(Y^n; J) + \sum_{i=1}^{n} [I(X_i; U_i) - I(Y_i; U_i)] \\
&\overset{(b)}{\geq} n\Delta_A + \sum_{i=1}^{n} [I(X_i; U_i) - I(Y_i; U_i)] - n\varepsilon_n \tag{24}
\end{aligned}
$$

where (a) follows from Lemma 14 and (b) is due to Fano's inequality and (15) (or equivalently from (17)).

Combining (22), (23) and (24), we can write

$$\begin{aligned}
R &\geq \Delta_A - \varepsilon_n \\
\Delta_A &\leq I(Y_Q; U_Q|Q) + \varepsilon_n = I(Y_Q; U_Q, Q) + \varepsilon_n \\
\Delta_M &\geq \Delta_A + I(X_Q; U_Q|Q) - I(Y_Q; U_Q|Q) - \varepsilon'_n \\
&= \Delta_A + I(X_Q; U_Q, Q) - I(Y_Q; U_Q, Q) - \varepsilon'_n
\end{aligned}$$

where $\varepsilon'_n := \varepsilon_n + \delta$ and Q is a random variable distributed uniformly over $\{1, 2, \ldots, n\}$ which is independent of (X, Y) and hence $I(Y_Q; U_Q|Q) = \frac{1}{n} \sum_{i=1}^{n} I(Y_i; U_i)$. The results follow by denoting $U := (U_Q, Q)$ and noting that Y_Q and X_Q have the same distributions as Y and X, respectively. $\square$

If the encoder does not have direct access to the private source X^n, then we can define the encoder mapping as $f_n : \mathcal{Y}^n \to \{1, 2, \ldots, s^{nR}\}$. The following corollary is an immediate consequence of Theorem 12.

Corollary 15. *If the encoder does not see the private source, then for all achievable dependence dilution triple* (R, Δ_A, Δ_M), *we have*

$$\begin{cases}
R \geq \Delta_A \\
\Delta_A \leq I(Y; U) \\
\Delta_M \geq I(X; U) - I(Y; U) + \Delta_A
\end{cases}$$

for some joint distribution $P_{XYU} = P_{XY} P_{U|Y}$ *where the auxiliary random variable* $U \in \mathcal{U}$ *satisfies* $|\mathcal{U}| \leq |\mathcal{Y}| + 1$.

Remark 5. If source Y is required to be amplified (according to (17)) at maximum rate, that is, $\Delta_A = I(Y; U)$ for an auxiliary random variable U which satisfies $X \multimap Y \multimap U$, then by Corollary 15, the best privacy performance one can expect from the dependence dilution setting is

$$\Delta_M^* = \min_{\substack{U: X \multimap Y \multimap U \\ I(Y;U) \geq \Delta_A}} I(X; U) \tag{25}$$

which is equal to the dual of $g_\varepsilon(X; Y)$ evaluated at Δ_A, $t_{\Delta_A}(X; Y)$, as defined in (1).

The dependence dilution problem is closely related to the discriminatory lossy source coding problem studied in [15]. In this problem, an encoder f observes (X^n, Y^n) and wants to describe this source to a decoder, g, such that g recovers Y^n within distortion level D and $I(f(X^n, Y^n); X^n) \leq n\Delta_M$. If the distortion level is Hamming measure, then the distortion constraint and the amplification constraint are closely related via Fano's inequality. Moreover, dependence dilution problem reduces to a secure lossless (list decoder of fixed size 1) source coding problem by setting $\Delta_A = H(H)$, which is recently studied in [43].

3.2. MMSE Estimation of Functions of Private Information

In this section, we provide a justification for the privacy guarantee $\rho_m^2(X; Z) \leq \varepsilon$. To this end, we recall the definition of the minimum mean squared error estimation.

Definition 16. Given random variables U and V, $\mathsf{mmse}(U|V)$ is defined as the minimum error of an estimate, $g(V)$, of U based on V, measured in the mean-square sense, that is

$$\mathsf{mmse}(U|V) := \inf_{g \in \mathscr{L}^2(\mathscr{V})} \mathbb{E}[(U - g(V))^2] = \mathbb{E}[(U - \mathbb{E}[U|V])^2] = \mathbb{E}[\mathsf{var}(U|V)] \tag{26}$$

where $\mathsf{var}(U|V)$ denotes the conditional variance of U given V.

It is easy to see that $\mathsf{mmse}(U|V) = 0$ if and only if $U = f(V)$ for some measurable function f and $\mathsf{mmse}(U|V) = \mathsf{var}(U)$ if and only if $U \perp\!\!\!\perp V$. Hence, unlike for the case of maximal correlation, a small value of $\mathsf{mmse}(U|V)$ implies a strong dependence between U and V. Hence, although it is not a "proper" measure of correlation, in a certain sense it measures how well one random variable can be predicted from another one.

Given a non-degenerate measurable function $f : \mathcal{X} \to \mathbb{R}$, consider the following constraint on $\mathrm{mmse}(f(X)|Y)$

$$(1 - \varepsilon)\mathrm{var}(f(X)) \leq \mathrm{mmse}(f(X)|Z) \leq \mathrm{var}(f(X)). \tag{27}$$

This guarantees that no adversary knowing Z can efficiently estimate $f(X)$. First consider the case where f is an identity function, i.e., $f(x) = x$. In this case, a direct calculation shows that

$$
\begin{aligned}
\mathrm{mmse}(X|Z) &\overset{(a)}{=} \mathbb{E}[(X - \mathbb{E}[X|Z])^2] = \mathbb{E}[X^2] - \mathbb{E}[(\mathbb{E}[X|Z])^2] \\
&= \mathrm{var}(X)(1 - \rho^2(X; \mathbb{E}[X|Z])) \\
&\overset{(b)}{\geq} \mathrm{var}(X)(1 - \rho_m^2(X; Z))
\end{aligned}
$$

where (a) follows from (26) and (b) is due to the definition of maximal correlation. Having imposed $\rho_m^2(X; Z) \leq \varepsilon$, we, can therefore conclude that the MMSE of estimating X given Z satisfies

$$(1 - \varepsilon)\mathrm{var}(X) \leq \mathrm{mmse}(X|Z) \leq \mathrm{var}(X) \tag{28}$$

which shows that $\rho_m^2(X; Z) \leq \varepsilon$ implies (27) for $f(x) = x$. However, in the following we show that the constraint $\rho_m^2(X; Z) \leq \varepsilon$ is, indeed, equivalent to (27) for *any* non-degenerate measurable $f : \mathcal{X} \to \mathbb{R}$.

Definition 17 ([44]). A joint distribution P_{UV} satisfies a *Poincaré inequality* with constant $c \leq 1$ if for all $f : \mathcal{U} \to \mathbb{R}$

$$c \cdot \mathrm{var}(f(U)) \leq \mathrm{mmse}(f(U)|V)$$

and the *Poincaré constant* for P_{UV} is defined as

$$\vartheta(U; V) := \inf_f \frac{\mathrm{mmse}(f(U)|V)}{\mathrm{var}(f(U))}$$

The privacy constraint (27) can then be viewed as

$$\vartheta(X; Z) \geq 1 - \varepsilon. \tag{29}$$

Theorem 18 ([44]). *For any joint distribution P_{UV}, we have*

$$\vartheta(U; V) = 1 - \rho_m^2(U; V)$$

In light of Theorem 18 and (29), the privacy constraint (27) is equivalent to $\rho_m^2(X; Z) \leq \varepsilon$, that is,

$$\rho_m^2(X; Z) \leq \varepsilon \iff (1 - \varepsilon)\mathrm{var}(f(X)) \leq \mathrm{mmse}(f(X)|Z) \leq \mathrm{var}(f(X))$$

for any non-degenerate measurable functions $f : \mathcal{X} \to \mathbb{R}$.

Hence, $\hat{g}_\varepsilon(X; Y)$ characterizes the maximum information extraction from Y such that no (non-trivial) function of X can be efficiently estimated, in terms of MMSE (27), given the extracted information.

4. Observation Channels for Minimal and Maximal $g_\varepsilon(X; Y)$

In this section, we characterize the observation channels which achieve the lower or upper bounds on the rate-privacy function in (4). We first derive general conditions for achieving the lower bound and then present a large family of observation channels $P_{Y|X}$ which achieve the lower bound. We also give a family of $P_{Y|X}$ which attain the upper bound on $g_\varepsilon(X; Y)$.

4.1. Conditions for Minimal $g_\varepsilon(X; Y)$

Assuming that $g_0(X; Y) = 0$, we seek a set of conditions on P_{XY} such that $g_\varepsilon(X; Y)$ is linear in ε, or equivalently, $g_\varepsilon(X; Y) = \varepsilon \frac{H(Y)}{I(X;Y)}$. In order to do this, we shall examine the slope of $g_\varepsilon(X; Y)$ at zero.

Recall that by concavity of $g_\varepsilon(X;Y)$, it is clear that $g_0'(X;Y) \geq \frac{H(Y)}{I(X;Y)}$. We strengthen this bound in the following lemmas. For this, we need to recall the notion of Kullback-Leibler divergence. Given two probability distribution P and Q supported over a finite alphabet $\mathcal{U}$,

$$D(P||Q) := \sum_{u \in \mathcal{U}} P(u) \log \left(\frac{P(u)}{Q(u)} \right) \tag{30}$$

Lemma 19. *For a given joint distribution $P_{XY} = P_Y \times P_{X|Y}$, if $g_0(X;Y) = 0$, then for any $\varepsilon \geq 0$*

$$g_0'(X;Y) \geq \max_{y \in \mathcal{Y}} \frac{-\log P_Y(y)}{D(P_{X|Y}(\cdot|y)||P_X(\cdot))}$$

Proof. The proof is given in Appendix A. □

Remark 6. Note that if for a given joint distribution P_{XY}, there exists $y_0 \in \mathcal{Y}$ such that $D(P_{X|Y}(\cdot|y_0)||P_X(\cdot)) = 0$, it implies that $P_{X|Y}(\cdot|y_0) = P_X(x)$. Consider the binary random variable $Z \in \{1, e\}$ constructed according to the distribution $P_{Z|Y}(1|y_0) = 1$ and $P_{Z|Y}(e|y) = 1$ for $y \in \mathcal{Y}\backslash\{y_0\}$. We can now claim that Z is independent of X, because $P_{X|Z}(x|1) = P_{X|Y}(x|y_0) = P_X(x)$ and

$$\begin{aligned}
P_{X|Z}(x|e) &= \sum_{y \neq y_0} P_{X|Y}(x|y)P_{Y|Z}(y|e) = \sum_{y \neq y_0} P_{X|Y}(x|y) \frac{P_Y(y)}{1 - P_Y(y_0)} \\
&= \frac{1}{1 - P_Y(y_0)} \sum_{y \neq y_0} P_{XY}(x, y) = P_X(x)
\end{aligned}$$

Clearly, Z and Y are not independent, and hence $g_0(X;Y) > 0$. This implies that the right-hand side of inequality in Lemma 19 can not be infinity.

In order to prove the main result, we need the following simple lemma.

Lemma 20. *For any joint distribution P_{XY}, we have*

$$\frac{H(Y)}{I(X;Y)} \leq \max_{y \in \mathcal{Y}} \frac{-\log P_Y(y)}{D(P_{X|Y}(\cdot|y)||P_X(x))}$$

where equality holds if and only if there exists a constant $c > 0$ such that $-\log P_Y(y) = cD(P_{X|Y}(\cdot|y)||P_X(x))$ for all $y \in \mathcal{Y}$.

Proof. It is clear that

$$\frac{H(Y)}{I(X;Y)} = \frac{-\sum_{y \in \mathcal{Y}} P_Y(y) \log P_Y(y)}{\sum_{y \in \mathcal{Y}} P_Y(y)D(P_{X|Y}(\cdot|y)||P_X(x))} \leq \max_{y \in \mathcal{Y}} \frac{-\log P_Y(y)}{D(P_{X|Y}(\cdot|y)||P_X(x))}$$

where the inequality follows from the fact that for any three sequences of positive numbers $\{a_i\}_{i=1}^n$, $\{b_i\}_{i=1}^n$ and $\{\lambda_i\}_{i=1}^n$ we have $\frac{\sum_{i=1}^n \lambda_i a_i}{\sum_{i=1}^n \lambda_i b_i} \leq \max_{1 \leq i \leq n} \frac{a_i}{b_i}$ where equality occurs if and only if $\frac{a_i}{b_i} = c$ for all $1 \leq i \leq n$. □

Now we are ready to state the main result of this subsection.

Theorem 21. *For a given (X, Y) with joint distribution $P_{XY} = P_Y \times P_{X|Y}$, if $g_0(X;Y) = 0$ and $\varepsilon \mapsto g_\varepsilon(X;Y)$ is linear for $0 \leq \varepsilon \leq I(X;Y)$, then for any $y \in \mathcal{Y}$*

$$\frac{H(Y)}{I(X;Y)} = \frac{-\log P_Y(y)}{D(P_{X|Y}(\cdot|y)||P_X(\cdot))}$$

Proof. Note that the fact that $g_0(X;Y) = 0$ and $g_\varepsilon(X;Y)$ is linear in ε is equivalent to $g_\varepsilon(X;Y) = \varepsilon\frac{H(Y)}{I(X;Y)}$. It is, therefore, immediate from Lemmas 19 and 20 that we have

$$g_0'(X;Y) \overset{(a)}{=} \frac{H(Y)}{I(X;Y)} \overset{(b)}{\leq} \max_{y \in \mathcal{Y}} \frac{-\log P_Y(y)}{D(P_{X|Y}(\cdot|y)||P_X(x))}$$

$$\overset{(c)}{\leq} g_0'(X;Y) \tag{31}$$

where (a) follows from the fact that $g_\varepsilon(X;Y) = \varepsilon\frac{H(Y)}{I(X;Y)}$ and (b) and (c) are due to Lemmas 20 and 19, respectively. The inequality in (31) shows that

$$\frac{H(Y)}{I(X;Y)} = \max_{y \in \mathcal{Y}} \frac{-\log P_Y(y)}{D(P_{X|Y}(\cdot|y)||P_X(x))} \tag{32}$$

According to Lemma 20, (32) implies that the ratio of $\frac{-\log P_Y(y)}{D(P_{X|Y}(\cdot|y)||P_X(x))}$ does not depend on $y \in \mathcal{Y}$ and hence the result follows.

This theorem implies that if there exists $y = y_1$ and $y = y_2$ such that $\frac{\log P_Y(y)}{D(P_{X|Y}(\cdot|y)||P_X(x))}$ results in two different values, then $\varepsilon \mapsto g_\varepsilon(X,Y)$ cannot achieve the lower bound in (4), or equivalently

$$g_\varepsilon(X;Y) > \varepsilon\frac{H(Y)}{I(X;Y)}$$

This, therefore, gives a necessary condition for the lower bound to be achievable. The following corollary simplifies this necessary condition.

Corollary 22. *For a given joint distribution $P_{XY} = P_Y \times P_{X|Y}$, if $g_0(X;Y) = 0$ and $\varepsilon \mapsto g_\varepsilon(X;Y)$ is linear, then the following are equivalent:*

(i) Y is uniformly distributed,
(ii) $D(P_{X|Y}(\cdot|y)||P_X(\cdot))$ is constant for all $y \in \mathcal{Y}$.

Proof. $(i) \Rightarrow (ii)$:
From Theorem 21, we have for all $y \in \mathcal{Y}$

$$\frac{H(Y)}{I(X;Y)} = \frac{-\log(P_Y(y))}{D\left(P_{X|Y}(\cdot|y)||P_X(\cdot)\right)} \tag{33}$$

Letting $D := D\left(P_{X|Y}(\cdot|y)||P_X(\cdot)\right)$ for any $y \in \mathcal{Y}$, we have $\sum_y P_Y(y)D = I(X;Y)$ and hence $D = I(X;Y)$, which together with (33) implies that $H(Y) = -\log(P_Y(y))$ for all $y \in \mathcal{Y}$ and hence Y is uniformly distributed.

$(ii) \Rightarrow (i)$:
When Y is uniformly distributed, we have from (33) that $I(X;Y) = D\left(P_{X|Y}(\cdot|y)||P_X(\cdot)\right)$ which implies that $D\left(P_{X|Y}(\cdot|y)||P_X(\cdot)\right)$ is constant for all $y \in \mathcal{Y}$. $\square$

Example 1. Suppose $P_{Y|X}$ is a binary symmetric channel (BSC) with crossover probability $0 < \alpha < 1$ and $P_X = \text{Bernoulli}(0.5)$. In this case, $P_{X|Y}$ is also a BSC with input distribution $P_Y = \text{Bernoulli}(0.5)$. Note that Corollary 11 implies that $g_0(X;Y) = 0$. We will show that $g_\varepsilon(X;Y)$ is linear as a function of $\varepsilon \geq 0$ for a larger family of symmetric channels (including BSC) in Corollary 24. Hence, the BSC with uniform input nicely illustrates Corollary 22, because $D(P_{X|Y}(\cdot|y)||P_X(\cdot)) = 1 - h(\alpha)$ for $y \in \{0,1\}$.

Example 2. Now suppose $P_{X|Y}$ is a binary asymmetric channel such that $P_{X|Y}(\cdot|0) = \text{Bernoulli}(\alpha_0)$, $P_{X|Y}(\cdot|1) = \text{Bernoulli}(\alpha_1)$ for some $0 < \alpha_0, \alpha_1 < 1$ and input distribution $P_Y = \text{Bernoulli}(p)$, $0 < p \leq 0.5$. It is easy to see that if $\alpha_0 + \alpha_1 = 1$ then $D(P_{X|Y}(\cdot|y)||P_X(\cdot))$ does not depend on y and hence we can conclude from Corollary 22 (noticing that $g_0(X;Y) = 0$) that in this case for any $p < 0.5$, $g_\varepsilon(X;Y)$ is not linear and hence for $0 < \varepsilon < I(X;Y)$

$$g_\varepsilon(X;Y) > \varepsilon \frac{H(Y)}{I(X;Y)}$$

In Theorem 21, we showed that when $g_\varepsilon(X;Y)$ achieves its lower bound, illustrated in (4), the slope of the mapping $\varepsilon \mapsto g_\varepsilon(X;Y)$ at zero is equal to $\frac{-\log P_Y(y)}{D(P_{X|Y}(\cdot|y)\|P_X(\cdot))}$ for any $y \in \mathcal{Y}$. We will show in the next section that the reverse direction is also true at least for a large family of binary-input symmetric output channels, for instance when $P_{Y|X}$ is a BSC, and thus showing that in this case,

$$g_0'(X;Y) = \frac{-\log P_Y(y)}{D(P_{X|Y}(\cdot|y)\|P_X(\cdot))}, \ \forall y \in \mathcal{Y} \Longleftrightarrow g_\varepsilon(X;Y) = \varepsilon \frac{H(Y)}{I(X;Y)}, \ 0 \le \varepsilon \le I(X;Y)$$

4.2. Special Observation Channels

In this section, we apply the results of last section to different joint distributions P_{XY}. In the first family of channels from X to Y, we look at the case where Y is binary and the reverse channel $P_{X|Y}$ has symmetry in a particular sense, which will be specified later. One particular case of this family of channels is when $P_{X|Y}$ is a BSC. As a family of observation channels which achieves the upper bound of $g_\varepsilon(X;Y)$, stated in (4), we look at the class of erasure channels from $X \to Y$, i.e., Y is an erasure version of X.

4.2.1. Observation Channels With Symmetric Reverse

The first example of P_{XY} that we consider for binary Y is the so-called *Binary Input Symmetric Output* (BISO) $P_{X|Y}$, see for example [45,46]. Suppose $\mathcal{Y} = \{0,1\}$ and $\mathcal{X} = \{0,\pm1,\pm2,\ldots,\pm k\}$, and for any $x \in \mathcal{X}$ we have $P_{X|Y}(x|1) = P_{X|Y}(-x|0)$. This clearly implies that $p_0 := P_{X|Y}(0|0) = P_{X|Y}(0|1)$. We notice that with this definition of symmetry, we can always assume that the output alphabet $\mathcal{X} = \{\pm1,\pm2,\ldots,\pm k\}$ has even number of elements because we can split $X = 0$ into two outputs, $X = 0^+$ and $X = 0^-$, with $P_{X|Y}(0^-|0) = P_{X|Y}(0^+|0) = \frac{p_0}{2}$ and $P_{X|Y}(0^-|1) = P_{X|Y}(0^+|1) = \frac{p_0}{2}$. The new channel is clearly essentially equivalent to the original one, see [46] for more details. This family of channels can also be characterized using the definition of *quasi-symmetric* channels [47, Definition 4.17]. A channel W is BISO if (after making $|\mathcal{X}|$ even) the transition matrix $P_{X|Y}$ can be partitioned along its columns into binary-input binary-output sub-arrays in which rows are permutations of each other and the column sums are equal. It is clear that binary symmetric channels and binary erasure channels are both BISO. The following lemma gives an upper bound for $g_\varepsilon(X,Y)$ when $P_{X|Y}$ belongs to such a family of channels.

Lemma 23. *If the channel $P_{X|Y}$ is BISO, then for $\varepsilon \in [0, I(X;Y)]$,*

$$\varepsilon \frac{H(Y)}{I(X;Y)} \le g_\varepsilon(X;Y) \le H(Y) - \frac{I(X;Y) - \varepsilon}{C(P_{X|Y})}$$

where $C(P_{X|Y})$ denotes the capacity of $P_{X|Y}$.

Proof. The lower bound has already appeared in (4). To prove the upper bound note that by Markovity $X \text{---} Y \text{---} Z$, we have for any $x \in \mathcal{X}$ and $z \in \mathcal{Z}$

$$P_{X|Z}(x|z) = P_{X|Y}(x|0)P_{Y|Z}(0|z) + P_{X|Y}(x|1)P_{Y|Z}(1|z) \tag{34}$$

Now suppose $\mathcal{Z}_0 := \{z : P_{Y|Z}(0|z) \le P_{Y|Z}(1|z)\}$ and similarly $\mathcal{Z}_1 := \{z : P_{Y|Z}(1|z) \le P_{Y|Z}(0|z)\}$. Then (34) allows us to write for $z \in \mathcal{Z}_0$

$$P_{X|Z}(x|z) = P_{X|Y}(x|0)h_b^{-1}(H(Y|Z=z)) + P_{X|Y}(x|1)(1 - h_b^{-1}(H(Y|Z=z))) \tag{35}$$

where $h_b^{-1} : [0,1] \to [0,0.5]$ is the inverse of binary entropy function, and for $z \in \mathcal{Z}_1$,

$$P_{X|Z}(x|z) = P_{X|Y}(x|0)(1 - h_b^{-1}(H(Y|Z = z))) + P_{X|Y}(x|1)h_b^{-1}(H(Y|Z = z)) \tag{36}$$

Letting $P \otimes h_b^{-1}(H(Y|z))$ and $\tilde{P} \otimes h_b^{-1}(H(Y|z))$ denote the right-hand sides of (35) and (36), respectively, we can, hence, write

$$
\begin{aligned}
H(X|Z) &= \sum_{z \in \mathcal{Z}} P_Z(z)H(X|Z = z) \\
&\overset{(a)}{=} \sum_{z \in \mathcal{Z}_0} P_Z(z)H(P \otimes h_b^{-1}(H(Y|Z = z))) + \sum_{z \in \mathcal{Z}_1} P_Z(z)H(\tilde{P} \otimes h_b^{-1}(H(Y|Z = z))) \\
&\overset{(b)}{\leq} \sum_{z \in \mathcal{Z}_0} P_Z(z)\left[(1 - H(Y|Z = z))H(P \otimes h_b^{-1}(0)) + H(Y|Z = z)H(P \otimes h_b^{-1}(1))\right] \\
&\quad + \sum_{z \in \mathcal{Z}_1} P_Z(z)\left[(1 - H(Y|Z = z))H(\tilde{P} \otimes h_b^{-1}(0)) + H(Y|Z = z)H(\tilde{P} \otimes h_b^{-1}(1))\right] \\
&\overset{(c)}{=} \sum_{z \in \mathcal{Z}_0} P_Z(z)\left[(1 - H(Y|Z = z))H(X|Y) + H(Y|Z = z)H(X_{\text{unif}})\right] \\
&\quad + \sum_{z \in \mathcal{Z}_1} P_Z(z)\left[(1 - H(Y|Z = z))H(X|Y) + H(Y|Z = z)H(X_{\text{unif}})\right] \\
&= H(X|Y)[1 - H(Y|Z)] + H(Y|Z)H(X_{\text{unif}})
\end{aligned}
$$

where $H(X_{\text{unif}})$ denotes the entropy of X when Y is uniformly distributed. Here, (a) is due to (35) and (36), (b) follows form convexity of $u \mapsto H(P \otimes h_b^{-1}(u)))$ for all $u \in [0,1]$ [48] and Jensen's inequality. In (c), we used the symmetry of channel $P_{X|Y}$ to show that $H(X|Y = 0) = H(X|Y = 1) = H(X|Y)$. Hence, we obtain

$$H(Y|Z) \geq \frac{H(X|Z) - H(X|Y)}{H(X_{\text{unif}}) - H(X|Y)} = \frac{I(X;Y) - I(X;Z)}{C(P_{X|Y})}$$

where the equality follows from the fact that for BISO channel (and in general for any quasi-symmetric channel) the uniform input distribution is the capacity-achieving distribution [47, Lemma 4.18]. Since $g_\varepsilon(X;Y)$ is attained when $I(X;Z) = \varepsilon$, the conclusion immediately follows. $\square$

This lemma then shows that the larger the gap between $I(X;Y)$ and $I(X;Y')$ is for $Y' \sim$ Bernoulli(0.5), the more $g_\varepsilon(X;Y)$ deviates from its lower bound. When $Y \sim$ Bernoulli(0.5), then $C(P_{Y|X}) = I(X;Y)$ and $H(Y) = 1$ and hence Lemma 23 implies that

$$\frac{\varepsilon}{I(X;Y)} \leq g_\varepsilon(X;Y) \leq 1 - \frac{I(X;Y) - \varepsilon}{I(X;Y)} = \frac{\varepsilon}{I(X;Y)}$$

and hence we have proved the following corollary.

Corollary 24. *If the channel $P_{X|Y}$ is BISO and $Y \sim$ Bernoulli(0.5), then for any $\varepsilon \geq 0$*

$$g_\varepsilon(X;Y) = \frac{1}{I(X;Y)} \min\{\varepsilon, I(X;Y)\}$$

This corollary now enables us to prove the reverse direction of Theorem 21 for the family of BISO channels.

Theorem 25. *If $P_{X|Y}$ is a BISO channel, then the following statements are equivalent:*

(i) $g_\varepsilon(X;Y) = \varepsilon\frac{H(Y)}{I(X;Y)}$ for $0 \leq \varepsilon \leq I(X;Y)$.
(ii) The initial efficiency of privacy-constrained information extraction is

$$g_0'(X;Y) = \frac{-\log P_Y(y)}{D(P_{X|Y}(\cdot|y)||P_X(\cdot))}, \quad \forall y \in \mathcal{Y}$$

Proof. $(i) \Rightarrow (ii)$.

This follows from Theorem 21.

$(ii) \Rightarrow (i)$.

Let $Y \sim$ Bernoulli(p) for $0 < p < 1$, and, as before, $\mathcal{X} = \{\pm 1, \pm 2, \ldots, \pm k\}$, so that $P_{X|Y}$ is determined by a $2 \times (2k)$ matrix. We then have

$$\frac{-\log P_Y(0)}{D(P_{X|Y}(\cdot|0)||P_X(\cdot))} = \frac{\log(1-p)}{H(X|Y) + \sum_{x=-k}^{k} P_{X|Y}(x|0) \log(P_X(x))} \tag{37}$$

and

$$\frac{-\log P_Y(1)}{D(P_{X|Y}(\cdot|1)||P_X(\cdot))} = \frac{\log(p)}{H(X|Y) + \sum_{x=-k}^{k} P_{X|Y}(x|1) \log(P_X(x))}. \tag{38}$$

The hypothesis implies that (37) is equal to (38), that is,

$$\frac{\log(1-p)}{H(X|Y) + \sum_{x=-k}^{k} P_{X|Y}(x|0) \log(P_X(x))} = \frac{\log(p)}{H(X|Y) + \sum_{x=-k}^{k} P_{X|Y}(x|1) \log(P_X(x))} \tag{39}$$

It is shown in Appendix B that (39) holds if and only if $p = 0.5$. Now we can invoke Corollary 24 to conclude that $g_\varepsilon(X;Y) = \varepsilon \frac{H(Y)}{I(X;Y)}$. □

This theorem shows that for any BISO $P_{X|Y}$ channel with uniform input, the optimal privacy filter is an erasure channel depicted in Figure 2. Note that if $P_{X|Y}$ is a BSC with uniform input $P_Y =$ Bernoulli(0.5), then $P_{Y|X}$ is also a BSC with uniform input $P_X =$ Bernoulli(0.5). The following corollary specializes Corollary 24 for this case.

Corollary 26. *For the joint distribution $P_X P_{Y|X} =$ Bernoulli(0.5) $\times$ BSC(α), the binary erasure channel with erasure probability (shown in Figure 4)*

$$\delta(\varepsilon, \alpha) := 1 - \frac{\varepsilon}{I(X;Y)} \tag{40}$$

for $0 \leq \varepsilon \leq I(X;Y)$, is the optimal privacy filter in (3). In other words, for $\varepsilon \geq 0$

$$g_\varepsilon(X;Y) = \frac{1}{I(X;Y)} \min\{\varepsilon, I(X;Y)\}$$

Moreover, for a given $0 < \alpha < \frac{1}{2}$, $P_X =$ Bernoulli(0.5) is the only distribution for which $\varepsilon \mapsto g_\varepsilon(X;Y)$ is linear. That is, for $P_X P_{Y|X} =$ Bernoulli$(p) \times$ BSC(α), $0 < p < 0.5$, we have

$$g_\varepsilon(X;Y) > \varepsilon \frac{H(Y)}{I(X;Y)}$$

Proof. As mentioned earlier, since $P_X =$ Bernoulli(0.5) and $P_{Y|X}$ is BSC(α), it follows that $P_{X|Y}$ is also a BSC with uniform input and hence from Corollary 24, we have $g_\varepsilon(X;Y) = \frac{\varepsilon}{I(X;Y)}$. As in this case $g_\varepsilon(X;Y)$ achieves the lower bound given in Lemma 1, we conclude from Figure 2 that BEC($\delta(\varepsilon, \alpha)$), where $\delta(\varepsilon, \alpha) = 1 - \frac{\varepsilon}{I(X;Y)}$, is an optimal privacy filter. The fact that $P_X =$ Bernoulli(0.5) is the only input distribution for which $\varepsilon \mapsto g_\varepsilon(X;Y)$ is linear follows from the proof of Theorem 25. In particular, we saw that a necessary and sufficient condition for $g_\varepsilon(X;Y)$ being linear is that the ratio $\frac{-\log P_Y(y)}{D(P_{X|Y}(\cdot|y)||P_X(\cdot))}$ is constant for all $y \in \mathcal{Y}$. As shown before, this is equivalent to $Y \sim$ Bernoulli(0.5). For the binary symmetric channel, this is equivalent to $X \sim$ Bernoulli(0.5). □

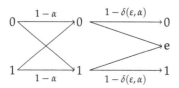

Figure 4. Optimal privacy filter for $P_{Y|X} = BSC(\alpha)$ with uniform X where $\delta(\varepsilon, \alpha)$ is specified in (40).

The optimal privacy filter for $BSC(\alpha)$ and uniform X is shown in Figure 4. In fact, this corollary immediately implies that the general lower-bound given in (4) is tight for the binary symmetric channel with uniform X.

4.2.2. Erasure Observation Channel

Combining (8) and Lemma 1, we have for $\varepsilon \leq I(X; Y)$

$$\varepsilon \frac{H(Y)}{I(X;Y)} + g_0(X;Y)\left[1 - \frac{\varepsilon}{I(X;Y)}\right] \leq g_\varepsilon(X;Y) \leq H(Y|X) + \varepsilon \tag{41}$$

In the following we show that the above upper and lower bound coincide when $P_{Y|X}$ is an erasure channel, i.e., $P_{Y|X}(x|x) = 1 - \delta$ and $P_{Y|X}(e|x) = \delta$ for all $x \in \mathcal{X}$ and $0 \leq \delta \leq 1$.

Lemma 27. *For any given* (X, Y), *if* $P_{Y|X}$ *is an erasure channel (as defined above), then*

$$g_\varepsilon(X;Y) = H(Y|X) + \min\{\varepsilon, I(X;Y)\}$$

for any $\varepsilon \geq 0$.

Proof. It suffices to show that if $P_{Y|X}$ is an erasure channel, then $g_0(X;Y) = H(Y|X)$. This follows, since if $g_0(X;Y) = H(Y|X)$, then the lower bound in (41) becomes $H(Y|X) + \varepsilon$ and thus $g_\varepsilon(X;Y) = H(Y|X) + \varepsilon$.

Let $|\mathcal{X}| = m$ and $\mathcal{Y} = \mathcal{X} \cup \{e\}$ where e denotes the erasure symbol. Consider the following privacy filter to generate $Z \in \mathcal{Y}$:

$$P_{Z|Y}(z|y) = \begin{cases} \frac{1}{m} & \text{if } y \neq e, z \neq e, \\ 1 & \text{if } y = z = e. \end{cases}$$

For any $x \in \mathcal{X}$, we have

$$P_{Z|X}(z|x) = P_{Z|Y}(z|x)P_{Y|X}(x|x) + P_{Z|Y}(z|e)P_{Y|X}(e|x) = \left[\frac{1-\delta}{m}\right]1_{\{z \neq e\}} + \delta 1_{\{z=e\}}$$

which implies $Z \perp\!\!\!\perp X$ and thus $I(X; Z) = 0$. On the other hand, $P_Z(z) = \left[\frac{1-\delta}{m}\right]1_{\{z \neq e\}} + \delta 1_{\{z=e\}}$, and therefore we have

$$\begin{aligned} g_0(X;Y) &\geq I(Y;Z) = H(Z) - H(Z|Y) = H\left(\frac{1-\delta}{m}, \ldots, \frac{1-\delta}{m}, \delta\right) - (1-\delta)\log(m) \\ &= h(\delta) = H(Y|X) \end{aligned}$$

It then follows from Lemma 1 that $g_0(X;Y) = H(Y|X)$, which completes the proof. $\square$

Example 3. In light of this lemma, we can conclude that if $P_{Y|X} = BEC(\delta)$, then the optimal privacy filter is a combination of an identity channel and a $BSC(\alpha(\varepsilon, \delta))$, as shown in Figure 5, where $0 \leq \alpha(\varepsilon, \delta) \leq \frac{1}{2}$ is the unique solution of

$$(1 - \delta)[h_b(\alpha * p) - h_b(\alpha)] = \varepsilon \tag{42}$$

where $X \sim$ Bernoulli(p), $p \leq 0.5$ and $a * b = a(1-b) + b(1-a)$. Note that it is easy to check that $I(X;Z) = (1-\delta)[h_b(\alpha * p) - h_b(\alpha)]$. Therefore, in order for this channel to be a valid privacy filter, the crossover probability, $\alpha(\varepsilon, \delta)$, must be chosen such that $I(X;Z) = \varepsilon$. We note that for fixed $0 < \delta < 1$ and $0 < p < 0.5$, the map $\alpha \mapsto (1-\delta)[h_b(\alpha * p) - h_b(\alpha)]$ is monotonically decreasing on $[0, \frac{1}{2}]$ ranging over $[0, (1-\delta)h_b(p)]$ and since $\varepsilon \leq I(X;Y) = (1-\delta)h_b(p)$, the solution of the above equation is unique.

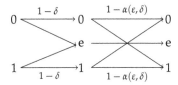

Figure 5. Optimal privacy filter for $P_{Y|X} = BEC(\delta)$ where $\delta(\varepsilon, \alpha)$ is specified in (42).

Combining Lemmas 1 and 27 with Corollary 26, we can show the following *extremal property* of the BEC and BSC channels, which is similar to other existing extremal properties of the BEC and the BSC, see, e.g., [46] and [45]. For $X \sim$ Bernoulli(0.5), we have for any channel $P_{Y|X}$,

$$g_\varepsilon(X;Y) \geq \frac{\varepsilon}{I(X;Y)} = g_\varepsilon(BSC(\hat{\alpha}))$$

where $g_\varepsilon(BSC(\alpha))$ is the rate-privacy function corresponding to $P_{XY} =$ Bernoulli$(0.5) \times BSC(\alpha)$ and $\hat{\alpha} := h_b^{-1}(H(X|Y))$. Similarly, if $X \sim$ Bernoulli(p), we have for any channel $P_{Y|X}$ with $H(Y|X) \leq 1$,

$$g_\varepsilon(X;Y) \leq H(Y|X) + \varepsilon = g_\varepsilon(BEC(\hat{\delta}))$$

where $g_\varepsilon(BEC(\delta))$ is the rate-privacy function corresponding to $P_{XY} =$ Bernoulli$(p) \times BEC(\delta)$ and $\hat{\delta} := h_b^{-1}(H(Y|X))$.

5. Rate-Privacy Function for Continuous Random Variables

In this section we extend the rate-privacy function $g_\varepsilon(X;Y)$ to the continuous case. Specifically, we assume that the private and observable data are continuous random variables and that the filter is composed of two stages: first Gaussian noise is added and then the resulting random variable is quantized using an M-bit accuracy uniform scalar quantizer (for some positive integer $M \in \mathbb{N}$). These filters are of practical interest as they can be easily implemented. This section is divided in two subsections, in the first we discuss general properties of the rate-privacy function and in the second we study the Gaussian case in more detail. Some observations on $\hat{g}_\varepsilon(X;Y)$ for continuous X and Y are also given.

5.1. General Properties of the Rate-Privacy Function

Throughout this section we assume that the random vector (X, Y) is absolutely continuous with respect to the Lebesgue measure on $\mathbb{R}^2$. Additionally, we assume that its joint density $f_{X,Y}$ satisfies the following.

(a) There exist constants $C_1 > 0$, $p > 1$ and bounded function $C_2 : \mathbb{R} \to \mathbb{R}$ such that

$$f_Y(y) \leq C_1|y|^{-p}$$

and also for $x \in \mathbb{R}$

$$f_{Y|X}(y|x) \leq C_2(x)|y|^{-p}$$

(b) $\mathbb{E}[X^2]$ and $\mathbb{E}[Y^2]$ are both finite,
(c) the differential entropy of (X, Y) satisfies $h(X, Y) > -\infty$,
(d) $H(\lfloor Y \rfloor) < \infty$, where $\lfloor a \rfloor$ denotes the largest integer ℓ such that $\ell \leq a$.

Note that assumptions (b) and (c) together imply that $h(X, Y)$, $h(X)$ and $h(Y)$ are finite, *i.e.*, the maps $x \mapsto f_X(x)|\log f_X(x)|$, $y \mapsto f_Y(y)|\log f_Y(y)|$ and $(x, y) \mapsto f_{X,Y}(x, y)|\log(f_{X,Y}(x, y))|$ are integrable. We also assume that X and Y are not independent, since otherwise the problem to characterize $g_\varepsilon(X; Y)$ becomes trivial by assuming that the displayed data Z can equal the observable data Y.

We are interested in filters of the form $\mathcal{Q}_M(Y + \gamma N)$ where $\gamma \geq 0$, $N \sim N(0, 1)$ is a standard normal random variable which is independent of X and Y, and for any positive integer M, $\mathcal{Q}_M$ denotes the M-bit accuracy uniform scalar quantizer, *i.e.*, for all $x \in \mathbb{R}$

$$\mathcal{Q}_M(x) = \frac{1}{2^M} \left\lfloor 2^M x \right\rfloor$$

Let $Z_\gamma = Y + \gamma N$ and $Z_\gamma^M = \mathcal{Q}_M(Z_\gamma) = \mathcal{Q}_M(Y + \gamma N)$. We define, for any $M \in \mathbb{N}$,

$$g_{\varepsilon,M}(X; Y) := \sup_{\substack{\gamma \geq 0, \\ I(X; Z_\gamma^M) \leq \varepsilon}} I(Y; Z_\gamma^M) \tag{43}$$

and similarly

$$g_\varepsilon(X; Y) := \sup_{\substack{\gamma \geq 0, \\ I(X; Z_\gamma) \leq \varepsilon}} I(Y; Z_\gamma) \tag{44}$$

The next theorem shows that the previous definitions are closely related.

Theorem 28. *Let $\varepsilon > 0$ be fixed. Then $\lim_{M \to \infty} g_{\varepsilon,M}(X; Y) = g_\varepsilon(X; Y)$.*

Proof. See Appendix C. □

In the limit of large M, $g_\varepsilon(X; Y)$ approximates $g_{\varepsilon,M}(X; Y)$. This becomes relevant when $g_\varepsilon(X; Y)$ is easier to compute than $g_{\varepsilon,M}(X; Y)$, as demonstrated in the following subsection. The following theorem summarizes some general properties of $g_\varepsilon(X; Y)$.

Theorem 29. *The function $\varepsilon \mapsto g_\varepsilon(X; Y)$ is non-negative, strictly-increasing, and satisfies*

$$\lim_{\varepsilon \to 0} g_\varepsilon(X; Y) = 0 \qquad \text{and} \qquad g_{I(X;Y)}(X; Y) = \infty$$

Proof. See Apendix C. □

As opposed to the discrete case, in the continuous case $g_\varepsilon(X; Y)$ is no longer bounded. In the following section we show that $\varepsilon \mapsto g_\varepsilon(X; Y)$ can be convex, in contrast to the discrete case where it is always concave.

We can also define $\hat{g}_{\varepsilon,M}(X; Y)$ and $\hat{g}_\varepsilon(X; Y)$ for continuous X and Y, similar to (43) and (44), but where the privacy constraints are replaced by $\rho_m^2(X; Z_\gamma^M) \leq \varepsilon$ and $\rho_m^2(X; Z_\gamma) \leq \varepsilon$, respectively. It is clear to see from Theorem 29 that $\hat{g}_0(X; Y) = g_0(X; Y) = 0$ and $\hat{g}_{\rho^2(X;Y)}(X; Y) = \infty$. However, although we showed that $g_\varepsilon(X; Y)$ is indeed the asymptotic approximation of $g_{\varepsilon,M}(X; Y)$ for M large enough, it is not clear that the same statement holds for $\hat{g}_\varepsilon(X; Y)$ and $\hat{g}_{\varepsilon,M}(X; Y)$.

5.2. Gaussian Information

The rate-privacy function for Gaussian Y has an interesting interpretation from an estimation theoretic point of view. Given the private and observable data (X, Y), suppose an agent is required to *estimate* Y based on the output of the privacy filter. We wish to know the effect of imposing a privacy constraint on the estimation performance.

The following lemma shows that $g_\varepsilon(X; Y)$ bounds the best performance of the predictability of Y given the output of the privacy filter. The proof provided for this lemma does not use the Gaussianity of the noise process, so it holds for any noise process.

Lemma 30. *For any given private data X and Gaussian observable data Y, we have for any $\varepsilon \geq 0$*

$$\inf_{\substack{\gamma \geq 0, \\ I(X;Z_\gamma) \leq \varepsilon}} \text{mmse}(Y|Z_\gamma) \geq \text{var}(Y)2^{-2g_\varepsilon(X;Y)}$$

Proof. It is a well-known fact from rate-distortion theory that for a Gaussian Y and its reconstruction $\hat{Y}$

$$I(Y;\hat{Y}) \geq \frac{1}{2}\log \frac{\text{var}(Y)}{\mathbb{E}[(Y-\hat{Y})^2]}$$

and hence by setting $\hat{Y} = \mathbb{E}[Y|Z_\gamma]$, where Z_γ is an output of a privacy filter, and noting that $I(Y;\hat{Y}) \leq I(Y;Z_\gamma)$, we obtain

$$\text{mmse}(Y|Z_\gamma) \geq \text{var}(Y)2^{-2I(Y;Z_\gamma)} \tag{45}$$

from which the result follows immediately. $\square$

According to Lemma 30, the quantity $\lambda_\varepsilon(X) := 2^{-2g_\varepsilon(X;Y)}$ is a parameter that bounds the difficulty of estimating Gaussian Y when observing an additive perturbation Z with privacy constraint $I(X;Z) \leq \varepsilon$. Note that $0 < \lambda_\varepsilon(X) \leq 1$, and therefore, provided that the privacy threshold is not trivial (i.e, $\varepsilon < I(X;Y)$), the mean squared error of estimating Y given the privacy filter output is bounded away from zero, however the bound decays exponentially at rate of $g_\varepsilon(X;Y)$.

To finish this section, assume that X and Y are jointly Gaussian with correlation coefficient ρ. The value of $g_\varepsilon(X;Y)$ can be easily obtained in closed form as demonstrated in the following theorem.

Theorem 31. *Let (X,Y) be jointly Gaussian random variables with correlation coefficient ρ. For any $\varepsilon \in [0, I(X;Y))$ we have*

$$g_\varepsilon(X;Y) = \frac{1}{2}\log\left(\frac{\rho^2}{2^{-2\varepsilon}+\rho^2-1}\right)$$

Proof. One can always write $Y = aX + N_1$ where $a^2 = \rho^2\frac{\text{var}(Y)}{\text{var}(X)}$ and N_1 is a Gaussian random variable with mean 0 and variance $\sigma^2 = (1-\rho^2)\text{var}(Y)$ which is independent of (X,Y). On the other hand, we have $Z_\gamma = Y + \gamma N$ where N is the standard Gaussian random variable independent of (X,Y) and hence $Z_\gamma = aX + N_1 + \gamma N$. In order for this additive channel to be a privacy filter, it must satisfy

$$I(X;Z_\gamma) \leq \varepsilon$$

which implies

$$\frac{1}{2}\log\left(\frac{\text{var}(Y)+\gamma^2}{\sigma^2+\gamma^2}\right) \leq \varepsilon$$

and hence

$$\gamma^2 \geq \frac{2^{-2\varepsilon}+\rho^2-1}{1-2^{-2\varepsilon}}\text{var}(Y) =: \gamma^*$$

Since $\gamma \mapsto I(Y;Z_\gamma)$ is strictly decreasing (cf., Appendix C), we obtain

$$\begin{aligned} g_\varepsilon(X;Y) &= I(Y;Z_{\gamma^*}) = \frac{1}{2}\log\left(1+\frac{\text{var}(Y)}{\gamma^2}\right) \\ &= \frac{1}{2}\log\left(1+\frac{1-2^{-2\varepsilon}}{2^{-2\varepsilon}+\rho^2-1}\right) \quad \square \end{aligned} \tag{46}$$

According to (46), we conclude that the optimal privacy filter for jointly Gaussian (X,Y) is an additive Gaussian channel with signal to noise ratio $\frac{1-2^{-2\varepsilon}}{2^{-2\varepsilon}+\rho^2-1}$, which shows that if perfect privacy is required, then the displayed data is independent of the observable data Y, i.e., $g_0(X;Y) = 0$.

Remark 7. We could assume that the privacy filter adds non-Gaussian noise to the observable data and define the rate-privacy function accordingly. To this end, we define

$$g_\varepsilon^f(X;Y) := \sup_{\substack{\gamma \geq 0, \\ I(X;Z_\gamma^f)}} I(Y;Z_\gamma^f)$$

where $Z_\gamma^f = Y + \gamma M_f$ and M_f is a noise process that has stable distribution with density f and is independent of (X,Y). In this case, we can use a technique similar to Oohama [49] to lower bound $g_\varepsilon^f(X;Y)$ for jointly Gaussian (X,Y). Since X and Y are jointly Gaussian, we can write $X = aY + bN$ where $a^2 = \rho^2 \frac{\text{var}(X)}{\text{var}(Y)}$, $b = \sqrt{(1-\rho^2)\text{var}X}$, and N is a standard Gaussian random variable that is independent of Y. We can apply the conditional entropy power inequality (cf., [42, Page 22]) for a random variable Z that is independent of N, to obtain

$$2^{2h(X|Z)} \geq 2^{2h(aY|Z)} + 2^{2h(N)} = a^2 2^{2h(Y|Z)} + 2\pi e(1-\rho^2)\text{var}(X)$$

and hence

$$2^{-2I(X;Z)} 2^{2h(X)} \geq a^2 2^{2h(Y)} 2^{-2I(Y;Z)} + 2\pi e(1-\rho^2)\text{var}(X)$$

Assuming $Z = Z_\gamma^f$ and taking infimum from both sides of above inequality over γ such that $I(X;Z_\gamma^f) \leq \varepsilon$, we obtain

$$g_\varepsilon^f(X;Y) \geq \frac{1}{2} \log\left(\frac{\rho^2}{2^{-2\varepsilon} + \rho^2 - 1}\right) = g_\varepsilon(X;Y)$$

which shows that for Gaussian (X,Y), Gaussian noise is the worst stable additive noise in the sense of privacy-constrained information extraction.

We can also calculate $\hat{g}_\varepsilon(X;Y)$ for jointly Gaussian (X,Y).

Theorem 32. *Let (X,Y) be jointly Gaussian random variables with correlation coefficient ρ. For any $\varepsilon \in [0,\rho^2)$ we have that*

$$\hat{g}_\varepsilon(X;Y) = \frac{1}{2} \log\left(\frac{\rho^2}{\rho^2 - \varepsilon}\right)$$

Proof. Since for the correlation coefficient between Y and Z_γ we have for any $\gamma \geq 0$,

$$\rho^2(Y;Z_\gamma) = \frac{\text{var}(Y)}{\text{var}(Y) + \gamma^2}$$

we can conclude that

$$\rho^2(X;Z_\gamma) = \frac{\rho^2 \text{var}(Y)}{\text{var}(Y) + \gamma^2}$$

Since $\rho_m^2(X;Z) = \rho^2(X;Z)$ (see, e.g., [34]), the privacy constraint $\rho_m^2(X;Z) \leq \varepsilon$ implies that

$$\frac{\rho^2 \text{var}(Y)}{\text{var}(Y) + \gamma^2} \leq \varepsilon$$

and hence

$$\gamma^2 \geq \frac{(\rho^2 - \varepsilon)\text{var}(Y)}{\varepsilon} =: \hat{\gamma}_\varepsilon^2$$

By monotonicity of the map $\gamma \mapsto I(Y;Z_\gamma)$, we have

$$\hat{g}_\varepsilon(X;Y) = I(Y;Z_{\hat{\gamma}_\varepsilon}) = \frac{1}{2} \log\left(1 + \frac{\text{var}(Y)}{\hat{\gamma}_\varepsilon^2}\right) = \frac{1}{2} \log\left(\frac{\rho^2}{\rho^2 - \varepsilon}\right) \qquad \square$$

Theorems 31 and 32 show that unlike to the discrete case (cf. Lemmas 2 and 8), $\varepsilon \mapsto g_\varepsilon(X;Y)$ and $\varepsilon \mapsto \hat{g}_\varepsilon(X;Y)$ are convex.

6. Conclusions

In this paper, we studied the problem of determining the maximal amount of information that one can extract by observing a random variable Y, which is correlated with another random variable X that represents sensitive or private data, while ensuring that the extracted data Z meets a privacy constraint with respect to X. Specifically, given two correlated discrete random variables X and Y, we introduced the rate-privacy function as the maximization of $I(Y;Z)$ over all stochastic "privacy filters" $P_{Z|Y}$ such that $pm(X;Z) \leq \epsilon$, where $pm(\cdot;\cdot)$ is a privacy measure and $\epsilon \geq 0$ is a given privacy threshold. We considered two possible privacy measure functions, $pm(X;Z) = I(X;Z)$ and $pm(X;Z) = \rho_m^2(X;Z)$ where ρ_m denotes maximal correlation, resulting in the rate-privacy functions $g_\varepsilon(X;Y)$ and $\hat{g}_\varepsilon(X;Y)$, respectively. We analyzed these two functions, noting that each function lies between easily evaluated upper and lower bounds, and derived their monotonicity and concavity properties. We next provided an information-theoretic interpretation for $g_\varepsilon(X;Y)$ and an estimation-theoretic characterization for $\hat{g}_\varepsilon(X;Y)$. In particular, we demonstrated that the dual function of $g_\varepsilon(X;Y)$ is a corner point of an outer bound on the achievable region of the dependence dilution coding problem. We also showed that $\hat{g}_\varepsilon(X;Y)$ constitutes the largest amount of information that can be extracted from Y such that no meaningful MMSE estimation of any function of X can be realized by just observing the extracted information Z. We then examined conditions on P_{XY} under which the lower bound on $g_\varepsilon(X;Y)$ is tight, hence determining the exact value of $g_\varepsilon(X;Y)$. We also showed that for any given Y, if the observation channel $P_{Y|X}$ is an erasure channel, then $g_\varepsilon(X;Y)$ attains its upper bound. Finally, we extended the notions of the rate-privacy functions $g_\varepsilon(X;Y)$ and $\hat{g}_\varepsilon(X;Y)$ to the continuous case where the observation channel consists of an additive Gaussian noise channel followed by uniform scalar quantization.

Acknowledgments: This work was supported in part by Natural Sciences and Engineering Council (NSERC) of Canada.

Author Contributions: All authors of this paper contributed equally. All authors have read and approved the final manuscript.

Conflicts of Interest: The authors declare no conflict of interest.

Appendix A. Proof of Lemma 19

Given a joint distribution P_{XY} defined over $\mathcal{X} \times \mathcal{Y}$ where $\mathcal{X} = \{1,2,\ldots,m\}$ and $\mathcal{Y} = \{1,2,\ldots,n\}$ with $n \leq m$, we consider a privacy filter specified by the following distribution for $\delta > 0$ and $\mathcal{Z} = \{k,e\}$

$$P_{Z|Y}(k|y) = \delta 1_{\{y=k\}} \tag{A1}$$
$$P_{Z|Y}(e|y) = 1 - \delta 1_{\{y=k\}} \tag{A2}$$

where $1_{\{\cdot\}}$ denotes the indicator function. The system of $X \multimap Y \multimap Z$ in this case is depicted in Figure 6 for the case of $k=1$.

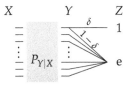

Figure 6. The privacy filter associated with (A1) and (A2) with $k=1$. We have $P_{Z|Y}(\cdot|1) = \text{Bernoulli}(\delta)$ and $P_{Z|Y}(\cdot|y) = \text{Bernoulli}(0)$ for $y \in \{2,3,\ldots,n\}$.

We clearly have $P_Z(k) = \delta P_Y(k)$ and $P_Z(e) = 1 - \delta P_Y(k)$, and hence

$$P_{X|Z}(x|k) = \frac{P_{XZ}(x,k)}{\delta P_Y(k)} = \frac{P_{XYZ}(x,k,k)}{\delta P_Y(k)} = \frac{\delta P_{XY}(x,k)}{\delta P_Y(k)} = P_{X|Y}(x|k)$$

and also,

$$
\begin{aligned}
P_{X|Z}(x|e) &= \frac{P_{XZ}(x,e)}{1 - \delta P_Y(k)} = \frac{\sum_y P_{XYZ}(x,y,e)}{1 - \delta P_Y(k)} \\
&= \frac{\sum_{y \neq k} P_{XYZ}(x,y) + (1-\delta)P_{XY}(x,k)}{1 - \delta P_Y(k)} = \frac{P_X(x) - \delta P_{XY}(x,k)}{1 - \delta P_Y(k)}
\end{aligned}
$$

It, therefore, follows that for $k \in \{1,2,\ldots,n\}$

$$H(X|Z = k) = H(X|Y = k)$$

and

$$H(X|Z = e) = H\left(\frac{P_X(1) - \delta P_{XY}(1,k)}{1 - \delta P_Y(k)}, \ldots, \frac{P_X(m) - \delta P_{XY}(m,k)}{1 - \delta P_Y(k)}\right) =: \hbar_X(\delta)$$

We then write

$$I(X;Z) = H(X) - H(X|Z) = H(X) - \delta P_Y(k)H(X|Y = k) - (1 - \delta P_Y(k))\hbar_X(\delta)$$

and hence,

$$\frac{d}{d\delta}I(X;Z) = -P_Y(k)H(X|Y = k) + P_Y(k)\hbar_X(\delta) - (1 - \delta P_Y(k))\hbar'_X(\delta)$$

where

$$\hbar'_X(\delta) = \frac{d}{d\delta}\hbar_X(\delta) = -\sum_{x=1}^{m} \frac{P_X(x)P_Y(k) - P_{XY}(x,k)}{[1 - \delta P_Y(k)]^2} \log\left(\frac{P_X(x) - \delta P_{XY}(x,y)}{1 - \delta P_Y(k)}\right)$$

Using the first-order approximation of mutual information for $\delta = 0$, we can write

$$
\begin{aligned}
I(X;Z) &= \frac{d}{d\delta}I(X;Z)|_{\delta=0}\delta + o(\delta) \\
&= \delta\left[\sum_{x=1}^{m} P_{XY}(x,k)\log\left(\frac{P_{XY}(x,k)}{P_X(x)P_Y(k)}\right)\right] + o(\delta) \\
&= \delta P_Y(k)D(P_{X|Y}(\cdot|k)||P_X(\cdot)) + o(\delta) \tag{A3}
\end{aligned}
$$

Similarly, we can write

$$
\begin{aligned}
I(Y;Z) &= h(Z) - \sum_{y=1}^{n} P_Y(y)h(Z|Y = y) = h(Z) - P_Y(k)h(\delta) = h(\delta P_Y(k)) - P_Y(k)h(\delta) \\
&= -\delta P_Y(k)\log(P_Y(k)) - \Psi(1 - \delta P_Y(k)) + P_Y(k)\Psi(1 - \delta)
\end{aligned}
$$

where $\Psi(x) := x \log x$ which yields

$$\frac{d}{d\delta}I(Y;Z) = -\Psi(P_Y(k)) + P_Y(k)\log\left(\frac{1 - \delta P_Y(k)}{1 - \delta}\right)$$

From the above, we obtain

$$
\begin{aligned}
I(Y;Z) &= \frac{d}{d\delta}I(Y;Z)|_{\delta=0}\delta + o(\delta) \\
&= -\delta\Psi(P_Y(k)) + o(\delta) \tag{A4}
\end{aligned}
$$

Clearly from (A3), in order for the filter $P_{Z|Y}$ specified in (A1) and (A2) to belong to $\mathscr{D}_\varepsilon(P_{XY})$, we must have

$$\frac{\varepsilon}{\delta} = P_Y(k)D(P_{X|Y}(\cdot|k)||P_X(\cdot)) + \frac{o(\delta)}{\delta}$$

and hence from (A4), we have

$$I(Y;Z) = \frac{-\Psi(P_Y(k))}{P_Y(k)D(P_{X|Y}(\cdot|k)||P_X(\cdot))}\varepsilon + o(\delta)$$

This immediately implies that

$$g_0'(X;Y) = \lim_{\varepsilon\downarrow 0}\frac{g_\varepsilon(X;Y)}{\varepsilon} \geq \frac{-\Psi(P_Y(k))}{P_Y(k)D(P_{X|Y}(\cdot|k)||P_X(\cdot))} = \frac{-\log(P_Y(k))}{D\left(P_{X|Y}(\cdot|k)||P_X(\cdot)\right)} \tag{A5}$$

where we have used the assumption $g_0(X,Y) = 0$ in the first equality.

Appendix B. Completion of Proof of Theorem 25

To prove that the equality (39) has only one solution $p = \frac{1}{2}$, we first show the following lemma.

Lemma 33. *Let P and Q be two distributions over $\mathscr{X} = \{\pm 1, \pm 2, \ldots, \pm k\}$ which satisfy $P(x) = Q(-x)$. Let $R_\lambda := \lambda P + (1-\lambda)Q$ for $\lambda \in (0,1)$. Then*

$$\frac{D(P||R_{1-\lambda})}{D(P||R_\lambda)} < \frac{\log(1-\lambda)}{\log(\lambda)} \tag{A6}$$

for $\lambda \in (0,\frac{1}{2})$ and

$$\frac{D(P||R_{1-\lambda})}{D(P||R_\lambda)} > \frac{\log(1-\lambda)}{\log(\lambda)} \tag{A7}$$

for $\lambda \in (\frac{1}{2},1)$.

Note that it is easy to see that the map $\lambda \mapsto D(P||R_\lambda)$ is convex and strictly decreasing and hence $D(P||R_\lambda) > D(P||R_{1-\lambda})$ when $\lambda \in (0,\frac{1}{2})$ and $D(P||R_\lambda) < D(P||R_{1-\lambda})$ when $\lambda \in (\frac{1}{2},1)$. Inequality (A6) and (A7) strengthen these monotonic behavior and show that $D(P||R_\lambda) > \frac{\log(\lambda)}{\log(1-\lambda)}D(P||R_{1-\lambda})$ and $D(P||R_\lambda) < \frac{\log(\lambda)}{\log(1-\lambda)}D(P||R_{1-\lambda})$ for $\lambda \in (0,\frac{1}{2})$ and $\lambda \in (\frac{1}{2},1)$, respectively.

Proof. Without loss of generality, we can assume that $P(x) > 0$ for all $x \in \mathscr{X}$. Let $\mathscr{X}_+ := \{x \in \mathscr{X}|P(X) > P(-x)\}$, $\mathscr{X}_- := \{x \in \mathscr{X}|P(X) < P(-x)\}$ and $\mathscr{X}_0 := \{x \in \mathscr{X}|P(X) = P(-x)\}$. We notice that when $x \in \mathscr{X}_+$, then $-x \in \mathscr{X}_-$, and hence $|\mathscr{X}_+| = |\mathscr{X}_-| = m$ for a $0 < m \leq k$. After relabelling if needed, we can therefore assume that $\mathscr{X}_+ = \{1,2,\ldots,m\}$ and $\mathscr{X}_- = \{-m,\ldots,-2,-1\}$. We can write

$$
\begin{aligned}
D(P||R_\lambda) &= \sum_{x=-k}^{k} \log\left(\frac{P(x)}{\lambda P(x) + (1-\lambda)Q(x)}\right) = \sum_{x=-k}^{k} \log\left(\frac{P(x)}{\lambda P(x) + (1-\lambda)P(-x)}\right)\\
&\overset{(a)}{=} \sum_{x=1}^{m}\left[P(x)\log\left(\frac{P(x)}{\lambda P(x) + (1-\lambda)P(-x)}\right) + P(-x)\log\left(\frac{P(-x)}{\lambda P(-x) + (1-\lambda)P(x)}\right)\right]\\
&\overset{(b)}{=} \sum_{x=1}^{m}\left[P(x)\log\left(\frac{1}{\lambda + (1-\lambda)\zeta_x}\right) + P(x)\zeta_x\log\left(\frac{1}{\lambda + \frac{(1-\lambda)}{\zeta_x}}\right)\right]\\
&\overset{(c)}{=} \sum_{x=1}^{m} P(x)\Xi(\lambda,\zeta_x)\log\left(\frac{1}{\lambda}\right)
\end{aligned}
$$

where (a) follows from the fact that for $x \in \mathcal{X}_0$, $\log\left(\frac{P(x)}{R_\lambda(x)}\right) = 0$ for any $\lambda \in (0,1)$, and in (b) and (c) we introduced $\zeta_x := \frac{P(-x)}{P(x)}$ and

$$\Xi(\lambda, \zeta) := \frac{1}{\log\left(\frac{1}{\lambda}\right)}\left(\log\left(\frac{1}{\lambda + (1-\lambda)\zeta}\right) + \zeta \log\left(\frac{1}{\lambda + \frac{(1-\lambda)}{\zeta}}\right)\right)$$

Similarly, we can write

$$
\begin{aligned}
D(P||R_{1-\lambda}) &= \sum_{x=-k}^{k} \log\left(\frac{P(x)}{(1-\lambda)P(x) + \lambda Q(x)}\right) = \sum_{x=-k}^{k} \log\left(\frac{P(x)}{(1-\lambda)P(x) + \lambda P(-x)}\right)\\
&= \sum_{x=1}^{m}\left[P(x)\log\left(\frac{P(x)}{(1-\lambda)P(x) + \lambda P(-x)}\right) + P(-x)\log\left(\frac{P(-x)}{(1-\lambda)P(-x) + \lambda P(x)}\right)\right]\\
&= \sum_{x=1}^{m}\left[P(x)\log\left(\frac{1}{1-\lambda + \lambda\zeta_x}\right) + P(x)\zeta_x\log\left(\frac{1}{1-\lambda + \frac{\lambda}{\zeta_x}}\right)\right]\\
&= \sum_{x=1}^{m}P(x)\Xi(1-\lambda, \zeta_x)\log\left(\frac{1}{1-\lambda}\right)
\end{aligned}
$$

which implies that

$$\frac{D(P||R_\lambda)}{-\log(\lambda)} - \frac{D(P||R_{1-\lambda})}{-\log(1-\lambda)} = \sum_{x=1}^{m}P(x)\left[\Xi(\lambda,\zeta_x) - \Xi(1-\lambda,\zeta_x)\right]$$

Hence, in order to show (A6), it suffices to verify that

$$\Phi(\lambda,\zeta) := \Xi(\lambda,\zeta) - \Xi(1-\lambda,\zeta) > 0 \tag{A8}$$

for any $\lambda \in (0,\frac{1}{2})$ and $\zeta \in (1,\infty)$. Since $\log(\lambda)\log(1-\lambda)$ is always positive for $\lambda \in (0,\frac{1}{2})$, it suffices to show that

$$h(\zeta) := \Phi(\lambda,\zeta)\log(1-\lambda)\log(\lambda) > 0 \tag{A9}$$

for $\lambda \in (0,\frac{1}{2})$ and $\zeta \in (1,\infty)$. We have

$$h''(\zeta) = A(\lambda,\zeta)B(\lambda,\zeta) \tag{A10}$$

where

$$A(\lambda,\zeta) := \frac{1+\zeta}{(1-\lambda+\lambda\zeta)^2(\lambda+(1-\lambda)\zeta)^2\zeta}$$

and

$$B(\lambda,\zeta) := \lambda^2(1 + \lambda(\lambda-2)(\zeta-1)^2 + \zeta(\zeta-1))\log(\lambda) - (1-\lambda)^2(\lambda^2(\zeta-1)^2 + \zeta)\log(1-\lambda).$$

We have

$$\frac{\partial^2}{\partial\zeta^2}B(\lambda,\zeta) = 2\lambda^2(1-\lambda)^2\log\left(\frac{\lambda}{1-\lambda}\right) < 0$$

because $\lambda \in (0,\frac{1}{2})$ and hence $\lambda < 1-\lambda$. This implies that the map $\zeta \mapsto B(\lambda,\zeta)$ is concave for any $\lambda \in (0,\frac{1}{2})$ and $\zeta \in (1,\infty)$. Moreover, since $\zeta \mapsto B(\lambda,\zeta)$ is a quadratic polynomial with negative leading coefficient, it is clear that $\lim_{\zeta\to\infty}B(\lambda,\zeta) = -\infty$. Consider now $g(\lambda) := B(\lambda,1) = \lambda^2\log(\lambda) - (1-\lambda)^2\log(1-\lambda)$. We have $\lim_{\lambda\to 0}g(\lambda) = g(\frac{1}{2}) = 0$ and $g''(\lambda) = 2\log\left(\frac{\lambda}{1-\lambda}\right) < 0$ for $\lambda \in (0,\frac{1}{2})$. It implies that $\lambda \mapsto g(\lambda)$ is concave over $(0,\frac{1}{2})$ and hence $g(\lambda) > 0$ over $(0,\frac{1}{2})$ which implies that $B(\lambda,1) > 0$. This together with the fact that $\zeta \mapsto B(\lambda,\zeta)$ is concave and it approaches to $-\infty$ as $\zeta \to \infty$ imply that there exists a real number $c = c(\lambda) > 1$ such that $B(\lambda,\zeta) > 0$ for all $\zeta \in (1,c)$ and $B(\lambda,\zeta) < 0$ for all $\zeta \in (c,\infty)$. Since $A(\lambda,\zeta) > 0$, it follows from (A10) that $\zeta \mapsto h(\zeta)$ is convex over $(1, c)$ and concave over (c, ∞). Since $h(1) = h'(1) = 0$ and $\lim_{\zeta \to \infty} h(\zeta) = \infty$, we can conclude that $h(\zeta) > 0$ over $(1, \infty)$. That is, $\Phi(\lambda, \zeta) > 0$ and thus $\Xi(\lambda, \zeta) - \Xi(1 - \lambda, \zeta) > 0$, for $\lambda \in (0, \frac{1}{2})$ and $\zeta \in (1, \infty)$.

The inequality (A7) can be proved by (A6) and switching λ to $1 - \lambda$. $\quad\square$

Letting $P(\cdot) = P_{X|Y}(\cdot|1)$ and $Q(\cdot) = P_{X|Y}(\cdot|0)$ and $\lambda = \Pr(Y = 1) = p$, we have $R_p(x) = P_X(x) = pP(x) + (1 - p)Q(x)$ and $R_{1-p} = P_X(-x) = (1 - p)P(x) + pQ(x)$. Since $D(P_{X|Y}(\cdot|0)||P_X(\cdot)) = D(P||R_{1-p})$, we can conclude from Lemma 33 that

$$\frac{D(P_{X|Y}(\cdot|0)||P_X(\cdot))}{-\log(1 - p)} < \frac{D(P_{X|Y}(\cdot|1)||P_X(\cdot))}{-\log(p)}$$

over $p \in (0, \frac{1}{2})$ and

$$\frac{D(P_{X|Y}(\cdot|0)||P_X(\cdot))}{-\log(1 - p)} > \frac{D(P_{X|Y}(\cdot|1)||P_X(\cdot))}{-\log(p)}$$

over $p \in (\frac{1}{2}, 1)$, and hence equation (39) has only solution $p = \frac{1}{2}$.

Appendix C. Proof of Theorems 28 and 29

The proof of Theorem 29 does not depend on the proof of Theorem 28, so, there is no harm in proving the former theorem first. The following version of the data-processing inequality will be required.

Lemma 34. *Let X and Y be absolutely continuous random variables such that X, Y and (X, Y) have finite differential entropies. If V is an absolutely continuous random variable independent of X and Y, then*

$$I(X; Y + V) \le I(X; Y)$$

with equality if and only if X and Y are independent.

Proof. Since $X - \!\!\circ\!\!- Y - \!\!\circ\!\!- (Y + V)$, the data processing inequality implies that $I(X; Y + V) \le I(X; Y)$. It therefore suffices to show that this inequality is tight if and only X and Y are independent. It is known that data processing inequality is tight if and only if $X - \!\!\circ\!\!- (Y + V) - \!\!\circ\!\!- Y$. This is equivalent to saying that for any measurable set $A \subset \mathbb{R}$ and for P_{Y+V} almost all z, $\Pr(X \in A|Y + V = z, Y = y) = \Pr(X \in A|Y + V = z)$. On the other hand, due to the independence of V and (X, Y), we have $\Pr(X \in A|Y + V = z, Y = y) = \Pr(X \in A|Y = z - v)$. Hence, the equality holds if and only if $\Pr(X \in A|Y + V = z) = \Pr(X \in A|Y = z - v)$ which implies that X and Y must be independent. $\quad\square$

Lemma 35. *In the notation of Section 5.1, the function $\gamma \mapsto I(Y; Z_\gamma)$ is strictly-decreasing and continuous. Additionally, it satisfies*

$$I(Y; Z_\gamma) \le \frac{1}{2} \log \left(1 + \frac{\operatorname{var}(Y)}{\gamma^2}\right)$$

with equality if and only if Y is Gaussian. In particular, $I(Y; Z_\gamma) \to 0$ as $\gamma \to \infty$.

Proof. Recall that, by assumption b), $\operatorname{var}(Y)$ is finite. The finiteness of the entropy of Y follows from assumption, the corresponding statement for $Y + \gamma N$ follows from a routine application of the entropy power inequality [50, Theorem 17.7.3] and the fact that $\operatorname{var}(Y + \gamma N) = \operatorname{var}(Y) + \gamma^2 < \infty$, and for $(Y, Y + \gamma N)$ the same conclusion follows by the chain rule for differential entropy. The data processing inequality, as stated in Lemma 34, implies

$$I(Y; Z_{\gamma+\delta}) \le I(Y; Y + \gamma N) = I(Y; Z_\gamma)$$

Clearly Y and $Y + \gamma N$ are not independent, therefore the inequality is strict and thus $\gamma \mapsto I(Y, Z_\gamma)$ is strictly-decreasing.

Continuity will be studied for $\gamma = 0$ and $\gamma > 0$ separately. Recall that $h(\gamma N) = \frac{1}{2} \log(2\pi e \gamma^2)$. In particular, $\lim_{\gamma \to 0} h(\gamma N) = -\infty$. The entropy power inequality shows then that $\lim_{\gamma \to 0} I(Y; Y + \gamma N) = \infty$.

This coincides with the convention $I(Y; Z_0) = I(Y; Y) = \infty$. For $\gamma > 0$, let $(\gamma_n)_{n \geq 1}$ be a sequence of positive numbers such that $\gamma_n \to \gamma$. Observe that

$$I(Y; Z_{\gamma_n}) = h(Y + \gamma_n N) - h(\gamma_n N) = h(Y + \gamma_n N) - \frac{1}{2}\log(2\pi e \gamma_n^2)$$

Since $\lim_{n \to \infty} \frac{1}{2}\log(2\pi e \gamma_n^2) = \frac{1}{2}\log(2\pi e \gamma^2)$, we only have to show that $h(Y + \gamma_n N) \to h(Y + \gamma N)$ as $n \to \infty$ to establish the continuity at γ. This, in fact, follows from de Bruijn's identity (cf., [50, Theorem 17.7.2]).

Since the channel from Y to Z_γ is an additive Gaussian noise channel, we have $I(Y; Z_\gamma) \leq \frac{1}{2}\log\left(1 + \frac{\text{var}(Y)}{\gamma^2}\right)$ with equality if and only if Y is Gaussian. The claimed limit as $\gamma \to 0$ is clear. $\square$

Lemma 36. *The function $\gamma \mapsto I(X; Z_\gamma)$ is strictly-decreasing and continuous. Moreover, $I(X; Z_\gamma) \to 0$ when $\gamma \to \infty$.*

Proof. The proof of the strictly-decreasing behavior of $\gamma \mapsto I(X; Z_\gamma)$ is proved as in the previous lemma.

To prove continuity, let $\gamma \geq 0$ be fixed. Let $(\gamma_n)_{n \geq 1}$ be any sequence of positive numbers converging to γ. First suppose that $\gamma > 0$. Observe that

$$I(X; Z_{\gamma_n}) = h(Y + \gamma_n N) - h(Y + \gamma_n N | X)$$

for all $n \geq 1$. As shown in Lemma 35, $h(Y + \gamma_n N) \to h(Y + \gamma N)$ as $n \to \infty$. Therefore, it is enough to show that $h(Y + \gamma_n N | X) \to h(Y + \gamma N | X)$ as $n \to \infty$. Note that by de Bruijn's identity, we have $h(Y + \gamma_n N | X = x) \to h(Y + \gamma N | X = x)$ as $n \to \infty$ for all $x \in \mathbb{R}$. Note also that since

$$h(Z_{\gamma_n} | X = x) \leq \frac{1}{2}\log\left(2\pi e \text{var}(Z_{\gamma_n} | x)\right)$$

we can write

$$h(Z_{\gamma_n} | X) \leq \mathbb{E}\left[\frac{1}{2}\log(2\pi e \text{var}(Z_{\gamma_n} | X))\right] \leq \frac{1}{2}\log\left(2\pi e \mathbb{E}[\text{var}(Z_{\gamma_n} | X)]\right)$$

and hence we can apply dominated convergence theorem to show that $h(Y + \gamma_n N | X) \to h(Y + \gamma N | X)$ as $n \to \infty$.

To prove the continuity at $\gamma = 0$, we first note that Linder and Zamir [51, Page 2028] showed that $h(Y + \gamma_n N | X = x) \to h(Y | X = x)$ as $n \to \infty$, then, as before, by dominated convergence theorem we can show that $h(Y + \gamma_n N | X) \to h(Y | X)$. Similarly [51] implies that $h(Y + \gamma_n N) \to h(Y)$. This concludes the proof of the continuity of $\gamma \mapsto I(X; Z_\gamma)$.

Furthermore, by the data processing inequality and previous lemma,

$$0 \leq I(X; Z_\gamma) \leq I(Y; Z_\gamma) \leq \frac{1}{2}\log\left(1 + \frac{\text{var}(Y)}{\gamma^2}\right)$$

and hence we conclude that $\lim_{\gamma \to \infty} I(X; Z_\gamma) = 0$. $\square$

Proof of Theorem 29. The nonnegativity of $g_\varepsilon(X; Y)$ follows directly from definition.

By Lemma 36, for every $0 < \varepsilon \leq I(X; Y)$ there exists a unique $\gamma_\varepsilon \in [0, \infty)$ such that $I(X; Z_{\gamma_\varepsilon}) = \varepsilon$, so $g_\varepsilon(X; Y) = I(Y; Z_{\gamma_\varepsilon})$. Moreover, $\varepsilon \mapsto \gamma_\varepsilon$ is strictly decreasing. Since $\gamma \mapsto I(Y; Z_\gamma)$ is strictly-decreasing, we conclude that $\varepsilon \mapsto g_\varepsilon(X; Y)$ is strictly increasing.

The fact that $\varepsilon \mapsto \gamma_\varepsilon$ is strictly decreasing, also implies that $\gamma_\varepsilon \to \infty$ as $\varepsilon \to 0$. In particular,

$$\lim_{\varepsilon \to 0} g_\varepsilon(X; Y) = \lim_{\varepsilon \to 0} I(Y; Z_{\gamma_\varepsilon}) = \lim_{\gamma_\varepsilon \to \infty} I(Y; Z_{\gamma_\varepsilon}) = \lim_{\gamma \to \infty} I(Y; Z_\gamma) = 0$$

By the data processing inequality we have that $I(X; Z_\gamma) \leq I(X; Y)$ for all $\gamma \geq 0$, i.e., any filter satisfies the privacy constraint for $\varepsilon = I(X; Y)$. Thus, $g_{I(X; Y)}(X; Y) \geq I(Y; Y) = \infty$. $\square$

In order to prove Theorem 28, we first recall the following theorem by Rényi [52].

Theorem 37 ([52]). *If U is an absolutely continuous random variable with density $f_U(x)$ and if $H(\lfloor U \rfloor) < \infty$, then*

$$\lim_{n \to \infty} H(n^{-1}\lfloor nU \rfloor) - \log(n) = -\int_{\mathbb{R}} f_U(x) \log f_U(x) dx$$

provided that the integral on the right hand side exists.

We will need the following consequence of the previous theorem.

Lemma 38. *If U is an absolutely continuous random variable with density $f_U(x)$ and if $H(\lfloor U \rfloor) < \infty$, then $H(\mathcal{Q}_M(U)) - M \geq H(\mathcal{Q}_{M+1}(U)) - (M+1)$ for all $M \geq 1$ and*

$$\lim_{n \to \infty} H(\mathcal{Q}_M(U)) - M = -\int_{\mathbb{R}} f_U(x) \log f_U(x) dx$$

provided that the integral on the right hand side exists.

The previous lemma follows from the fact that $\mathcal{Q}_{M+1}(U)$ is constructed by refining the quantization partition for $\mathcal{Q}_M(U)$.

Lemma 39. *For any $\gamma \geq 0$,*

$$\lim_{M \to \infty} I(X; Z_\gamma^M) = I(X; Z_\gamma) \qquad \text{and} \qquad \lim_{M \to \infty} I(Y; Z_\gamma^M) = I(Y; Z_\gamma)$$

Proof. Observe that

$$
\begin{aligned}
I(X; Z_\gamma^M) &= I(X; \mathcal{Q}_M(Y + \gamma N)) \\
&= H(\mathcal{Q}_M(Y + \gamma N)) - H(\mathcal{Q}_M(Y + \gamma N)|X) \\
&= [H(\mathcal{Q}_M(Y + \gamma N)) - M] - \int_{\mathbb{R}} f_X(x)[H(\mathcal{Q}_M(Y + \gamma N)|X = x) - M]dx
\end{aligned}
$$

By the previous lemma, the integrand is decreasing in M, and thus we can take the limit with respect to M inside the integral. Thus,

$$\lim_{M \to \infty} I(X; Z_\gamma^M) = h(Y + \gamma N) - h(Y + \gamma N|X) = I(X; Z_\gamma)$$

The proof for $I(Y; Z_\gamma^M)$ is analogous. $\square$

Lemma 40. *Fix $M \in \mathbb{N}$. Assume that $f_Y(y) \leq C|y|^{-p}$ for some positive constant C and $p > 1$. For integer k and $\gamma \geq 0$, let*

$$p_{k,\gamma} := \Pr\left(\mathcal{Q}_M(Y + \gamma N) = \frac{k}{2^M}\right)$$

Then

$$p_{k,\gamma} \leq \frac{C2^{(p-1)M+p}}{k^p} + 1_{\{\gamma > 0\}} \frac{\gamma 2^{M+1}}{k\sqrt{2\pi}} e^{-k^2/2^{2M+3}\gamma^2}$$

Proof. The case $\gamma = 0$ is trivial, so we assume that $\gamma > 0$. For notational simplicity, let $r_a = \frac{a}{2^M}$ for all $a \in \mathbb{Z}$. Assume that $k \geq 0$. Observe that

$$
\begin{aligned}
p_{k,\gamma} &= \int_{-\infty}^{\infty} \int_{-\infty}^{\infty} f_{\gamma N}(n) f_Y(y) 1_{[r_k, r_{k+1})}(y + n) dy dn \\
&= \int_{-\infty}^{\infty} \frac{e^{-n^2/2\gamma^2}}{\sqrt{2\pi\gamma^2}} \Pr\left(Y \in [r_k, r_{k+1}) - n\right) dn
\end{aligned}
$$

We will estimate the above integral by breaking it up into two pieces.

First, we consider

$$\int_{-\infty}^{\frac{r_k}{2}} \frac{e^{-n^2/2\gamma^2}}{\sqrt{2\pi\gamma^2}} \Pr\left(Y \in [r_k, r_{k+1}) - n\right) dn$$

When $n \leq \frac{r_k}{2}$, then $r_k - n \geq r_k/2$. By the assumption on the density of Y,

$$\Pr\left(Y \in [r_k, r_{k+1}) - n\right) \leq \frac{C}{2^M}\left(\frac{r_k}{2}\right)^{-p}$$

(The previous estimate is the only contribution when $\gamma = 0$.) Therefore,

$$\int_{-\infty}^{\frac{r_k}{2}} \frac{e^{-n^2/2\gamma^2}}{\sqrt{2\pi\gamma^2}} \Pr\left(Y \in [r_k, r_{k+1}) - n\right) dn \leq \frac{C}{2^M}\left(\frac{r_k}{2}\right)^{-p} \int_{-\infty}^{\frac{r_k}{2}} \frac{e^{-n^2/2\gamma^2}}{\sqrt{2\pi\gamma^2}} dn$$

$$\leq \frac{C 2^{(p-1)M+p}}{k^p}$$

Using the trivial bound $\Pr\left(Y \in [r_k, r_{k+1}) - n\right) \leq 1$ and well known estimates for the error function, we obtain that

$$\int_{\frac{r_k}{2}}^{\infty} \frac{e^{-n^2/2\gamma^2}}{\sqrt{2\pi\gamma^2}} \Pr\left(Y \in [r_k, r_{k+1}) - n\right) dn < \frac{1}{\sqrt{2\pi}} \frac{2\gamma}{r_k} e^{-r_k^2/8\gamma^2}$$

$$= \frac{\gamma 2^{M+1}}{k\sqrt{2\pi}} e^{-k^2/2^{2M+3}\gamma^2}$$

Therefore,

$$p_{k,\gamma} \leq \frac{C 2^{(p-1)M+p}}{k^p} + \frac{\gamma 2^{M+1}}{k\sqrt{2\pi}} e^{-k^2/2^{2M+3}\gamma^2}$$

The proof for $k < 0$ is completely analogous. $\square$

Lemma 41. *Fix $M \in \mathbb{N}$. Assume that $f_Y(y) \leq C|y|^{-p}$ for some positive constant C and $p > 1$. The mapping $\gamma \mapsto H(\mathcal{Q}_M(Y + \gamma N))$ is continuous.*

Proof. Let $(\gamma_n)_{n \geq 1}$ be a sequence of non-negative real numbers converging to γ_0. First, we will prove continuity at $\gamma_0 > 0$. Without loss of generality, assume that $\gamma_n > 0$ for all $n \in \mathbb{N}$. Define $\gamma_* = \inf\{\gamma_n | n \geq 1\}$ and $\gamma^* = \sup\{\gamma_n | n \geq 1\}$. Clearly $0 < \gamma_* \leq \gamma^* < \infty$. Recall that

$$p_{k,\gamma} = \int_{\mathbb{R}} \frac{e^{-z^2/2\gamma^2}}{\sqrt{2\pi\gamma^2}} \Pr\left(Y \in \left[\frac{k}{2^M}, \frac{k+1}{2^M}\right) - z\right) dz$$

Since, for all $n \in \mathbb{N}$ and $z \in \mathbb{R}$,

$$\frac{e^{-z^2/2\gamma_n^2}}{\sqrt{2\pi\gamma_n^2}} \Pr\left(Y \in \left[\frac{k}{2^M}, \frac{k+1}{2^M}\right) - z\right) \leq \frac{e^{-z^2/2(\gamma^*)^2}}{\sqrt{2\pi\gamma_*^2}}$$

the dominated convergence theorem implies that

$$\lim_{n \to \infty} p_{k,\gamma_n} = p_{k,\gamma_0} \tag{A11}$$

The previous lemma implies that for all $n \geq 0$ and $|k| > 0$,

$$p_{k,\gamma_n} \leq \frac{C 2^{(p-1)M+p}}{k^p} + \frac{\gamma_n 2^{M+1}}{k\sqrt{2\pi}} e^{-k^2/2^{2M+3}\gamma_n^2}$$

Thus, for k large enough, $p_{k,\gamma_n} \leq \dfrac{A}{k^p}$ for a suitable positive constant A that does not depend on n. Since the function $x \mapsto -x\log(x)$ is increasing in $[0, 1/2]$, there exists $K' > 0$ such that for $|k| > K'$

$$-p_{k,\gamma_n} \log(p_{k,\gamma_n}) \leq \frac{A}{k^p} \log(A^{-1}k^p)$$

Since $\displaystyle\sum_{|k|>K'} \frac{A}{k^p} \log(A^{-1}k^p) < \infty$, for any $\epsilon > 0$ there exists K_ϵ such that

$$\sum_{|k|>K_\epsilon} \frac{A}{k^p} \log(A^{-1}k^p) < \epsilon$$

In particular, for all $n \geq 0$,

$$H(\mathcal{Q}(Y + \gamma_n N)) - \sum_{|k| \leq K_\epsilon} -p_{k,\gamma_n} \log(p_{k,\gamma_n}) = \sum_{|k| > K_\epsilon} -p_{k,\gamma_n} \log(p_{k,\gamma_n}) < \epsilon$$

Therefore, for all $n \geq 1$,

$$|H(\mathcal{Q}(Y + \gamma_n N)) - H(\mathcal{Q}(Y + \gamma_0 N))|$$

$$\leq \sum_{|k|>K_\epsilon} -p_{k,\gamma_n} \log(p_{k,\gamma_n}) + \left| \sum_{|k| \leq K_\epsilon} p_{k,\gamma_0} \log(p_{k,\gamma_0}) - p_{k,\gamma_n} \log(p_{k,\gamma_n}) \right| + \sum_{|k|>K_\epsilon} -p_{k,\gamma_0} \log(p_{k,\gamma_0})$$

$$\leq \epsilon + \left| \sum_{|k| \leq K_\epsilon} p_{k,\gamma_0} \log(p_{k,\gamma_0}) - p_{k,\gamma_n} \log(p_{k,\gamma_n}) \right| + \epsilon$$

By continuity of the function $x \mapsto -x\log(x)$ on $[0, 1]$ and equation (A11), we conclude that

$$\limsup_{n \to \infty} |H(\mathcal{Q}(Y + \gamma_n N)) - H(\mathcal{Q}(Y + \gamma_0 N))| \leq 3\epsilon$$

Since ϵ is arbitrary,

$$\lim_{n \to \infty} H(\mathcal{Q}(Y + \gamma_n N)) = H(\mathcal{Q}(Y + \gamma_0 N))$$

as we wanted to prove.

To prove continuity at $\gamma_0 = 0$, observe that equation (A11) holds in this case as well. The rest is analogous to the case $\gamma_0 > 0$. $\square$

Lemma 42. *The functions $\gamma \mapsto I(X; Z_\gamma^M)$ and $\gamma \mapsto I(Y; Z_\gamma^M)$ are continuous for each $M \in \mathbb{N}$.*

Proof. Since $H(\mathcal{Q}_M(Y + \gamma N)|Y = y)$ and $H(\mathcal{Q}_M(Y + \gamma N)|X = x)$ for $x, y \in \mathbb{R}$ are bounded by M, and $f_{Y|X}(y|x)$ satisfies assumption (b), the conclusion follows from the dominated convergence theorem. $\square$

Proof of Theorem 28. For every $M \in \mathbb{N}$, let $\Gamma_\epsilon^M := \{\gamma \geq 0 | I(X; Z_\gamma^M) \leq \epsilon\}$. The Markov chain $X \to Y \to Z_\gamma \to Z_\gamma^{M+1} \to Z_\gamma^M$ and the data processing inequality imply that

$$I(X; Z_\gamma) \geq I(X; Z_\gamma^{M+1}) \geq I(X; Z_\gamma^M)$$

and, in particular,

$$\epsilon = I(X; Z_{\gamma_\epsilon}) \geq I(X; Z_{\gamma_\epsilon}^{M+1}) \geq I(X; Z_{\gamma_\epsilon}^M)$$

where γ_ϵ is as defined in the proof of Theorem 29. This implies then that

$$\gamma_\epsilon \in \Gamma_\epsilon^{M+1} \subset \Gamma_\epsilon^M \tag{A12}$$

and thus

$$I(Y; Z_{\gamma_\epsilon}^M) \le g_{\epsilon,M}(X; Y)$$

Taking limits in both sides, Lemma 39 implies

$$g_\epsilon(X; Y) = I(Y; Z_{\gamma_\epsilon}) \le \liminf_{M \to \infty} g_{\epsilon,M}(X; Y) \tag{A13}$$

Observe that

$$
\begin{aligned}
g_{\epsilon,M}(X; Y) &= \sup_{\gamma \in \Gamma_\epsilon^M} I(Y; Z_\gamma^M) \\
&\le \sup_{\gamma \in \Gamma_\epsilon^M} I(Y; Z_\gamma) \\
&= I(Y; Z_{\gamma_{\epsilon,min}^M}) \tag{A14}
\end{aligned}
$$

where inequality follows from Markovity and $\gamma_{\epsilon,min}^M := \inf_{\Gamma_\epsilon^M} \gamma$. By equation (A12), $\gamma_\epsilon \in \Gamma_\epsilon^{M+1} \subset \Gamma_\epsilon^M$ and in particular $\gamma_{\epsilon,min}^M \le \gamma_{\epsilon,min}^{M+1} \le \gamma_\epsilon$. Thus, $\{\gamma_{\epsilon,min}^M\}$ is an increasing sequence in M and bounded from above and, hence, has a limit. Let $\gamma_{\epsilon,min} = \lim_{M \to \infty} \gamma_{\epsilon,min}^M$. Clearly

$$\gamma_{\epsilon,min} \le \gamma_\epsilon \tag{A15}$$

By the previous lemma we know that $I(X; Z_\gamma^M)$ is continuous, so Γ_ϵ^M is closed for all $M \in \mathbb{N}$. Thus, we have that $\gamma_{\epsilon,min}^M = \min_{\Gamma_\epsilon^M} \gamma$ and in particular $\gamma_{\epsilon,min}^M \in \Gamma_\epsilon^M$. By the inclusion $\Gamma_\epsilon^{M+1} \subset \Gamma_\epsilon^M$, we have then that $\gamma_{\epsilon,min}^{M+n} \in \Gamma_\epsilon^M$ for all $n \in \mathbb{N}$. By closedness of Γ_ϵ^M we have then that $\gamma_{\epsilon,min} \in \Gamma_\epsilon^M$ for all $M \in \mathbb{N}$. In particular,

$$I(X; Z_{\gamma_{\epsilon,min}}^M) \le \epsilon$$

for all $M \in \mathbb{N}$. By Lemma 39,

$$I(X; Z_{\gamma_{\epsilon,min}}) \le \epsilon = I(X; Z_{\gamma_\epsilon})$$

and by the monotonicity of $\gamma \mapsto I(X; Z_\gamma)$, we obtain that $\gamma_\epsilon \le \gamma_{\epsilon,min}$. Combining the previous inequality with (A15) we conclude that $\gamma_{\epsilon,min} = \gamma_\epsilon$. Taking limits in the inequality (A14)

$$\limsup_{M \to \infty} g_{\epsilon,M}(X; Y) \le \limsup_{M \to \infty} I(Y; Z_{\gamma_{\epsilon,min}^M}) = I(Y; Z_{\gamma_{\epsilon,min}})$$

Plugging $\gamma_{\epsilon,min} = \gamma_\epsilon$ in above we conclude that

$$\limsup_{M \to \infty} g_{\epsilon,M}(X; Y) \le I(Y; Z_{\gamma_\epsilon}) = g_\epsilon(X; Y)$$

and therefore $\lim_{M \to \infty} g_{\epsilon,M}(X; Y) = g_\epsilon(X; Y)$. $\square$

References

1. Asoodeh, S.; Alajaji, F.; Linder, T. Notes on information-theoretic privacy. In Proceedings of the 52nd Annual Allerton Conference on Communication, Control, and Computing, Monticello, IL, USA, 30 September–3 October 2014; pp. 1272–1278.

2. Asoodeh, S.; Alajaji, F.; Linder, T. On maximal correlation, mutual information and data privacy. In Proceedings of the IEEE 14th Canadian Workshop on Information Theory (CWIT), St. John's, NL, Canada, 6–9 July 2015; pp. 27–31.

3. Warner, S.L. Randomized Response: A Survey Technique for Eliminating Evasive Answer Bias. *J. Am. Stat. Assoc.* **1965**, *60*, 63–69.

4. Blum, A.; Ligett, K.; Roth, A. A learning theory approach to non-interactive database privacy. In Proceedings of the Fortieth Annual ACM Symposium on the Theory of Computing, Victoria, BC, Canada, 17–20 May 2008; pp. 1123–1127.

5. Dinur, I.; Nissim, K. Revealing information while preserving privacy. In Proceedings of the Twenty-Second Symposium on Principles of Database Systems, San Diego, CA, USA, 9–11 June 2003; pp. 202–210.
6. Rubinstein, P.B.; Bartlett, L.; Huang, J.; Taft, N. Learning in a large function space: Privacy-preserving mechanisms for SVM learning. *J. Priv. Confid.* **2012**, *4*, 65–100.
7. Duchi, J.C.; Jordan, M.I.; Wainwright, M.J. Privacy aware learning. **2014**, arXiv: 1210.2085.
8. Dwork, C.; McSherry, F.; Nissim, K.; Smith, A. Calibrating noise to sensitivity in private data analysis. In Proceedings of the Third Conference on Theory of Cryptography (TCC'06), New York, NY, USA, 5–7 March 2006; pp. 265–284.
9. Dwork, C. Differential privacy: A survey of results. In *Theory and Applications of Models of Computation, Proceedings of the 5th International Conference, TAMC 2008, Xi'an, China, 25–29 April 2008*; Agrawal, M., Du, D., Duan, Z., Li, A., Eds.; Springer: Berlin/Heidelberg, Germany, 2008; Lecture Notes in Computer Science, Volume 4978; pp. 1–19.
10. Dwork, C.; Lei, J. Differential privacy and robust statistics. In Proceedings of the 41st Annual ACM Symposium on the Theory of Computing, Bethesda, MD, USA, 31 May–2 June 2009; pp. 437–442.
11. Kairouz, P.; Oh, S.; Viswanath, P. Extremal mechanisms for local differential privacy. **2014**, arXiv: 1407.1338v2.
12. Calmon, F.P.; Varia, M.; Médard, M.; Christiansen, M.M.; Duffy, K.R.; Tessaro, S. Bounds on inference. In Proceedings of the 51st Annual Allerton Conference on Communication, Control, and Computing, Monticello, IL, USA, 2–4 October 2013; pp. 567–574.
13. Yamamoto, H. A source coding problem for sources with additional outputs to keep secret from the receiver or wiretappers. *IEEE Trans. Inf. Theory* **1983**, *29*, 918–923.
14. Sankar, L.; Rajagopalan, S.; Poor, H. Utility-privacy tradeoffs in databases: An information-theoretic approach. *IEEE Trans. Inf. Forensics Secur.* **2013**, *8*, 838–852.
15. Tandon, R.; Sankar, L.; Poor, H. Discriminatory lossy source coding: side information privacy. *IEEE Trans. Inf. Theory* **2013**, *59*, 5665–5677.
16. Calmon, F.; Fawaz, N. Privacy against statistical inference. In Proceedings of the 50th Annual Allerton Conference on Communication, Control, and Computing, Monticello, IL, USA, 1–5 October 2012; pp. 1401–1408.
17. Rebollo-Monedero, D.; Forne, J.; Domingo-Ferrer, J. From t-closeness-like privacy to postrandomization via information theory. *IEEE Trans. Knowl. Data Eng.* **2010**, *22*, 1623–1636.
18. Makhdoumi, A.; Salamatian, S.; Fawaz, N.; Médard, M. From the information bottleneck to the privacy funnel. In Proceedings of the IEEE Information Theory Workshop (ITW), Hobart, Australia, 2–5 November 2014; pp. 501–505.
19. Tishby, N.; Pereira, F.C.; Bialek, W. The information bottleneck method. **2000**, arXiv: physics/0004057.
20. Calmon, F.P.; Makhdoumi, A.; Médard, M. Fundamental limits of perfect privacy. In Proceedings of the IEEE Int. Symp. Inf. Theory (ISIT), Hong Kong, China, 14–19 June 2015; pp. 1796–1800.
21. Wyner, A.D. The Wire-Tap Channel. *Bell Syst. Tech. J.* **1975**, *54*, 1355–1387.
22. Makhdoumi, A.; Fawaz, N. Privacy-utility tradeoff under statistical uncertainty. In Proceedings of the 51st Annual Allerton Conference on Communication, Control, and Computing, Monticello, IL, USA, 2–4 October 2013; pp. 1627–1634.
23. Li, C.T.; El Gamal, A. Maximal correlation secrecy. **2015**, arXiv: 1412.5374.
24. Ahlswede, R.; Gács, P. Spreading of sets in product spaces and hypercontraction of the Markov operator. *Ann. Probab.* **1976**, *4*, 925–939.
25. Anantharam, V.; Gohari, A.; Kamath, S.; Nair, C. On maximal correlation, hypercontractivity, and the data processing inequality studied by Erkip and Cover. **2014**, arXiv:1304.6133v1.
26. Courtade, T. Information masking and amplification: The source coding setting. In Proceedings of the IEEE Int. Symp. Inf. Theory (ISIT), Boston, MA, USA, 1–6 July 2012; pp. 189–193.
27. Goldwasser, S.; Micali, S. Probabilistic encryption. *J. Comput. Syst. Sci.* **1984**, *28*, 270–299.
28. Rockafellar, R.T. *Convex Analysis*; Princeton Univerity Press: Princeton, NJ, USA, 1997.
29. Csiszár, I.; Körner, J. *Information Theory: Coding Theorems for Discrete Memoryless Systems*; Cambridge University Press: Cambridge, UK, 2011.
30. Shulman, N.; Feder, M. The uniform distribution as a universal prior. *IEEE Trans. Inf. Theory* **2004**, *50*, 1356–1362.

31. Rudin, W. *Real and Complex Analysis*, 3rd ed.; McGraw Hill: New York, NY, USA, 1987.

32. Gebelein, H. Das statistische Problem der Korrelation als Variations- und Eigenwert-problem und sein Zusammenhang mit der Ausgleichungsrechnung. *Zeitschrift fur Angewandte Mathematik und Mechanik* **1941**, *21*, 364–379. (In German)

33. Hirschfeld, H.O. A connection between correlation and contingency. *Camb. Philos. Soc.* **1935**, *31*, 520–524.

34. Rényi, A. On measures of dependence. *Acta Mathematica Academiae Scientiarum Hungarica* **1959**, *10*, 441–451.

35. Linfoot, E.H. An informational measure of correlation. *Inf. Control* **1957**, *1*, 85–89.

36. Csiszár, I. Information-type measures of difference of probability distributions and indirect observation. *Studia Scientiarum Mathematicarum Hungarica* **1967**, *2*, 229–318.

37. Zhao, L. Common randomness, efficiency, and actions. Ph.D. Thesis, Stanford University, Stanford, CA, USA, 2011.

38. Berger, T.; Yeung, R. Multiterminal source encoding with encoder breakdown. *IEEE Trans. Inf. Theory* **1989**, *35*, 237–244.

39. Kim, Y.H.; Sutivong, A.; Cover, T. State mplification. *IEEE Trans. Inf. Theory* **2008**, *54*, 1850–1859.

40. Merhav, N.; Shamai, S. Information rates subject to state masking. *IEEE Trans. Inf. Theory* **2007**, *53*, 2254–2261.

41. Ahlswede, R.; Körner, J. Source coding with side information and a converse for degraded broadcast channels. *IEEE Trans. Inf. Theory* **1975**, *21*, 629–637.

42. Kim, Y.H.; El Gamal, A. *Network Information Theory*; Cambridge University Press: Cambridge, UK, 2012.

43. Asoodeh, S.; Alajaji, F.; Linder, T. Lossless secure source coding, Yamamoto's setting. In Proceedings of the 53rd Annual Allerton Conference on Communication, Control, and Computing, Monticello, IL, USA, 30 September–2 October 2015.

44. Raginsky, M. Logarithmic Sobolev inequalities and strong data processing theorems for discrete channels. In Proceedings of the IEEE Int. Sym. Inf. Theory (ISIT), Istanbul, Turkey, 7–12 July 2013; pp. 419–423.

45. Geng, Y.; Nair, C.; Shamai, S.; Wang, Z.V. On broadcast channels with binary inputs and symmetric outputs. *IEEE Trans. Inf. Theory* **2013**, *59*, 6980–6989.

46. Sutskover, I.; Shamai, S.; Ziv, J. Extremes of information combining. *IEEE Trans. Inf. Theory* **2005**, *51*, 1313–1325.

47. Alajaji, F.; Chen, P.N. *Information Theory for Single User Systems, Part I*; Course Notes, Queen's University. Available online: http://www.mast.queensu.ca/math474/it-lecture-notes.pdf (accessed on 4 March 2015).

48. Chayat, N.; Shamai, S. Extension of an entropy property for binary input memoryless symmetric channels. *IEEE Trans.Inf. Theory* **1989**, *35*, 1077–1079.

49. Oohama, Y. Gaussian multiterminal source coding. *IEEE Trans. Inf. Theory* **1997**, *43*, 2254–2261.

50. Cover, T.M.; Thomas, J.A. *Elements of Information Theory*; Wiley: New York, NY, USA, 2006.

51. Linder, T.; Zamir, R. On the asymptotic tightness of the Shannon lower bound. *IEEE Trans. Inf. Theory* **2008**, *40*, 2026–2031.

52. Rényi, A. On the dimension and entropy of probability distributions. *Acta Mathematica Academiae Scientiarum Hungarica* **1959**, *10*, 193–215.

7

Throughput Capacity of Selfish Wireless *Ad Hoc* Networks with General Node Density

Qiuming Liu [1], Yong Luo [1], Yun Ling [1] and Jun Zheng [2,*]

[1]   Jiangxi University of Science and Technology, 1180 Shuanggang Road, Nanchang 330013, China;
      liuqiuming@jxust.edu.cn (Q.L.); luoyong@jxust.edu.cn (Y.Lu.); lingyun.jxust@gmail.com (Y.Li.)
[2]   School of Science, Zhejiang A&F University, 88 Huancheng Road, Lin'An City, Hangzhou 311300, China
*   Correspondence: junzheng@hust.edu.cn

Academic Editor: Willy Susilo

Abstract: In this paper, we study the throughput capacity of wireless networks considering the selfish feature of interaction between nodes. In our proposed network model, each node has a probability of cooperating to relay transmission. According to the extent of selfishness, we, by the application of percolation theory, construct a series of highways crossing the network. The transmission strategy is then divided into three consecutive phases. Comparing the rate in each phase, we find the bottleneck of rate is always in the highway phase. Finally, the result reveals that the node's selfishness degrades the throughput with a factor of square root of the cooperative probability, whereas the node density has trivial impact on the throughput.

Keywords: network capacity; selfish behavior; general node density; percolation theory

1. Introduction

Wireless *ad hoc* networks (WANETs) are an emerging networking technology, which are widely used in environmental monitoring, emergency communication, and military applications, *etc.* The unique feature of such networks is formed by the huge number of nodes. Each node communicates over a wireless channel without any centralized control. One of the problems in WANETs is the routing protocol. Much work has been done on this issue; for example, Zuhairi *et al.* [1] studied the routing protocol in Machine-to-Machine communication network, and the case of vehicular applications was investigated by Cho *et al.* [2]. The routing protocol in mobile WANETs was analyzed by Zaman *et al.* [3]. The other problem is the network capacity. Gupta and Kumar [4] gave an outstanding result on the scaling law of wireless network capacity. They considered n nodes randomly located in a unit network area, each node randomly selected a destination and derived a capacity upper bound of $O\left(\frac{1}{\sqrt{n}}\right)$ and a lower bound of $\Theta\left(\frac{1}{\sqrt{n\log n}}\right)$, respectively. (Given two functions $f(n)$ and $g(n)$: $f(n) = o(g(n))$ means $\lim_{n\to\infty} f(n)/g(n) = 0$; $f(n) = O(g(n))$ means $\lim_{n\to\infty} f(n)/g(n) = c < \infty$; if $g(n) = O(f(n))$, $f(n) = \Omega(g(n))$ *w.h.p.* ; if both $f(n) = \Omega(g(n))$ and $f(n) = O(g(n))$, $f(n) = \Theta(g(n))$; $f(n) = \widetilde{\Theta}(g(n))$ means $f(n) = \Theta(g(n))$ when logarithmic terms are ignored.) The results showed that the per-node rate decreases as the number of nodes increases. This pessimistic result is a milestone work of wireless network capacity proceeding. Motivated by [4], Franceschetti *et al.* [5] exploited percolation theory and variable transmission radius to construct a highway system in the network. Based on highways systems, a per-node rate of $\Omega\left(\frac{1}{\sqrt{n}}\right)$ was achieved. The result closed the capacity gap in Kumar's work [4]. Since mobility plays an important role in wireless networks, Grossglauser *et al.* [6] found that mobility can increase the throughput of networks. They demonstrated that a per-node rate of $\Theta(1)$ can be achieved while the transmission delay was up to $\Theta(n)$. Due to the results on network capacity, many researchers became devoted to solving the problem of capacity and delay; most of these works can be generalized into two categories: (1) Increase the number of simultaneous transmission; (2) Decrease the count of hops from source nodes to destination nodes. For the first case, some advanced technologies were employed, such as directional antennas (DA) [7,8], multi-packet reception (MPR) [9] and Multi-input Multi-output (MIMO) [10]. With regard to the second case, infrastructure or base station and nodes mobility were explored; for example, in [11,12], the authors added a base station into the networks. By constructing an optimized transmission scheme, the distance between source and destination can be decreased. Mobility can increase the throughput capacity to $\Theta(1)$, but at the cost of increasing the delay to $\Theta(n)$. Therefore, the work on the tradeoff between throughput and delay was elaborated in [13–16].

However, most of the previous works on network capacity of WANETs assumed that node was cooperative [17–19]. That is, whenever a node receives a request to relay traffic, it will forward the packets on no condition. This ignores the nodes' viewpoint. In addition, previous works either focused on dense or extended networks; that is, the node density is n or 1. They do not consider the impact of node density on the throughput. Therefore, the question remained: what is the throughput capacity of the network if the node exposed selfishness and the node density is general? In this work, we study the throughput of wireless *ad hoc* networks with selfish nodes under general node density. We denote these networks as SWANETs, which were widely researched in connectivity [20] and routing protocol [21]. Minho Jo [22] *et al.* proposed an easy and efficient cooperative of neighboring (COOPON) technique to detect the selfish cognitive radio attack. It is known that selfishness always comes with a price. The price may be tolerable in small-scale WANETs, but it may dominate the consumption of scarce network resources in large-scale WANETs. This situation makes the investigation of throughput with selfish characteristic in large scale WANETs an important open challenge.

In this paper, we consider n nodes randomly and independently distributed in an area with dimension of $\sqrt{A} \times \sqrt{A}$. The communication between source and destination nodes uses multi-hops transmission. we define $p(n)$ as the probability that a node will forward a packet. When $p(n) < 1$, in general, there is network performance degradation because we require all communications to operate on partial nodes, and some network resources (*i.e.*, the selfish nodes) cannot be utilized compared to WANETs. Therefore, it is natural to ask the following: What is the price of selfishness (performance degradation) we have to pay in SWANETs? We formally characterize the relation between the probability $p(n)$, node density ζ, and network performance. Then, we answer these questions with rigorous analysis based on reasonable assumptions on SWANETs.

The main contributions of this paper can be summarized as follows:

(1) Comparing to previous research, we firstly consider the model of selfish wireless *ad hoc* network, which is more realistic.
(2) We derive the asymptotic throughput capacity of the network combining selfish feature and general node density, which is different from the previous works of dense or extended networks.
(3) We observe that the selfishness degrades the achievable throughput with a factor $\sqrt{p(n)}$, where $p(n)$ is the probability of forwarding transmission. In addition, the node density impacts the throughput trivially.

The roadmap of the paper is as follows. In Section 2 we introduce the network model in detail. The achievable rate is derived in Section 3. In Section 4, we discuss the results and conclude the paper in Section 5.

2. System Assumption

In this paper, we construct a random SWANET with the general node density $\zeta \in [1, n]$. The general node density includes the case of random dense networks where $\zeta = n$ and random extended networks where $\zeta = 1$. The other features of the system model we considered are as follows:

(1) We assume n static nodes uniformly and independently placed over an area $\mathbb{A} = [0, \sqrt{A}] \times [0, \sqrt{A}]$, where $A = n/\zeta$.

(2) The node is classified by whether it will forward other transmission. As shown in Figure 1, if a node will forward other transmission, we define the node as an altruistic node (AN, empty points in Figure 1). Otherwise the node is a Selfish Node (SN, solid points in Figure 1). In this work, we assume each node may be selfish, and define the probability that a node i will forward other transmission as $p_i(n)$. For simplicity, we assume the probability that each node forwards other transmission is $p(n)$.

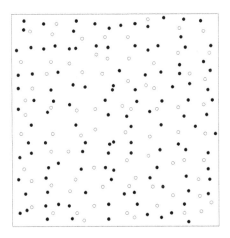

Figure 1. Network model of selfish wireless *ad hoc* networks (SWANETs). Solid points are selfish nodes, and empty points denote altruistic nodes.

(3) Each node randomly chooses a destination node and each node is the destination of exactly one node.

(4) The transmission model we adopted is General Physical Model [4], where the channel gain ignores shadowing and fading, and only depends on the distance between the transmitter and receiver. Let S denote the subset of nodes transmitting simultaneously. Based on the point-to-point coding and decoding [4], the transmission rate $R_{i,j}$ between node i to node j is:

$$R_{i,j} = \log\left(1 + \frac{P_i \cdot d_{ij}^{-\alpha}}{N_0 + \sum_{k \in S \setminus \{i\}} P_k \cdot d_{kj}^{-\alpha}}\right) \text{ bit/s} \tag{1}$$

where P_i is the transmission power of node i. We assume each employs identical power P to transmit. d_{ij} denotes the distance between an arbitrary pair of nodes i and j. N_0 is the ambient noise power at the receiver. α is the path loss exponent, and $\alpha > 2$. The notations of this paper are summarized in Table 1.

(5) We say that the throughput capacity of a network [4] is of the order $O(f(n))$ bits per second if there is a deterministic constant $c_1 < +\infty$ such that

$$\liminf_{n \to +\infty} \text{Pro}(T(n) = c_1 f(n) \text{ is feasible}) < 1$$

and is of order $\Theta(f(n))$ bits per second if there are deterministic constants $0 < c_2 < c_3 < +\infty$ such that

$$\liminf_{n \to +\infty} \text{Pro}(T(n) = c_2 f(n) \text{ is feasible}) = 1,$$

$$\liminf_{n \to +\infty} \text{Pro}(T(n) = c_3 f(n) \text{ is feasible}) < 1$$

Table 1. Notations.

Notation	Definition
n	Total number of nodes in the network.
ζ	Node density.
A	Network area; $A = n/\zeta$.
$p(n)$	Probability that a node will forward other transmission.
S	Set of simultaneous nodes.
$R_{i,j}$	Point to point rate.
P	Power of transmission.
d_{ij}	The distance between node i and j.
N_0	Power of noise.
α	Path loss exponent.
$T(n)$	The achievable throughput.

3. Achievable Rate

In order to derive the per-node rate of the networks, we leverage the routing strategy illustrated in [5] and show that there also exists a routing scheme in SWNETs.

Without loss of generality, the strategy of obtaining per-node achievable rate operates as follows: Firstly, using percolation theory, we construct a backbone network which is composed of many horizontal and vertical highways. Then, according to the density of AN, we partition the network area dynamically to ensure each square contains an AN *w.h.p.*, such that the transmission would not be terminated by the selfish nodes. Since we begin with percolation theory in the SWNETs model, we will take a brief look at it here.

Percolation theory [23,24] is a field of mathematics and statistical physics that provides models of phase transition phenomena. For example, assume that water is poured on top of a porous stone—will the water be able to make its way from hole to hole and reach the bottom? By modeling the stone as a square grid, each edge can be open and traversed by water with probability p, or closed with probability $1 - p$, and they are assumed to be independent. For a given p, what is the probability that an open path exists from the top to the bottom? That is, is there a path of connected points of infinite length through the network? In fact, there exists a critical p_c below which the probability is always 0 and above which the probability is always 1. In some cases p_c may be calculated explicitly; for example, in a two-dimensional square lattice $\mathbf{Z}^2$, when $p > 1/2$, water percolates through the stone with a probability of one. One can then ask at what rate the water percolates and how it depends on p. In other words, how rich in disjoint paths are the connected component of open edges? To maximize the information flow, we want to operate the network at $p > 1/2$, above the percolation threshold, so that we can guarantee the existence of many disjoint paths that traverse the network.

In this paper, we merely consider the case of $\frac{1}{n} \leq p(n) \leq 1$. When $p(n) < \frac{1}{n}$, following the Chernoff Bound, we know that there are few ANs in the network, and each node transmits the packets directly to the destination or via constant hops by increasing the power. In this case, the asymptotic throughput is similar to the broadcast capacity [25], which is $\Theta\left(\frac{1}{n}\right)$.

3.1. Construction of the Backbone Network

According to percolation theory, a square is said to be open if it contains at least one AN, and closed otherwise. To construct the backbone of the network, we divide the network area into squares of dimensions $l(n) \times l(n)$, where $l(n) = c_0 \sqrt{\frac{1}{\zeta p(n)}}$. By appropriately choosing the constant c_0, we can adjust the probability that a square contains at least one AN:

$$P(\text{a square contains at least one AN}) = 1 - e^{-c_0^2} \equiv p_o \qquad (2)$$

Note that squares are open (closed) with probability p_o, related to $p(n)$ and ζ and independently of each other. As Figure 2 shows, in each square we draw a horizontal edge (thick lines) across it, and in the vertical direction as well. An edge is said to be open if there exists at least one AN in the square and closed otherwise. On the basis of construction, we establish a bond percolation model [23]. Consequently, the probability that an edge is open is p_o. Since the number of nodes located in a given square follows Poisson random process with parameter $\frac{1}{\zeta p(n)}$, we can get Lemma 1:

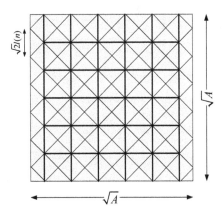

Figure 2. A new square system. We partition the network with side length $l(n)$, and the thick line represents that there is at least one altruistic node in the square.

Lemma 1. *Let N_i denote the number of node contained in a given square s_i. Let E_i be the event $\frac{1}{8p(n)} \leq N_i \leq \frac{2}{p(n)}, \forall i$. Then,*

$$p_a(n) \equiv P(E_i) > 1 - 16\,(2/e)^{1/4p(n)} \tag{3}$$

Proof. The lemma can be proven simply by applying the Chernoff bound and the Union bound. $\square$

According to the backbone construction, we use $m(n)$ to denote the number of horizontal (vertical) edges which compose the side length of the area $\mathbb{A}$. Then,

$$m(n) = \frac{\sqrt{A}}{\sqrt{2}l(n)} = \sqrt{c_1 n p(n)} \tag{4}$$

Notice that $m(n) \to \infty$ as $n \to \infty$, and c_1 is a constant.

Next we divide the area $\mathbb{A}$ into horizontal rectangular slabs with dimensions $\sqrt{A} \times \sqrt{2}l(n)\,(\kappa \log m(n) + \epsilon_n)$, where $\kappa > 0$, as shown in Figure 3. Let R_n^i denote the i-th slab, where $i \leq \frac{m(n)}{\kappa \log m(n) + \epsilon_n}$. The parameter ϵ_n is the smallest nonnegative number, as the number of rectangular slabs $\frac{m(n)}{\kappa \log m(n) + \epsilon_n}$ is an integer.

As proven in Theorem 1 of [5], many open paths from left to right exist inside each slab. Let C_N^i be the maximal number of disjoint left-to-right crossing paths in rectangle R_n^i and $N_n = \min_i C_n^i$. The following lemma shows that there exists a large number of crossing paths in each horizontal rectangular slab of $\mathbb{A}$.

Lemma 2. *For all $\kappa > 0$, there exists a δ satisfying $0 < \delta < \kappa$ such that*

$$\lim_{n \to \infty} P\left(N_n \leq \delta \log m(n)\right) = 0 \tag{5}$$

Proof. According to Theorem 5 in [5], we note that when $p > \frac{5}{6}$ for large n. Taking the limits as $n \to \infty$, the inequality (16) in [5] derives the condition $0 < \delta < \kappa$.

Similarly, by dividing $\mathbb{A}$ into rectangular slabs of sides $\sqrt{2}l(n)$ $(\kappa \log m(n) + \epsilon_n) \times \sqrt{A}$ in the vertical direction, we can show that there exists $\delta \log m(n)$ top-to-bottom crossing paths in each vertical slab. Therefore, by exploiting the union bound, we can get that there exists $\Omega(m(n))$ left-to-right and top-to-bottom crossing paths (*i.e.*, highways) in the area of $\mathbb{A}$ *w.h.p.* □

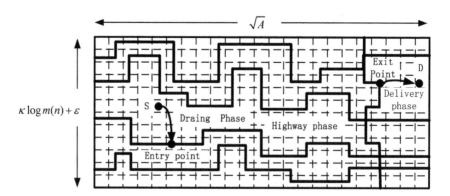

Figure 3. There are at least $\delta \log m(n)$ disjoint highways in each slab. And the three phase routing scheme is illustrated.

3.2. Routing Protocol

We now elaborate on the detailed operation in each phase of routing scheme. As shown in Figure 3, the routing scheme involves three phases: *Draining phase, Highway phase, and Delivery phase.*

(1) *Draining phase:* In the draining phase, source node s drops packets to an entry point on the nearest horizontal crossing highway.

(2) *Highway phase:* In the highway phase, packets are first moved along horizontal highway, and then along the vertical highway until they arrive at an exit point that is close to the destination node D.

(3) *Delivery phase:* In this phase, packets are delivered to the destination node D from the exit point located on the highway.

3.3. The Rate for Transporting a Packet

To achieve the rate of transmit a packet, we use the Time Division Multiplex (TDM) strategy. The idea of the TDM strategy is that when a node transmits along a path, other nodes which are far away can simultaneously transmit without causing excessive interference, as shown in Figure 4.

The following Theorem introduces the fact that the rate can be obtained *w.h.p.* on the path simultaneously. The theorem is stated in slightly more general terms considering nodes at distance d in the edge percolation grid, where d is not the Euclidean distance but the number of d squares away.

Theorem 3. *In each square, for any integer $d > 0$, the rate that source-destination pair can be obtained is*

$$R(d) = \begin{cases} \Omega\left(\left(\frac{d}{\sqrt{\zeta p(n)}}\right)^{-\alpha-2}\right) & \text{if } dl(n) = \Omega(1) \\ \Omega\left(d^{-2}\right) & \text{if } dl(n) = O(1) \end{cases} \tag{6}$$

Proof. As depicted in Figure 4, we partition the network into squares and divide the time frame into k^2 successive slots, where $k = 2(d + 1)$. Then, the disjoint set of squares of s_i can transmit simultaneously.

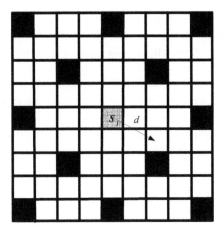

Figure 4. The time division multiplex (TDM) strategy and the case $d = 3$. Gray squares can transmit simultaneously. Notice that around each grey square there is a "silent" region of squares that are not allowed to transmit in the given time slot.

For a specific square s_i, a node in square s_i transmits toward a destination node located in a square at distance d away. At the same time slot, there are four closest squares located at Euclidean distance at least $l(n)(d + 1)$ from the receiver, the next eight closest squares are at least $l(n)(3d + 3)$ Euclidean distance, and so on. By extending the sum of the interference of the network area, we can calculate the upper bound of the interference at the receiver as

$$I(d,n) \leq \sum_{j=1}^{\infty} 4j \cdot P(l(n)(2j-1)(d+1))^{-\alpha} \leq P(l(n)(d+1))^{-\alpha} \times \sum_{j=1}^{\infty} 4j(2j-1)^{-\alpha} \qquad (7)$$

where P is the transmission power, and we notice that this sum is converged if the path loss exponent $\alpha > 2$. Thus, we can get that $I(d,n) = O\left((dl(n))^{-\alpha}\right)$.

Next we will give a lower bound of the signal received from the transmitter. According to the interference mode, we notice that the distance between transmitter and receiver is at most $\sqrt{2}l(n)(d+1)$. Hence, the lower bound of the signal $S(d)$ at the receiver is

$$S(d,n) \geq P\left(\sqrt{2}(d+1)l(n)\right)^{-\alpha} \qquad (8)$$

Next, By General Physical Model [4], combining the interference and the receive signal, we can achieve transmission rate at receiver located d squares away is

$$R(d) = \lim_{n\to\infty} \log\left(1 + \frac{S(d,n)}{N_0 + I(d,n)}\right) = \begin{cases} \Omega\left((dl(n))^{-\alpha}\right) & \text{if } dl(n) = \Omega(1) \\ \Omega(1) & \text{if } dl(n) = O(1) \end{cases} \qquad (9)$$

This means that there is a threshold on the rate, which is related to d and square length $l(n)$.

In addition, based on the TDM strategy we adopted, there are $k^2 = 4(d+1)^2$ time slots in our TDM strategy. Thus, the actual rate available needs to be divided by k^2. Correspondingly,

$$R(d) = \begin{cases} \Omega\left(l^{-\alpha}(n)d^{-\alpha-2}\right) & \text{if } dl(n) = \Omega(1) \\ \Omega\left(d^{-2}\right) & \text{if } dl(n) = O(1) \end{cases} \qquad (10)$$

□

Equation (10) acts as the groundwork to compute the rate in this work. Since node in this paper is distributed with general node density and nodes are possibly selfish, it makes it more complicated than previous works. In particular, we partition the square dynamically to ensure there exists an AN in each square $w.h.p$. The rate between transmitter and receiver is associated with the node density ζ and probability of altruist $p(n)$.

According to Theorem 3, we can derive the achievable rate in each phase. Comparing the achievable rate of each phase, we get the rate bottleneck.

(1) *Draining phase:* Since the network is divided into squares with side length of $l(n) = c_0\sqrt{\frac{1}{\zeta p(n)}}$, we partition the network area into slices with dimension $\sqrt{A} \times l(n)$. Similar to Lemma 2 in [5], we bound the number of nodes N_s in each slice uniformly, which bounds the number of nodes accessing a crossing highway. Note that there are a total of $\frac{\sqrt{A}}{\sqrt{2}l(n)}$ slices, each node in the i-th slice transmits directly to an entry point located on the i-th crossing highway, as shown in Figure 2.

Lemma 4. *Let N_s denote the number of nodes in each slice. Then,*

$$\lim_{n\to\infty} P\left(N_s \le 2\sqrt{2n/p(n)}, \ \forall s\right) = 1 \tag{11}$$

Proof. The proof follows from the Chernoff and Union bound. $\square$

The next lemma illustrates the achievable rate in the draining phase.

Lemma 5. *The transmitter inside each square can achieve a rate to an entry node on the highway of*

$$R^{Dr} = \begin{cases} \Omega\left(p(n)\left(\frac{\log^2 np(n)}{\sqrt{\zeta p(n)}}\right)^\alpha \right) & \text{if } l(n) = \Omega(\log np(n)) \\ \Omega\left(\frac{p(n)}{\log^2 np(n)}\right) & \text{if } l(n) = O(\log np(n)) \end{cases} \tag{12}$$

Proof. Similar to [5], the area $\mathbb{A}$ is divided into rectangular slabs of dimensions $\sqrt{A} \times \sqrt{2}l(n)(\kappa \log m(n) + \epsilon_n)$, where $m(n)$ is defined in (4) and κ is chosen such that there are at least $\lceil \delta \log m(n)\rceil$ crossing paths in each slab. The crossing paths are denoted as $1, \cdots, N_n$. In order to balance the load across the highways, we slice the each slab into $\delta \log m(n)$ smaller strips, each of dimensions $\sqrt{A} \times \sqrt{2}\omega l(n)$, where ω is a constant and chosen appropriately. Note that each crossing highway may not be fully contained in its corresponding strip, but it may deviate from it. Once the source nodes are mapped to crossing paths, we choose the entry points for each source as follows: The entry point is chosen from only these open squares containing one AN. The transmitter drains the information to the entry point directly, and each transmitter finds its highway within the same slab. Hence, the distance between transmitter and entry point is never larger than $\kappa l(n) \log m(n) + \sqrt{2}l(n)$. To compute the rate that node can transport to the entry point on the highway, let $d = \kappa l(n) \log m(n) + \sqrt{2}l(n)$ and apply the Theorem 3. We can obtain that a node can communicate to its entry point at rate

$$R^{Dr} = R\left(\kappa l(n) \log m(n) + \sqrt{2}l(n)\right) = R\left(\kappa l(n) \log\left(\sqrt{np(n)}\right) + \sqrt{2}l(n)\right)$$

$$= \begin{cases} \Omega\left(\left(\frac{\log^2 np(n)}{\sqrt{\zeta p(n)}}\right)^\alpha \right) & \text{if } l(n) = \Omega(\log np(n)) \\ \Omega\left(1/\log^2 np(n)\right) & \text{if } l(n) = O(\log np(n)) \end{cases} \tag{13}$$

$\square$

Next, we derive the achievable rate on the highway phase.

Lemma 6. *The information along the highways can achieve a per-node rate of R^H w.h.p., where R^H is*

$$R^H = \begin{cases} \Omega\left(\frac{1}{\sqrt{n}}p^{\frac{1}{2}}(n)(\zeta p(n))^{\alpha}\right) & \text{if } l(n) = \Omega(1) \\ \Omega\left(\frac{1}{\sqrt{n}}p^{\frac{1}{2}}(n)\right) & \text{if } l(n) = O(1) \end{cases} \tag{14}$$

Proof. The information transported on the highway is forwarded by multi-hop routing. Under the pairwise coding and decoding, the transporting is performed along the horizontal highways first, until it reaches the crossing with the target vertical highway. Then, the same is performed along the vertical highways until it reaches the appropriate exit point for delivery.

According to Lemma 2, a node on the horizontal highway must relay for at most $2l(n)\sqrt{A}$ nodes, and the maximal distance between two hops is $\sqrt{2}l(n)$. Using Theorem 3, we can conclude that an achievable rate along the horizontal highways is

$$R^{Hh} = \begin{cases} \Omega\left(l^{-\alpha}(n)\left(\frac{p(n)}{n}\right)^{1/2}\right) & \text{if } l(n) = \Omega(1) \\ \Omega\left(\left(\frac{p(n)}{n}\right)^{1/2}\right) & \text{if } l(n) = O(1) \end{cases} \tag{15}$$

Similarly, the rate on vertical highways is

$$R^{Hv} = \begin{cases} \Omega\left(l^{-\alpha}(n)\left(\frac{p(n)}{n}\right)^{1/2}\right) & \text{if } l(n) = \Omega(1) \\ \Omega\left(\left(\frac{p(n)}{n}\right)^{1/2}\right) & \text{if } l(n) = O(1) \end{cases} \tag{16}$$

Combining Equations (15) and (16), we finish the proof of Lemma 6. $\square$

The following lemma illustrates the achievable rate of the delivery phase.

Lemma 7. *The receiver can attain a rate of R^{Dl} from an exit point on the highway, where R^{Dl} is*

$$R^{Dl} = \begin{cases} \Omega\left(p(n)\left(\frac{\log^2 np(n)}{\sqrt{\zeta p(n)}}\right)^{\alpha}\right) & \text{if } l(n) = \Omega(\log np(n)) \\ \Omega\left(\frac{p(n)}{\log^2 np(n)}\right) & \text{if } l(n) = O(\log np(n)) \end{cases} \tag{17}$$

Proof. The delivery phase is an opposite process to the draining phase, while the transmission is from highways to the destination. $\square$

Combining the Lemma 5, Lemma 6 and Lemma 7, we can derive the rate bottleneck of SWANETs

Theorem 8. *Comparing the achievable rate of each phase, we get the rate of per-node in SWANETs with general nodes density is*

$$T(n) = \begin{cases} \Omega\left(\frac{1}{\sqrt{n}}p^{\frac{1}{2}}(n)(\zeta p(n))^{\alpha}\right) & \text{if } l(n) = \Omega(1) \\ \Omega\left(\frac{1}{\sqrt{n}}p^{\frac{1}{2}}(n)\right) & \text{if } l(n) = O(1) \end{cases} \tag{18}$$

4. Discussion

In this section, we will discuss the results we obtained. By comparing our results with previous literature, we get the price of selfishness and the impact of node density on the throughput capacity of WANETs.

Firstly, our results can unify previous works [4,5], when we set $p(n) = 1$ and $\zeta = 1$ or $\zeta = n$.

Secondly, As shown in Figure 5, Figure 5a depicts the relation of throughput capacity with the probability $p(n)$ and node density ζ. From Figure 5a, we find that selfish nodes can severely impact the achievable per-node rate. In particular, when the square length $l(n) = \Omega(1)$, a degradation factor of $p^{\frac{1}{2}}(n)(\zeta p(n))^{\alpha}$ emerged, while for the case of $l(n) = O(1)$, the degradation factor is $p^{\frac{1}{2}}(n)$. In addition, node density has a trivial impact on the throughput. If the node density $\zeta > \frac{1}{p(n)}$, there is no impact on the throughput, while for the case of $\zeta > \frac{1}{p(n)}$, the throughput loss caused by node density is ζ^{α}. The reason for the performance degradation is that, due to the selfish nodes, all communications operate on partial nodes, and the selfish nodes cannot be utilized. Thus, it is hard for a node to find a relay node. With the extent of selfish nodes increasing, a transmitter needs to enlarge its transmission radius to find a relay node. From [4], we know that the network capacity is decreased with increasing transmission radius, since the number of simultaneous transmissions is decreased. We can enhance the transmission power to offset the impact of node density, which also provides sufficient conditions to guarantee the connectivity of the network [20]. In addition, we also give a comparison with previous works in Figure 5b. Figure 5b demonstrates that there exists a throughput loss caused by selfish nodes and node density. This insightful result is quite important because it provides valuable insight on the desirable operating point that balances selfish nodes and node density with throughput. We need to increase $p(n)$ in order to get more altruistic nodes, but as a node itself, it is quite the opposite. Hence, for future work, we will use Game Theory to solve the benefit between nodes and network performance.

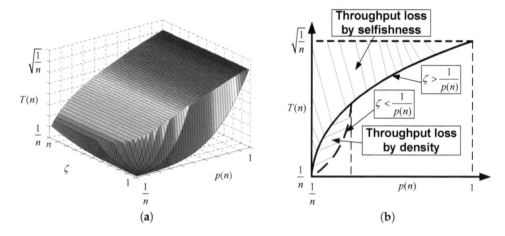

Figure 5. (a) shows the asymptotic throughput capacity of WANETs under the impact of selfish nodes and node density. (b) is a section of (a); We note that there exists a threshold for node density ζ. Comparing with previous literature, we can notice the throughput loss caused by selfish nodes or node density intuitively. The scales of the axes are in terms of the order in n.

5. Conclusions

This paper introduces a modeling framework for SWANETs under general node density. We consider various scope of selfish behavior for each node. Moreover, different node density is considered. A percolation model is adopted to construct a series of highway systems to connect the transmission. The computation of throughput capacity is conducted under the model which gives a more realistic description of SWANETs. The result reveals that, although a selfish node can save resources for the node itself, it degrades the network performance significantly.

Acknowledgments: This work was supported in part by the Specialized Research Fund for Jiangxi University of Science and Technology (Grant No. JXXJ11178).

Author Contributions: Qiuming Liu proposed the idea, derived the results and wrote the paper. Yong Luo proposed the circular percolation model. Yun Ling assisted in revising the paper. Jun Zheng proof-read the paper. All authors have read and approved the final manuscript.

Conflicts of Interest: The authors declare no conflict of interest.

References

1. Zuhairi, M.; Zafar, H.; Harle, D. Wireless Machine-to-Machine Routing Protocol with Unidirectional Links. *Smart Comput. Rev.* **2011**, *1*, 58–68.
2. Cho, K.H.; Ryu, M.W. A survey of greedy routing protocols for vehicular ad hoc networks. *Smart Comput. Rev.* **2012**, *2*, 125–137.
3. Zaman, K.; Shafiq, M.; Choi, J.G.; Iqbal, M. The Life Cycle of Routing in Mobile Ad Hoc Networks. *Smart Comput. Rev.* **2015**, *5*, 135–150.
4. Gupta, P.; Kumar, P.R. The capacity of wireless networks. *IEEE Trans. Inf. Theory* **2000**, *46*, 388–404.
5. Franceschetti, M.; Dousse, O.; David, N.C. Closing the gap in the capacity of wireless networks via percolation theory. *IEEE Trans. Inf. Theory* **2007**, *53*, 1009–1018.
6. Grossglauser, M.; Tse, D. Mobility increases the capacity of ad-hoc wireless networks. In Proceedings of the Twentieth Annual Joint Conference of the IEEE Computer and Communications Societies (INFOCOM), Anchorage, AK, USA, 22–26 April 2001; volume 3, pp. 1360–1369.
7. Li, P.; Zhang, C.; Fang, Y. The capacity of wireless ad hoc networks using directional antennas. *IEEE Trans. Mob. Comput.* **2011**, *10*, 1374–1387.
8. Zhang, G.; Xu, Y.; Wang, X. Capacity of hybrid wireless networks with directional antenna and delay constraint. *IEEE Trans. Commun.* **2010**, *58*, 2097–2106.
9. Sadjadpour, H.R; Wang, Z.; Garcia-Luna-Aceves, J.J. The capacity of wireless ad hoc networks with multi-packet reception. *IEEE Trans. Commun.* **2010**, *58*, 600–610.
10. Ozgur, A.; Leveque, O.; Tse, D.N.C. Hierarchical cooperation achieves optimal capacity scaling in ad hoc networks. *IEEE Trans. Inf. Theory* **2007**, *53*, 3549–3572.
11. Shin, W.Y.; Jeon, S.W.; Devroye, N. Improved capacity scaling in wireless networks with infrastructure. *IEEE Trans. Inf. Theory* **2011**, *57*, 5088–5102.
12. Shila, D.M.; Cheng, Y. Ad hoc wireless networks meet the infrastructure: Mobility, capacity and delay. In Proceedings of the 2012 Proceedings IEEE INFOCOM, Orlando, FL, USA, 25–30 March 2012; pp. 3031–3035.
13. Gamal, A.E.; Mammen, J.; Prabhakar, B. Throughput-delay trade-off in wireless networks. In Progress of the Twenty-Third Annual Joint Conference of the IEEE Computer and Communications Societies, Hong Kong, China, 7–11 March 2004.
14. Lin, X.; Shroff, N.B. The fundamental capacity-delay tradeoff in large mobile ad hoc networks. In Proceedings of the Third Annual Mediterranean Ad Hoc Networking Workshop, Bodrum, Turkey, 27–30 June 2004.
15. Yao, S.; Wang, X.; Tian, X.; Zhang, Q. Delay-Throughput Tradeoff with Correlated Mobility of Ad-Hoc Networks. In Proceedings of the 2014 Proceedings IEEE INFOCOM, Toronto, ON, Canada, 27 April–2 May 2014 .
16. Neely, M.J.; Modiano, E. Capacity and delay tradeoffs for ad hoc mobile networks. *IEEE Trans. Inf. Theory* **2005**, *51*, 1917–1937.
17. Lu, N.; Shen, X. Scaling Laws for Throughput Capacity and Delay in Wireless Networks—A Survey. *IEEE Commun. Surveys Tutor.* **2014**, *16*, 642–657.
18. Jiang, C.; Shi, Y.; Hou, Y.; Lou, W.; Kompella, S.; Midkiff, S.F. Toward Simple Criteria to Establish Capacity Scaling Laws for Wireless Networks. In Proceedings of the IEEE INFOCOM, Orlando, FL, USA, 25–30 March 2012.
19. Mao, G.; Lin, Z.; Ge, X.; Yang, Y. Towards a Simple Relationship to Estimate the Capacity of Static and Mobile Wireless Networks. *IEEE Trans. Wirel. Commun.* **2013**, *12*, 3883–3895.
20. Liu, E.; Zhang, Q.; Leung, K.K. Connectivity in selfish, cooperative networks. *IEEE Commun. Lett.* **2010**, *14*, 936–938.

21. Lee, S.; Levin, D.; Gopalakrishnan, V. Backbone construction in selfish wireless networks. *ACM SIGMETRICS Perform. Eval. Rev.* **2007**, *35*, 121–132.

22. Jo, M.; Han, L.; Kim, D.; In, H.P. Selfish attacks and detection in cognitive radio ad-hoc networks. *IEEE Netw.* **2013**, *27*, 46–50.

23. Kesten, H. The critical probability of bond percolation on the square lattice equals 1/2. *Commun. Math. Phys.* **1980**, *74*, 41–59.

24. Stauffer, D.; Aharony, A. *Introduction to Percolation Theory*; CRC Press: Boca Raton, FL, USA, 1994.

25. Keshavarz-Haddad, A.; Ribeiro, V.; Riedi, R. Broadcast capacity in multihop wireless networks. In Proceedings of the 12th Annual International Conference on Mobile Computing and Networking, Los Angeles, CA, USA, 24–29 September 2006; pp. 239–250.

8

Communication-Theoretic Model of Power Talk for a Single-Bus DC Microgrid

Marko Angjelichinoski [1,*], **Čedomir Stefanović** [1], **Petar Popovski** [1] and **Frede Blaabjerg** [2]

1   Department of Electronic Systems, Aalborg University, Aalborg 9220, Denmark; cs@es.aau.dk (Č.S.); petarp@es.aau.dk (P.P.)

2   Department of Energy Technology, Aalborg University, Aalborg 9220, Denmark; fbl@et.aau.dk

*   Correspondence: maa@es.aau.dk

Academic Editors: Mikael Skoglund, Lars K. Rasmussen and Tobias Oechtering

Abstract: Power talk is a method for communication among voltage control sources (VSCs) in DC microgrids (MGs), achieved through variations of the supplied power that is incurred by modulation of the parameters of the primary control. The physical medium upon which the communication channel is established is the voltage supply level of the common MG bus. In this paper, we show how to create power talk channels in all-to-all communication scenarios and implement the signaling and detection techniques, focusing on the construction and use of the constellations or arbitrary order. The main challenge to the proposed communication method stems from random shifts of the loci of the constellation symbols, which are due to random load variations in the MG. We investigate the impact that solutions that combat the effects of random load variations by re-establishing the detection regions have on the power talk rate.

Keywords: power talk; DC microgrids; microgrid communications

---

1. Introduction

One of the key paradigm shifts in the smart grid (SG) [1–3] is the introduction of the concept of microgrid (MG), which emerged as a result of the penetration of distributed energy resources (DERs), *i.e.*, small-scale distributed generators (DGs), including renewables and energy storage systems (ESSs). MGs are clusters of DERs and loads that span relatively small geographical areas (e.g., a single suburban neighborhood), which can operate connected to the main grid or autonomously, in islanded, self-sustaining mode. An example of a simple single bus DC MG system in a basic architectural configuration is shown in Figure 1. The DER units interface the common bus through flexible *power electronic converters* that support digital signal processing (Figure 1); the high penetration of flexible and programmable power electronic interfaces represents a distinguishing characteristic of MGs with respect to the traditional power grid.

The converters implement a set of control mechanisms with different control bandwidths to regulate the power flow in the MG and to balance the power supply and demand. The control mechanisms can be implemented in a decentralized manner, using only locally-observable quantities without any communication and providing strictly suboptimal control references (e.g., the droop control on primary control level). To enable optimal control in MGs, information exchange between units in the system is required. Traditionally, in power grid applications, external communication systems are used to provide communication capabilities, including power line communications [4,5]. The design approach where the feedback loops of the optimal controllers are enabled by an external communication system inherently reduces the reliability of the control system. In contrast, recent approaches for MG control avoid (crucially) relying on external communication networks [6–8] due to the availability and reliability requirements and advocate the use of the capabilities of the power electronic interfaces, foremost the capability to perform digital signal processing, as potential communication enablers. Notable examples are the *bus signaling* solutions that have been proposed to address specific aspects of distributed control in DC and AC MGs [8–12].

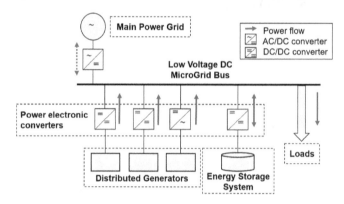

Figure 1. Architecture of a single bus DC microgrid (MG) system.

In this paper, we present a novel communication method designed for DC MGs termed *power talk* [13,14] that exploits the flexibility of the power electronic converters, enables a general digital communication interface to support optimal MG control without necessitating external hardware and has the same reliability and availability as the MG system itself. The main idea behind power talk is to modulate information in the parameters of the primary control loops that are implemented in the power electronic converters that regulate the voltage of the MG buses. This incurs bus voltage deviations that can be detected by other MG units, resulting in information transfer; the effective physical medium used for communication is bus voltage level, jointly maintained by all units in the system through primary control. As a result, the induced power talk channel exhibits some challenging properties from the communication perspective. The achievable rates of the power talk are limited by the response times of primary control loops, which are at the order of tens of milliseconds. Nevertheless, such rates may prove sufficient for the communication requirement of the MG control applications. On the other hand, power talk is, in essence, as reliable as the MG power control system itself, since all units connected to the same bus measure the bus voltage. Unlike existing bus signaling solutions whose application is limited to a narrow set of predefined coordination strategies, power talk offers a generic digital communication interface, able to support the communication demands of the majority of optimization and coordination mechanisms. As an example, the core mechanism in standard bus signaling solutions [8–12] relies on assigning several predefined bus voltage/frequency thresholds; whenever the thresholds are crossed, the units in the system performed predefined and coordinated actions (e.g., back up generators are turned on when the bus voltage falls beneath a predefined threshold, signaling that the system is overloaded). Evidently, the bus signaling solutions are not actually designed to transmit information messages. Thus, their implementation is application specific; this is the main limitation of existing bus signaling solutions that power talk aims to alleviate. Finally, since power talk is implemented in primary control loops, it only demands software modifications in the power electronic converters, a major advantage over other communication solutions, including standard off-the-shelf power line communications that require the installation of additional hardware.

Power talk has been introduced in [13,14], in a basic setup with two MG units and in a one-way communication scenario. The focus of [13] is on enabling reliable communication without precise knowledge of the system configuration and of the load; it is shown that using a special input symbol in the role of a pilot transforms the MG bus into some of the known communication channels. The work in [14] represents the unknown system configuration and load variations through a Thevenin equivalent, whose parameters determine the channel state and can be estimated, enabling the design of power talk constellations that perform optimally in terms of symbol error probability.

In this paper, we investigate strategies for designing *multiple access* power talk communication channels over the MG bus voltage. We focus on a single-bus DC MG systems with multiple control units that perform a higher layer control application, which requires exchanges of short messages, and develop a corresponding power talk framework. In particular, we investigate the construction of symbol constellations of arbitrary order at the transmitter, taking into account limitations related to power control and supply, and the construction of detection spaces used at the receiver, in which the symbol detection is performed. The above transmission and reception techniques are reviewed using the time division multiple access (TDMA) strategy for all-to-all communication setup. The main challenge of the power talk is posed by the random shifts of the constellation points due to the random variations of the loads in the system. In the paper, we assess the impact of two approaches to remedy the effects of random load variations by reestablishing the detection regions on the power talk rate. The first approach is based on periodic resetting of the detection regions, while the other is an on-demand scheme that is activated when a change in the load has been detected. We show that there is a basic trade-off between the number of communicating units, the rate of the load change and the order of modulation on one side and the attainable net rate of power talk.

The rest of the paper is organized as follows: Section 2 briefly introduces the basic terminology in MG technology, an overview of its control hierarchy with the related communication requirements and sets the design cornerstones of the power talk concept. Section 3 formalizes the operation of power talk in a TDMA framework. Section 4 introduces the concepts of signaling and detection spaces under power-related constraints and discusses the basic structural aspects. Section 5 briefly reviews the aspects of building power talk protocols that are able to cope with load changes. Section 6 presents a related evaluation of the power talk performance. Section 7 discusses the general power channel and outlines several of its interesting properties. Section 8 concludes the paper. Table 1 gives a non-exhaustive listing of the notation system and the abbreviations used throughout the manuscript.

Table 1. List of symbols and abbreviations.

Notations	
Symbols	**Meaning**
Electrical Parameters	
$V_{min} \leq v^* \leq V_{max}$	Bus voltage level
$0 \leq i_k \leq I_{k,max}$	Output current of unit k
$P_{k,max} = v^* i_k$	Output power of unit k
v_k	Reference voltage of the droop control
$r_{d,k}$	Virtual resistance of the droop control
$r \in [R_{min}, R_{max}]$	Resistive part of the load
P_{CP}	Constant power part of the load
Power Talk-related Parameters	
T_S	Symbol slot duration
$\mathbf{b}_k$	The bit combination sent bu unit k
$\mathbf{x}_k$	Power talk symbol representing $\mathbf{b}_k$
$w_H(\mathbf{b}_k)$	The Hamming weight of $\mathbf{b}_k$
$\mathbf{s}_j$	Power talk symbol received by unit j
$\mathcal{X}$	Signaling space
$\mathcal{C}$	Constraint space
$\delta_j(\mathbf{x}_k)$	Relative power deviation of unit j when unit k transmits
η, μ	Transmission, reception rate
Abbreviations	
Smart grid	SG
Direct current, alternate current	DC, AC
Microgrid	MG
Distributed energy resource	DER
Distributed generator	DG
Energy storage system	ESS
Time division multiple access	TDMA
Voltage source converter	VSC
Current source converter	CSC
Piecewise Linear Electrical Circuit Simulation	PLECS

2. Brief Overview of Microgrids' Control

Before proceeding to describe the communication channel defined by power talk and to motivate its development, we review the basic principles of control in DC MGs.

2.1. Control Architecture

The notion of control is central in MGs, especially when it operates in islanded mode. The control mechanisms in MG are usually organized in a layered, hierarchical structure [6,7] comprising three levels: *primary*, *secondary* and *tertiary*.

Primary control: The primary control level defines fully-decentralized mechanisms for harmonized operation of different DERs in the MG and enables adequate, load-dependent power sharing among them. Depending on the configuration of the primary control loops, the power electronically-controlled DERs fall into two categories [6,7,18]: voltage source converters (VSCs), which perform voltage regulation, and current source converters (CSCs), which do not perform voltage regulation usually configured to supply/consume constant power to/from the MG. Figure 2 shows the primary control diagram of a unit k that operates as VSC. The inner control loops (also known as *zero level control*) of the VSC units are usually fast (of the order of kHz), enforcing the output current i_k and voltage v_k^* to follow the predefined references, as shown in Figure 2. The bus voltage reference v_k^* that is fed to the inner voltage control loop of the unit k is set according to the *droop law* [15–18]:

$$v_k^* = v_k - r_{d,k} i_k, \tag{1}$$

where v_k and $r_{d,k}$ are the droop parameters, namely the *reference voltage* and the *virtual resistance* (also referred to as *droop slope*), and i_k is the output current. Evidently, the point (v_k^*, i_k) moves along the droop line with load changes maintaining the bus voltage within predefined limits, denoted with V_{min} and V_{max}, not violating the current rating of the unit $I_{k,max}$ and meeting the new power demand. Parameters v_k and $r_{d,k}$ are controllable; in standalone mode, the value v_k is set to the target bus voltage level, while $r_{d,k}$ is set to enable proportional power sharing based on the ratings of the units. In steady-state, the VSC units can be represented with equivalent voltage sources with parameters v_k and $r_{d,k}$. On the other hand, CSC units are usually constant power units that either consume or supply power. They do not implement the inner voltage control loop; instead, the reference for the inner current control loop is provided by upper control layers, and it is determined by the amount of power that the unit is willing to supply/consume. A unit can, in principle, switch between the VSC and CSC modes seamlessly; therefore, we consider only VSC units in the paper, as their task is to control the bus voltage and power sharing in the standalone mode.

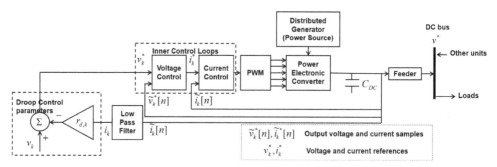

Figure 2. Primary control loops of power electronically-controlled DER.

Secondary and tertiary controls: The primary controls, when implemented in a distributed manner using the droop method, introduce steady-state voltage deviation (refer to (1)). In light of this, the secondary control level is introduced to restore the steady-state voltage level to the nominal [6,7]. This control level is only optional, since many MG applications do not require tight voltage regulation and can handle the voltage drops introduced by the droop control. Finally, the tertiary control level deals with MG optimization (operational, economic, reliability optimization, optimal power flow, *etc.*) and related processing tasks (such as topology discovery, equivalent impedance estimation, *etc.*) [6,7]. This is the highest control level and is also active when the MG operates in grid-connected mode, enabling the transfer of energy between the MG and the main grid, determining the MG operation set points and providing the reference values for the lower controls. Although optional as the secondary level, for long-term sustainability, the presence of tertiary control is required to improve the overall efficiency and reliability of the system.

2.2. Communications for Microgrid Control

As discussed above, the primary control level works only with local voltage and current measurements v_k^* and i_k, *i.e.*, no communication is necessary for the basic operation of the MG system. Oppositely, the tertiary (and also the secondary when present) requires information about the status of other/all units to operate properly. There is extensive literature on defining the upper level control mechanisms and optimization algorithms, including the type and the format of the information messages that should be exchanged among the units and (possibly) to a central controller [6–12,18,23,24]. An interesting result is presented in [24]; there, besides showing how to implement the optimal dispatch (standard control application on the tertiary level) in a distributed manner without a central controller, the authors also rigorously show that the sufficient information that is necessary to optimally assign duties to each DER is the average values of the disposable power, the power demand and the power cost in the system.

Summarizing the above discussion, it can be concluded that the resulting messages that need to be exchanged in MG systems are inherently very small. Moreover, the control messages are exchanged infrequently; as an example, the time period for which certain dispatch is valid is usually on the scale of tens of minutes or even more [24]. Therefore, we strive to design easily implementable, reliable and inexpensive communication solutions for the MG system that meets the information exchange needs of the system and avoids the need to install additional hardware.

2.3. How Power Talk Can Help

The principle of power talk communication is illustrated in Figures 3 and 4. The basic idea is to modulate, *i.e.*, change the droop control parameters v_k and $r_{d,k}$ in a controlled manner. This will result in slight deviations of the output bus voltage v^* and the output current i_k of the unit. Since all units are connected to the same bus and measure the output bus voltage, they can detect the deviations. Thus, the process of varying the droop control parameters enables information transfer in the droop-controlled DC MG.

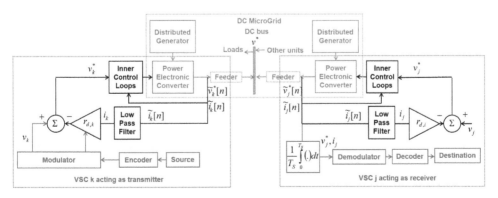

Figure 3. Power talk: the MG as the communication system.

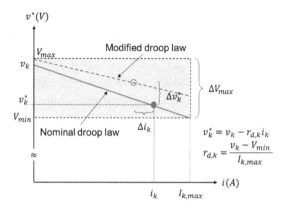

Figure 4. Modifying the droop control.

Since droop control is valid only in the steady state, power talk is inherently a low-rate communication solution, which can be well suited for standard upper level control applications in MGs. Thus, power talk can serve as a general purpose communication enabler for the upper level control applications that trigger its activation whenever a specific control unit needs to send data to other peers in the system. As an example, power talk is activated in coordination scenarios whenever a specific unit, e.g., a renewable source or battery, experiences low levels of maximum output power and needs to notify other units in the system, which take predefined actions upon receiving the notification. Furthermore, in standard periodic economic dispatch applications, power talk will be activated at each VSC-operated DG unit periodically and to enable the exchange of dispatch-related data. The inherent advantage of power talk as opposed to the majority of the communication solutions considered for MG control is its implementation in primary control loops in the power electronic converters, circumventing the need for the installation of additional communication hardware over the MG system.

3. Power Talk in DC Microgrids

3.1. Preliminaries and Assumptions

Here, we state the assumptions used throughout the manuscript. The system model is presented in Figure 5, which is a small, localized, single bus MG system with K DER units. This means that we do not consider the effect of transmission lines, neglecting the losses. All DERs are operated as VSC units that implement droop control with reference voltages v_k and virtual resistances $r_{d,k}$, $k = 1, ..., K$; see (1). The units are connected to the common bus through feeder lines with negligible losses; therefore, *all* units observe the same bus voltage denoted with $v_k^* = v^*, k = 1, ..., K$. The droop parameters in nominal mode, *i.e.*, when the system is not power talking, are denoted with v_k^n and $r_{d,k}^n$, $k = 1, ..., K$. v_k^n are usually set to the value of the target bus voltage, while $r_{d,k}^n$ are set to enable proportional power sharing. The bus feeds a collection of loads of different types, *i.e.*, they can be either purely resistive or constant power loads. The loads represents the variable power demand of the system that changes randomly through time. Under the above assumptions, the bus voltage in steady state is a nonlinear function in the reference voltages and the virtual resistances. We assume that the load consists of the variable resistive part denoted with r and the variable constant power part, which consumes power P_{CP}. The constant power load can be modeled with current source $I_{CP} = 2P_{CP}/v^*$ and parallel negative resistance $r_{CP} = -(v^*)/P_{CP}$. Writing the current balance law for the bus of the MG, we have the following (Figure 5):

$$\sum_{k=1}^{K} i_k + I_{CP} = \frac{v^*}{r} + \frac{v^*}{r_{CP}}, \tag{2}$$

where:

$$i_k = \frac{v_k - v^*}{r_{d,k}} \qquad (3)$$

is the output current of VSC unit k in steady state and is uniquely determined by v_k and v^*. From the above equation, the bus voltage in the steady state can be written as follows:

$$v^* = \frac{\sum_{k=1}^K \frac{v_k}{r_{d,k}} + \sqrt{(\sum_{k=1}^K \frac{v_k}{r_{d,k}})^2 - 4P_{CP}(\frac{1}{r} + \sum_{k=1}^K \frac{1}{r_{d,k}})}}{2(\frac{1}{r} + \sum_{k=1}^K \frac{1}{r_{d,k}})}. \qquad (4)$$

Evidently, in the general case, the bus voltage is a nonlinear function in v_k and $r_{d,k}$. Note that $P_k = v^* i_k$ is the power supplied by VSC k to the bus. The power in nominal mode, *i.e.*, the nominal power, is denoted with P_k^n.

For the reasons outlined above, the VSC units *do not* have knowledge of the system configuration, *i.e.*, the states/operating points of the other MG units. This is in line with the underlying assumption used in primary control: each unit makes its primary control decisions based on locally-observable quantities, *i.e.*, the bus voltage v^* and the output current i_k. Therefore, we develop power talk using the concept of detection space for each VSC unit k (see Section 4.2) as a local map of all possible values for the bus voltage and output current combinations (v^*, i_k) when the system is in power talk mode.

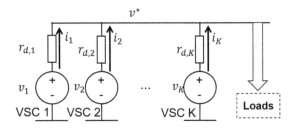

Figure 5. Single bus DC MG system with K VSC units in the steady state.

To test the performance of the developed techniques, we use PLECS integrated with Simulink as the standard simulation tool for testing the performance of power electronically-controlled systems. In the simulation, we use booster converters operated as VSCs with an output current and voltage sampling frequency f_0 (usually of the order of kHz). Specifically, we simulate a low voltage DC MG system with allowable voltage deviation on the main bus $V_{min} \le v^* \le V_{max}$. The current ratings of the DER units are denoted with $I_{k,max}$. In the simulation, we assume that the loads can be represented with pure resistance $r \in [R_{min}, R_{max}]$; however, we note that the developed techniques are applicable to any type of load, since the structure of the detection space is independent of the load types. We assume that the time axis is slotted, with slot duration T_S. In each slot, the VSC units modify their droop control parameters to transmit information. The slot duration is assumed to be 10 ms, which is the duration that allows the bus to reach steady state. We assume that all units maintain synchronization at the slot level. Finally, we assume the all-to-all communication scenario where each unit transmits data to all other units. The values of the parameters used in the simulation are summarized in Table 2.

Table 2. DC MG parameters simulated with PLECS.

T_s	f_0	V_{max}	V_{min}	$I_{k,max}$	$(v_k^n, r_{d,k}^n)$	R_{min}	R_{max}
10 ms	10 kHz	400 V	390 V	5 A	(400 V, 2 Ω)	50 Ω	250 Ω

3.2. All-to-All Power Talk: Time Division Multiple Access

We assume that the scheduling of the units is done in some predetermined manner, such that in each time slot, only one VSC transmits information over the MG, while the rest operate in the nominal mode, performing the role of receivers. The transmitting VSC inputs power talk symbols on the shared bus, while the receiving VSCs at the same time observe the corresponding output symbols.

3.2.1. Input Symbols

Denote the droop parameters of VSC k as the input $\mathbf{x}_k$:

$$\mathbf{x}_k = (v_k, r_{d,k}), \ k = 1, ..., K. \tag{5}$$

When transmitting, VSC k chooses from Q different droop combinations $\mathbf{x}_k^q$, $q = 0, ..., Q - 1$, where every droop combination represents a combination of $\log_2 Q$ transmit bits, denoted with $\mathbf{b}_k^q \in \{0, 1\}^{\log_2 Q}$:

$$\mathbf{x}_k^q = (v_k^q, r_{d,k}^q) \ \leftrightarrow \ \mathbf{b}_k^q, \ k = 1, ..., K, \ q = 0, ..., Q - 1. \tag{6}$$

We refer to combination $\mathbf{x}_k^q, q = 0, ..., Q - 1$ as a power talk input symbol. Note that the mapping (6) can be done arbitrarily on a VSC basis; for the sake of simplicity in the rest of the paper, we focus on the case where all units use the same symbols for signaling:

$$\mathbf{x}_k^q \equiv \mathbf{x}^q, \ k = 1, ..., K, \ q = 0, ..., Q - 1. \tag{7}$$

In principle, the symbols $\mathbf{x}^q$ can be also chosen arbitrarily, as long as they comply to the operational constraints, as elaborated in Section 4.1. Without losing generality, we assume that the input symbols $\mathbf{x}^q$ and the corresponding mappings $\mathbf{x}^q \longleftrightarrow \mathbf{b}^q$ are chosen to satisfy the following condition when unit k transmits and all others operate in a nominal mode:

$$P_k(\mathbf{x}_k^0) < ... < P_k(\mathbf{x}_k^{\frac{Q}{2}-1}) < P_k^n < P_k(\mathbf{x}_k^{\frac{Q}{2}}) < ... < P_k(\mathbf{x}_k^{Q-1}), \tag{8}$$

$k = 1, ..., K$, while the Hamming weights of $\mathbf{b}_k^q$ satisfy:

$$w_H(\mathbf{b}_k^0) \leq ... \leq w_H(\mathbf{b}_k^{\frac{Q}{2}-1}) \leq w_H(\mathbf{b}_k^{\frac{Q}{2}}) \leq ... \leq w_H(\mathbf{b}_k^{Q-1}). \tag{9}$$

$P_k(\mathbf{x}_k^{q_k})$ is the supplied power to the bus by VSC k when using the droop control combination $\mathbf{x}_k^{q_k}$ while all other units $\sim k$ use $\mathbf{x}_{\sim k}^n$; P_k^n is the supplied power when all units operate in nominal mode. Thus, VSC k inserts more power than nominally in the slot when transmitting a bit combination that has a higher Hamming weight. As an example, consider $Q = 2$. Then, the input symbols satisfy $P_k(\mathbf{x}_k^0) < P_k^n < P_k(\mathbf{x}_k^1)$, and the bit to symbol mappings are as follows: $\mathbf{x}_k^0 \longleftrightarrow$ "0", $\mathbf{x}_k^1 \longleftrightarrow$ "1". As another example, fix $Q = 4$. The input symbols satisfy $P_k(\mathbf{x}_k^0) < P_k(\mathbf{x}_k^1) < P_k^n < P_k(\mathbf{x}_k^2) < P_k(\mathbf{x}_k^3)$, and the bit to symbol mappings are as follows: $\mathbf{x}_k^0 \longleftrightarrow$ "00", $\mathbf{x}_k^1 \longleftrightarrow$ "01", $\mathbf{x}_k^2 \longleftrightarrow$ "10", $\mathbf{x}_k^3 \longleftrightarrow$ "11". Further, an example of a power talk symbol constellation satisfying (8) is the following: keep the virtual resistances fixed to their nominal values, *i.e.*, $r_{d,k} = r_{d,k}^n, k = 1, ..., K$, and use the following reference voltage constellation:

$$v^0 = v_k^n - \frac{(Q-1)\Delta v_k}{2}$$

$$\vdots$$

$$v^{\frac{Q}{2}-2} = v_k^n - \frac{3\Delta v_k}{2}$$

$$v^{\frac{Q}{2}-1} = v_k^n - \frac{\Delta v_k}{2}$$

$$v^{\frac{Q}{2}} = v_k^n + \frac{\Delta v_k}{2}$$

$$v^{\frac{Q}{2}+1} = v_k^n + \frac{3\Delta v_k}{2}$$

$$\vdots$$

$$v^{Q-1} = v_k^n + \frac{(Q-1)\Delta v_k}{2}. \tag{10}$$

i.e., the reference voltage constellation is antipodal with respect to v_k^n. Δv_k is a small term (usually $< 2\,\text{V}$ or even less for a modulation of higher order) chosen to satisfy (7). Figure 6 shows the bus voltage and the output current in an example system of two VSC units that use (10) with $Q = 2$. Evidently, the main impairment is the sporadic, random load variations.

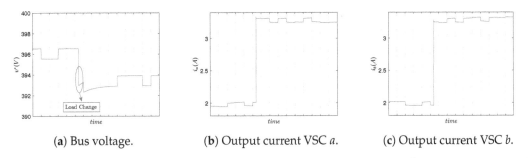

(a) Bus voltage.   (b) Output current VSC a.   (c) Output current VSC b.

Figure 6. TDMA-based binary power talk: two VSC units (obtained with PLECS® simulation of the system shown in Figure 5, $r_d = 2\,\Omega$, $v_a^n = v_b^n = 400\,\text{V}$, $r_{d,a}^n = r_{d,b}^n = 2\,\Omega$, $v^0 = 398\,\text{V}$, $v^1 = 402\,\text{V}$, $r = 100\,\Omega$ changing to $r = 60\,\Omega$).

The subsequent sections present the concept of detection space and show how to design effective detection mechanisms by observing the output voltage and current from each unit locally (*i.e.*, by observing the waveforms shown in Figure 6).

3.2.2. Output Symbols

The receiving units j, $j \neq k$, use the nominal droop parameter combination $\mathbf{x}_j^n$ and locally observe a voltage and current combination, denoted as the output symbol $\mathbf{s}_j$:

$$\mathbf{s}_j = (\bar{v}^*, \bar{i}_j), \; j = 1, ..., K, \; j \neq k, \tag{11}$$

where $\bar{y} = \sum_{l=0}^{f_0 T_S} y[l]$ denotes the time average of y over a single slot that is obtained by unit j. Each $\mathbf{s}_j$ is associated with the average output power $P_j = \bar{v}^* \bar{i}_j$, which depends on: (i) the nominal droop parameters of VSC j; (ii) the droop parameters of the other VSC unit including the transmitting one; and (iii) the momentary power demand of the loads. Assume that the loads do not change during the slot. Then, by measuring its own supplied power P_j, VSC j can infer which droop parameter combination is the input of the transmitting unit. This is equivalent to tracking the point $(\overline{v}^*, \overline{i}_j)$ in the local $v - i$ diagram, as it determines how much power VSC j is providing. Henceforth, we refer to the $v - i$ diagram as the *detection space*. Since the local output $\mathbf{s}_j$ is determined by $\mathbf{x}^{q_k}$, we use the following notation for TDMA power talk:

$$\mathbf{s}_j = \mathbf{s}_j(\mathbf{x}^{q_k}) = \mathbf{s}_j(\mathbf{b}^{q_k}) = \mathbf{s}_j(q_k)$$
$$P_j = P_j(\mathbf{x}^q) = P_j(\mathbf{b}^{q_k}) = P_j(q_k), \ j = 1, ..., K, \ q_k = 0, ..., Q - 1, \tag{12}$$

where $j \neq k$ is a receiving unit and $\mathbf{b}^{q_k}$ is the information bit block represented by input symbol q and transmitted by VSC k. Figure 7 illustrates the detection spaces for a system of two VSCs ($K = 2$), denoted with VSC a and VSC b, assuming that VSC a is active for $Q = 2$ and $Q = 4$.

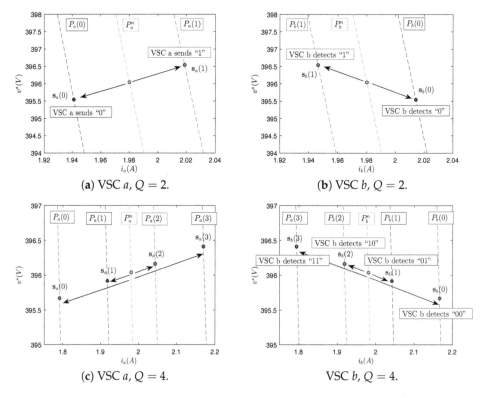

Figure 7. $v - i$ diagram for TDMA-based binary power talk: two VSC units **(a,b)** $v^0 = 399$ V, $v^1 = 401$ V, **(c,d)** $v^0 = 399.25$ V, $v^1 = 399.75$ V, $v^2 = 400.25$ V, $v^3 = 400.47$ V (obtained with PLECS® simulation of the system shown in Figure 5, $r_d = 2 \ \Omega$, $v_a^n = v_b^n = 400$ V, $r_{d,a}^n = r_{d,b}^n = 2 \ \Omega$, $r = 100 \ \Omega$).

When $Q = 2$, if VSC a inserts $\mathbf{x}^0$, it supplies less power than nominally, i.e., $P_a("0") < P_a^n$. At the same time, VSC b observes $\mathbf{s}_b(0)$, detects that it supplies more than the nominal power $P_b("0") > P_b^n$ and concludes that VSC a is signaling "0". Similarly, if VSC a inserts $\mathbf{x}^1$, VSC b observes $\mathbf{s}_b(1)$, detects that $P_b("1") < P_b^n$ and concludes that VSC a is signaling "1". The TDMA scheme described above can be easily generalized to an arbitrary number of units and arbitrary constellation orders. Note that we have not assumed a specific input-output relation between $\mathbf{x}^{q_k}$ and $\mathbf{s}_j$; in general, such a relation would be nonlinear. At this point, we also note that, in general, VSC j observes noisy versions of $\mathbf{s}_j$. However, in this work, the effect of the noise is neglected due to several reasons: (1) the dominant impairment of power talk as communication techniques over the power lines, implemented in primary control, is the variability of the load that changes randomly; (2) investigations have shown that the voltage/current measurements error of standard power electronic equipment available on the market is low [21,23–26]; and (3) since we use the average values of the bus voltage and the current to define the output symbol, the noise will be even further reduced due to averaging. Accounting for the Gaussian noise can rely on standard digital communication theory, while in this paper, we are focusing on the properties of a new multi-user channel that operates under power constraints.

To conclude this section, we list the main challenges in power talk as described above:

- The described communication protocol requires prior knowledge of all possible points s_j in the detection space of VSC j. As the detailed configuration of the MG is not known *a priori*, these values have to be learned, e.g., in a predefined training phase, during which each VSC constructs the detection space. This is analogous to the case of channel estimation in a standard communication system where a linear relation between the input and the output can be postulated. Power talk does not use such a relation; instead, in the training phase, each unit learns each possible output in the detection space and identifies which input combination causes the respective inputs.
- The output power of a VSC can also vary as a result of the load change, which happens arbitrarily and randomly. In particular, the current values of the loads can be seen as determining the state of the system or the state of the communication channel. Whenever they change, the structure of the detection space also changes, leading to incorrect decisions at the receivers if the detection space prior to change is still used. A strategy to deal with random state variations is to periodically repeat the training phase or to provide a mechanism that tracks the state changes and re-initiates the training phase whenever a change is detected. Section 5 outlines possible strategies to deal with this challenge.

4. Constraining Power Talk

Here, we introduce the concept of signaling space to capture the effect that the operating constraints of the MG have on the power talk schemes. We then investigate the structure of the detection space and its dynamics due to the load changes, as this is vital for implementing reliable power talk solutions.

4.1. The Signaling Space

Every MG is subject to operational constraints that may not be violated. Denote by C a set that consists of all operational constraints. The signaling space $\mathcal{X}$ for Q-ary power talk is the set of all possible symbols x^q, $q = 0, \ldots, Q - 1$, that jointly satisfy the constraints in C for any value of the loads:

$$\mathcal{X} = \left\{ x^q = (v^q, r_d^q), \, q = 0, ..., Q - 1 : C, \, k = 1, ..., K, \text{ for any value of the loads} \right\}. \tag{13}$$

In this paper, we focus on the bus voltage and output current constraints as the most important:

$$C = \left\{ V_{min} \leq v^* \leq V_{max}; I_{k,min} \leq i_k \leq I_{k,max}, k = 1, \ldots, K \right\} \tag{14}$$

where V_{min} and V_{max} are the minimum and maximum allowable bus voltages and where $I_{k,min}$ and $I_{k,max}$ are the minimum and maximum output currents of VSC k; usually, $I_{k,min} = 0$, and $I_{k,max}$ is the current rating of the unit.

To illustrate the signaling space, assume that the load is purely resistive $r \in [R_{min}, R_{max}]$. Then, under the constraints (14), the steady-state model (4) and (3), the symbols $\mathbf{x}^q$ when unit k is transmitting should jointly satisfy:

$$r_d^q \frac{V_{min} - \frac{\sum_{i \neq k} \frac{v_i^n}{r_{d,i}^n}}{\left(\frac{1}{R_{min}} + \sum_{i \neq k} \frac{1}{r_{d,i}^n}\right)}}{\left(\frac{1}{R_{min}} + \sum_{i \neq k} \frac{1}{r_{d,i}^n}\right)^{-1}} + V_{min} \leq v^q \leq r_d^q \frac{V_{max} - \frac{\sum_{i \neq k} \frac{v_i^n}{r_{d,i}^n}}{\left(\frac{1}{R_{max}} + \sum_{i \neq k} \frac{1}{r_{d,i}^n}\right)}}{\left(\frac{1}{R_{max}} + \sum_{i \neq k} \frac{1}{r_{d,i}^n}\right)^{-1}} + V_{max}, \tag{15}$$

$$\frac{\sum_{i \neq k} \frac{v_i^n}{r_{d,i}^n}}{\left(\frac{1}{R_{max}} + \sum_{i \neq k} \frac{1}{r_{d,i}^n}\right)} \leq v^q \leq r_d^q I_{k,max} + \frac{I_{k,max}}{\left(\frac{1}{R_{min}} + \sum_{i \neq k} \frac{1}{r_{d,i}^n}\right)} + \frac{\sum_{i \neq k} \frac{v_i^n}{r_{d,i}^n}}{\left(\frac{1}{R_{min}} + \sum_{i \neq k} \frac{1}{r_{d,i}^n}\right)}, \tag{16}$$

for $q = 0, ..., Q-1$ and $k = 1, ..., K$. Note that when the symbols satisfy (8), (15) and (16) are satisfied for $q = 0$ and $q = Q-1$; then, they are also satisfied by $q = 1, ..., Q-2$.

It can be shown that the signaling space given with (15) and (16) can be equivalently written as follows:

$$r_d^q \left(\frac{V_{min} - G_k(R_{min})}{H_k(R_{min})}\right) + V_{min} \leq v^q \leq r_d^q \left(\frac{V_{max} - G_k(R_{max})}{H_k(R_{max})}\right) + V_{max}, \tag{17}$$

$$G_k(R_{max}) \leq v^q \leq r_d^q I_{a,max} + H_k(R_{min}) I_{a,max} + G_k(R_{min}), \tag{18}$$

where $G_k(r)$ and $H_k(r)$ are the voltage and the resistance of the Thevenin equivalent as seen from the transmitting VSC, calculated for input $\mathbf{x}^q$ when the load value is r. Thus, from (17) and (18), it follows that the units do not need precise knowledge of the system (*i.e.*, the function (4)); to determine the signaling space when transmitting, they only need the equivalent response of the system at minimum and maximum load.

Further, every input symbol $\mathbf{x}^q, q = 0, ..., Q-1$ results in different power $P_j(q_k)$ supplied by VSC j. To account for this effect, we introduce the relative power deviation of unit j when unit k is transmitting, respective to its supplied power P_j^n when all units operate nominally:

$$\delta_j(q_k) = \frac{\sqrt{\mathbb{E}_R \left\{ (P_j(q_k) - P_j^n)^2 \right\}}}{\mathbb{E}_R \left\{ P_j^n \right\}}, \quad j = 1, \ldots, K, \ q_k = 0, \ldots, Q-1, \tag{19}$$

where the averaging is performed over the load r, modeled as a random variable with some distribution $p_R(r)$. Then, the average supplied power deviation per unit δ, for TDMA-based power talk, is calculated as:

$$\delta = \frac{1}{K^2} \sum_{j \in \mathcal{X}} \sum_{k \in \mathcal{X}} \left(\frac{1}{Q} \sum_{q_k=0}^{Q-1} \delta_j(q_k) \right), \tag{20}$$

where, for given j and given k, we first average over all possible Q symbols $\mathbf{x}^Q, q = 1, ..., Q-1$ unit k inputs; then, we also average over all k for a given j, and the final averaging is over all possible j. Finally, we introduce average power deviation limit γ, requiring that:

$$\delta \leq \gamma, \tag{21}$$

i.e., the average power deviation per unit w.r.t. the nominal mode of operation is bound by γ.

Figure 8 depicts the signaling space $\mathcal{X}$ for a two-unit system, when VSC a transmits, while VSC b operates in nominal mode, for system parameters listed in Table 2 and the uniform distribution of the load $\mathcal{U}[R_{min}, R_{max}]$. The figure also depicts the relative power deviation of VSC a, $\delta_a(q_a)$ as a function of the input symbol $\mathbf{x}^{q_a}$. Evidently, $\delta_a(q_a)$ increases when the input symbol $\mathbf{x}^{q_a}$ is placed far from $\mathbf{x}^n$.

Figure 9 shows that the signaling space and the average power deviation δ for binary power talk and have fixed droop slope $r_d^1 = r_d^0$ and $v^1 > v^0$. δ is obtained by averaging as in (20) with equiprobable bits. Evidently, the available signaling spaces decrease as the number of units increases.

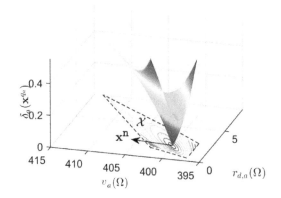

Figure 8. The signaling space $\mathcal{X}$ and the relative power deviation $\delta_a(q_a)$ in a two-unit system.

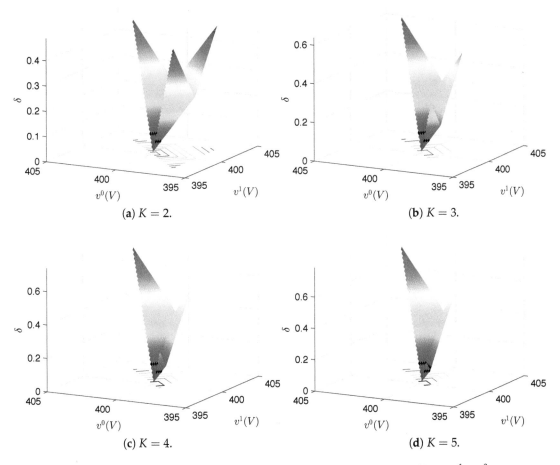

Figure 9. The signaling space and average power deviation, $Q = 2$, fixed r_d constellation, $r_d^1 = r_d^0 = 2\,\Omega$, equiprobable bit values.

4.2. The Detection Space

As already introduced, the detection space $\mathcal{S}_j$ for receiving VSC j when VSC k is transmitting $(j \neq k)$ is defined as the set of points $\mathbf{s}_j = (v^*, i_j)$, where v^* is the output voltage, equal to the bus voltage when the line resistance is negligible, and i_j is the output current of VSC j. By observing $\mathbf{s}_j$, VSC j gathers information about the symbols/powers of other units.

We outline the general structure of the detection space, illustrated in Figure 10. All outputs of VSC j lie on the line $v^* = -r_{d,j}i_j + v_j$ where $(v_j, r_{d,j})$ is the symbol VSC j is inserting. When VSC k is transmitting, $\mathbf{x}_j = \mathbf{x}_j^n = (v_j^n, r_{d,j}^n), j \neq k$, and the output symbols lie on a single line, as shown in Figure 10. The actual loci of output symbols of VSC j, i.e., $\mathbf{s}_j = (v^*, i_j)$, are in the intersection of $v^* = -r_{d,j}i_k + v_j$ and $v^* = \frac{P_j}{i_j}$, where P_j is the output power. As the load in the system varies, the points $\mathbf{s}_j$ in $\mathcal{S}_j$ shift along $v^* = -r_{d,j}i_j + v_j$; see Figure 10b. Comparing Figure 10c to Figure 10a, it is apparent that under a constant average power deviation constraint, increasing the number of units reduces the distance among the symbols.

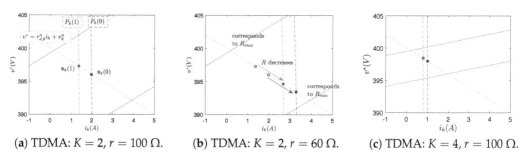

(a) TDMA: $K = 2, r = 100\ \Omega$.   (b) TDMA: $K = 2, r = 60\ \Omega$.   (c) TDMA: $K = 4, r = 100\ \Omega$.

Figure 10. The detection space of VSC j, fixed r_d constellation, $\gamma = 0.2$, $Q = 2$ and resistive load r. The dashed lines represent the output power $P_j = v^* i_j$, and the dashed-dotted line $v^* = -r_{d,j}i_j + v_j$ represents the symbol $\mathbf{x}_j$ that VSC j is inserting. The loci of output symbols $\mathbf{s}_j$ are on the intersection between the lines corresponding to output powers and the local inputs. As r varies, $\mathbf{s}_j$ slide along the dashed-dotted lines between the bounds (dotted lines) defined by operational constraints on the load.

5. Dealing with Random Load Changes

In this section, we present techniques that complement the basic power talk operation, as described in the previous sections, required to design a fully-operational communication protocol. To evaluate their efficiency, we use the net reception rate per unit $\bar{\mu}$, i.e., the average number of information bits received per unit per time slot, calculated as follows:

$$\bar{\mu} = (K - 1)\eta \tag{22}$$

where η is the transmission rate that is equal to, for each VSC k, $k = 1, ..., K$ and where the term $K - 1$ reflects the fact that a VSC unit is in receiving mode $K - 1$ times more than in transmitting mode when TDMA is used. The following bound holds:

$$\eta \leq \frac{\log_2 Q}{K}, k = 1, ..., K \tag{23}$$

with equality when the load is perfectly know. However, all VSCs have to maintain a layout of the detection space that matches the current value of the loads. A simple and effective strategy for the construction of the detection space is to conduct a training phase during which the units input predefined training sequences. We think of the number of time slots used for training sequences as a necessary cost in order to "learn" the respective power talk channels. We assume that each unit builds its detection space separately, in order to take into account the imperfections of the MG system, such as small resistances of the feeder lines and the common bus. Therefore, a unit has to learn Q points in its detection space for each of the remaining units. Assuming that a point is learned during M dedicated slots, the training phase length is QMK slots. The training phase can be performed by sequential transmission of $\mathbf{x}^q, q = 0, ..., Q - 1$, by one of the units, while the remaining units operate nominally and construct their detection spaces.

Finally, we review potential schemes for the activation of the training phase. We assume that the rate of change of the loads in the system is much lower than the power talk signaling rate. A simple solution for training phase activation would be to perform training periodically and to update the detection spaces of the units. This is a robust and stable solution; however, load changes during the data phase might lead to lost data, which would require retransmissions. A more involved approach would be to employ a model change detector that tracks the bus voltage and, if a change is detected, initiates the training phase. Using this approach, no data are lost; however, it necessitates a model change detector with high fidelity performance since all units have to detect the load change with very high probability [28].

6. Performance Evaluation

Here, we evaluate the performance of power in terms of the net reception rate, and we show that there is an inherent trade-off between the number of units, the order of the power talk modulation and the rate of load change. We simulate a DC MG system as described in Section 3.1. We assume that the load is purely resistive and model the load changes through a Poisson process, whose intensity λ is the expected number of load changes per time slot. As the slot duration T_S is of the order of milliseconds, one can expect that $\lambda \ll 1$ in practice. We also assume that whenever the load changes, the detection spaces are completely destroyed for all units. Thus, when the training sequences are inserted periodically, if a load change occurs in the data transmission phase, all bits after the change are assumed to be lost. This is essentially the worst case scenario, since very small load changes will cause a negligible shift of the points in the detection spaces. Additionally, since we neglect the noise, we assume a perfect model change detector for the on-demand training sequence insertion approach.

Figure 11 depicts the simulation results for the net reception rate for TDMA power talk. For a given order of modulation, the net reception rate of TDMA power talk is upper bounded with $(K - 1) \log_2 Q/K$. We observe that the net reception rate decreases as the rate of load change increases. This is due to the detection space establishment cost. For the periodic insertion approach, the increase in the load change rate will result in more lost data, while with the on-demand approach, the training sequence will be inserted more frequently. Comparing Figure 11a,b to Figure 11c,d, we see that for the same rate of load changes, higher net reception rates can be achieved with the on-demand training sequence insertion approach. This is the expected result since when inserting the training sequences only when necessary, we are using the available time resources more efficiently. Additionally, from Figure 11, there exist an optimum number of units that maximizes the net reception rate for a fixed load change rate and a fixed constellation size; nevertheless, we can observe that the reduction of the net reception rate for K larger than the optimum is not dramatic. For a given load change rate, there exists an optimum number of constellation points that maximizes the net reception rate; the optimal Q increases as the load change rate decreases. Finally, with the on-demand training sequence insertion approach, we can in general use higher order constellations for a fixed number of units and a fixed load change rate and achieve higher net reception rates.

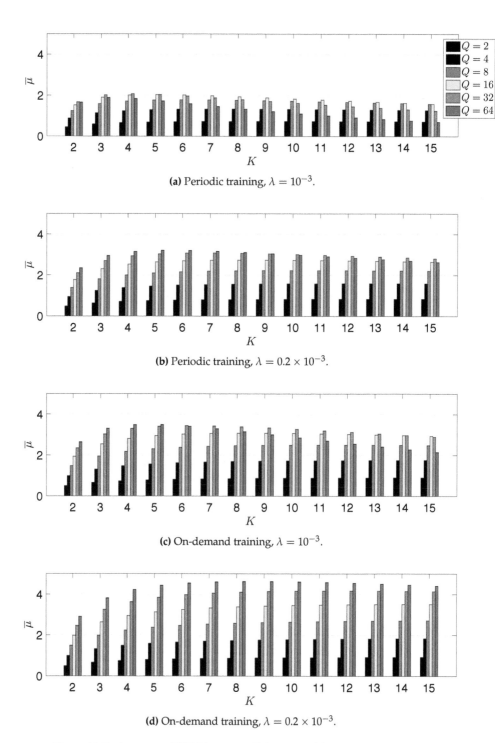

(a) Periodic training, $\lambda = 10^{-3}$.

(b) Periodic training, $\lambda = 0.2 \times 10^{-3}$.

(c) On-demand training, $\lambda = 10^{-3}$.

(d) On-demand training, $\lambda = 0.2 \times 10^{-3}$.

Figure 11. Performance of TDMA power talk in terms of the net reception rate.

7. On the General Power Talk Channel Model

Finally, here, we discuss some unique aspects of the general power talk channel model, established over the voltage supply level. For a single bus DC MG system, where all units are connected to the same bus and observe the same bus voltage, the input-output relation of the channel is given by (4). As is evident, all units jointly determine the output of the channel (through their droop control parameters); on the other hand, the output also varies sporadically as the load changes, representing the main communication impairment. If the load variations are seldom, with a lower rate than the power talk communication rate, then they can be modeled as a random channel state that remains fixed during multiple transmission slots. So far, we have treated the TDMA strategy over (4), where in each slot, only one unit transmits, while all other units operate in nominal mode x_k^n. In Section 4.1, we showed that when constraining the input using the signaling space, essentially all units (the transmitting and the receiving) jointly constrain the individual input of the transmitting unit; the signaling space (15) and (16), as well as the average power deviation (20) clearly illustrate this aspect. Having a joint constraint on the transmitters is a remarkable property in power talk channels created over the bus voltage level in the MG, not found in the conventional communication model, where it is common to have an individual constraint per transmitter. The property is strongly pronounced in full duplex scenarios where all units transmit and receive at the same time; in this case, the assignment of equivalent power deviation budgets for each unit will be done by solving a joint optimization problem over all droop control units in the MG.

Another major aspect of (4) is its non-linearity of v^* in the inputs $x_k, k = 1, ..., K$. In this paper, we presented a solution based on detection spaces; this way, we were are able to eliminate some of the issues stemming from the non-linearity of (4) and its dependence on the values of the loads. Another possible approach is to use very small droop deviations around the nominal value, i.e., $x_k = x_k^n + \Delta x_k$ with $\Delta x_k = (\Delta v_k, \Delta r_{d,k})$ satisfying $\frac{|\Delta v_k|}{v_k^n} << 1$, $\frac{|\Delta r_{d,k}|}{r_{d,k}^n} << 1$. Then, we can linearize (4) around $x_k^n, k = 1, ..., K$. This solution will significantly limit the space of all possible input combinations; nevertheless, it leads to some particularly interesting observations. Specifically, the resulting signal model is a linear combination of the input droop deviations (that carry the information in this case); however, the coefficients of the linear combination are functions of the nominal droop parameters $x_k^n, k = 1, ..., K$, and their values can be modified through $x_k^n, k = 1, ..., K$. This is an interesting feature of the linearized power talk channel, which opens a multitude of possibilities to optimize the performance of the power talk communication, and it is part of our ongoing work. Moreover, it can be also shown that in the linearized channel, each unit obtains its input constraint as a solution of the linear program, solved over all participating units; the coefficients of the program are also functions of x_k^n, opening another possible way of optimizing the power talk channels.

8. Conclusions and Discussion

In the paper, we presented power talk, a method for communication among VSC units in a microgrid. We have shown that by modifying the parameters of the primary control loops of VSC units, it is possible to design signaling constellations that conform to the operating constraints and limits to the power deviations with respect to the nominal operation.

The main challenge of power talk is the arbitrary variations of load. We investigated the impact that the techniques that counter-effect load changes have on the power talk rate, showing that there exists a dependence between the number of communication units, constellation size and load-change rate.

The future work will focus on more advanced power talk solutions that effectively address the non-linearity of the general problem and more efficiently exploit the available communication resources. A possible approach is to let all VSC units communicate at the same time in a full duplex fashion, where each unit is at the same time a transmitter and a receiver. Our initial investigations have shown that in such a case, under mild assumptions on the input symbol constellations, the resulting power talk channel is an integer adder multiple access channel for which efficient uniquely decodable codes can be applied. Another approach would be to use linearization strategies on (4) to obtain a linear input-output model. The preliminary investigations have shown that if only the reference voltage is modulated, the droop slopes are kept fixed, and the output is linearized in the input reference voltage deviations, the resulting channel is linear with channel coefficients that depend on the droop slopes, and thus, they can be controlled. In this regard, one of our goals is to find optimal communication strategies for power talking DC MGs.

Acknowledgments: The work presented in this paper was supported in part by the EU, under Grant Agreement No. 607774 "ADVANTAGE".

Author Contributions: Marko Angjelichinoski, Čedomir Stefanović and Petar Popovski conceived the theoretical content of the paper. Marko Angjelichinoski carried out the analysis, formulated the representations of signaling and detection spaces, carried out the simulations and analyzed the simulation data. Čedomir Stefanović and Petar Popovski proposed the investigation of the trade-off between the net reception rate of TDMA power talk, the order of the constellation, the number of communicating units and the rate of load changes. Frede Blaabjerg proposed the simulation environment, as well as provided consultations regarding the implementation details.

Conflicts of Interest: The authors declare no conflict of interest.

References

1. Lasseter, R. Microgrids. In Proceedings of the IEEE Power Engineering Society Winter Meeting, New York, NY, USA, 27–31 January 2002; pp. 305–308.
2. Hatziargyriou, N. *Microgrids: Architectures and Control*; Wiley-IEEE Press: New York, NY, USA, 2014.
3. Bush, S.F. *Smart Grid: Communication-Enabled Intelligence for the Electric Power Grid*; John Wiley & Sons: New York, NY, USA, 2014.
4. Yan, Y.; Qian, Y.; Sharif, H.; Tipper, D. A survey on smart grid communication infrastructures: Motivations, requirements and challenges. *IEEE Commun. Surveys Tutor.* **2013**, *15*, 15–20.
5. Galli, S.; Scaglione, A.; Wang, Z. For the grid and through the grid: The role of power line communications in the smart grid. *IEEE Proc.* **2011**, *99*, 998–1027.
6. Guerrero, J.; Vasquez, J.; Matas, J.; de Vicuna, L.G.; Castilla, M. Hierarchical control of droop-controlled AC and DC microgrids—A general approach toward standardization. *IEEE Trans. Ind. Electron.* **2011**, *58*, 158–172.
7. Guerrero, J.; Chandorkar, M.; Lee, T.; Loh, P. Advanced control architectures for intelligent microgrids; part i: Decentralized and hierarchical control. *IEEE Trans. Ind. Electron.* **2013**, *60*, 1254–1262.
8. Jin, C.; Wang, P.; Xiao, J.; Tang, Y.; Choo, F.H. Implementation of hierarchical control in DC microgrids. *IEEE Trans. Ind. Electron.* **2014**, *68*, 4032–4042.
9. Schonberger, J.; Duke, R.; Round, S. DC-bus signaling: A distributed control strategy for a hybrid renewable nanogrid. *IEEE Trans. Ind. Electron.* **2006**, *53*, 1453–1460.
10. Chen, D.; Xu, L.; Yao, L. DC voltage variation based autonomous control of DC microgrids. *IEEE Trans. Power Deliv.* **2013**, *28*, 637–648.
11. Vandoorn, T.; Renders, B.; Degroote, L.; Meersman, B.; Vandevelde, L. Active load control in islanded microgrids based on the grid voltage. *IEEE Trans. Smart Grid* **2011**, *2*, 139–151.
12. Sun, K.; Zhang, L.; Xing, Y.; Guerrero, J. A distributed control strategy based on DC bus signaling for modular photovoltaic generation systems with battery energy storage. *IEEE Trans. Power Electron.* **2011**, *26*, 3032–3045.
13. Angjelichinoski, M.; Stefanovic, C.; Popovski, P.; Liu, H.; Loh, P.; Blaabjerg, F. Power talk: How to modulate data over a DC micro grid bus using power electronics. In Proceedings of the 6th IEEE International Conference on Smart Grid Communications (SmartGridComm 2015), Miami, FL, USA, 2–5 November 2015.
14. Angjelichinoski, M.; Stefanovic, C.; Popovski, P.; Blaabjerg, F. Power talk in DC micro grids: Constellation design and error probability performance. **2015**, arXiv:1507.02598.
15. Pogaku, N.; Prodanovic, M.; Green, T. Modeling, analysis and testing of autonomous operation of an inverter-based microgrid. *IEEE Trans. Power Electron.* **2007**, *22*, 613–625.
16. Mohamed, Y.-R.; El-Saadany, E. Adaptive decentralized droop controller to preserve power sharing stability of paralleled inverters in distributed generation microgrids. *IEEE Trans. Power Electron.* **2008**, *23*, 2806–2816.
17. Blaabjerg, F.; Chen, Z.; Kjaer, S. Power electronics as efficient interface in dispersed power generation systems. *IEEE Trans. Power Electron.* **2004**, *19*, 1184–1194.
18. Dragicevic, T.; Guerrero, J.; Vasquez, J.; Skrlec, D. Supervisory control of an adaptive-droop regulated DC microgrid with battery management capability. *IEEE Trans. Power Electron.* **2014**, *29*, 695–706.

19. Giannakis, G.; Kekatos, V.; Gatsis, N.; Kim, S.-J.; Zhu, H.; Wollenberg, B. Monitoring and Optimization for Power Grids: A Signal Processing Perspective. *IEEE Signal Process. Mag.* **2013**, *30*, 107–128.

20. Liang, H.; Choi, B.J.; Abdrabou, A.; Zhuang, W.; Shen, X. Decentralized Economic Dispatch in Microgrids via Heterogeneous Wireless Networks. *IEEE J. Sel. Areas Commun.* **2012**, *30*, 1061–1074.

21. Sangswang, A.; Nwankpa, C. Effects of switching-time uncertainties on pulsewidth-modulated power converters: Modeling and analysis. *IEEE Trans. Circuits Syst. I* **2003**, *50*, 1006–1012.

22. Cobreces, S.; Bueno, E.; Pizarro, D.; Rodriguez, F.; Huerta, F. Grid impedance monitoring system for distributed power generation electronic interfaces. *IEEE Trans. Instrum. Meas.* **2009**, *58*, 3112–3121.

23. Midya, P.; Krein, P. Noise properties of pulse-width modulated power converters: Open-loop effects. *IEEE Trans. Power Electron.* **2000**, *15*, 1134–1143.

24. Mazumder, S.; Nayfeh, A.; Boroyevich, D. Theoretical and experimental investigation of the fast- and slow-scale instabilities of a DC-DC converter. *IEEE Trans. Power Electron.* **2001**, *16*, 201–216.

25. Cavallini, A.; Montanari, G.; Cacciari, M. Stochastic evaluation of harmonics at network buses. *IEEE Trans. Power Deliv.* **1995**, *10*, 1606–1613.

26. Sangswang, A.; Nwankpa, C. Random noise in switching DC-DC converter: Verification and analysis. In Proceedings of the 2003 IEEE International Symposium on Circuits and Systems (ISCAS 2003), Bangkok, Thailand, 25–28 May 2003.

27. Sanchez, S.; Molinas, M. Large signal stability analysis at the common coupling point of a DC microgrid: A grid impedance estimation approach based on a recursive method. *IEEE Trans. Energy Convers.* **2015**, *30*, 122–131.

28. Kay, S. *Fundamentals of Statistical Signal Processing: Estimation Theory*; Prentice-Hall: Upper Saddle River, NJ, USA, 1998.

9

A Big Network Traffic Data Fusion Approach Based on Fisher and Deep Auto-Encoder

Xiaoling Tao [1,2,*], Deyan Kong [1], Yi Wei [2,*] and Yong Wang [2,3]

1   Key Laboratory of Cognitive Radio and Information Processing, Guilin University of Electronic Technology, Guilin 541004, China; kcykdy@163.com
2   Guangxi Colleges and Universities Key Laboratory of Cloud Computing and Complex Systems, Guilin University of Electronic Technology, Guilin 541004, China; wang@guet.edu.cn
3   Guangxi Key Laboratory of Trusted Software, Guilin University of Electronic Technology, Guilin 541004, China
*   Correspondence: txl@guet.edu.cn (X.T.); 4128wy@163.com (Y.W.)

Academic Editors: Yong Yu, Yu Wang and Willy Susilo

Abstract: Data fusion is usually performed prior to classification in order to reduce the input space. These dimensionality reduction techniques help to decline the complexity of the classification model and thus improve the classification performance. The traditional supervised methods demand labeled samples, and the current network traffic data mostly is not labeled. Thereby, better learners will be built by using both labeled and unlabeled data, than using each one alone. In this paper, a novel network traffic data fusion approach based on Fisher and deep auto-encoder (DFA-F-DAE) is proposed to reduce the data dimensions and the complexity of computation. The experimental results show that the DFA-F-DAE improves the generalization ability of the three classification algorithms (J48, back propagation neural network (BPNN), and support vector machine (SVM)) by data dimensionality reduction. We found that the DFA-F-DAE remarkably improves the efficiency of big network traffic classification.

Keywords: big network traffic data; data fusion; Fisher; deep auto-encoder

1. Introduction

Nowadays, to enhance network security, a variety of security devices are used, such as firewall, intrusion detection system (IDS), intrusion prevention system (IPS), antivirus software, security audit, *etc.* Though all kinds of monitoring approaches and reporting mechanisms provide big data for network management personnel, the lack of effective network traffic data fusion has become a stumbling block to solve different issues in network security situation awareness (NSSA) In such circumstances, the research on data fusion as one of the next generation security solutions has enough academic value and comprehensive practical value.

Data fusion in NSSA aims to effectively eliminate the redundancy of big network traffic data by feature extraction, classification, and integration. Thereby network management personnel can realize situational awareness quickly. Therefore, how to build a suitable data fusion algorithm is one of the important issues in NSSA. Feature extraction is the key of the data fusion algorithm because its performance directly affects the result of fusion. The feature extraction, as a preprocessing method to overcome dimension disaster, aims at extracting a few features that can represent the original data from big data by analyzing its internal characteristics. The classic methods include principal components analysis (PCA) [1], linear discriminant analysis (LDA) [2], Fisher score [3], *etc.*

In 2006, the significant technological achievement to effective training tactics for deep architectures [4] came with the unsupervised greedy layer-wise pre-training algorithm that was closed behind supervised fine-tuning. Since then, denoising auto-encoders [5], convolutional neural networks [6], deep belief networks [7], *etc.*, and other deep learning models have been put forward as well. Currently, deep learning theory has been successfully applied to a variety of real-world applications, including face/image recognition, voice search, speech-to-text (transcription), spam filtering (anomaly detection), E-commerce fraud detection, regression, and other machine learning fields.

In this paper, a novel network traffic data fusion approach based on Fisher and deep auto-encoder (DFA-F-DAE) is proposed to reduce the data dimensions and the complexity of computation, and it is helpful for handling big network traffic data validly. The experimental results indicate that, the proposed approach improves the generalization ability of the classification algorithms by data dimensionality reduction. Furthermore, it can reduce the redundancy of big network traffic data. Under the premise of ensuring the classification accuracy, the DFA-F-DAE reduces the time complexity of classification.

The rest of this paper is organized as follows. Section 2 describes related works. Section 3 reviews the concept of Fisher and deep auto-encoder. In Section 4, the data fusion based on Fisher and the deep auto-encoder is proposed. The experimental results and discussion are covered in Section 5. Finally, the conclusion and future work are presented in Section 6.

2. Related Work

Network security issues are more prominent with each passing day, which has become a key research topic which needs to be dealt with urgently [8]. In 1999, Bass proposed the concept of NSSA [9]. Its main goal is to obtain the macro level of information from multiple network security information by extracting, refining, and fusing. Then it can help administrators to deal with various kinds of security problems in the network. Soon after, Bass proposed a framework of intrusion detection based on multi-sensor data fusion, and pointed out that the next generation network management system and intrusion detection system will interact in the unified model. Thus it can fuse the data into information to help the network administrators make decisions. Since the objects of NSSA mostly are data information, the research of data fusion in NSSA [10,11] has gradually become a developmental trend.

Data fusion technology dated from 1970s, it was mainly engaged in the military area. As the technology is developing in a high speed, data fusion technology gradually extended to civilian areas, and has been widely employed in urban mapping [12], forest-related studies [13], oil slick detection and characterization [14], disaster management [15], remote sensing [16] and other fields. Of course, all sorts of data fusion approaches were proposed. Li *et al.* [17] proposed a fusion mechanism MCMR based on trust, which considered historical and time correlation and draws up situation trust awareness rule on historical trust and current data correlation. Papadopoulos *et al.* [18] used a data fusion method to present SIES, a scheme that solves exact SUM queries through a combination of homomorphic encryption and secret sharing. A distributed data fusion technique is provided by Akselrod *et al.* [19] in multi-sensor multi-target tracking. A few examples which introduce Fisher into data fusion are as follows. Zeng *et al.* [20] proposed a sensor fusion framework based adaptive activity recognition and dynamic heterogeneous, and they incorporated it into popular feature transformation algorithms, e.g., marginal Fisher's analysis, and maximum mutual information in the proposed framework. Chen *et al.* [21] introduced the finite mixture of Von Mises-Fisher (VMF) distribution for observations that are invariant to actions of a spherical symmetry group. The approach reduced the computation time by a factor of 2. Yong Wang [3] described an interpolation family that generalizes the Fisher scoring method and proposed a general Monte Carlo approach in dimensionality reduction.

Recently, deep learning has attracted wide attention again since the efficient layer-wise unsupervised learning strategy is proposed to retrain this kind of deep architecture. Deep learning focuses on the deep structure of neural networks, with the purpose of realizing a machine which has cognitive capabilities similar to those of the human brains. In 2006, Hinton *et al.* proposed deep belief nets (DBN) [4], which were composed of multiple logistic belief neural networks and one restricted Boltzmann machine (RBM). In recent years, deep learning has been successfully applied to various applications, such as dimensionality reduction, object recognition, and natural language processing. For example, Bu *et al.* [22] proposed to fuse the different modality data of 3D shapes into a deep learning framework, which combined intrinsic and extrinsic features to provide complementary information so better discriminability could be reached. It is better to mine the deep correlations of different modalities. Gu *et al.* [23] used the quasi-Newton method, conjugate gradient method and the Levenberg-Marquardt algorithm to improve the traditional BP neural network algorithm, and eventually got converged data, as well as improved traffic flow accuracy. Furthermore, in [24], speech features were used as input into a pre-trained DBN in order to extract BN features, though the DBN hybrid system outperforms the BN system. Although varieties of deep learning algorithms have been applied in the field of data fusion, there are a few studies of auto-encoder algorithms in the data fusion field. Felix *et al.* [25] investigated blind feature space de-reverberation and deep recurrent de-noising auto-encoders (DAE) in an early fusion scheme. Then they proposed early feature level fusion with model-based spectral de-reverberation and showed that this further improves performance. A sparse auto encoder (SAE) has proven to be an effective way for dimension reduction and data reconstruction in practices [26].

3. Preliminaries

3.1. Fisher Score

Classical Fisher Score is a well-known method to establish a linear transformation that maximizes the ratio of between-class scatter to average within-class scatter in the lower-dimensional space. The Fisher Score [27] is a classical algorithm widely engaged in statistics, pattern recognition, and machine learning. In statistical pattern recognition, the Fisher Score is used to reduce the dimension of a given statistical model, by searching for a transform. F is the class-to-class variation of the detected signal divided by the sum of the within-class variations of the signal, and F is defined as follows [28].

$$F = \frac{\sigma_{between}}{\sigma_{within}} \tag{1}$$

where $\sigma_{between}$ is the class-to-class variation, and σ_{within} is the within-class variation.

$$\sigma_{between} = \sum \frac{(\bar{x}_i - \bar{x})n_i}{(k-1)} \tag{2}$$

where n_i is the number of measurements in the ith class, $\bar{x}_i$ is the mean of the ith class, $\bar{x}$ is the overall mean, and k is the number of classes.

$$\sigma_{within} = \frac{\sum \left(\sum (\bar{x}_{ij} - \bar{x})^2\right) - (\sum (\bar{x}_i - \bar{x})n_i)}{(N-k)} \tag{3}$$

where $\bar{x}_{ij}$ is the ith measurement of the jth class, and N is the total number of sample profiles.

3.2. Deep Auto-Encoder

An auto-encoder (AE) is a professional neural network composed of three layers, including an input layer, hidden layer (because its values are not observed in the training set), and an output layer. The output of the second layer acts as a compact representation or "code" for the input data. The function of AE is much like principal component analysis (PCA) but AE works in a non-linear fashion. Auto-encoders are unsupervised learning algorithms that attempt to reconstruct visible layer data in the reconstruction layer. The idea of AE was extended to several other variants such as deep AE [29], sparse AE, denoising AE [5] and contractive AE [30]. All of these ideas have been formalized and successfully applied to various applications, and have even taken an important part of deep learning. An AE is shown in Figure 1.

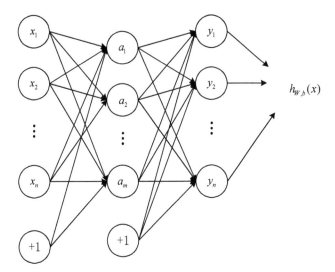

Figure 1. The architecture of auto-encoder.

Suppose a set of unlabeled training samples $x = (x_1, x_2, \cdots, x_i)$, $i \in (1, 2, \cdots, n)$, where $x_i \in \Re^n$. AE neural network is an unsupervised learning algorithm that utilizes backpropagation, setting the target values to be equal to the inputs. This means $y_i = x_i$. AE attempts to learn a function $h_{W,b}(x) \approx x$, i.e., it is attempting to learn an approximation to the identity function. In Figure 1, the circles labeled "+1" are called bias units, and correspond to the intercept term.

In our scheme, we choose $f(\bullet)$ to be the sigmoid function:

$$f(z) = \frac{1}{1 + \exp(-z)} \tag{4}$$

l denotes the number of layers in our network. $W_{ij}^{(l)}$ denotes the parameter (or weight) associated with the connection between unit j in layer l, and unit i in layer $l + 1$. Also, $b_i^{(l)}$ is the bias associated with unit i in layer $l + 1$. s_l denotes the number of nodes in layer l (not counting the bias unit).

$a_i^{(l)}$ denotes the activation (meaning output value) of unit i in layer l. For $l = 1$, we also make use of $a_i^{(1)} = x_i$ to denote the ith input. Given a fixed setting of the parameters (W, b), our neural network defines a hypothesis $h_{W,b}(x)$ that outputs a real number. Particularly, the calculation is given by:

$$h_{W,b}(x) = a_i^{(l+1)} = f(z_i^{(l)}) = f(\sum_{j=1}^{m} W_{ji}^l + b_j^l) \tag{5}$$

where m is the number of hidden nodes.

Suppose that given a fixed training set of n training examples. The definition of the overall cost function is as follows:

$$J(W, b) = [\frac{1}{n} \sum_{i=1}^{n} (\frac{1}{2} || h_{W,b}(x_i) - y_i ||^2)] + \frac{\lambda}{2} \sum_{k=1}^{l-1} \sum_{i=1}^{s_l} \sum_{j=1}^{s_l+1} \left(W_{ji}^{(l)} \right)^2 \tag{6}$$

where λ is weight decay parameter. The first term in the definition of $J(W,b)$ is an average sum-of-squares error term. The second term is a regularization term (also called a weight decay term) that tends to decrease the magnitude of the weights, and helps to prevent overfitting.

3.3. Fine-Tune

In order to minimize $J(W,b)$ according to the function of W and b, we initialized every parameter $W_{ij}^{(1)}$ and every $b_i^{(1)}$ to a small random value closed to 0. Then we use a Fine-tune algorithm, for instance, batch gradient descent (BGD). Gradient descent is likely to lead to local optima because $J(W,b)$ is a non-convex function. However, gradient descent usually works quite well in practice. Eventually, noted that it is important to initialize the parameters randomly, rather than to all 0's. The random initialization avoids symmetry breaking.

One iteration of gradient descent updates the parameters $W^{(l)}$, $b^{(l)}$ as follows:

Firstly, compute the error term:

$$\delta^{(l)} = ((W^{(l)})^T \delta^{(l+1)}) f'(z^{(l)}) \tag{7}$$

Secondly, compute the desired partial derivatives:

$$\nabla_{W^{(l)}} J(W,b) = \delta^{(l+1)} (a^{(l)})^T \tag{8}$$

$$\nabla_{b^{(l)}} J(W,b) = \delta^{(l+1)} \tag{9}$$

Thirdly, update $\Delta W^{(l)}$, $\Delta b^{(l)}$:

$$\Delta W^{(l)} := \Delta W^{(l)} + \nabla_{W^{(l)}} J(W,b) \tag{10}$$

$$\Delta b^{(l)} := \Delta b^{(l)} + \nabla_{b^{(l)}} J(W,b) \tag{11}$$

Finally, reset $W^{(l)}$, $b^{(l)}$:

$$W^{(l)} = W^{(l)} - \alpha[(\frac{1}{m}\Delta W^{(l)} + \lambda W^{(l)})] \tag{12}$$

$$b^{(l)} = b^{(l)} - \alpha[\frac{1}{m}\Delta b^{(l)}] \tag{13}$$

where α is the learning rate.

4. Data Fusion Approach Based on Fisher and Deep Auto-Encoder (DFA-F-DAE)

The machine-learning methods generally are divided into two categories: supervised and unsupervised. In the supervised methods, the training data is fully labeled and the goal is to find a mapping from input features to output classes. On the contrary, unsupervised methods devote itself to discovering patterns in unlabeled data such that the traffic with similar characteristics is grouped without any prior guidance from class labels. The unsupervised methods need to be further transformed into a classifier for the online classifying stage. In general, the supervised methods are more precise than the unsupervised. Instead, unsupervised methods have some significant advantages such as the elimination of requirements for fully labeled training data sets and the ability to discover hidden classes that might represent unknown applications. Furthermore, unlabeled data is not only cheap but also requires experts and special devices. It is not practical to use the traditional feature extraction method to deal with it. Therefore, in this paper, combined the robustness of traditional feature extraction method (Fisher) with the unsupervised learning advantages of deep auto-encoder, we propose a novel network traffic data fusion approach. In particular, Fisher score, as a high-efficiency filter-based supervised feature selection method, according to the feature selection criteria of the minimum intra-cluster distance and the maximum inter-cluster distance, evaluates and sorts the features by the internal properties of single feature. The architecture of DFA-F-DAE is shown in Figure 2.

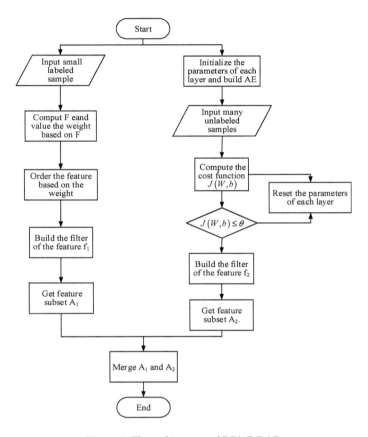

Figure 2. The architecture of DFA-F-DAE.

The DFA-F-DAE aims to fuse network traffic data by two approaches (Fisher and DAE). The details are below.

Fisher:

  I Input small labeled set sample.

  II Use the Formula (1) to compute F and value the weight based on F.

  III Order the feature based on the weight.

  IV Build the filter of the feature f_1 and get feature subset A_1.

DAE:

  I Initialize the parameters of each layer and build the model of AE.

  II Input a large number of unlabeled samples.

  III Set up the threshold value θ, then compute the cost function according to Formula (6).

  IV If $J(W,b) \leqslant \theta$, the process continues. However, if $J(W,b) > \theta$, reset the parameters of each layer until $J(W,b) \leqslant \theta$.

  V Build the filter of the feature f_2 and get feature subset A_2.

In the end:

Merge A_1 and A_2.

5. The Experiment Design and the Result Analysis

Below we present the datasets, experimental environment, and experimental results. The classifier is used in our experiments for the evaluation criteria.

5.1. Dataset

The 1999 DARPA IDS data set [31], or KDD99 for short, is well known as standard network security dataset, which was collected at MIT Lincoln Labs. The attacks types were divided into four categories: (1) Denial-Of-Service (DOS): Denial of service; (2) Surveillance or Probe (Probe): Surveillance and other probing; (3) User to Root (U2R): unauthorized access to local super user (root) privileges; (4) Remote to Local (R2L): unauthorized access from a remote machine. The experiment used repeated sampling to randomly extract 10,000 flows from KDD99 as train-set. Besides, the test-set contains of 500,000 flows. Since the Normal type is easy to be mistaken, we increased the proportion of Normal type in the test-set, and the other types are randomly selected. The composition of data set is shown in Table 1.

Table 1. The composition of data set.

Attacks Types	Train-Set		Test-Set	
	Number	Percentage	Number	Percentage
Normal (0)	2146	21.46%	348,413	69.6826%
Probe (1)	2092	20.92%	19,395	3.879%
DOS (2)	5164	51.64%	131,605	26.321%
U2R (3)	25	0.25%	25	0.005%
R2L (4)	573	5.73%	562	0.1124%

5.2. Experimental Environment

Experimental environment: Matlab version 8.0.0 (The MathWorks Inc., Natick, MA, USA) and Weka version 3.7.13 (University of Waikato, Waikato, New Zealand) were used as the tools in data processing and analysis in the experiments. The configuration information of node is as shown in Table 2.

Table 2. Node configuration information.

Information	
CPU	Intel i7-3770@ 3.40 GHz
Memory	16 GB
Hard Drive	256 G SSD
Operating System	Windows 7 64-bit
Java Environment	JDK 1.7.0
Matlab	version 8.0.0
Weka	version 3.7.13

5.3. Experimental Results

In order to verify the validity of the proposed DFA-F-DAE, our experimental evaluation considers two standards of classification: one is classification accuracy which symbolizes the effect of classification, while another is classification time which symbolizes the efficiency of classification.

5.3.1. Classification Accuracy under Different Dimensionalities

In order to choose proper dimensionalities by the DFA-F-DAE, we measure the performance of three classification algorithms (J48, BPNN, and SVM) under different dimensionalities. Matlab 8.0.0

and Weka 3.7.13 were used as the tools in data processing and analysis. The classification accuracy under different dimensionalities (J48, BPNN, and SVM) is described in Figure 3.

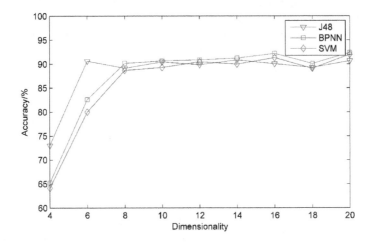

Figure 3. The classification accuracy under different dimensionalities.

It is clear that with the increasing of the number of dimensionalities, the classification accuracy performs better and better, and all the curves tend to be stable after eight dimensionalities. In addition, undesired accuracy is exhibited under smaller dimensionalities, which means that one cannot reduce the dimension infinitely. What is more, all the algorithms (J48, BPNN, and SVM) perform well under more than eight dimensionalities. So the result indicates that the DFA-F-DAE improves the generalization ability of the three algorithms by data dimensionality reduction.

5.3.2. Classification Time

For proving the effectiveness of the proposed DFA-F-DAE in terms of classification efficiency, we apply it in big network traffic data classification. The experiment compared classification times of three algorithms, which are respectively J48, BPNN, and SVM. Table 3 describes the classification time for different scale sets, which the test set increases by a factor of 1/2/3/4/5, and classification time contains of the time before fusing (B-time) and the time after fusing (A-time).

Table 3. The comparison of classification time.

Algorithm		J48	BPNN	SVM
500,000	B-time	7.8 s	43.23 s	51.04 s
	A-time	2.71 s	3.42 s	2.73 s
1,000,000	B-time	15.68 s	86.32 s	104.47 s
	A-time	5.12 s	6.91 s	5.75 s
1,500,000	B-time	24.96 s	130.48 s	158.81 s
	A-time	7.86 s	10.08 s	7.98 s
2,000,000	B-time	30.73 s	169.65 s	214.39 s
	A-time	10.47 s	14.12 s	10.78 s
2,500,000	B-time	39.83 s	217.42 s	256.76 s
	A-time	13.81 s	17.46 s	15.52 s
3,000,000	B-time	47.9 s	263.03 s	319.53 s
	A-time	16.58 s	20.41 s	18.41 s

From Table 3, it can be seen that the classification times of three algorithms after data fusion all show a sharp decline, when compare the classification times before data fusion. This is because DFA-F-DAE reduces the dimensionalities, furthermore reduces the time complexity of classification. Note that classification time of BPNN and SVM decreased more severely than that of J48, since that the dimensionalities of the test-set have a great influence on the nonlinear computation, whereas BPNN and SVM need a large number of nonlinear computation. Obviously, the DFA-F-DAE remarkably improves the efficiency of big network traffic classification.

6. Conclusions

In recent years, a few methods for data fusion have been proposed by utilized the machine learning approach, such as Dempster–Shafer (D-S), principal components analysis (PCA), *etc.* Although these methods have shown their promising potential and robustness, there are still several challenges such as the curse of dimensionality because datasets are often of high dimension. The architecture of DFA-F-DAE has been proven useful to overcome this drawback that how to reduce dimensionality and generalization error. The experimental study shows that the proposed architecture outperforms traditional methods in terms of the classification time and classification accuracy. Our future work is studying the influence of DFA-F-DAE on the classification results, which is an interesting research topic is to realize the data fusion of big data by MapReduce.

Acknowledgments: This work is supported by the National Natural Science Foundation of China (61163058 and 61363006), Guangxi Key Laboratory of Trusted Software (No. KX201306), and Guangxi Colleges and Universities Key Laboratory of Cloud Computing and Complex Systems (No. 14104).

Author Contributions: The work presented here was a collaboration of all the authors. All authors contributed to designing the methods and experiments. Deyan Kong performed the experiments. Xiaoling Tao, Yi Wei, and Yong Wang analyzed the data and interpreted the results. Xiaoling Tao and Yi Wei wrote the paper. All authors have read and approved the final manuscript.

Conflicts of Interest: The authors declare no conflict of interest.

References

1.   Li, X.; Pang, Y.; Yuan, Y. L1-Norm-Based 2DPCA. *IEEE Trans. Syst. Man Cybern.* **2010**, *40*, 1170–1175.
2.   Lu, G.; Zou, J.; Wang, Y. Incremental complete LDA for face recognition. *Pattern Recognit.* **2012**, *45*, 2510–2521. [CrossRef]
3.   Wang, Y. Fisher scoring: An interpolation family and its Monte Carlo implementations. *Comput. Stat. Data Anal.* **2010**, *54*, 1744–1755. [CrossRef]
4.   Hinton, G.E.; Salakhutdinov, R.R. Reducing the dimensionality of data with neural networks. *Science* **2006**, *313*, 504–507. [CrossRef] [PubMed]
5.   Wang, D.; Tan, X. Label-Denoising Auto-encoder for Classification with Inaccurate Supervision Information. In Proceedings of the Pattern Recognition (ICPR), Stockholm, Sweden, 24–28 August 2014; pp. 3648–3653.
6.   Baccouche, M.; Mamalet, F.; Wolf, C.; Garcia, C.; Baskurt, A. Sequential Deep Learning for Human Action Recognition. In *Human Behavior Understanding*; Springer: Berlin/Heidelberg, Germany, 2011; Volume 7065, pp. 29–39.
7.   Tamilselvan, P.; Wang, Y.; Wang, P. Deep Belief Network Based State Classification for Structural Health Diagnosis. In Proceedings of the Aerospace Conference, Big Sky, MT, USA, 3–10 March 2012; pp. 1–11.
8.   Liu, Z.; Yang, S. A Hybrid Intelligent Optimization Algorithm to Assess the NSS Based on FNN Trained by HPS. *J. Netw.* **2010**, *5*, 1076–1083. [CrossRef]
9.   Tim, B. Intrusion detection systems and multi-sensor data fusion: Creating cyberspace situational awareness. *Commun. ACM* **2000**, *43*, 99–105.
10. Kokar, M.; Endsley, M. Situation awareness and cognitive modeling. *IEEE Intell. Syst.* **2012**, *27*, 91–96. [CrossRef]
11. Parvar, H.; Fesharaki, M.; Moshiri, B. Shared Situation Awareness System Architecture for Network Centric Environment Decision Making. In Proceedings of the Second International Conference on Computer and Network Technology (ICCNT), Bangkok, Thailand, 23–25 April 2010; pp. 372–376.

12. Gamba, P. Human settlements: A global challenge for EO data processing and interpretation. *Proc. IEEE* **2013**, *101*, 570–581. [CrossRef]

13. Delalieux, S.; Zarco-Tejada, P.J.; Tits, L.; Jimenez-Bello, M.A.; Intrigliolo, D.S.; Somers, B. Unmixing-based fusion of hyperspatial and hyperspectral airborne imagery for early detection of vegetation stress. *Sel. Top. Appl. Earth Obs. Remote Sen.* **2014**, *7*, 2571–2582. [CrossRef]

14. Fingas, M.; Brown, C. Review of oil spill remote sensing. *Mar. Pollut. Bull.* **2014**, *83*, 9–23. [CrossRef] [PubMed]

15. Dell, A.F.; Gamba, P. Remote sensing and earthquake damage assessment: Experiences, limits, perspectives. *Proc. IEEE* **2012**, *100*, 2876–2890. [CrossRef]

16. Dalla, M.M.; Prasad, S.; Pacifici, F.; Gamba, P.; Chanussot, J.; Benediktsson, J.A. Challenges and opportunities of multimodality and data fusion in remote sensing. *Proc. IEEE* **2015**, *103*, 1585–1601. [CrossRef]

17. Li, F.; Nie, Y.; Liu, F.; Zhu, J.; Zhang, H. Event-centric situation trust data aggregation mechanism in distributed wireless network. *Int. J. Distrib. Sens. Netw.* **2014**, *2014*, 585302. [CrossRef]

18. Papadopoulos, S.; Kiayisa, A.; Papadias, D. Exact in-network aggregation with integrity and confidentiality. *Comput. Inf. Syst.* **2012**, *24*, 1760–1773. [CrossRef]

19. Akselrod, D.; Sinha, A.; Kirubarajan, T. Information flow control for collaborative distributed data fusion and multisensory multitarget tracking. *IEEE Syst. Man Cybern. Soc.* **2012**, *42*, 501–517. [CrossRef]

20. Zeng, M.; Wang, X.; Nguyen, L.T.; Mengshoel, O.J.; Zhang, J. Adaptive Activity Recognition with Dynamic Heterogeneous Sensor Fusion. In Proceedings of the 6th International Conference on Mobile Computing, Applications and Services (MobiCASE), Austin, TX, USA, 6–7 November 2014; pp. 189–196.

21. Chen, Y.; Wei, D.; Neastadt, G.; DeGraef, M.; Simmons, J.; Hero, A. Statistical Estimation and Clustering of Group-Invariant Orientation Parameters. In Proceedings of the 18th International Conference on Information Fusion (Fusion), Washington, DC, USA, 6–9 July 2015; pp. 719–726.

22. Bu, S.; Cheng, S.; Liu, Z.; Han, J. Multimodal feature fusion for 3D shape recognition and retrieval. *IEEE MultiMed.* **2014**, *21*, 38–46. [CrossRef]

23. Gu, Y.; Wang, X.; Xu, J. Traffic data fusion research based on numerical optimization BP neural network. *Appl. Mech. Mater.* **2014**, *513–517*, 1081–1087. [CrossRef]

24. Yu, D.; Seltzer, M.L. Improved bottleneck features using pretrained deep neural networks. *Interspeech* **2011**, *237*, 234–240.

25. Felix, W.; Shigetaka, W.; Yuuki, T.; Schuller, B. Deep Recurrent De-noising Auto-encoder and Blind De-Reverberation for Reverberated Speech Recognition. In Proceedings of the IEEE International Conference on Acoustics, Speech and Signal Processing (ICASSP), Florence, Italy, 4–9 May 2014; pp. 4623–4627.

26. Coates, A.; Ng, A.Y.; Lee, H. An analysis of single-layer networks in unsupervised feature learning. *J. Mach. Learn. Res.* **2011**, *15*, 215–223.

27. Chen, B.; Wang, S.; Jiao, L.; Stolkin, R.; Liu, H. A three-component Fisher-based feature weighting method for supervised PolSAR image classification. *Geosci. Remote Sens. Lett.* **2015**, *12*, 731–735. [CrossRef]

28. Marney, L.C.; Siegler, W.C.; Parsons, B.A. Tile-based Fisher-ratio software for improved feature selection analysis of comprehensive two-dimensional gas chromatography–time-of-flight mass spectrometry data. *Talanta* **2013**, *115*, 887–895. [CrossRef] [PubMed]

29. Lange, S.; Riedmiller, M. Deep Auto-Encoder Neural Networks in Reinforcement Learning. In Proceedings of the 2010 International Joint Conference on Neural Networks (IJCNN 2010), Barcelona, Spain, 18–23 July 2010; pp. 1–8.

30. Muller, X.; Glorot, X.; Bengio, Y.; Rifai, S.; Vincent, P. Contractive auto-encoders: Explicit invariance during feature extraction. In Proceedings of the 28th International Conference on Machine Learning (ICML-11), Bellevue, WA, USA, 28 June–2 July 2011; pp. 833–840.

31. KDD Cup 1999 Data. Available online: http://kdd.ics.uci.edu/databases/kddcup99/kddcup99.html (accessed on 11 October 2015).

10

An Approach to the Match between Experts and Users in a Fuzzy Linguistic Environment

Ming Li * and Mengyue Yuan

School of Business Administration, China University of Petroleum, Beijing 102249, China; moriayuan@126.com
* Correspondence: limingzyq@cup.edu.cn

Academic Editor: Willy Susilo

Abstract: Knowledge management systems are widely used to manage the knowledge in organizations. Consulting experts is an effective way to utilize tacit knowledge. The paper aims to optimize the match between users and experts to improve the efficiency of tacit knowledge-sharing. Firstly, expertise, trust and feedback are defined to characterize the preference of users for experts. Meanwhile, factors including trust, relationship and knowledge distance are defined to characterize the preference of experts for users. Then, a new method for the measurement of satisfaction based on the principle of axiomatic design is proposed. Afterwards, in order to maximize the satisfaction of both experts and users, the optimization model is constructed and the optimal solution is shown in the matching results. The evaluation results show the approach is feasible and performs well. The approach provides new insights for research on tacit knowledge-sharing. It can be applied as a tool to match experts with users in the development of knowledge management systems. The fuzzy linguistic method facilitates the expression of opinions, and as a result, the users-system interaction is improved.

Keywords: fuzzy linguistic method; tacit knowledge; experts matching; knowledge management systems

1. Introduction

In today's highly competitive environment, knowledge is a kind of strategic resource for organizations [1,2]. It can enhance an organization's advantage in responding to new and unusual situations. The knowledge management system (KMS) has been widely implemented to serve the needs of managing the valuable knowledge in organizations [2,3].

Tacit knowledge such as know-how and experience exists in experts' minds. It is subjective and difficult to formalize. Tacit knowledge is more important to a produce competitive advantage since it is harder to imitate than explicit knowledge [4–6]. Consulting experts is an efficient way to share tacit knowledge [7–10].

Many approaches have been proposed to help consult experts. For example, expert profiles are constructed manually or automatically, and are stored in the knowledge repository by systems administrators or system users [11–13]. Users search for a suitable expert for help by categories, passively. For a specific category, the list of information about experts is provided to users. In order to ease the burden of browsing categories one by one, the list is provided to users actively based on their needs [14–17]. Then they can choose the expert from the list for help manually.

These approaches are based on the assumption that experts are willing to help any person without discrimination. Experts' preferences are ignored. Moreover, these approaches only focus on knowledge needs and other preferences of users are neglected. In fact, consulting experts is a communication process between experts and users. Tacit knowledge is transferred by face-to-face interactions. Many factors affect knowledge-sharing in the communication. Besides expertise, users care about trust [18–20] and feedback [18]. Factors including trust [18–20], relationship [21] and knowledge distance [18] influence the willingness of experts to share their knowledge [18,21].

Satisfying both experts and users from types of preferences facilitates the communication and promotes knowledge-sharing [18]. Being instructed by favorable experts can result in a higher satisfaction of users. Meanwhile, experts are glad to help preferred users. Therefore, the first problem arises as how to characterize preferences of both experts and users comprehensively. Meanwhile, a method is required for making the global optimum match between experts and users. Intuitively, choosing done by users and experts themselves directly may derive the match. However, the user who is satisfied with the expert may not be preferred by the chosen expert, and *vice versa*. Moreover, the number of users that one expert can help is restricted because of limited time and spirit. In the condition, only a few matches can be made. Other experts and users are excluded from the match. Therefore, there needs to be a matching method for satisfying both users and experts as much as possible to derive the maximum satisfaction globally.

In order to resolve the above problems, in this paper, an approach to the match between experts and users in a fuzzy linguistic environment is proposed. Factors including expertise, trust, relationship, knowledge distance and feedback are defined in the fuzzy linguistic environment. Then methods for the measurement of satisfaction and for the match between experts and users are constructed. The remainder of this paper is organized as follows. In the next section, related works are reviewed. In Section 3, we present the approach to matching between experts and users. Then, in Section 4, the evaluation of the proposed approach is given. Finally, conclusions are presented.

2. Related Works

2.1. Tacit Knowledge-Sharing

Knowledge is divided into tacit knowledge and explicit knowledge [1]. Explicit knowledge refers to knowledge that can be codified. On the contrary, knowledge which is difficult to codify is called tacit knowledge. Since tacit knowledge resides in owners' brains, it is often shared and transferred via instruction or face-to-face interactions [2]. Information technologies for supporting tacit knowledge-sharing focus on assisting users in finding appropriate experts and facilitating communications between them.

In the initial stage, the expert database is built, in which the expert profile is constructed and stored. Each expert belongs to a category. Users who are in need of help search related categories for appropriate experts. The focus of research in the field is on profiling experts. In most previous research [11,12], experts have been profiled manually by system administrators or system users. Afterwards, the automatic expert profiling method based on registered documents is proposed [13]. However, it will fail when there are no or few documents, especially in the early stage of the implementation of knowledge management systems.

With the increasing complexity of tasks, categories develop rapidly. At the same time, more and more tasks are involved in multiple categories. It consumes more time to find the appropriate experts by searching categories. In order to ease the burden of finding experts passively, researchers propose methods for providing a list of experts to users actively according to the needs of users [14–17]. Then users can choose the expert from the list for help manually. In most studies, the needs of users only refer to knowledge needs. In fact, besides knowledge needs, users care about many other factors. Moreover, these studies are based on the assumption that experts are willing to help users without discrimination. However, tacit knowledge is transferred through a mutual communication process and it resides in experts' brains [18,20]. Experts' satisfaction is more important in tacit knowledge-sharing. However, in the previous research, experts' preferences have been ignored. Considering these limitations, it is ideal to match users with experts by integrating both experts' and users' preferences.

2.2. Fuzzy Linguistic Method

The fuzzy linguistic method is used to handle linguistic information [22]. Linguistic terms are often represented by fuzzy numbers such as triangular and trapezoidal fuzzy numbers [23,24].

A triangular fuzzy number is a special case of a trapezoidal fuzzy number. When the two vertexes of the trapezoidal fuzzy number have the same value, the trapezoidal fuzzy number becomes a triangular fuzzy number [24]. It can be used to cope with more general situations. In the following, the trapezoidal fuzzy number and corresponding operators are reviewed [25].

A trapezoidal fuzzy number can be defined as $\tilde{A} = (a, b, c, d)$, where $a \leqslant b \leqslant c \leqslant d$. The corresponding membership function $\mu_{\tilde{A}}$ of $\tilde{A}$ is shown in Figure 1,

$$\mu_{\tilde{A}} = \begin{cases} \frac{x-a}{b-a} & (a \leqslant x \leqslant b) \\ 1 & (b \leqslant x \leqslant c) \\ \frac{d-x}{d-c} & (c \leqslant x \leqslant d) \end{cases} \tag{1}$$

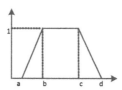

Figure 1. A trapezoidal fuzzy number.

Let $\tilde{A}$ and $\tilde{B}$ be two positive trapezoidal fuzzy numbers parameterized by (a_1, b_1, c_1, d_1) and (a_2, b_2, c_2, d_2). Some algebraic operations of trapezoidal fuzzy numbers $\tilde{A}$ and $\tilde{B}$ can be expressed as follows [26,27].

Definition 1. Addition operator

$$\tilde{A} \oplus \tilde{B} = (a_1, b_1, c_1, d_1) + (a_2, b_2, c_2, d_2) = (a_1 + a_2, b_1 + b_2, c_1 + c_2, d_1 + d_2) \tag{2}$$

Definition 2. Subtraction operator

$$\tilde{A} \ominus \tilde{B} = (a_1, b_1, c_1, d_1) - (a_2, b_2, c_2, d_2) = (a_1 - a_2, b_1 - b_2, c_1 - c_2, d_1 - d_2) \tag{3}$$

Definition 3. Multiplication operator

$$\tilde{A} \otimes \tilde{B} = (a_1, b_1, c_1, d_1) \otimes (a_2, b_2, c_2, d_2) = (a_1 a_2, b_1 b_2, c_1 c_2, d_1 d_2) \tag{4}$$

Definition 4. Division operator

$$\tilde{A}/\tilde{B} = (a_1, b_1, c_1, d_1) / (a_2, b_2, c_2, d_2) = (a_1/a_2, b_1/b_2, c_1/c_2, d_1/d_2) \tag{5}$$

Definition 5. Multiplication operator of real number k and a trapezoidal fuzzy number

$$k\tilde{A} = (ka_1, kb_1, kc_1, kd_1) \tag{6}$$

Definition 6. Reciprocal operator

$$(\tilde{A})^{-1} = (1/d_1, 1/c_1, 1/b_1, 1/a_1) \tag{7}$$

Definition 7. Defuzzification operator

$$N = D(\tilde{A}) = \frac{(a_1 + 2b_1 + 2c_1 + d_1)}{6} \tag{8}$$

where N is the defuzzified crisp value.

2.3. Axiomatic Design

Axiomatic design (AD) principles are proposed to provide the systematic scientific basis for designers in the area of product design and software design [28,29]. The advantage of AD principles is that not only the best alternative but also the most appropriate alternative can be selected.

Information axiom is one of concepts in AD principles. The principle states that the alternative that has the smallest information content is deemed the best design. The information axiom provides a way to select appropriate alternatives. It is symbolized by the information content which refers to the probability of reaching design goals. Information content (I) is defined as [28–31]

$$I = \log_2 \frac{1}{p} \tag{9}$$

where p is the probability of meeting a specific function requirement.

When there is more than one function requirement, the information content can be derived by summing all probabilities,

$$I = \sum_{i=1}^{t} I_i = -\log_2 \left(\prod_{i=1}^{t} p_i \right) \tag{10}$$

The probability of meeting the function requirement is given by the design range, the system range and the common area. Design range refers to the object of the design and the system range is the capacity that the system achieves. The common area is the intersection area of the design range and the system range, which is just the acceptable solution, as is shown in Figure 2 [28].

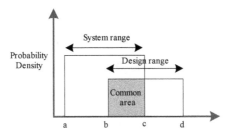

Figure 2. Design range, system range and common area of the function requirement.

Therefore, the information content I can be defined as [28]

$$I = \log_2 \frac{1}{p} = \log_2 \frac{1}{\frac{\text{Common range}}{\text{System range}}} = \log_2 \frac{\text{System range}}{\text{Common range}} \tag{11}$$

3. Approach to the Match between Experts and Users

3.1. Establishing Criteria for the Match

The establishment of the proper criteria is the basis of the match between users and experts. For evaluating users, trust, relationship and knowledge distance are considered. Meanwhile, expertise, trust and feedback are used to evaluate experts. In the following, the detailed definitions of the criteria are given.

3.1.1. Expertise

As a consulting expert is there to learn from, his expertise with regard to knowledge needs of users is the first criterion for users to evaluate experts.

The expert is always involved in multiple knowledge areas with different expertise levels. The predefined expertise level of expert E_j in knowledge area K_j is denoted as $\widetilde{VE}_{ji}$.

In order to identify knowledge needs, user U_i is required to rate the relevance of completed tasks to knowledge needs. Based on linguistic evaluations, the relevant degree $\widetilde{VN}_{ik}$ of user U_i's knowledge needs to the knowledge area K_k can be obtained by

$$\widetilde{VN}_{ik} = \frac{\sum_{T_t \in STS_i} \tilde{\epsilon}_{ti} \times \widetilde{VT}_{tk}}{\sum_{T_t \in STS_i} \tilde{\epsilon}_{ti}} \tag{12}$$

where STS_i is the set of retrieved similar completed tasks, $\tilde{\epsilon}_{ti}$ is the rating of completed task T_t to the knowledge needs of user U_i on relevance, and $\widetilde{VT}_{tk}$ is the belonging degree of task T_t to the knowledge area K_k.

The degree $\widetilde{VM}_{ij}$ of the match of the expertise between expert E_j and the knowledge needs of user U_i is determined by

$$\widetilde{VM}_{ij} = \frac{\sum_{k=1}^{n} \left(\widetilde{VP}_{ik} \times \widetilde{VN}_{jk} \right)}{\sum_{k=1}^{n} \left(\widetilde{VN}_{jk} \right)} \tag{13}$$

where n is the number of knowledge areas, and $\widetilde{VP}_{jk}$ is the expertise level of expert E_j in knowledge area K_k.

3.1.2. Trust

Trust is people's subject belief in the other people, which includes ambiguity and subjectivity [18]. In the evaluation of experts, trust represents the subject belief in the expert which is generated from authority and reputation. When evaluating users, trust means the expert has confidence in the user that the user will not misuse knowledge and take unjust credit for it.

Users and experts are allowed to rate trust in each other with linguistic terms directly. When there are unrated experts and users, for the unrated trust people, the max-min aggregation method [32] among shorted paths is extended to propagate indirect trust in others.

Firstly, the strength of the trust path from expert E_j to user U_i is obtained through

$$\widetilde{ST}_{j,t} = \max_{u_k \in OTS(e_j)} [min\{\tilde{\rho}_{j,k}, \widetilde{ST}_{k,t}\}] \tag{14}$$

where $OTS(u_i)$ is the set of users whom user U_i directly trusts, and $\tilde{\rho}_{j,k}$ is the direct linguistic rating of user U_k given by expert E_j on trust.

Then, among the inlink-neighbor of U_i, the user who is trusted most by U_i can be derived by

$$U_{t*} = \arg \max_{u_t \in ITS(u_i)} \widetilde{ST}_{j,t} \tag{15}$$

where $ITS(u_i)$ is the set of users who trust user U_i.

Afterwards, expert E_j's indirect trust $\tilde{T}_{j,i}$ in user U_i is estimated by

$$\tilde{T}_{j,i} = min \left\{ \widetilde{ST}_{j,t*}^{*}, \tilde{\omega}_{t*,i} \right\} \tag{16}$$

where $\tilde{\omega}_{t*,i}$ is the direct linguistic rating of user U_i given by user U_{t*}.

In the same way, user U_i's indirect trust $\tilde{T}_{i,j}$ in expert E_j can be estimated by

$$\tilde{T}_{i,j} = min \left\{ \widetilde{ST}_{i,t*}^{*}, \tilde{\omega}_{t*,j} \right\} \tag{17}$$

$$E_{t*} = \arg \max_{e_t \in ITS(e_j)} \widetilde{ST}_{i,t} \tag{18}$$

$$\widetilde{ST}_{i,t} = \max_{e_k \in OTS(u_i)} [min\{\tilde{\rho}_{i,k}, \widetilde{ST}_{k,t}\}] \tag{19}$$

where $\tilde{\omega}_{t*,j}$ is the direct linguistic rating of expert E_j given by expert E_{t*}, $ITS(e_j)$ is the set of experts who trust expert e_j, $OTS(u_i)$ is the set of experts whom user U_i directly trusts, $\tilde{\rho}_{i,k}$ is the direct linguistic rating of expert E_k given by user U_i on trust.

3.1.3. Relationship

In organizations, especially in inter-organizations, there often exist relationships such as cooperative relationships and competitive relationships between experts and users. These relationships determine by expected benefits of knowledge-sharing and influence experts' willingness to share the knowledge [21]. Thus, relationship is selected as the criterion for experts to evaluate users.

Experts are allowed to use linguistic terms to declare the relationship with users or groups. A user may join in more than one group and there probably exist conflicts in relationships of groups that the user belongs to. The relationship $\tilde{R}_{ij}$ of expert E_i with user U_j is aggregated by

$$\tilde{R}_{ij} = \begin{cases} \max_{O_h \in OC_j} \tilde{c}'_{ih}, & \text{if the expert has the generous preference.} \\ \min_{O_h \in OC_j} \tilde{c}'_{ih}, & \text{if the expert has the cautious preference.} \end{cases} \tag{20}$$

where OC_j is the collection of groups that user U_j belongs to, and $\tilde{c}'_{ih}$ is the linguistic declaration of the relationship given by expert E_i to group O_h.

3.1.4. Feedback

Consulting the same expert who was used to ask for help can ease the burden of introducing background information repeatedly, and more personalized help can be given. The feedback of the user denotes whether he is willing to get help from the expert next time. Experts with a higher degree of feedback will be matched with the user in a higher priority.

As an expert may be consulted and rated more than once and the effect decreases as time goes on, by integrating the time factor [33], the aggregated rating $\tilde{F}_{ij}$ of expert E_j on feedback given by user U_i can be derived by

$$\tilde{F}_{ij} = \frac{\sum_{k=1}^{m} \tilde{f}'_{ijk} \times \frac{1}{e^{\tau(t_{now}-t_k)}}}{\sum_{k=1}^{m} \frac{1}{e^{\tau(t_{now}-t_k)}}}, \tag{21}$$

where $\tilde{f}'_{ijk}$ is the linguistic rating given by user U_i to expert E_j at the kth time, t_{now} is the present date, t_k is the date of the rating at the kth time, and τ is a tunable parameter.

3.1.5. Knowledge Distance

The efficiency of consultation will decrease because of the lower knowledge level of recipients. The expert has his own preference for a user with a certain level of knowledge. Thus, knowledge distance is used as the criterion for the expert to evaluate users. It can be derived by calculating the gap between experts' expected knowledge level of users and the real knowledge level of users.

In the aggregation of knowledge distances, the knowledge needs are used as weights. The distance $\tilde{D}_{ij}$ between expert E_i and user U_j is defined by

$$\tilde{D}_{ij} = \sum_{k=1}^{n} distance\left(\widetilde{VE}_{ik}, \widetilde{VU}_{jk}\right) \tilde{w}_{jk} \tag{22}$$

where $\tilde{w}_{jk}$ denotes the weight of the knowledge needs of user U_j in knowledge area K_k, and $\widetilde{VE}_{ik}$ and $\widetilde{VU}_{jk}$ represent expert E_i's expected knowledge level for users and the actual knowledge level of user U_j in knowledge area K_k, respectively.

3.2. *Constructing the Matching Approach*

The architecture of the proposed matching approach is shown in Figure 3. Among the five criteria, only the criterion of trust can be used directly. For the criteria feedback, the direct ratings need to be aggregated along with the rating time. For the criteria expertise, knowledge distance and relationship, values need to be derived from the linguistic ratings with respect to the indirect criteria. These indirect criteria include the relevance of completed tasks to knowledge needs (task relevance), the relationship with users or groups (direct relationship) and the expected expertise level of users (expected level of expertise). In the proposed approach, firstly, besides trust and feedback, users and experts are required to rate each other with respect to the indirect criteria. Then the rating values are processed. Afterwards, based on the processed values, the satisfactions are measured. Finally, the optimization model is constructed to derive the optimal match.

The detail of these modules is presented in the following sections.

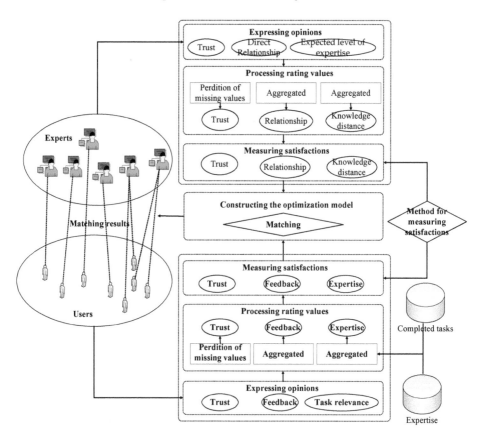

Figure 3. Structure of the matching approach.

Let $E = \{E_1, E_2, \cdots, E_p\}$ and $U = \{U_1, U_2, \cdots, U_q\}$ be collections of experts and users, and $\tilde{W} = \{\tilde{w}_1, \tilde{w}_2, \cdots, \tilde{w}_p\}$ and $\tilde{V} = \{\tilde{v}_1, \tilde{v}_2, \cdots, \tilde{v}_q\}$ be corresponding weights. The criteria $C^e = \{C_1^e = \text{expertise}, C_2^e = \text{trust}, C_3^e = \text{feedback}\}$ are used to evaluate experts. In order to evaluate users, the criteria $C^u = \{C_1^u = \text{trust}, C_2^u = \text{relationship}, C_3^u = \text{knowledge distance}\}$ are taken into account. The predefined profile of expert E_j is $VP_j = \left(\widetilde{vp}_{j1}, \widetilde{vp}_{j2}, \cdots, \widetilde{vp}_{jn}\right)$ and the predefined profile of user U_i is $VU_i = (\widetilde{vu}_{i1}, \widetilde{vu}_{i2}, \cdots, \widetilde{vu}_{in})$. The predefined relevance of completed task T_t to knowledge areas is $VT_t = \left(\widetilde{vt}_{it}, \widetilde{vt}_{it}, \cdots, \widetilde{vt}_{tn}\right)$. The collection of groups that user U_i belongs to is denoted by OC_i. The set of user U_i's retrieved completed tasks is denoted by STS_i.

3.2.1. Expressing Opinions and Processing Rating Values

The weight vector of criteria C^u given by expert E_j is denoted by $\tilde{\zeta}_j = \{\tilde{\zeta}_{j1}, \tilde{\zeta}_{j2}, \tilde{\zeta}_{j3}\}$. The weight vector of criteria C^e given by user U_i is denoted by $\tilde{\eta}_i = \{\tilde{\eta}_{i1}, \tilde{\eta}_{i2}, \tilde{\eta}_{i3}\}$.

Besides the criteria of trust and feedback, experts and users rate each other using linguistic terms with respect to the corresponding indirect criteria. Meanwhile, they are also required to give their opinions on the value of goals.

As for the criterion of expertise, the linguistic rating of completed task T_t to the knowledge needs on relevance given by user U_i is denoted by $\tilde{e}_{ti}$. With Equations (12) and (13), the evaluation value of expert E_j on expertise given by user U_i. can be derived by

$$\widetilde{VE}_{ij} = \frac{\sum_{k=1}^{n}\left(\widetilde{VE}_{ik} \times \frac{\sum_{T_t \in STS_i} \tilde{e}_{ti} \times \widehat{VT}_{tk}}{\sum_{T_t \in STS_i} \tilde{e}_{ti}}\right)}{\frac{\sum_{T_t \in STS_i} \tilde{e}_{ti} \times \widehat{VT}_{tk}}{\sum_{T_t \in STS_i} \tilde{e}_{ti}}} \tag{23}$$

With respect to the criterion of knowledge distance, expert E_j's expected knowledge level of users is denoted by $\widetilde{VE}_{jk}$. With Equation (22), the distance $\tilde{D}_{ji}$ between the expert E_j and the user U_i is derived by

$$\tilde{D}_{ji} = \sum_{k=1}^{n} distance\left(\widetilde{VE}_{jk}, \widetilde{VU}_{ik}\right)\tilde{w}_{ik} \tag{24}$$

Concerning the criterion relationship, the linguistic declaration of the relationship given by expert E_j with group O_h is denoted by $\tilde{c}_{jh}$, and OC_i is the collection of groups that user U_i belongs to. According to Equation (20), the relationship $\tilde{R}_{ji}$ of expert E_j with user U_i is aggregated by

$$\tilde{R}_{ji} = \begin{cases} \max\limits_{O_h \in OC_i} \tilde{c}_{jh}, & \text{if the expert has the generous preference.} \\ \min\limits_{O_h \in OC_i} \tilde{c}_{jh}, & \text{if the expert has the cautious preference.} \end{cases} \tag{25}$$

With regard to the criterion of feedback, the linguistic rating given by user U_i to expert E_j at the kth time is denoted by $\tilde{f}'_{ijk}$. With Equation (21), the evaluation value of expert E_j on feedback can be aggregated by

$$\tilde{F}_{ij} = \frac{\sum_{k=1}^{m} \tilde{f}'_{ijk} \times \frac{1}{e^{\tau(t_{now}-t_k)}}}{\sum_{k=1}^{m} \frac{1}{e^{\tau(t_{now}-t_k)}}} \tag{26}$$

For the criterion of trust, it can be rated directly. If expert E_j does not rate user U_i on trust, then the missing value needs to be propagated with Equations (14)–(16). $ITS(u_i)$ is the set of users who trust user U_i, $OTS(u_i)$ is the set of users whom user U_i directly trusts. The direct linguistic rating of user U_i given by user U_{t*} is represented by $\tilde{\omega}_{t*,i}$, and the direct linguistic rating of user U_k given by expert E_j on trust is denoted by $\tilde{\rho}_{i,k}$. Firstly, with Equation (14), the strength $\widetilde{ST}_{j,t}$ of the trust path from expert E_j to user U_i is obtained. Then the reliable inlink-neighbor of U_i is derived by $U_{t*} = \arg\max\limits_{u_t \in ITS(u_i)} \widetilde{ST}_{j,t}$. Finally, with Equation (16), expert e_j's indirect trust $\tilde{T}_{j,i}$ in user u_i is estimated by $\tilde{T}_{j,i} = \min\left\{\widetilde{ST}^*_{j,t*}, \tilde{\omega}_{t*,i}\right\}$.

3.2.2. Measuring the Satisfaction

Let the value derived from the ratings of user U_i given expert E_j on the criterion C_y^u be represented $\tilde{u}_{jyi} = (a_1, a_2, a_3, a_4)$ and the corresponding value of the goal provided by expert E_j be $\tilde{G}_{jy}^{u*} = (A_1, A_2, A_3, A_4)$. If the value of goals is not provided, the default value is set by

$$\tilde{G}_{jy}^{u*} = \max_i \{\tilde{u}_{jyi}\} \tag{27}$$

As the value of a goal and the rating value are both represented by trapezoidal fuzzy numbers, the common area [24] can be used as the satisfaction area to measure the satisfaction, as is shown in Figure 4.

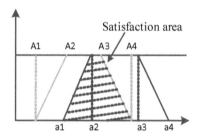

Figure 4. Satisfaction area.

The smaller the gap area is, the less the dissatisfaction is.

The information content of expert E_j's satisfaction with the user U_i with respect to the criterion C_y^u can be defined as

$$S_{jyi} = \log_2 \frac{\text{System Area}}{\text{Satisfaction Area}}$$
$$= \begin{cases} \log_2 \frac{(a_4-a_1+a_3-a_2)\times(A_2-A_1-a_3+a_4)}{(a_4-A_1)^2} & if\ (A_2 \geqslant a_3) \wedge (A_1 < a_4) \\ \log_2 \frac{(a_4-a_1)+(a_3-a_2)}{(a_3-A_2)+(a_4-A_1)} & if\ (A_3 \geqslant a_3 \geqslant A_2) \\ \log_2 \frac{(a_4-a_1)+(a_3-a_2)}{(A_3-a_2)+(A_4-a_1)} & if\ (A_3 \geqslant a_2 \geqslant A_2) \\ \log_2 \frac{(a_4-a_1+a_3-a_2)(a_2-a_1-A_3+A_4)}{(A_4-a_1)^2} & if\ (A_3 \leqslant a_2) \wedge (A_4 > a_1) \end{cases} \tag{28}$$

When there are no common areas, the gap area [31] between the system area and design area represents dissatisfactions, and the gap area can be used as a dissatisfaction area, as is shown in Figure 5. The smaller the dissatisfaction area is, the less the dissatisfaction is.

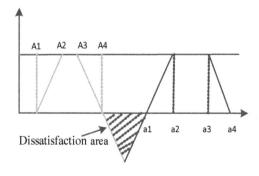

Figure 5. Dissatisfaction area.

Thus, the information content of expert E_j's dissatisfaction with user U_i with respect to criterion C_y^u is defined as

$$\widetilde{DF}_{jyi} = \begin{cases} \log_2 \frac{(a_4-a_1+a_3-a_2)(A_3-A_4-a_2+a_1)}{(a_1-A_4)^2} & if \ (a_1 > A_4) \\ \log_2 \frac{(a_4-a_1+a_3-a_2)(a_3-a_4-A_2+A_1)}{(A_1-a_4)^2} & if \ (a_4 < A_1) \end{cases} \qquad (29)$$

In fact, the opposite number of the information content of dissatisfaction indicates the information content of satisfaction. Thus, the information content of expert E_j's satisfaction with user U_i can be defined as

$$S_{jyi} = \begin{cases} \log_2 \frac{(a_4-a_1+a_3-a_2)\times(A_2-A_1-a_3+a_4)}{(a_4-A_1)^2} & if \ (A_2 \geqslant a_3) \wedge (A_1 < a_4) \\ \log_2 \frac{(a_4-a_1)+(a_3-a_2)}{(a_3-A_2)+(a_4-A_1)} & if \ (A_3 \geqslant a_3 \geqslant A_2) \\ \log_2 \frac{(a_4-a_1)+(a_3-a_2)}{(A_3-a_2)+(A_4-a_1)} & if \ (A_3 \geqslant a_2 \geqslant A_2) \\ \log_2 \frac{(a_4-a_1+a_3-a_2)(a_2-a_1-A_3+A_4)}{(A_4-a_1)^2} & if \ (A_3 \leqslant a_2) \wedge (A_4 > a_1) \\ -\log_2 \frac{(a_4-a_1+a_3-a_2)(A_3-A_4-a_2+a_1)}{(a_1-A_4)^2} & if \ (a_1 > A_4) \\ -\log_2 \frac{(a_4-a_1+a_3-a_2)(a_3-a_4-A_2+A_1)}{(A_1-a_4)^2} & if \ (a_4 < A_1) \\ \log_2 \frac{(a_4-a_1)+(a_3-a_2)}{2\varepsilon} & if \ a_1 = A_4 \ or \ a_4 = A_1 \end{cases} \qquad (30)$$

where ε is the positive value that is far smaller than the minimal common area.

Accordingly, user U_i's satisfaction with expert E_j with respect to each criterion can be measured in the same way.

The overall satisfaction can be measured by summing the information content with regard to each criterion along with the corresponding weights. The overall information content of expert E_j's satisfaction with user U_i can be derived by

$$\alpha_{ji} = D\left(\sum_{y=1}^{m} \widetilde{\zeta}_{jy} \times S_{jyi}\right) \qquad (31)$$

Correspondingly, the overall information content of user U_j's satisfaction with expert E_i can be derived by

$$\beta_{ij} = D\left(\sum_{z=1}^{n} \widetilde{\eta}_{iz} \times S_{izj}\right) \qquad (32)$$

3.2.3. Constructing the Optimization Model

The match is optimal when the sum of the information content of the satisfaction is at its minimum [30]. Let x_{ij} $(i = 1, 2, \cdots, p, j = 1, 2, \cdots, q)$ be a binary variable that denotes whether expert E_j $(j = 1, 2, \cdots, p)$ is matched with user U_i $(i = 1, 2, \cdots, q)$ or not, i.e., if expert E_j $(j = 1, 2, \cdots, p)$ is matched with user U_i $(i = 1, 2, \cdots, q)$, then $x_{ji} = 1$; otherwise, $x_{ji} = 0$. The optimization model is established as

$$\min Z = \sum_{i=1}^{q} \sum_{j=1}^{p} D\left(\alpha_{ji} \times \tilde{w}_j\right) \times x_{ji} + \sum_{i=1}^{q} \sum_{j=1}^{p} D\left(\beta_{ij} \times \tilde{v}_i\right) \times x_{ji}$$

s.t.

$$\sum_{i=1}^{q} x_{ji} \leqslant \eta_j^{max}$$

$$\eta_j^{min} \leqslant \sum_{i=1}^{q} x_{ji} \tag{33}$$

$$\sum_{j=1}^{p} x_{ji} \leqslant \lambda_i^{max}$$

$$\lambda_i^{min} \leqslant \sum_{j=1}^{p} x_{ji}$$

$$x_{ji} \in \{0,1\}, j = 1,2,\cdots,p,\ i = 1,2,\cdots,q$$

where η_j^{max} and η_j^{min} are the maximum and minimum numbers of users that can be accepted by expert E_j, λ_i^{max} and λ_i^{min} are the maximum and minimum numbers of experts that user U_i can consult. By resolving the model, according to the value of variable x_{ji}, the optimal match with the global highest level of satisfaction can be obtained.

4. Evaluations

In this section, the feasibility and effectiveness of the proposed approach are evaluated. The experiment is carried out with the match between users and experts in a scene of information system design and development. Novices are users and the people that have rich experience in system design and development are experts. Each user and each expert is required to use linguistic terms in Table 1 to express their opinions.

Table 1. Linguistic terms.

Linguistic Variables	Fuzzy Numbers
Very low (VL)	(0,1,2,3)
Low (L)	(1,2,3,4)
Medium (M)	(3,4,5,6)
High (H)	(4,5,6,7)
Very low (VH)	(5,6,7,8)

The criteria of expertise (C_1^e), trust (C_2^e) and feedback (C_3^e) are used to evaluate experts and trust (C_1^u), relationship (C_2^u) and knowledge distance (C_3^u) are used to evaluate users. Since the expertise, knowledge distance and relationship cannot be rated directly, the corresponding indirect criteria, which include task relevance ($C_1^{\prime e}$), direct relationship ($C_2^{\prime u}$) and expected expertise ($C_3^{\prime u}$), are used. The criteria of trust and feedback are rated directly. Besides the criteria of trust and feedback, users and experts give ratings with respect to the indirect criteria. The rating values are processed to drive the value of ratings with respect to the criteria.

In the following, the definition and measurement of criteria in a fuzzy linguistic setting along with the calculation of satisfaction degrees are explained.

The derived information content of users' satisfaction with experts is shown in Table 2. In the table, we can see the level of satisfaction with respect to each criterion. The smaller the value is, the higher the level of satisfaction is. For example, considering criterion C_1^e, user U_6 is more satisfied with expert E_1 than expert E_2.

Table 2. Information content of users' satisfaction with experts.

User	E_1			E_2			E_3			E_4		
	C_1^e	C_2^e	C_3^e	C_1^e	C_2^e	C_3^e	C_1^e	C_2^e	C_3^e	C_1^e	C_2^e	C_3^e
U_1	0.14	1.00	1.00	0.41	3.00	1.00	0.37	0.00	1.00	−6.65	3.00	3.00
U_2	0.14	1.00	0.00	0.36	1.00	0.00	0.22	0.00	0.00	−5.06	1.00	0.00
U_3	0.15	1.00	1.00	0.37	4.99	3.00	0.28	0.00	0.00	−4.96	1.00	3.00
U_4	0.11	0.00	0.00	0.39	1.00	3.00	0.31	0.00	0.00	−6.04	1.00	3.00
U_5	0.18	1.00	1.00	0.38	0.00	1.00	0.28	0.00	0.00	−5.35	3.00	3.00
U_6	0.22	1.00	3.00	0.33	3.00	3.00	0.20	0.00	3.00	−3.94	0.00	0.00
U_7	0.21	0.00	3.00	0.38	0.00	0.00	0.23	0.00	1.00	−5.03	3.00	3.00
U_8	0.05	3.00	1.00	0.43	3.00	1.00	0.50	0.00	1.00	−14.09	3.00	1.00
U_9	0.19	1.00	0.00	0.39	3.00	3.00	0.30	1.00	0.00	−5.44	1.00	3.00
U_{10}	0.19	3.00	1.00	0.38	3.00	0.00	0.21	0.00	0.00	−4.99	1.00	3.00
U_{11}	0.21	0.00	1.00	0.40	1.00	3.00	0.24	0.00	1.00	−5.23	1.00	1.00
U_{12}	0.14	0.00	0.00	0.40	0.00	1.00	0.36	0.00	0.00	−6.39	3.00	1.00

User	E_5			E_6			E_7			E_8		
	C_1^e	C_2^e	C_3^e	C_1^e	C_2^e	C_3^e	C_1^e	C_2^e	C_3^e	C_1^e	C_2^e	C_3^e
U_1	0.88	3.00	3.00	0.30	1.00	3.00	0.00	0.00	3.00	1.95	3.00	3.00
U_2	0.68	1.00	0.00	0.28	1.00	3.00	0.00	1.00	3.00	1.64	1.00	0.00
U_3	0.58	1.00	3.00	0.25	0.00	3.00	0.00	0.00	1.00	1.56	4.99	−3.00
U_4	0.83	1.00	3.00	0.26	0.00	3.00	0.00	0.00	1.00	1.80	1.00	−3.00
U_5	0.69	1.00	3.00	0.29	−3.00	3.00	0.00	0.00	3.00	1.81	−3.00	3.00
U_6	0.38	3.00	3.00	0.12	3.00	3.00	0.00	1.00	3.00	1.50	1.00	3.00
U_7	0.56	−3.00	3.00	0.24	−3.00	3.00	0.00	1.00	3.00	1.74	1.00	3.00
U_8	1.16	1.00	1.00	0.51	0.00	3.00	0.05	0.00	3.00	2.10	−3.00	1.00
U_9	0.69	3.00	3.00	0.29	1.00	1.00	0.00	0.00	1.00	1.85	0.00	3.00
U_{10}	0.54	3.00	−3.00	0.23	1.00	3.00	0.00	1.00	1.00	1.64	3.00	−3.00
U_{11}	0.53	0.00	3.00	0.24	4.99	1.00	0.00	0.00	1.00	1.73	4.99	0.00
U_{12}	0.88	1.00	3.00	0.29	0.00	1.00	0.00	0.00	1.00	1.94	−3.00	3.00

In order to measure the satisfaction of users on expertise (C_1^e), users are required to evaluate the relevance of completed tasks to knowledge needs. For example, U_6's ratings of the four completed tasks are L, L, VH and VH. The predefined belonging degrees of the four completed tasks to each knowledge area are (L, L, VL, VH, L), (VL, VH, VH, M, M), (VH, L, H, M, M) and (VL, VL, VL, L, VH), respectively. Then, with Equation (12), the knowledge needs of user U_6 can be derived as

$$\widetilde{VN}_6$$
$$= \left(\frac{L\otimes L\oplus L\otimes VL\oplus VH\otimes VH\oplus VH\otimes VL}{L\oplus L\oplus VH\oplus VH}, \frac{L\otimes L\oplus L\otimes VL\oplus VH\otimes VH\oplus VH\otimes VL}{L\oplus L\oplus VH\oplus VH}, \right.$$
$$\left. \frac{L\otimes L\oplus L\otimes VL\oplus VH\otimes VH\oplus VH\otimes VL}{L\oplus L\oplus VH\oplus VH}, \frac{L\otimes L\oplus L\otimes VL\oplus VH\otimes VH\oplus VH\otimes VL}{L\oplus L\oplus VH\oplus VH}, \frac{L\otimes L\oplus VL\oplus VH\otimes VH\oplus VH\otimes VL}{L\oplus L\oplus VH\oplus VH} \right)$$
$$= ((2.10, 2.93, 3.83, 4.77), (1.00, 2.21, 3.33, 4.41), (2.10, 3.14, 4.17, 5.18), (2.40, 3.57, 4.67, 5.73), (3.60, 4.43, 5.33, 6.27))$$

The predefined profile of expert E_1 is (VL, VH, VH, H, H). With Equation (13), the value of expertise (C_1^e) of expert E_1 for user U_6 can be obtained by

$$\widetilde{VM}_{6,1}$$
$$= \frac{\begin{array}{c}(2.10, 2.93, 3.83, 4.77) \otimes VL \oplus (1.00, 2.21, 3.33, 4.41) \otimes VH \oplus (2.10, 3.14, 4.17, 5.18) \otimes VH \oplus (2.40, 3.57, 4.67, 5.73) \otimes H \\ \oplus (3.60, 4.43, 5.33, 6.27) \otimes H\end{array}}{(2.10,2.93,3.83,4.77)\oplus(1.00,2.21,3.33,4.41)\oplus(2.10,3.14,4.17,5.18)\oplus(2.40,3.57,4.67,5.73)\oplus(3.60,4.43,5.33,6.27)}$$
$$= (3.53, 4.61, 5.63, 6.64)$$

In the same way, the values of expertise (C_1^e) of other experts for user U_6 are derived. The derived maximum value is (3.84, 4.87, 5.88, 6.87). Based on Equation (30), the information content of user U_6's satisfaction with expert E_1 on expertise (C_1^e) is obtained by

$$S_{6,1,1} = \log_2 \frac{\text{System Area}}{\text{Satisfaction Area}}$$
$$= \log_2 \frac{(6.64-3.53+5.63-4.61) \times (4.87-3.84-5.63+6.64)}{(6.64-3.53)^2}$$
$$= 0.22$$

User U_6 consulted with expert E_4 once and the rating value is VH. With Equation (21), the aggregated rating of expert E_4 for user U_6 on feedback (C_3^e) can be derived by

$$\widetilde{F}_{6,4}^u = \frac{VH\left(\frac{1}{e^{\tau(12-10)}}\right)}{\left(\frac{1}{e^{\tau(12-10)}}\right)} = VH = (5,6,7,8)$$

Likewise, the derived maximum value of feedback for user U_6 is VH. According to Equation (29), the information content of user U_6's satisfaction with expert E_4 on feedback (C_3^e) is obtained by

$$S_{6,2,4} = \log_2 \frac{(8-5)+(7-6)}{(7-6)+(8-5)} = 0$$

For trust (C_2^e), the rating value of expert E_1 given by user U_6 is missing. The direct rating of expert E_2 and expert E_4 on trust given by user U_6 are M and VH, respectively. Meanwhile, the direct trust rating of E_1 given by experts E_2 and E_4 are M and H. Therefore, Equations (14)–(16) are used to predict trust rating values as follows:

$$E_* = \operatorname{argmax}\left\{\widetilde{ST}_{6,2}, \widetilde{ST}_{6,4}\right\} = \operatorname{argmax}\{M, VH\} = E_4$$

$$\widetilde{T}_{6,1} = \min\left\{\max\left\{\widetilde{ST}_{6,2}, \widetilde{ST}_{6,4}\right\}, \omega_{*,1}\right\} = \min\{VH, H\} = H$$

As the derived maximum value of U_6's trust on experts is VH, according to Equation (21), the information content of user U_6's satisfaction with expert E_1 on trust (C_2^e) is 1.

The derived information content of experts' satisfaction with users is shown in Table 3.

Table 3. Information content of experts' satisfaction with users.

Expert	U_1			U_2			U_3			U_4		
	C_1^u	C_2^u	C_3^u	C_1^u	C_2^u	C_3^u	C_1^u	C_2^u	C_3^u	C_1^u	C_2^u	C_3^u
E_1	0.00	2.00	2.23	1.00	2.00	0.64	1.00	2.00	1.74	1.00	2.00	2.37
E_2	4.99	−0.25	0.59	1.00	−0.25	2.29	1.00	−0.25	0.93	1.00	−0.25	0.67
E_3	0.00	1.00	1.80	0.00	1.00	1.86	0.00	1.00	1.98	0.00	1.00	0.22
E_4	0.00	−0.25	2.87	1.00	−0.25	0.59	1.00	−0.25	1.51	1.00	−0.25	3.00
E_5	0.00	2.00	2.43	1.00	2.00	0.17	0.00	2.00	2.52	0.00	2.00	1.17
E_6	0.00	1.00	0.44	3.00	1.00	3.54	1.00	1.00	0.71	3.00	1.00	2.13
E_7	0.00	−0.25	2.31	1.00	−0.25	0.18	1.00	−0.25	1.74	1.00	−0.25	1.81
E_8	0.00	2.00	3.00	1.00	2.00	0.26	0.00	2.00	2.00	0.00	2.00	1.11

Expert	U_5			U_6			U_7			U_8		
	C_1^u	C_2^u	C_3^u	C_1^u	C_2^u	C_3^u	C_1^u	C_2^u	C_3^u	C_1^u	C_2^u	C_3^u
E_1	1.00	2.00	1.65	1.00	1.00	1.84	4.99	1.00	0.68	0.00	1.00	0.50
E_2	0.00	−0.25	1.95	1.00	2.00	1.37	4.99	2.00	1.71	0.00	2.00	0.23
E_3	3.00	1.00	0.76	3.00	2.00	2.46	3.00	2.00	0.50	0.00	2.00	−0.69
E_4	1.00	−0.25	0.12	0.00	2.00	−0.59	1.00	2.00	1.63	1.00	2.00	0.50
E_5	1.00	2.00	2.59	1.00	1.00	3.79	1.00	1.00	2.79	0.00	1.00	−0.19
E_6	1.00	1.00	−0.72	−3.00	2.00	0.81	0.00	2.00	−1.01	1.00	2.00	0.68
E_7	1.00	−0.25	−1.41	1.00	2.00	−0.97	1.00	2.00	−0.93	0.00	2.00	1.27
E_8	1.00	2.00	2.20	1.00	1.00	2.52	1.00	1.00	1.40	0.00	1.00	0.50

Expert	U_9			U_{10}			U_{11}			U_{12}		
	C_1^u	C_2^u	C_3^u	C_1^u	C_2^u	C_3^u	C_1^u	C_2^u	C_3^u	C_1^u	C_2^u	C_3^u
E_1	1.00	1.00	2.03	0.00	1.00	2.71	1.00	1.00	2.03	0.00	2.00	2.52
E_2	1.00	2.00	0.93	0.00	2.00	−1.07	0.00	2.00	1.77	0.00	−0.25	1.21
E_3	0.00	2.00	−0.05	0.00	2.00	−1.98	3.00	2.00	0.78	3.00	1.00	0.26
E_4	1.00	2.00	−0.10	1.00	2.00	−0.50	1.00	2.00	4.02	1.00	−0.25	3.52
E_5	1.00	1.00	1.62	1.00	1.00	2.22	1.00	1.00	2.87	0.00	2.00	3.31
E_6	0.00	2.00	1.44	0.00	2.00	−0.47	3.00	2.00	0.51	−3.00	1.00	0.00
E_7	0.00	2.00	0.85	0.00	2.00	0.33	1.00	2.00	1.98	0.00	−0.25	1.68
E_8	0.00	1.00	1.67	1.00	1.00	2.33	1.00	1.00	2.58	0.00	2.00	3.09

The rating of user U_6 given by expert E_4 with respect to relationship (C_2^u) is VH. The expert chooses the caution preference. According to Equation (20), the corresponding value is obtained by

$$\tilde{R}_{4,6} = \max (VH) = VH$$

The derived maximum value of expert E_4's relationship with users is VH. With Equation (30), the obtained information content of the corresponding satisfaction is 0.

The rating of the expected knowledge level of users given by expert E_4 in the five knowledge areas is (VL, VL, L, M, VH) and the predefined profile of user U_6 is (VL, VL, VL, M, VL). The information content of user E_4's satisfaction with expert U_6 on knowledge distance (C_3^u) in each knowledge area can be calculated directly with Equation (30). The calculation results are 0, 0, 1, 0 and 4. The knowledge needs of user U_6 in each knowledge area are used as weights. With Equation (22), the weighted overall information content can be derived by

$$S'_{4,3,6} = \frac{(0 \times 3.40 + 0 \times 2.75 + 1 \times 3.65 + 0 \times 4.10 - 4 \times 4.90)}{3.40 + 2.75 + 3.65 + 4.10 + 4.90} = -0.59$$

The weights of criteria are given directly by experts and users. The weight of the criteria for evaluating experts and the weight of the criteria for evaluating users are shown in Tables 4 and 5 respectively. Each person has his or her own preference about the importance. The two tables show the importance of the criteria for each person. In Table 4, we see that user U_1. thinks the first two criteria are more important for him. In the calculation of his satisfaction degrees, the two criteria play more important roles.

Table 4. Weight of the criteria for evaluating experts given by users.

	U_1	U_2	U_3	U_4	U_5	U_6	U_7	U_8	U_9	U_{10}	U_{11}	U_{12}
C_1^e	VH	H	VH	H	VH	VH	H	VH	H	VH	M	VH
C_2^e	VH	VH	VH	H	H	VH	M	M	VH	M	M	H
C_3^e	H	VH	H	H	VH	H	L	M	VH	VH	M	VH

Table 5. Weight of the criteria for evaluating users given by experts.

	E_1	E_2	E_3	E_4	E_5	E_6	E_7	E_8
C_1^u	VH	H	H	H	H	M	L	M
C_2^u	M	H	VL	M	M	VL	VH	M
C_3^u	M	M	M	H	M	VH	H	H

In the evaluation, weights of experts and users are equal. In order to guarantee each user can get help and avoid the selection of experts from the matching results again, the values of λ_i^{min} and λ_i^{max} ($j = 1, 2, \cdots, 12$) are set to 1, which means one user can only accept one expert. In order to avoid concentrating on the small number of experts, the value of η_j^{max} ($j = 1, 2, \cdots, 8$) is set to 2 and the value of η_j^{min} ($j = 1, 2, \cdots, 8$) is set to 1. Each expert can accept two users at most.

According to Equation (33), the objective function is defined as

$$\min Z' = \sum_{j=1}^{8} \sum_{i=1}^{12} \sum_{y=1}^{3} D\left(\tilde{\zeta}_{jy} \times S_{jyi}\right) \times x_{ji} + \sum_{j=1}^{8} \sum_{i=1}^{12} \sum_{z=1}^{3} D\left(\tilde{\eta}_{iz} \times S_{izj}\right) \times x_{ji}$$

Thus, the optimal model is constructed as

$$
\min Z' = \sum_{j=1}^{8} \sum_{i=1}^{12} \left(\sum_{y=1}^{3} D\left(\tilde{\zeta}_{iy} \times S_{jyi}\right) + \sum_{z=1}^{3} D\left(\tilde{\eta}_{jz} \times S_{izj}\right) \right) \times x_{ji}
$$

$$
\begin{aligned}
= \; & 31.90x_{11} + 25.62x_{12} + 36.30x_{13} + 26.78x_{14} + 36.06x_{15} + 43.69x_{16} + 48.69x_{17} + 25.09x_{18} \\
& + 27.69x_{19} + 37.88x_{110} + 25.61x_{111} + 21.23x_{112} + 56.49x_{21} + 22.92x_{22} \\
& + 59.68x_{23} + 31.26x_{24} + 16.39x_{25} + 60.77x_{26} + 48.29x_{27} + 33.27x_{28} \\
& + 61.82x_{29} + 22.15x_{210} + 38.73x_{211} + 13.19x_{212} + 18.02x_{31} + 11.61x_{32} \\
& + 12.25x_{33} + 4.67x_{34} + 34.81x_{35} + 48.35x_{36} + 26.03x_{37} + 8.14x_{38} + 11.37x_{39} \\
& - 3.98x_{310} + 29.00x_{311} + 22.03x_{312} + 93.92x_{41} + 41.94x_{42} + 67.88x_{43} \\
& + 76.11x_{44} + 75.83x_{45} + 31.36x_{46} + 72.16x_{47} - 56.37x_{48} + 69.88x_{49} \\
& + 68.17x_{410} + 69.14x_{411} + 88.29x_{412} + 61.71x_{51} + 25.59x_{52} + 47.33x_{53} \\
& + 40.91x_{54} + 55.77x_{55} + 65.78x_{56} + 19.78x_{57} + 20.20x_{58} + 60.24x_{59} \\
& + 17.72x_{510} + 38.98x_{511} + 54.64x_{512} + 13.40x_{61} + 46.00x_{62} + 28.71x_{63} \\
& + 47.30x_{64} + 6.20x_{65} + 31.523x_{66} - 8.24x_{67} + 15.72x_{68} + 26.97x_{69} \\
& + 25.46x_{610} + 47.91x_{611} - 3.02x_{612} + 11.08x_{71} + 8.38x_{72} + 15.94x_{73} \\
& + 16.33x_{74} + 12.63x_{75} + 33.18x_{76} + 22.38x_{77} + 20.11x_{78} + 24.18x_{79} \\
& + 25.84x_{710} + 30.89x_{711} + 14.10x_{712} + 74.15x_{81} + 30.46x_{82} + 46.12x_{83} \\
& + 14.05x_{84} + 40.37x_{85} + 55.59x_{86} + 38.24x_{87} + 11.89x_{88} + 43.39x_{89} \\
& + 26.49x_{810} + 53.47x_{811} + 41.58x_{812}
\end{aligned}
$$

s.t.

$$
1 \leqslant \sum_{i=1}^{12} x_{ji} \leqslant 2, j = 1, 2, \cdots, 8
$$

$$
\sum_{j=1}^{8} x_{ji} = 1, i = 1, 2, \cdots, 12
$$

$$
x_{ji} \in \{0, 1\}, j = 1, 2, \cdots 8; i = 1, 2, \cdots, 12.
$$

By resolving the model, the derived optimal match is $\{(U_1, E_7), (U_2, E_5), (U_3, E_7), (U_4, E_8), (U_5, E_2), (U_6, E_4), (U_7, E_6), (U_8, E_4), (U_9, E_3), (U_{10}, E_3), (U_{11}, E_1), (U_{12}, E_6)\}$.

The matching results are based on ratings given by experts and users. With the optimized matching results, the maximum satisfaction degree can be obtained. It is the only optimum solution. Therefore, this match is better than any other one.

Compared with the manual selection of experts, both experts and users are more satisfied with the proposed approach.

(1)   With the proposed approach, the needs of both users and experts are identified more comprehensively because of the expression of preferences from multiple aspects. The burden of finding experts is reduced. The only requirements of users are to express their preferences instead of strenuously searching each category and browsing the descriptions of experts. Since the match is made based not only on users' preferences but also on experts' preferences, the experts' satisfaction with users is improved. As a result, experts are more willing to help the users and users can get more fitting help with higher quality. Moreover, searching and contacting experts repeatedly when the one-sided chosen expert is reluctant to help the user due to disagreement with their preferences or limited interest is avoided.

(2)   For experts, especially those whose expertise level is higher, the amount of users that ask them for help is reduced and the matched users are better fits for the experts' preferences. It eases the burden of experts and makes the matched users more acceptable. As the match is based on the rating with respect to the criteria but not rating the people directly, users can be matched with suitable but unfamiliar experts. These unfamiliar experts will be consulted and will not be

excluded from the tacit knowledge-sharing. The valuable tacit knowledge resources are utilized fully and efficiently.

It can be deduced that deriving the optimized match with the integration of preferences of both users and experts leads to a higher level of satisfaction and superior performance.

5. Conclusions

In this paper, we propose an approach to matching experts and users in a fuzzy linguistic environment. The criteria for the matching are constructed and defined in the fuzzy linguistic environment. Satisfaction of both experts and users is measured based on the AD. The optimal match is made by maximizing the overall satisfaction of both experts and users. The evaluation results show that the proposed approach performs well and reveals a better satisfaction of users and experts. This study has important implications both for the development of the knowledge management system and the research of tacit knowledge-sharing. Consulting the appropriate expert is the key for tacit knowledge-sharing. With the proposed approach, the satisfaction of both users and experts is improved and the sharing of tacit knowledge is promoted.

Acknowledgments: The research is supported by the National Natural Science Foundation of China under Grant No. 71101153, 71571191, and Science Foundation of China University of Petroleum, Beijing (No. 2462015YQ0722), Humanity and Social Science Youth Foundation of Ministry of Education in China (Project No. 15YJCZH081, 13YJC790112).

Author Contributions: Ming Li and Mengyue Yuan designed the approach. Ming Li completed the paper. Mengyue Yuan refined the manuscript and revised the final draft of the manuscript. Both authors have read and approved the final manuscript.

Conflicts of Interest: The authors declare no conflict of interest.

References

1. Nonaka, I.; Hirotaka, T. *The Knowledge-Creating Company: How Japanese Companies Create the Dynamics of Innovation*; Oxford University Press: Oxford, UK, 1995.
2. Alavi, M.; Leidner, D.E. Knowledge management systems: Issues, challenges, and benefits. *Commun. AIS* **1999**, *1*, 1.
3. Liao, S.H. Knowledge Management Technologies and Applications—Literature Review from 1995 to 2002. *Exper. Syst. Appl.* **2003**, *25*, 155–164. [CrossRef]
4. Cavusgil, S.T.; Calantone, R.J.; Zhao, Y. Tacit knowledge transfer and firm innovation capability. *J. Bus. Ind. Mark.* **2003**, *18*, 6–21. [CrossRef]
5. Hansen, M.T.; Nohria, N.; Tierney, T. What's your strategy for managing knowledge? *Harv. Bus. Rev.* **1999**, *77*, 106–116. [PubMed]
6. Polanyi, M. The Tacit Dimension. In *Knowledge in Organizations*; Prusak, L., Ed.; Butterworth-Heinemann: Boston, MA, USA, 1997; pp. 135–146.
7. Arnett, D.B.; Wittmann, C.M. Improving marketing success: The role of tacit knowledge exchange between sales and marketing. *J. Bus. Res.* **2014**, *67*, 324–331. [CrossRef]
8. Haldin-Herrgard, T. Difficulties in diffusion of tacit knowledge in organizations. *J. Intellect. Cap.* **2000**, *1*, 357–365. [CrossRef]
9. Nash, C.; Collins, D. Tacit knowledge in expert coaching: Science or art? *Quest* **2006**, *58*, 465–477. [CrossRef]
10. Alavi, M.; Leidner, D.E. Review: Knowledge management and knowledge management systems: Conceptual foundations and research issues. *MIS Q.* **2001**, *25*, 107–136. [CrossRef]
11. Irma, B.F. *Expert Seeker: A People-Finder Knowledge Management System*; Florida International University: Miami, FL, USA, 2000.
12. Microsoft SharePoint products and technologies. Available online: http://www.microsoft.com/sharepoint/ (accessed on 8 April 2016).
13. Yang, K.-W.; Huh, S.-Y. Automatic expert identification using a text categorization technique in knowledge management systems. *Exper. Syst. Appl.* **2008**, *34*, 1445–1455. [CrossRef]

14. Chen, Y.J.; Chen, Y.M.; Wu, M.S. An expert recommendation system for product empirical knowledge consultation. In Proceedings of the IEEE International Conference on Computer Science and Information Technology, Chengdu, China, 9–11 July 2010; pp. 23–27.

15. Yukawa, T.; Kasahara, K.; Kato, T.; Kita, T. An expert recommendation system using concept-based relevance discernment. In Proceedings of the 13th International Conference on Tools with Artificial Intelligence, Dallas, TX, USA, 7–9 November 2001; pp. 257–264.

16. Zhu, H.; Cao, H.; Xiong, H.; Chen, E.; Tian, J. Towards expert finding by leveraging relevant categories in authority ranking. In Proceedings of the 20th ACM International Conference on Information and Knowledge Management, Glasgow, UK, 24–28 October 2011; pp. 2221–2224.

17. Ehrlich, K.; Lin, C.Y.; Griffiths-Fisher, V. Searching for experts in the enterprise: Combining text and social network analysis. In Proceedings of the 2007 International ACM Conference on Supporting Group Work, Sanibel Island, FL, USA, 4–7 November 2007; pp. 117–126.

18. Duan, Y.; Nie, W.; Coakes, E. Identifying key factors affecting transnational knowledge transfer. *Inf. Manag.* **2010**, *47*, 356–363. [CrossRef]

19. Gupta, B.; Iyer, L.S.; Aronson, J.E. Knowledge management: Practices and challenges. *Ind. Manag. Data Syst.* **2000**, *100*, 17–21. [CrossRef]

20. Robertson, M.; O'Malley Hammersley, G. Knowledge management practices within a knowledge-intensive firm: The significance of the people management dimension. *J. Eur. Ind. Train.* **2000**, *24*, 241–253. [CrossRef]

21. Riege, A. Three-dozen knowledge-sharing barriers managers must consider. *J. Knowl. Manag.* **2005**, *9*, 18–35. [CrossRef]

22. Soheil, S.N.; Kaveh, K.D. Application of a fuzzy TOPSIS method base on modified preference ratio and fuzzy distance measurement in assessment of traffic police centers performance. *Appl. Soft Comput.* **2010**, *10*, 1028–1039.

23. Dong, M.; Li, S.; Zhang, H. Approaches to group decision making with incomplete information based on power geometric operators and triangular fuzzy AHP. *Exper. Syst. Appl.* **2015**, *42*, 7846–7857. [CrossRef]

24. Zheng, G.; Zhu, N.; Tian, Z.; Chen, Y.; Sun, B. Application of a trapezoidal fuzzy AHP method for work safety evaluation and early warning rating of hot and humid environments. *Saf. Sci.* **2012**, *50*, 228–239. [CrossRef]

25. Deng, Y.; Chan, F.T.; Wu, Y.; Wang, D. A new linguistic MCDM method based on multiple-criterion data fusion. *Exper. Syst. Appl.* **2011**, *38*, 6985–6993. [CrossRef]

26. Zimmermann, H.-J. *Fuzzy Set Theory—And Its Applications*; Kluwer Academic Publishers: Boston, MA, USA, 1991.

27. Sanayei, A.; Mousavi, S.F.; Yazdankhah, A. Group decision making process for supplier selection with VIKOR under fuzzy environment. *Exper. Syst. Appl.* **2010**, *37*, 24–30. [CrossRef]

28. Kulak, O.; Cebi, S.; Kahraman, C. Applications of axiomatic design principles: A literature review. *Expert Syst. Appl.* **2010**, *37*, 6705–6717. [CrossRef]

29. Suh, N.P. Design of thinking design machine. *CIRP Ann.* **1990**, *39*, 145–148. [CrossRef]

30. Chen, X.; Fan, Z. Problem of Two-sided Matching between Venture Capitalists and Venture Enterprises Based on Axiomatic Design. *Syst. Eng.* **2010**, *28*, 9–16.

31. Li, M.; Liu, L.; Li, C.B. Method for Knowledge Management System Selection Based on Improved Fuzzy Information Axiom. *Ind. Eng. J.* **2010**, *13*, 15–18.

32. Kim, Y.A.; Song, H.S. Strategies for predicting local trust based on trust propagation in social networks. *Knowledge- Based Syst.* **2011**, *24*, 1360–1371. [CrossRef]

33. Zhang, J.; Ackerman, M.S.; Adamic, L. Expertise networks in online communities: Structure and algorithms. In Proceedings of the 16th International Conference on World Wide Web, Banff, AB, Canada, 8–12 May 2007; pp. 221–230.

11

Super-Activation as a Unique Feature of Secure Communication in Malicious Environments

Rafael F. Schaefer [1,*,†], **Holger Boche** [2,†] and **H. Vincent Poor** [3,†]

[1] Information Theory and Applications Chair, Technische Universität Berlin, 10587 Berlin, Germany
[2] Institute of Theoretical Information Technology, Technische Universität München, 80333 Munich, Germany; boche@tum.de
[3] Department of Electrical Engineering, Princeton University, Princeton, NJ 08544, USA; poor@princeton.edu
[*] Correspondence: rafael.schaefer@tu-berlin.de
[†] These authors contributed equally to this work.

Academic Editor: Willy Susilo

Abstract: The wiretap channel models secure communication between two users in the presence of an eavesdropper who must be kept ignorant of transmitted messages. This communication scenario is studied for arbitrarily varying channels (AVCs), in which the legitimate users know only that the true channel realization comes from a pre-specified uncertainty set and that it varies from channel use to channel use in an arbitrary and unknown manner. This concept not only captures the case of channel uncertainty, but also models scenarios in which malevolent adversaries influence or jam the transmission of the legitimate users. For secure communication over orthogonal *arbitrarily varying wiretap channels* (AVWCs) it has been shown that the phenomenon of super-activation occurs; that is, there are orthogonal AVWCs, each having zero secrecy capacity, which allow for transmission with positive rate if they are used together. It is shown that for such orthogonal AVWCs super-activation is generic in the sense that whenever super-activation is possible, it is possible for all AVWCs in a certain neighborhood as well. As a consequence, a super-activated AVWC is robust and continuous in the uncertainty set, although a single AVWC might not be. Moreover, it is shown that the question of super-activation and the continuity of the secrecy capacity solely depends on the legitimate link. Accordingly, the single-user AVC is subsequently studied and it is shown that in this case, super-activation for non-secure message transmission is not possible making it a unique feature of secure communication over AVWCs. However, the capacity for message transmission of the single-user AVC is shown to be super-additive including a complete characterization. Such knowledge is important for medium access control and in particular resource allocation as it determines the overall performance of a system.

Keywords: wiretap channel; arbitrarily varying channel (AVC); secrecy capacity; super-activation; super-additivity; active attacks; malicious behavior

1. Introduction

The architecture of today's communication systems is designed such that data encryption and error correction are clearly separated. Data encryption is based on cryptographic principles and usually implemented at higher layers which abstracts out the underlying communication channel as an ideal bit pipe. The error correction is performed at the physical layer by adding redundancy into the message bits in order to combat the noisy channel. Such separation based approaches have been the typical solution in current communication systems.

In recent years there has been a growing interest in complementary approaches that realize security directly at the physical layer. Such *information theoretic approaches to security* establish data confidentiality and reliable communication jointly at the physical layer by exploiting the noisy and imperfect nature of the communication channel. This line of thinking goes back to Wyner, who introduced the so-called wiretap channel in [1]. This area of research provides a promising approach to achieve secrecy and to embed secure communication into wireless networks. Not surprisingly, it has drawn considerable attention recently [2–7] and has also been identified by operators of communication systems and national agencies as a key technique to secure future communication systems [8–10].

These studies are in particular relevant for wireless communication systems as the open nature of the wireless medium makes such systems inherently vulnerable for eavesdropping: Transmitted signals are received not only by intended users, but also easily eavesdropped upon by non-legitimate receivers. A common assumption of many studies is that all channels to the intended receivers and also to the non-legitimate eavesdroppers are known perfectly to all users. However, practical systems will always be limited in the availability of channel state information (CSI) due to nature of the wireless medium but also due to practical limitations such as estimation/feedback inaccuracy. In addition to that, the assumption of knowing the eavesdropper's channel is often hard to justify in practice since malevolent eavesdroppers will not share any information about their channels to make eavesdropping even harder. Accordingly, such approaches to security must incorporate imperfect CSI assumptions to yield practically meaningful insights. A recent survey on secure communication under channel uncertainty and adversarial attacks can be found in [11].

In this paper, we model the uncertainty in CSI by assuming *arbitrarily varying channels* (AVCs) [12–14]. This concept assumes that the actual channel realization is unknown; rather, it is only known that this realization is from a known uncertainty set and that it may vary in an arbitrary and unknown manner from channel use to channel use. The concept of AVCs provides a very general and powerful framework as it not only models the case of channel uncertainty, but also captures scenarios with malevolent adversaries who maliciously influence or jam the legitimate transmission.

Secure communication over AVCs is then modeled by the *arbitrarily varying wiretap channel* (AVWC) which has been studied in [15–22]. It has been shown that it makes a substantial difference whether unassisted or common randomness (CR) assisted codes are used by the transmitter and the legitimate receiver. Specifically, if the AVC to the legitimate receiver possesses the so-called symmetrizability property, then the unassisted secrecy capacity is zero, while the CR-assisted secrecy capacity may be positive. A complete characterization of how unassisted and CR-assisted secrecy capacity relate to each other is given in [16,21]. However, a single-letter characterization of the secrecy capacity itself remains open. Only a multi-letter description of the CR-assisted secrecy capacity has been recently established in [20].

Wireless communication systems are usually composed of orthogonal sub-systems such as those that arise via orthogonal frequency division multiplexing (OFDM) or time division multiplexing (TDM). And the important issue in such systems is how the available resources should be allocated to these orthogonal sub-systems. Common sense tells us that the overall capacity of such a system is given by the sum of the capacities of all orthogonal sub-systems. The inherent world view of the additivity of classical resources is also reflected by Shannon who conjectured in [23] the additivity of the zero error capacity for orthogonal discrete memoryless channels (DMCs). This was later restated by Lovász in ([24], Problem 2) and recently further highlighted in [25].

To this end, let us consider a system consisting of two orthogonal ordinary DMCs W_1 and W_2. If both channels are accessed in an orthogonal way by using independent encoders and decoders, we obtain $C(W_1) + C(W_2)$ as an achievable transmission rate, where $C(\cdot)$ denotes the capacity of the corresponding channel.

An interesting question is: Are there gains in capacity to be had by bonding the orthogonal channels and jointly accessing the resulting system $W_1 \otimes W_2$ by using a joint encoder and decoder? From the operational definition of the capacity it is clear that we have

$$C(W_1 \otimes W_2) \geq C(W_1) + C(W_2) \tag{1}$$

since a joint use of both channels can only increase the capacity. However, it is known that the capacity of ordinary DMCs is *additive* under the average error criterion so that Equation (1) is actually satisfied with equality, *i.e.*,

$$C(W_1 \otimes W_2) = C(W_1) + C(W_2). \tag{2}$$

This means that joint encoding and decoding over orthogonal channels does not provide any gains in capacity and the overall capacity of an OFDM system is indeed given by the sum of the capacities of all orthogonal sub-channels.

Although this verifies what one usually would expect for the capacity of orthogonal channels, the question of additivity of the capacity function is in general by no means obvious or trivial to answer. As already mentioned, Shannon for example asked this question in 1956 for the zero error capacity [23]. He conjectured that the zero error capacity C_0 is additive, thus possessing the same behavior as ordinary DMCs: $C_0(W_1 \otimes W_2) = C_0(W_1) + C_0(W_2)$; similar to Equation (2). This problem was subsequently studied by Haemers [26] and later by Alon [27] who explicitly constructed counter-examples. Thus, there exist channels for which the zero error capacity is strictly greater when encoding and decoding are done jointly instead of independently. This means that the zero error capacity is *super-additive* and there exist channels for which "$\geq$" in Equation (1) can actually be replaced by "$>$" so that

$$C_0(W_1 \otimes W_2) > C_0(W_1) + C_0(W_2)$$

holds. To date, only certain explicit examples are known that possess this property of super-additivity. A general characterization of which channels are super-additive or what further properties such channels possess remains open. In 1970 it was Ahlswede who showed that the capacity of the AVC under the maximum error criterion includes the characterization of the zero error capacity as a special case [28]. This is only one example demonstrating that Shannon's question of additivity of the zero error capacity considerably influenced the research in discrete mathematics and graph theory, *cf.* for example ([29], Chapter 41). Thus, Shannon's zero error capacity is closely related to AVCs, making it worth studying this question also from an AVC perspective.

The extreme case of non-additivity in Equation (1) occurs when for a system consisting of two orthogonal "useless" channels, *i.e.*, having zero capacity $C(W_1) = C(W_2) = 0$, it holds that $C(W_1 \otimes W_2) > 0$. This phenomenon is called *super-activation*: Two channels each with zero capacity can be used together to super-activate the whole system giving it a positive capacity. This phenomenon has been observed and studied in particular in the area of quantum information theory [30,31].

Very recently the phenomenon of super-activation has been observed for classical communication as well. Super-activation can occur for secure communication over AVCs and there exist orthogonal "useless" AVWCs, *i.e.*, having zero secrecy capacity, whose overall secrecy capacity is strictly positive [17]. This phenomenon of super-activation and its resulting secrecy capacity have then been completely characterized in [21].

In this paper we further explore the phenomenon of super-activation for AVWCs and its contributions are as follows. After introducing the system model in Section 2, we show that super-activation is not an isolated phenomenon in the sense that whenever two AVWCs can be super-activated, this is also true for all AVWCs in a certain neighborhood. As a consequence, we show that the secrecy capacity of a super-activated AVWC is continuous in the underlying uncertainty set, although this might not be the case for one of the AVWCs itself. Furthermore, we show that the question of whether super-activation is possible or not depends only on the legitimate channel, making it independent of the eavesdropper channel. This is the content of Section 3.

From a super-activation and continuity perspective, the legitimate AVC is more important than the eavesdropper AVC. Accordingly, we subsequently study these issues for the single-user AVC in detail in Section 4. Surprisingly, this has not been done so far to the best of our knowledge and we show that super-activation is not possible for public message transmission, making this a unique phenomenon of secure communication over AVWCs. However, we show that the single-user AVC indeed possesses the property of super-additivity which means that a joint use of orthogonal AVCs can provide gains in capacity. With this we provide a complete characterization of super-additivity and super-activation for the capacity of a single-user AVC. Finally, a discussion is given in Section 5.

Notation

Discrete random variables are denoted by capital letters and their realizations and ranges by lower case and script letters, respectively; all logarithms and information quantities are taken to the base 2; $X - Y - Z$ denotes a Markov chain of random variables X, Y, and Z in this order; $\mathcal{P}(\mathcal{X})$ is the set of all probability distributions on $\mathcal{X}$; the mutual information between the input random variable X and the output random variable Y of a channel W is denoted by $I(X;Y) = I(P_X, W)$, where the latter notation is interchangeably used to emphasize the dependence on the input distribution P_X and the channel.

2. Arbitrarily Varying Wiretap Channels

In this section we introduce the problem of secure communication over arbitrarily varying channels [12–14]. Such channel conditions appear for example in fast fading environments but also, more importantly, in scenarios in which malevolent adversaries actively influence or jam the legitimate transmission. This is the AVWC [15–22] which is depicted in Figure 1.

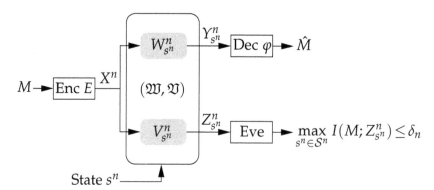

Figure 1. Arbitrarily varying wiretap channel. The transmitter encodes the message M into the codeword $X^n = E(M)$ and transmits it over the AVWC to the legitimate receiver, which has to decode its intended message $\hat{M} = \varphi(Y_{s^n}^n)$ for any state sequence $s^n \in \mathcal{S}^n$. At the same time, the eavesdropper must be kept ignorant of M by requiring $\max_{s^n \in \mathcal{S}^n} I(M; Z_{s^n}^n) \leq \delta_n$.

2.1. System Model

The channel state may vary in an unknown and arbitrary manner from channel use to channel use and this uncertainty in CSI is modeled with the help of a finite state set $\mathcal{S}$. Then the communication links to the legitimate receiver and the eavesdropper are given by stochastic matrices $W : \mathcal{X} \times \mathcal{S} \to \mathcal{P}(\mathcal{Y})$ and $V : \mathcal{X} \times \mathcal{S} \to \mathcal{P}(\mathcal{Z})$ with $\mathcal{X}$ the finite input alphabet and $\mathcal{Y}$ and $\mathcal{Z}$ the finite output alphabets at the legitimate receiver and eavesdropper respectively. We interchangeably also write $W_s : \mathcal{X} \to \mathcal{P}(\mathcal{Y})$ and $V_s : \mathcal{X} \to \mathcal{P}(\mathcal{Z})$ with $s \in \mathcal{S}$.

For a fixed state sequence $s^n = (s_1, s_2, ..., s_n) \in \mathcal{S}^n$ of length n, the discrete memoryless channel to the legitimate receiver is given by $W_{s^n}^n(y^n|x^n) = W^n(y^n|x^n, s^n) = \prod_{i=1}^n W(y_i|x_i, s_i)$ for all input and output sequences $x^n \in \mathcal{X}^n$ and $y^n \in \mathcal{Y}^n$.

Definition 1. The *arbitrarily varying channel (AVC)* $\mathfrak{W}$ to the legitimate receiver is defined as the family of channels for all state sequences $s^n \in \mathcal{S}^n$ as

$$\mathfrak{W} = \{W_{s^n}^n : s^n \in \mathcal{S}^n\}.$$

We further need the definition of an *averaged channel* which is defined for any probability distribution $q \in \mathcal{P}(\mathcal{S})$ as

$$\overline{W}_q(y|x) = \sum_{s \in \mathcal{S}} W(y|x,s)q(s) \tag{3}$$

for all $x \in \mathcal{X}$ and $y \in \mathcal{Y}$. An important property of an AVC is the so-called concept of symmetrizability as introduced next.

Definition 2. An AVC $\mathfrak{W}$ is called *symmetrizable* if there exists a channel (stochastic matrix) $\sigma : \mathcal{X} \to \mathcal{P}(\mathcal{S})$ such that

$$\sum_{s \in \mathcal{S}} W(y|x,s)\sigma(s|x') = \sum_{s \in \mathcal{S}} W(y|x',s)\sigma(s|x) \tag{4}$$

holds for all $x, x' \in \mathcal{X}$ and $y \in \mathcal{Y}$.

Roughly speaking, symmetrizability means that the AVC can "simulate" a valid channel input which makes it impossible for the receiver to decide on the correct codeword sent by the transmitter. This can be seen by writing the left hand side of Equation (4) as $\widetilde{W}(y|x,x') = \sum_{s \in \mathcal{S}} W(y|x,s)\sigma(s|x')$. Now symmetrizability means that this channel is symmetric in both inputs x and x', i.e., $\widetilde{W}(y|x,x') = \widetilde{W}(y|x',x)$.

In a similar way we can define the channel to the eavesdropper. For fixed $s^n \in \mathcal{S}^n$ the discrete memoryless channel is given by $V_{s^n}^n(z^n|x^n) = V^n(z^n|x^n, s^n) = \prod_{i=1}^{n} V(z_i|x_i, s_i)$. We also set $\mathfrak{V} = \{V_{s^n}^n : s^n \in \mathcal{S}^n\}$ and $\overline{V}_q(z|x) = \sum_{s \in \mathcal{S}} V(z|x,s)q(s)$ for $q \in \mathcal{P}(\mathcal{S})$.

Definition 3. The *arbitrarily varying wiretap channel (AVWC)* $(\mathfrak{W}, \mathfrak{V})$ is given by its marginal AVCs $\mathfrak{W}$ and $\mathfrak{V}$ with common input as

$$(\mathfrak{W}, \mathfrak{V}) = (\{W_{s^n}^n : s^n \in \mathcal{S}^n\}, \{V_{s^n}^n : s^n \in \mathcal{S}^n\}).$$

Finally, we need a concept to measure the distance between two channels. As in [22] we define the distance between two channels $W_1, W_2 : \mathcal{X} \to \mathcal{P}(\mathcal{Y})$ based on the total variation distance as

$$d(W_1, W_2) = \max_{x \in \mathcal{X}} \sum_{y \in \mathcal{Y}} |W_1(y|x) - W_2(y|x)|. \tag{5}$$

Now, this generalizes to a distance between two AVCs as follows. For two AVWCs $\mathfrak{W}_1$ and $\mathfrak{W}_2$ with finite state sets $\mathcal{S}_1$ and $\mathcal{S}_2$ we define uncertainty sets $\mathcal{W}_1 = \{W_{s_1} : s_1 \in \mathcal{S}_1\}$ and $\mathcal{W}_2 = \{W_{s_2} : s_2 \in \mathcal{S}_2\}$. Then the distance between these two sets of channels is

$$d_1(\mathcal{W}_1, \mathcal{W}_2) = \max_{s_2 \in \mathcal{S}_2} \min_{s_1 \in \mathcal{S}_1} d(W_{s_1}, W_{s_2})$$

$$d_2(\mathcal{W}_1, \mathcal{W}_2) = \max_{s_1 \in \mathcal{S}_1} \min_{s_2 \in \mathcal{S}_2} d(W_{s_1}, W_{s_2})$$

so that the distance between the AVCs $\mathfrak{W}_1$ and $\mathfrak{W}_2$ is given as

$$D(\mathfrak{W}_1, \mathfrak{W}_2) = \max\{d_1(\mathcal{W}_1, \mathcal{W}_2), d_2(\mathcal{W}_1, \mathcal{W}_2)\}.$$

Roughly speaking, the distance $D(\mathfrak{W}_1, \mathfrak{W}_2)$ between two AVCs $\mathfrak{W}_1$ and $\mathfrak{W}_2$ is given by the largest distance in Equation (5) between all possible channel realizations in the corresponding state sets.

The distance $D(\mathfrak{V}_1, \mathfrak{V}_2)$ between two eavesdropper AVCs is defined accordingly so that the distance between two AVWCs $(\mathfrak{W}_1, \mathfrak{V}_1)$ and $(\mathfrak{W}_2, \mathfrak{V}_2)$ is finally given by

$$D((\mathfrak{W}_1, \mathfrak{V}_1), (\mathfrak{W}_2, \mathfrak{V}_2)) = \max\{D(\mathfrak{W}_1, \mathfrak{W}_2), D(\mathfrak{V}_1, \mathfrak{V}_2)\}.$$

2.2. Code Concepts

For communication over AVCs it makes a substantial difference whether unassisted (deterministic) or more sophisticated code concepts based on *common randomness (CR)* are used. Indeed, the unassisted capacity of an AVC can be zero, while the corresponding CR-assisted capacity is positive [12–14].

2.2.1. Unassisted Codes

Unassisted codes refer to codes whose encoder and decoder are pre-specified and fixed prior to the transmission as shown in Figure 1.

Definition 4. An *unassisted* (n, M_n)-*code* $\mathcal{C}$ consists of a stochastic encoder at the transmitter

$$E : \mathcal{M} \to \mathcal{P}(\mathcal{X}^n) \tag{6}$$

with a set of messages $\mathcal{M} = \{1, ..., M_n\}$ and a deterministic decoder at the legitimate receiver

$$\varphi : \mathcal{Y}^n \to \mathcal{M}. \tag{7}$$

Remark 1. Since the encoder in Equation (6) and the decoder in Equation (7) are fixed prior to the transmission of the message, they must be universally valid for all possible state sequences $s^n \in \mathcal{S}^n$ simultaneously.

The average probability of error of such a code for a given state sequence $s^n \in \mathcal{S}^n$ is given by

$$\bar{e}_n(s^n) = \frac{1}{|\mathcal{M}|} \sum_{m \in \mathcal{M}} \sum_{x^n \in \mathcal{X}^n} \sum_{y^n : \varphi(y^n) \neq m} W^n(y^n | x^n, s^n) E(x^n | m).$$

The confidentiality of the message is ensured by requiring $\max_{s^n \in \mathcal{S}^n} I(M; Z_{s^n}^n) \leq \delta_n$ for some $\delta_n > 0$ with M the random variable uniformly distributed over the set of messages $\mathcal{M}$ and $Z_{s^n}^n = (Z_{s_1}, Z_{s_2}, ..., Z_{s_n})$ the output at the eavesdropper for state sequence $s^n \in \mathcal{S}^n$. This criterion is termed *strong secrecy* [32,33] and the reasoning is to control the total amount of information leaked to the eavesdropper. This yields the following definition.

Definition 5. A rate $R_S > 0$ is an *achievable secrecy rate* for the AVWC $(\mathfrak{W}, \mathfrak{V})$ if for all $\tau > 0$ there exists an $n(\tau) \in \mathbb{N}$, positive null sequences $\{\lambda_n\}_{n \in \mathbb{N}}$, $\{\delta_n\}_{n \in \mathbb{N}}$, and a sequence of (n, M_n)-codes $\{\mathcal{C}_n\}_{n \in \mathbb{N}}$ such that for all $n \geq n(\tau)$ we have $\frac{1}{n} \log M_n \geq R_S - \tau$,

$$\max_{s^n \in \mathcal{S}^n} \bar{e}_n(s^n) \leq \lambda_n,$$

and

$$\max_{s^n \in \mathcal{S}^n} I(M; Z_{s^n}^n) \leq \delta_n.$$

The *unassisted secrecy capacity* $C_S(\mathfrak{W}, \mathfrak{V})$ of the AVWC $(\mathfrak{W}, \mathfrak{V})$ is given by the maximum of all achievable rates R_S.

Unfortunately, it has been shown that unassisted codes with a pre-specified encoder and decoder will not work for symmetrizable channels, *cf.* Definition 2. Thus the unassisted capacity will be zero [14] and more sophisticated code concepts based on CR are needed.

2.2.2. CR-Assisted Codes

CR is a powerful coordination resource and can be realized for example based on a common synchronization procedure or a satellite signal. It is modeled by a random variable Γ which takes values in a finite set $\mathcal{G}_n$ according to a distribution $P_\Gamma \in \mathcal{P}(\mathcal{G}_n)$. This enables the transmitter and the receiver to choose their encoder in Equation (6) and decoder in Equation (7) according to the actual realization $\gamma \in \mathcal{G}_n$ as shown in Figure 2.

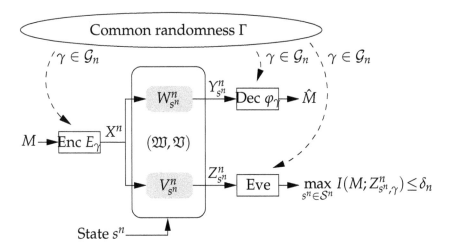

Figure 2. CR is available to all users including the eavesdropper. The transmitter and receiver can adapt their encoder and decoder according to the actual CR realization $\gamma \in \mathcal{G}_n$.

Definition 6. A *CR-assisted* $(n, M_n, \mathcal{G}_n, P_\Gamma)$-*code* $\mathcal{C}_{\mathbf{CR}}$ is given by a family of unassisted codes

$$\{\mathcal{C}(\gamma) : \gamma \in \mathcal{G}_n\}$$

together with a random variable Γ taking values in $\mathcal{G}_n$ with $|\mathcal{G}_n| < \infty$ according to $P_\Gamma \in \mathcal{P}(\mathcal{G}_n)$.

The reliability and secrecy constraints extend to CR-assisted codes in a natural way: The mean average probability of error is

$$\bar{e}_{\mathrm{CR}} = \max_{s^n \in \mathcal{S}^n} \frac{1}{|\mathcal{M}|} \sum_{m \in \mathcal{M}} \sum_{\gamma \in \mathcal{G}_n} \sum_{x^n \in \mathcal{X}^n} \sum_{y^n : \varphi_\gamma(y^n) \neq m} W^n(y^n | x^n, s^n) E_\gamma(x^n | m) P_\Gamma(\gamma)$$

where E_γ and φ_γ indicate that the encoder and decoder are chosen according to the CR realization $\gamma \in \mathcal{G}_n$. Accordingly, the secrecy criterion becomes

$$\max_{s^n \in \mathcal{S}^n} \sum_{\gamma \in \mathcal{G}_n} I(M; Z^n_{s^n, \gamma}) P_\Gamma(\gamma) \leq \delta_n \tag{8}$$

where $Z^n_{s^n, \gamma}$ indicates that the observed output at the eavesdropper depends on the chosen encoder $E_\gamma, \gamma \in \mathcal{G}_n$.

Remark 2. Note that the secrecy criterion Equation (8) can further be strengthened by requiring

$$\max_{s^n \in \mathcal{S}^n} \max_{\gamma \in \mathcal{G}_n} I(M; Z^n_{s^n, \gamma}) \leq \delta_n,$$

i.e., the average over all CR in Equation (8) is replaced by the maximum. Surprisingly, this strengthening comes at no cost and does not decrease the secrecy capacity, *cf.* [20]. The stronger criterion has the advantage that it protects the message even in the scenario in which the eavesdropper is aware of the CR realization $\gamma \in \mathcal{G}_n$, *cf.* Figure 2.

Then the definitions of a *CR-assisted achievable secrecy rate* and the *CR-assisted secrecy capacity* $C_{S,CR}(\mathfrak{W}, \mathfrak{V})$ of the AVWC $(\mathfrak{W}, \mathfrak{V})$ follow accordingly.

2.3. Capacity Results

There has been some work done in order to understand the secrecy capacity of the AVWC [15–22] which is briefly reviewed in the following. If CR is available, the transmitter and the legitimate receiver can coordinate their choice of encoder and decoder. This scenario has been studied in [15–18,20,22], but despite these efforts a single-letter characterization remains unknown to date (if it exists at all). Only a multi-letter description has been found in [20].

Theorem 1 ([20]). *A multi-letter description of the CR-assisted secrecy capacity* $C_{S,CR}(\mathfrak{W}, \mathfrak{V})$ *of the AVWC* $(\mathfrak{W}, \mathfrak{V})$ *is*

$$C_{S,CR}(\mathfrak{W}, \mathfrak{V}) = \lim_{n \to \infty} \frac{1}{n} \max_{U - X^n - (\overline{Y}_q^n, Z_{s^n}^n)} \left(\min_{q \in \mathcal{P}(\mathcal{S})} I(U; \overline{Y}_q^n) - \max_{s^n \in \mathcal{S}^n} I(U; Z_{s^n}^n) \right)$$

with $\overline{Y}_q^n$ *the random variable associated with the output of the averaged channel* $\overline{W}_q^n = \sum_{s^n \in \mathcal{S}^n} q^n(s^n) W_{s^n}$, $q \in \mathcal{P}(\mathcal{S})$.

If CR is not available to the transmitter and legitimate receiver, unassisted codes must be used and the corresponding unassisted secrecy capacity has been completely characterized in terms of its CR-assisted secrecy capacity [16,21].

Theorem 2 ([16,21]). *The unassisted secrecy capacity* $C_S(\mathfrak{W}, \mathfrak{V})$ *of the AVWC* $(\mathfrak{W}, \mathfrak{V})$ *possesses the following symmetrizability properties:*

1. *If* $\mathfrak{W}$ *is symmetrizable, then* $C_S(\mathfrak{W}, \mathfrak{V}) = 0$.
2. *If* $\mathfrak{W}$ *is non-symmetrizable, then* $C_S(\mathfrak{W}, \mathfrak{V}) = C_{S,CR}(\mathfrak{W}, \mathfrak{V})$.

The unassisted secrecy capacity displays a dichotomous behavior similar to the capacity of the single-user AVC: The unassisted secrecy capacity $C_S(\mathfrak{W}, \mathfrak{V})$ either equals its CR-assisted secrecy capacity $C_{S,CR}(\mathfrak{W}, \mathfrak{V})$ or else is zero.

From Theorem 2 we see that it is only the symmetrizability of the legitimate AVC $\mathfrak{W}$ that controls whether the unassisted secrecy capacity is zero or positive. However, it does not specify the sensitivity, meaning how rapidly the AVC $\mathfrak{W}$ can change from symmetrizable to non-symmetrizable. This is addressed by the next result.

Theorem 3 ([21]). *If the unassisted secrecy capacity* $C_S(\mathfrak{W}, \mathfrak{V})$ *of the AVWC* $(\mathfrak{W}, \mathfrak{V})$ *satisfies* $C_S(\mathfrak{W}, \mathfrak{V}) > 0$, *then there is an* $\epsilon > 0$ *such that for all AVWCs* $(\mathfrak{W}', \mathfrak{V}')$ *satisfying* $D((\mathfrak{W}, \mathfrak{V}), (\mathfrak{W}', \mathfrak{V}')) \leq \epsilon$ *we have* $C_S(\mathfrak{W}', \mathfrak{V}') > 0$.

This result shows the stability of positivity of the unassisted secrecy capacity: Wherever it is positive, *i.e.*, $C_S(\mathfrak{W}, \mathfrak{V}) > 0$, it remains positive in a certain neighborhood, *i.e.*, $C_S(\mathfrak{W}', \mathfrak{V}') > 0$ for $D((\mathfrak{W}, \mathfrak{V}), (\mathfrak{W}', \mathfrak{V}')) \leq \epsilon$. Thus, if the AVC $\mathfrak{W}$ is non-symmetrizable, small changes in the uncertainty set will not make it symmetrizable.

To further explore the question of continuity for the AVWC, we need the function

$$F(\mathfrak{W}) = \min_{\sigma: \mathcal{X} \to \mathcal{P}(\mathcal{S})} \left(\max_{x \neq x'} \sum_{y \in \mathcal{Y}} \left| \sum_{s \in \mathcal{S}} W(y|x', s)\sigma(s|x) - \sum_{s \in \mathcal{S}} W(y|x, s)\sigma(s|x') \right| \right). \tag{9}$$

This function generalizes ideas from the concept of symmetrizability, *cf.* Definition 2. It is a continuous function of the legitimate AVC $\mathfrak{W}$ and the AVC $\mathfrak{W}$ is symmetrizable if and only if

$F(\mathfrak{W}) = 0$. This yields a characterization of when the unassisted secrecy capacity $C_S(\mathfrak{W}, \mathfrak{V})$ is discontinuous: The AVC $\mathfrak{W}$ changes from non-symmetrizable to symmetrizable and the capacity breaks down to zero.

That the unassisted secrecy capacity is indeed discontinuous has been observed in [22] for the first time by constructing a simple example of dimensions $|\mathcal{X}| = 2$, $|\mathcal{Y}| = 3$, and $|\mathcal{S}| = 2$. It is noteworthy that a state set consisting of two different states only is already sufficient to get a discontinuous behavior. From an adversarial point of view this means that two different strategies for the adversary suffice to break down the system. On the other hand, reducing the state set to have only one element, i.e., $|\mathcal{S}| = 1$, the AVWC becomes a compound wiretap channel [34–36] (as the state remains constant for the entire duration of transmission) and the corresponding secrecy capacity becomes continuous [22]. Subsequently, the discontinuous behavior was then completely characterized in [21].

Theorem 4 ([21]). *The unassisted secrecy capacity $C_S(\mathfrak{W}, \mathfrak{V})$ of the AVWC $(\mathfrak{W}, \mathfrak{V})$ possesses the following discontinuity properties:*

1. *The AVWC $(\mathfrak{W}, \mathfrak{V})$ is a discontinuity point of $C_S(\mathfrak{W}, \mathfrak{V})$ if and only if the following holds: First, $C_{S,CR}(\mathfrak{W}, \mathfrak{V}) > 0$, and second, $F(\mathfrak{W}) = 0$ but for every $\epsilon > 0$ there is a finite $\mathfrak{W}'$ with $D(\mathfrak{W}, \mathfrak{W}') \leq \epsilon$ and $F(\mathfrak{W}') > 0$.*
2. *If $C_S(\mathfrak{W}, \mathfrak{V})$ is discontinuous in the point $(\mathfrak{W}, \mathfrak{V})$ then it is discontinuous for all $\mathfrak{V}'$ for which $C_{S,CR}(\mathfrak{W}, \mathfrak{V}') > 0$.*

This result has the following important consequence: Since the second condition relates the question of discontinuity to the function $F(\mathfrak{W})$ and therewith solely to the symmetrizability of the legitimate AVC $\mathfrak{W}$, the unassisted secrecy capacity $C_S(\mathfrak{W}, \mathfrak{V})$ is always a continuous function of the eavesdropper AVC $\mathfrak{V}$, while the discontinuity comes from the legitimate AVC $\mathfrak{W}$ only.

3. Super-Activation and Robustness

Medium access control and in particular resource allocation is one of the most important issues for wireless communication systems as it determines the overall performance of a system. For example, the overall capacity of an OFDM system is given by the sum of the capacities of all orthogonal sub-channels. To this end, a system consisting of two orthogonal ordinary DMCs, where both are "useless" in the sense of having zero capacity, the capacity of the whole system is zero as well. This reflects the world view of classical additivity of resources in the sense that "$0 + 0 = 0$."

Recently, it was shown in [17] that the additivity of basic resources does not hold anymore for secure communication over AVCs. Specifically, it was demonstrated that two orthogonal AVWCs which are themselves useless can be used jointly to allow for secure transmission with positive rate, i.e., "$0 + 0 > 0$." This phenomenon of super-activation was then further studied in [21], which in particular provides a characterization of when super-activation is possible.

3.1. Secure Communication over Orthogonal AVWCs

To continue this line of research, we now introduce the corresponding system model in detail.

For finite state sets $\mathcal{S}_i$, input alphabets $\mathcal{X}_i$, and output alphabets $\mathcal{Y}_i$ and $\mathcal{Z}_i$, $i = 1, 2$, we define two AVWCs $(\mathfrak{W}_1, \mathfrak{V}_1)$ and $(\mathfrak{W}_2, \mathfrak{V}_2)$ exactly as in Section 2.1, cf. Definitions 1 and 3. Then the parallel use of both AVWCs $(\mathfrak{W}_1, \mathfrak{V}_1)$ and $(\mathfrak{W}_2, \mathfrak{V}_2)$ creates a combined AVWC

$$(\widetilde{\mathfrak{W}}, \widetilde{\mathfrak{V}}) = (\mathfrak{W}_1, \mathfrak{V}_1) \otimes (\mathfrak{W}_2, \mathfrak{V}_2)$$
$$= (\mathfrak{W}_1 \otimes \mathfrak{W}_2, \mathfrak{V}_1 \otimes \mathfrak{V}_2),$$

where the notation $\otimes$ indicates the orthogonal use of $(\mathfrak{W}_1, \mathfrak{V}_1)$ and $(\mathfrak{W}_2, \mathfrak{V}_2)$. Now, for given state sequences $s^n = (s_1^n, s_2^n) \in \mathcal{S}_1^n \times \mathcal{S}_2^n$, the discrete memoryless channel to the legitimate receiver is

$$
\begin{aligned}
\widetilde{W}^n(y^n | x^n, s^n) &= W_{1,s_1^n}^n(y_1^n | x_1^n) W_{2,s_2^n}^n(y_2^n | x_2^n) \\
&= W_1^n(y_1^n | x_1^n, s_1^n) W_2^n(y_2^n | x_2^n, s_2^n) \\
&= \prod_{i=1}^{n} W_1(y_{1,i} | x_{1,i}, s_{1,i}) \prod_{i=1}^{n} W_2(y_{2,i} | x_{2,i}, s_{2,i})
\end{aligned}
\tag{10}
$$

with $x^n = (x_1^n, x_2^n) \in \mathcal{X}_1^n \times \mathcal{X}_2^n$ and $y^n = (y_1^n, y_2^n) \in \mathcal{Y}_1^n \times \mathcal{Y}_2^n$. Accordingly, the AVC $\widetilde{\mathfrak{W}}$ is then given by

$$
\begin{aligned}
\widetilde{\mathfrak{W}} &= \left\{ \widetilde{W}_{s^n}^n : s^n \in \mathcal{S}_1^n \times \mathcal{S}_2^n \right\} \\
&= \left\{ W_{1,s_1^n}^n W_{2,s_2^n}^n : s_1^n \in \mathcal{S}_1^n, s_2^n \in \mathcal{S}_2^n \right\}
\end{aligned}
\tag{11}
$$

and the AVWC $(\widetilde{\mathfrak{W}}, \widetilde{\mathfrak{V}})$ by

$$
(\widetilde{\mathfrak{W}}, \widetilde{\mathfrak{V}}) = \left(\{ \widetilde{W}_{s^n}^n : s^n \in \mathcal{S}_1^n \times \mathcal{S}_2^n \}, \{ \widetilde{V}_{s^n}^n : s^n \in \mathcal{S}_1^n \times \mathcal{S}_2^n \} \right)
$$

with $\widetilde{\mathfrak{V}}$ the AVC to the eavesdropper defined accordingly as in Equation (11).

Note that a parallel use of both AVWCs $(\mathfrak{W}_1, \mathfrak{V}_1)$ and $(\mathfrak{W}_2, \mathfrak{V}_2)$ means that for each $(\mathfrak{W}_i, \mathfrak{V}_i)$ we have individual encoders $E_i : \mathcal{M}_i \to \mathcal{P}(\mathcal{X}_i^n)$ and decoders $\varphi_i : \mathcal{Y}_i^n \to \mathcal{M}_i$, $i = 1, 2$, according to Definitions 4 and 6. On the other hand, a joint use of both AVWCs results in a joint encoder $E : \mathcal{M} \to \mathcal{P}(\mathcal{X}_1^n \times \mathcal{X}_2^n)$ and a joint decoder $\varphi : \mathcal{Y}_1^n \times \mathcal{Y}_2^n \to \mathcal{M}$.

3.2. Super-Activation of Orthogonal AVWCs

For orthogonal AVWCs as described above, the phenomenon of super-activation has been completely characterized in [21].

Theorem 5 ([21]). *Let $(\mathfrak{W}_1, \mathfrak{V}_1)$ and $(\mathfrak{W}_2, \mathfrak{V}_2)$ be two orthogonal AVWCs. Then the following properties hold:*

1. *If $C_S(\mathfrak{W}_1, \mathfrak{V}_1) = C_S(\mathfrak{W}_2, \mathfrak{V}_2) = 0$, then*

$$
C_S(\mathfrak{W}_1 \otimes \mathfrak{W}_2, \mathfrak{V}_1 \otimes \mathfrak{V}_2) > 0
$$

if and only if $\mathfrak{W}_1 \otimes \mathfrak{W}_2$ is non-symmetrizable and $C_{S,CR}(\mathfrak{W}_1 \otimes \mathfrak{W}_2, \mathfrak{V}_1 \otimes \mathfrak{V}_2) > 0$. If $(\mathfrak{W}_1, \mathfrak{V}_1)$ and $(\mathfrak{W}_2, \mathfrak{V}_2)$ can be super-activated it holds that

$$
C_S(\mathfrak{W}_1 \otimes \mathfrak{W}_2, \mathfrak{V}_1 \otimes \mathfrak{V}_2) = C_{S,CR}(\mathfrak{W}_1 \otimes \mathfrak{W}_2, \mathfrak{V}_1 \otimes \mathfrak{V}_2).
$$

2. *If $C_{S,CR}$ shows no super-activation for $(\mathfrak{W}_1, \mathfrak{V}_1)$ and $(\mathfrak{W}_2, \mathfrak{V}_2)$, then super-activation of C_S can only happen if $\mathfrak{W}_1$ is non-symmetrizable and $\mathfrak{W}_2$ is symmetrizable and $C_{S,CR}(\mathfrak{W}_1, \mathfrak{V}_1) = 0$ and $C_{S,CR}(\mathfrak{W}_2, \mathfrak{V}_2) > 0$. The statement is independent of the specific labeling.*
3. *There exist AVWCs that exhibit the behavior described by the second property.*

To give some intuition into why super-activation can happen, let us consider the following scenario: Assume there are two orthogonal AVWCs each having zero unassisted secrecy capacity. To this end, assume that one of the unassisted secrecy capacities is zero because the corresponding legitimate AVC is symmetrizable and the other capacity is zero because the eavesdropper AVC is "stronger" than the legitimate AVC. Since the latter legitimate AVC supports a positive rate (although non-secure), it can be used to transmit information to the legitimate receiver (and eavesdropper) to generate CR. Then the legitimate users can use CR-assisted codes to achieve a positive CR-assisted secrecy rate.

Theorem 5 provides a complete characterization of when super-activation can happen. In the following, we want to further explore this phenomenon. To this end, we first show that super-activation is generic in the sense that whenever two orthogonal AVWCs can be super-activated, it is possible for all AVWCs in a certain neighborhood as well.

Theorem 6. *Let $(\mathfrak{W}_1, \mathfrak{V}_1)$ and $(\mathfrak{W}_2, \mathfrak{V}_2)$ be two useless AVWCs that can be super-activated, i.e., $C_S(\mathfrak{W}_1, \mathfrak{V}_1) = C_S(\mathfrak{W}_2, \mathfrak{V}_2) = 0$ and $C_S(\mathfrak{W}_1 \otimes \mathfrak{W}_2, \mathfrak{V}_1 \otimes \mathfrak{V}_2) > 0$. Then there exists an $\epsilon > 0$ such that for all useless AVWCs $(\mathfrak{W}_1', \mathfrak{V}_1')$ and $(\mathfrak{W}_2', \mathfrak{V}_2')$ with*

$$D((\mathfrak{W}_i, \mathfrak{V}_i), (\mathfrak{W}_i', \mathfrak{V}_i')) < \epsilon, \quad i = 1, 2,$$

we have

$$C_S(\mathfrak{W}_1' \otimes \mathfrak{W}_2', \mathfrak{V}_1' \otimes \mathfrak{V}_2') > 0,$$

i.e., all channels in the neighborhood of $(\mathfrak{W}_1, \mathfrak{V}_1)$ and $(\mathfrak{W}_2, \mathfrak{V}_2)$ can be super-activated as well.

Proof. Let $(\mathfrak{W}_1, \mathfrak{V}_1)$ and $(\mathfrak{W}_2, \mathfrak{V}_2)$ be two useless orthogonal AVWCs that can be super-activated and let $(\mathfrak{W}_1', \mathfrak{V}_1')$ and $(\mathfrak{W}_2', \mathfrak{V}_2')$ be two useless AVWCs with $D((\mathfrak{W}_i, \mathfrak{V}_i), (\mathfrak{W}_i', \mathfrak{V}_i')) < \epsilon, i = 1, 2$. Then it holds that

$$\sum_{y_1 \in \mathcal{Y}_1} \sum_{y_2 \in \mathcal{Y}_2} \left| W_1(y_1|x_1, s_1) W_2(y_2|x_2, s_2) - W_1'(y_1|x_1, s_1') W_2'(y_2|x_2, s_2') \right|$$

$$= \sum_{y_1 \in \mathcal{Y}_1} \sum_{y_2 \in \mathcal{Y}_2} \Big| W_1(y_1|x_1, s_1) W_2(y_2|x_2, s_2) - W_1'(y_1|x_1, s_1') W_2(y_2|x_2, s_2)$$

$$+ W_1'(y_1|x_1, s_1') W_2(y_2|x_2, s_2) - W_1'(y_1|x_1, s_1') W_2'(y_2|x_2, s_2') \Big|$$

$$\leq \sum_{y_1 \in \mathcal{Y}_1} \sum_{y_2 \in \mathcal{Y}_2} \left| (W_1(y_1|x_1, s_1) - W_1'(y_1|x_1, s_1')) W_2(y_2|x_2, s_2) \right|$$

$$+ \sum_{y_1 \in \mathcal{Y}_1} \sum_{y_2 \in \mathcal{Y}_2} \left| (W_2(y_2|x_2, s_2) - W_2'(y_2|x_2, s_2')) W_1'(y_1|x_1, s_1') \right|$$

$$= \sum_{y_1 \in \mathcal{Y}_1} \left| W_1(y_1|x_1, s_1) - W_1'(y_1|x_1, s_1') \right| + \sum_{y_2 \in \mathcal{Y}_2} \left| W_2(y_2|x_2, s_2) - W_2'(y_2|x_2, s_2') \right|.$$

Since $D((\mathfrak{W}_i, \mathfrak{V}_i), (\mathfrak{W}_i', \mathfrak{V}_i')) < \epsilon, i = 1, 2$, by assumption, we have

$$D((\mathfrak{W}_1 \otimes \mathfrak{W}_2, \mathfrak{V}_1 \otimes \mathfrak{V}_2)), (\mathfrak{W}_1' \otimes \mathfrak{W}_2', \mathfrak{V}_1' \otimes \mathfrak{V}_2') < 2\epsilon. \tag{12}$$

Now we can apply the stability result in Theorem 3. From this we know that for all AVWCs $(\widetilde{\mathfrak{W}}, \widetilde{\mathfrak{V}})$ with $\widetilde{W} : \mathcal{X}_1 \times \mathcal{X}_2 \times \mathcal{S}_1 \times \mathcal{S}_2 \to \mathcal{P}(\mathcal{Y}_1 \times \mathcal{Y}_2)$ and $\widetilde{V} : \mathcal{X}_1 \times \mathcal{X}_2 \times \mathcal{S}_1 \times \mathcal{S}_2 \to \mathcal{P}(\mathcal{Z}_1 \times \mathcal{Z}_2)$ and

$$D((\mathfrak{W}_1 \otimes \mathfrak{W}_2, \mathfrak{V}_1 \otimes \mathfrak{V}_2), (\widetilde{\mathfrak{W}}, \widetilde{\mathfrak{V}})) < \tilde{\epsilon}$$

we have

$$C_S(\widetilde{\mathfrak{W}}, \widetilde{\mathfrak{V}}) > 0.$$

Now we choose ϵ in Equation (12) small such that $2\epsilon < \tilde{\epsilon}$ holds. With this we obtain the desired positivity for all AVWCs $(\mathfrak{W}_1', \mathfrak{V}_1')$ and $(\mathfrak{W}_2', \mathfrak{V}_2')$ for which Equation (12) is satisfied. This completes the proof. $\square$

This result shows that super-activation is not an isolated phenomenon of orthogonal AVWCs. In fact, whenever super-activation is possible for two AVWCs, it occurs for all AVWCs that are sufficiently close to them.

Corollary 1. *Let $(\mathfrak{W}_1, \mathfrak{V}_1)$ and $(\mathfrak{W}_2, \mathfrak{V}_2)$ be two useless orthogonal AVWCs that can be super-activated. Then $(\mathfrak{W}_2, \mathfrak{V}_2)$ super-activates all AVWCs $(\mathfrak{W}_1', \mathfrak{V}_1')$ that are close enough to $(\mathfrak{W}_1, \mathfrak{V}_1)$.*

Proof. The result follows immediately from Theorem 6. Note that we can even choose $\epsilon = \tilde{\epsilon}$ in this case to obtain the desired result.   □

The previous result of Theorem 6 can even be strengthened. This formulation is more involved than the previous one, but the advantage is that it reveals the following behavior: The AVC to the legitimate receiver is much more important than the AVC to the eavesdropper in terms of super-activation. Specifically, there is no need of an explicit requirement on the distance between the eavesdropper channels. We obtain the following result.

Theorem 7. *Let $(\mathfrak{W}_1, \mathfrak{V}_1)$ and $(\mathfrak{W}_2, \mathfrak{V}_2)$ be two useless orthogonal AVWCs that can be super-activated. Then there exists an $\epsilon > 0$ such that all useless orthogonal AVWCs $(\mathfrak{W}_1', \mathfrak{V}_1')$ and $(\mathfrak{W}_2', \mathfrak{V}_2')$ that satisfy*

$$D(\mathfrak{W}_1, \mathfrak{W}_1') < \epsilon, \qquad D(\mathfrak{W}_2, \mathfrak{W}_2') < \epsilon,$$

and

$$C_{S,CR}(\mathfrak{W}_1' \otimes \mathfrak{W}_2', \mathfrak{V}_1' \otimes \mathfrak{V}_2') > 0,$$

can be super-activated as well.

Proof. We know that the combined AVC $\mathfrak{W}_1 \otimes \mathfrak{W}_2$ is non-symmetrizable, since otherwise super-activation would not be possible, *cf.* Theorem 5. Similarly as in the proof of Theorem 6 we can then show that $D(\mathfrak{W}_1 \otimes \mathfrak{W}_2, \mathfrak{W}_1' \otimes \mathfrak{W}_2') < 2\epsilon$ holds. Next we consider the function $F(\mathfrak{W}_1 \otimes \mathfrak{W}_2)$, *cf.* Equation (9). Since $\mathfrak{W}_1 \otimes \mathfrak{W}_2$ is non-symmetrizable, we have $F(\mathfrak{W}_1 \otimes \mathfrak{W}_2) > 0$. In addition, since the function F depends in a continuous way on the channel, for all AVCs $\widetilde{\mathfrak{W}}$ with $\widetilde{W} : \mathcal{X}_1 \times \mathcal{X}_2 \times \mathcal{S}_1 \times \mathcal{S}_2 \to \mathcal{P}(\mathcal{Y}_1 \times \mathcal{Y}_2)$ and $D(\mathfrak{W}_1 \otimes \mathfrak{W}_2, \widetilde{\mathfrak{W}}) < \tilde{\epsilon}$ we always have $F(\widetilde{\mathfrak{W}}) > 0$. Here we have to choose $\tilde{\epsilon} > 0$ sufficiently small depending on $\mathfrak{W}_1 \otimes \mathfrak{W}_2$. Since $F(\widetilde{\mathfrak{W}}) > 0$, the AVC $\widetilde{\mathfrak{W}}$ is non-symmetrizable and from Theorem 2 it follows that

$$C_S(\mathfrak{W}_1' \otimes \mathfrak{W}_2', \mathfrak{V}_1' \otimes \mathfrak{V}_2') = C_{S,CR}(\mathfrak{W}_1' \otimes \mathfrak{W}_2', \mathfrak{V}_1' \otimes \mathfrak{V}_2') > 0$$

which proves that these AVWCs can be super-activated. This completes the proof.   □

In the following we briefly present an example in which super-activation is possible for all orthogonal AVWCs in a certain neighborhood. This example is based on an example given in ([22], Section V-C). This constructs suitable AVWCs, whose unassisted secrecy capacities are zero in a certain neighborhood, but who all can be super-activated to allow for secure communication at a positive rate.

Example 1. First, we construct an AVWC $(\mathfrak{W}^*, \mathfrak{V}^*)$ with $|\mathcal{X}| = 2$, $|\mathcal{Y}| = 3$, $|\mathcal{Z}| = 2$, and $|\mathcal{S}| = 2$ for which in a set of AVWCs $(\mathfrak{W}, \mathfrak{V})$ around this channel we always have $C_{S,CR}(\mathfrak{W}^*, \mathfrak{V}^*) > 0$ and $C_S(\mathfrak{W}, \mathfrak{V}) = C_S(\mathfrak{W}^*, \mathfrak{V}^*) = 0$. To do so, we define the legitimate AVC as $\mathfrak{W}^* = \{W_1^*, W_2^*\}$ with

$$W_1^* = \begin{pmatrix} \frac{1}{2} & \frac{1}{2} & 0 \\ \frac{1}{4} & 0 & \frac{3}{4} \end{pmatrix} \quad \text{and} \quad W_2^* = \begin{pmatrix} 0 & 0 & 1 \\ 0 & 1 & 0 \end{pmatrix}$$

and the eavesdropper AVC as $\mathfrak{V}^* = \{V^*, V^*\}$ with

$$V^* = \begin{pmatrix} \frac{1}{2} & \frac{1}{2} \\ \frac{1}{2} & \frac{1}{2} \end{pmatrix}. \tag{13}$$

With this choice, the eavesdropper channel is fixed, while the legitimate channel allows appropriate variations. In particular, it is easy to show that $\mathfrak{W}^*$ is symmetrizable so that $C_S(\mathfrak{W}^*, \mathfrak{V}^*) = 0$ but $C_{S,CR}(\mathfrak{W}^*, \mathfrak{V}^*) > 0$, cf. ([22], Section V-C). Further, for all AVWCs $(\mathfrak{W}, \mathfrak{V})$ with $D(\mathfrak{W}^*, \mathfrak{W}) < \epsilon$ for some $\epsilon > 0$ it holds that $C_S(\mathfrak{W}^*, \mathfrak{V}^*) = 0$ but $C_{S,CR}(\mathfrak{W}^*, \mathfrak{V}^*) > 0$, cf. ([22], Theorem 6), which means that all AVWCs in a certain neighborhood have zero unassisted secrecy capacity. Now we can find another orthogonal AVWC $(\widetilde{\mathfrak{W}}, \widetilde{\mathfrak{V}})$ that super-activates the original AVWC $(\mathfrak{W}^*, \mathfrak{V}^*)$, but also all other AVWCs $(\mathfrak{W}, \mathfrak{V})$ with $D(\mathfrak{W}^*, \mathfrak{W}) < \epsilon$, cf. Corollary 1 and Theorem 7.

Remark 3. The previous considerations show that bonding of orthogonal resources can increase the performance significantly. Such bonding gains do not only appear if both unassisted secrecy capacities are equal to zero (super-activation), but also if only one of these is zero while the other one is positive (super-additivity). This follows by an easy adaptation of the discussion above.

Next we want to show that bonding of orthogonal resources reveals further effects and properties that are practically relevant. This is discussed in the following result.

Theorem 8. *Let $(\mathfrak{W}_1, \mathfrak{V}_1)$ and $(\mathfrak{W}_2, \mathfrak{V}_2)$ be two useless orthogonal AVWCs that can be super-activated. Then the unassisted secrecy capacity $C_S(\mathfrak{W}_1' \otimes \mathfrak{W}_2', \mathfrak{V}_1' \otimes \mathfrak{V}_2')$ depends in a continuous way on the channels $(\mathfrak{W}_1', \mathfrak{V}_1')$ and $(\mathfrak{W}_2', \mathfrak{V}_2')$ with $D(\mathfrak{W}_i, \mathfrak{W}_i') < \epsilon$, $i = 1, 2$. Here, ϵ depends only on the orthogonal AVCs $\mathfrak{W}_1$ and $\mathfrak{W}_2$.*

Proof. Since the AVWCs $(\mathfrak{W}_1, \mathfrak{V}_1)$ and $(\mathfrak{W}_2, \mathfrak{V}_2)$ can be super-activated, we know that $C_S(\mathfrak{W}_1 \otimes \mathfrak{W}_2, \mathfrak{V}_1 \otimes \mathfrak{V}_2) > 0$. Then we know that this is also true for all AVWCs $(\widetilde{\mathfrak{W}}, \widetilde{\mathfrak{V}})$ with $\widetilde{W} : \mathcal{X}_1 \times \mathcal{X}_2 \times \mathcal{S}_1 \times \mathcal{S}_2 \to \mathcal{P}(\mathcal{Y}_1 \times \mathcal{Y}_2)$ and $\widetilde{V} : \mathcal{X}_1 \times \mathcal{X}_2 \times \mathcal{S}_1 \times \mathcal{S}_2 \to \mathcal{P}(\mathcal{Z}_1 \times \mathcal{Z}_2)$ that are sufficiently close to $(\mathfrak{W}_1, \mathfrak{V}_1)$ and $(\mathfrak{W}_2, \mathfrak{V}_2)$, cf. Theorem 3, so that

$$C_S(\widetilde{\mathfrak{W}}, \widetilde{\mathfrak{V}}) = C_{S,CR}(\widetilde{\mathfrak{W}}, \widetilde{\mathfrak{V}})$$

holds. Since $C_{S,CR}(\widetilde{\mathfrak{W}}, \widetilde{\mathfrak{V}})$ is a continuous function, cf. [20,22], the desired result follows then from Theorem 6. □

Remark 4. The unassisted secrecy capacity $C_S(\mathfrak{W}_1 \otimes \mathfrak{W}_2, \mathfrak{V}_1 \otimes \mathfrak{V}_2)$ need not necessarily be continuous in $(\mathfrak{W}_1, \mathfrak{V}_1)$ or $(\mathfrak{W}_2, \mathfrak{V}_2)$. In particular, there are examples with a discontinuous behavior as discussed above.

Remark 5. We see that bonding of orthogonal resources can also lead to a more robust system which is continuous. On the other hand, for a single AVC such continuous behavior cannot be guaranteed in general.

In the following we briefly present an example that demonstrates these effects. This example is based on an example in ([22], Section V-A). This constructs suitable AVWCs, whose unassisted secrecy capacity is continuous after super-activation although the unassisted secrecy capacity of one AVWC itself has a discontinuity point.

Example 2. First, we construct an AVWC $(\mathfrak{W}(\lambda), \mathfrak{V})$ for $0 \leq \lambda \leq 1$ with $|\mathcal{X}| = 2$, $|\mathcal{Y}| = 3$, $|\mathcal{Z}| = 2$, and $|\mathcal{S}| = 2$, whose unassisted secrecy capacity has a discontinuity point. To do so, for $0 \leq \lambda \leq 1$ we define the legitimate AVC as $\mathfrak{W}(\lambda) = \{W_1(\lambda), W_2(\lambda)\}$ with

$$W_1(\lambda) = \begin{pmatrix} 1 & 0 & 0 \\ 0 & \lambda & 1-\lambda \end{pmatrix} \text{ and } W_2(\lambda) = \begin{pmatrix} \lambda & 0 & 1-\lambda \\ 0 & 1 & 0 \end{pmatrix}$$

and the eavesdropper AVC as $\mathfrak{V} = \{V^*, V^*\}$ with V^* the useless channel as in (13) of Example 1. It can be shown that the unassisted secrecy capacity of the AVWC $(\mathfrak{W}(\lambda), \mathfrak{V})$ has a discontinuity point at $\lambda = 0$, i.e., we have $C_S(\mathfrak{W}(0), \mathfrak{V}) = 0$, but $\lim_{\lambda \searrow 0} C_S(\mathfrak{W}(0), \mathfrak{V}) > 0$, cf. ([22], Theorem 4). Now we can find another orthogonal AVWC $(\widetilde{\mathfrak{W}}, \widetilde{\mathfrak{V}})$ that super-activates the original AVWC $(\mathfrak{W}(\lambda), \mathfrak{V})$. Then we know from Theorem 8 that the unassisted secrecy capacity of this super-activated AVWC is continuous.

4. Communication over Orthogonal AVCs

The previous results and in particular Theorem 7 have shown that super-activation of AVWCs is robust in the eavesdropper AVC. Specifically, it is sufficient to require the eavesdropper AVC to be such that the CR-assisted secrecy capacity of the corresponding AVWC is positive. Then this capacity is continuous in the eavesdropper AVC. As a consequence, the phenomenon of super-activation depends particularly on the legitimate AVC. Accordingly, it is interesting to drop the eavesdropper and the security requirement for a while and study reliable message transmission over single-user AVCs in more detail.

4.1. Capacity Results

The single-user AVC is given as in Section 2.1 by considering only the legitimate AVC between the transmitter and legitimate receiver. Reliable message transmission for the single-user AVC has been well studied and its capacity has been established for both unassisted [13,14] and CR-assisted [12] codes.

Theorem 9 ([12]). *The* CR-assisted capacity $C_{CR}(\mathfrak{W})$ *of the AVC* $\mathfrak{W}$ *is*

$$C_{CR}(\mathfrak{W}) = \max_{P_X \in \mathcal{P}(\mathcal{X})} \inf_{q \in \mathcal{P}(\mathcal{S})} I(X; \overline{Y}_q) \tag{14}$$

where $\overline{Y}_q$ *denotes the random variable associated with the output of the averaged channel* $\overline{W}_q$, $q \in \mathcal{P}(\mathcal{S})$, *cf. Equation (3).*

The unassisted capacity is then completely characterized in terms of its CR-assisted capacity.

Theorem 10 ([13,14]). *The unassisted capacity* $C(\mathfrak{W})$ *of the AVC* $\mathfrak{W}$ *is*

$$C(\mathfrak{W}) = \begin{cases} C_{CR}(\mathfrak{W}) & \text{if } \mathfrak{W} \text{ is non-symmetrizable} \\ 0 & \text{if } \mathfrak{W} \text{ is symmetrizable.} \end{cases}$$

To the best of our knowledge, reliable message transmission over orthogonal AVCs has not been studied previously. This is surprising as this is already implicitly addressed by Shannon's question of the additivity of the zero error capacity [23]. Specifically, Ahlswede showed in [28] that the capacity of the AVC under the maximum error criterion includes the characterization of the zero error capacity as a special case. To this end, Alon's example in [27] for the super-additivity of the capacity of reliable message transmission over orthogonal AVCs under the maximum error criterion can be seen as the first contribution towards understanding the behavior of the capacity of orthogonal AVCs. In the following, we completely characterize the behavior of the capacity of orthogonal AVCs for the average error criterion.

4.2. Additivity of CR-Assisted Capacity

We start with the CR-assisted capacity and show that it is additive. This means that the CR-assisted capacity of two orthogonal AVCs is the sum of its CR-assisted capacities.

Theorem 11. *Let $\mathfrak{W}_1$ and $\mathfrak{W}_2$ be two orthogonal AVCs. Then the CR-assisted capacity is additive, i.e.,*

$$C_{CR}(\mathfrak{W}_1 \otimes \mathfrak{W}_2) = C_{CR}(\mathfrak{W}_1) + C_{CR}(\mathfrak{W}_2). \tag{15}$$

Proof. From the definition of capacity it follows immediately that

$$C_{CR}(\mathfrak{W}_1 \otimes \mathfrak{W}_2) \geq C_{CR}(\mathfrak{W}_1) + C_{CR}(\mathfrak{W}_2) \tag{16}$$

is satisfied since joint encoding and decoding over both AVCs can only increase the capacity compared to an individual encoding and decoding for both channels. Thus, to show equality in Equation (15) it remains to prove that the reversed inequality is also true, *i.e.*, $C_{CR}(\mathfrak{W}_1 \otimes \mathfrak{W}_2) \leq C_{CR}(\mathfrak{W}_1) + C_{CR}(\mathfrak{W}_2)$.

For the following argumentation it is beneficial to write the CR-assisted capacity in Equation (14) as

$$
\begin{aligned}
C_{CR}(\mathfrak{W}) &= \max_{P_X \in \mathcal{P}(\mathcal{X})} \inf_{q \in \mathcal{P}(\mathcal{S})} I(X; \overline{Y}_q) \\
&= \max_{P_X \in \mathcal{P}(\mathcal{X})} \min_{q \in \mathcal{P}(\mathcal{S})} I(P_X, \overline{W}_q)
\end{aligned}
$$

as the mutual information term is completely determined by the input distribution $P_X \in \mathcal{P}(\mathcal{X})$ and the averaged channel $\overline{W}_q$, $q \in \mathcal{P}(\mathcal{S})$, *cf.* Equation (3).

With this notation, the CR-assisted capacity of the combined AVC $\mathfrak{W}_1 \otimes \mathfrak{W}_2$, *cf.* also Equations (10) and (11), is given by

$$C_{CR}(\mathfrak{W}_1 \otimes \mathfrak{W}_2) = \max_{P_{X_1 X_2} \in \mathcal{P}(\mathcal{X}_1 \times \mathcal{X}_2)} \min_{q_{12} \in \mathcal{P}(\mathcal{S}_1 \times \mathcal{S}_2)} I(P_{X_1 X_2}, \overline{W}_{q_{12}}) \tag{17}$$

where $\overline{W}_{q_{12}}$, $q_{12} \in \mathcal{P}(\mathcal{S}_1 \times \mathcal{S}_2)$, denotes the corresponding averaged channel.

Now, this mutual information quantity in Equation (17) is continuous, concave in $P_{X_1 X_2}$, and convex in $\overline{W}_{q_{12}}$ so that the order of max and min can be exchanged to obtain

$$
\begin{aligned}
C_{CR}(\mathfrak{W}_1 \otimes \mathfrak{W}_2) &= \min_{q_{12} \in \mathcal{P}(\mathcal{S}_1 \times \mathcal{S}_2)} \max_{P_{X_1 X_2} \in \mathcal{P}(\mathcal{X}_1 \times \mathcal{X}_2)} I(P_{X_1 X_2}, \overline{W}_{q_{12}}) \\
&\leq \max_{P_{X_1 X_2} \in \mathcal{P}(\mathcal{X}_1 \times \mathcal{X}_2)} I(P_{X_1 X_2}, \overline{W}_{\hat{q}_1 \otimes \hat{q}_2})
\end{aligned}
$$

for some arbitrary but fixed $\hat{q}_1 \in \mathcal{P}(\mathcal{S}_1)$ and $\hat{q}_2 \in \mathcal{P}(\mathcal{S}_2)$. In addition, we have

$$
\begin{aligned}
\overline{W}_{\hat{q}_1 \otimes \hat{q}_2}(y_1, y_2 | x_1, x_2) &= \left(\sum_{s_1 \in \mathcal{S}_1} \hat{q}_1(s_1) W_{1,s_1}(y_1 | x_1) \right) \left(\sum_{s_2 \in \mathcal{S}_2} \hat{q}_2(s_2) W_{2,s_2}(y_2 | x_2) \right) \\
&= \overline{W}_{1,\hat{q}_1}(y_1 | x_1) \overline{W}_{2,\hat{q}_2}(y_2 | x_2)
\end{aligned}
$$

so that

$$\overline{W}_{\hat{q}_1 \otimes \hat{q}_2} = \overline{W}_{1,\hat{q}_1} \otimes \overline{W}_{2,\hat{q}_2}.$$

Since for ordinary DMCs under the average error criterion we have additivity, it holds that

$$\max_{P_{X_1 X_2} \in \mathcal{P}(\mathcal{X}_1 \times \mathcal{X}_2)} I(P_{X_1 X_2}, \overline{W}_{\hat{q}_1 \otimes \hat{q}_2}) = \max_{P_{X_1} \in \mathcal{P}(\mathcal{X}_1)} I(P_{X_1}, \overline{W}_{1,\hat{q}_1}) + \max_{P_{X_2} \in \mathcal{P}(\mathcal{X}_2)} I(P_{X_2}, \overline{W}_{2,\hat{q}_2}).$$

Since $\hat{q}_1 \in \mathcal{P}(\mathcal{S}_1)$ and $\hat{q}_2 \in \mathcal{P}(\mathcal{S}_2)$ are arbitrary, we obtain

$$
\begin{aligned}
C_{CR}(\mathfrak{W}_1 \otimes \mathfrak{W}_2) &\leq \min_{\hat{q}_1 \in \mathcal{P}(\mathcal{S}_1), \hat{q}_2 \in \mathcal{P}(\mathcal{S}_2)} \left(\max_{P_{X_1} \in \mathcal{P}(\mathcal{X}_1)} I(P_{X_1}, \overline{W}_{1,\hat{q}_1}) + \max_{P_{X_2} \in \mathcal{P}(\mathcal{X}_2)} I(P_{X_2}, \overline{W}_{2,\hat{q}_2}) \right) \\
&= \min_{\hat{q}_1 \in \mathcal{P}(\mathcal{S}_1)} \max_{P_{X_1} \in \mathcal{P}(\mathcal{X}_1)} I(P_{X_1}, \overline{W}_{1,\hat{q}_1}) + \min_{\hat{q}_2 \in \mathcal{P}(\mathcal{S}_2)} \max_{P_{X_2} \in \mathcal{P}(\mathcal{X}_2)} I(P_{X_2}, \overline{W}_{2,\hat{q}_2}) \\
&= C_{CR}(\mathfrak{W}_1) + C_{CR}(\mathfrak{W}_2) \tag{18}
\end{aligned}
$$

where the last step follows again from the fact that the mutual information is concave in the input distribution and convex in the channel which allows an exchange of min and max.

Now the inequalities in Equations (16) and (18) establish the desired additivity of the CR-assisted capacity, thereby proving the result. □

This result shows that the CR-assisted capacity is always additive and therewith confirms Shannon's conviction of the additivity of the capacity. The consequence is that joint encoding and decoding for both AVCs does not yield any gains in terms of CR-assisted capacity.

4.3. Super-Additivity of Unassisted Capacity

Next, we consider the unassisted capacity of two orthogonal AVCs.

Proposition 1. *Let $\mathfrak{W}_1$ and $\mathfrak{W}_2$ be two orthogonal AVCs. If the unassisted capacities satisfy $C(\mathfrak{W}_1) > 0$ and $C(\mathfrak{W}_2) > 0$, then the unassisted capacity is additive, i.e.,*

$$
C(\mathfrak{W}_1 \otimes \mathfrak{W}_2) = C(\mathfrak{W}_1) + C(\mathfrak{W}_2). \tag{19}
$$

Proof. From the additivity of the CR-assisted capacity, *cf.* Theorem 11, we have

$$
\begin{aligned}
C(\mathfrak{W}_1 \otimes \mathfrak{W}_2) &\leq C_{CR}(\mathfrak{W}_1 \otimes \mathfrak{W}_2) \\
&= C_{CR}(\mathfrak{W}_1) + C_{CR}(\mathfrak{W}_2) \\
&= C(\mathfrak{W}_1) + C(\mathfrak{W}_2) \tag{20}
\end{aligned}
$$

where the last equality follows from Theorem 10. On the other hand we have

$$
\begin{aligned}
C(\mathfrak{W}_1 \otimes \mathfrak{W}_2) &\geq C(\mathfrak{W}_1) + C(\mathfrak{W}_2) \\
&= C_{CR}(\mathfrak{W}_1) + C_{CR}(\mathfrak{W}_2) \\
&= C_{CR}(\mathfrak{W}_1 \otimes \mathfrak{W}_2) \\
&= C(\mathfrak{W}_1 \otimes \mathfrak{W}_2) \tag{21}
\end{aligned}
$$

where the first equality is again due to Theorem 10 since $C(\mathfrak{W}_1) > 0$ and $C(\mathfrak{W}_2) > 0$, and the second equality follows from Theorem 11. Equations (20) and (21) yield the desired equality in Equation (19), thereby proving the result. □

Proposition 2. *Let $\mathfrak{W}_1$ and $\mathfrak{W}_2$ be two orthogonal AVCs. If the unassisted capacities satisfy $C(\mathfrak{W}_1) = C(\mathfrak{W}_2) = 0$, then the unassisted capacity is additive, i.e.,*

$$
C(\mathfrak{W}_1 \otimes \mathfrak{W}_2) = C(\mathfrak{W}_1) + C(\mathfrak{W}_2).
$$

Proof. If $C(\mathfrak{W}_1) = C(\mathfrak{W}_2) = 0$, then both AVCs are symmetrizable according to Definition 2. This means there exist stochastic matrices $\sigma_i : \mathcal{X}_i \to \mathcal{P}(\mathcal{S}_i), i = 1, 2$, such that

$$\sum_{s_i \in \mathcal{S}_i} W_i(y_i|x_i, s_i)\sigma_i(s_i|x_i') = \sum_{s_i \in \mathcal{S}_i} W_i(y_i|x_i', s_i)\sigma_i(s_i|x_i)$$

holds for all $x_i, x_i' \in \mathcal{X}_i$ and $y_i \in \mathcal{Y}_i, i = 1, 2$.

Then, the AVC $\mathfrak{W}_1 \otimes \mathfrak{W}_2$ is symmetrizable as well and

$$\sum_{s_1 \in \mathcal{S}_1} \sum_{s_2 \in \mathcal{S}_2} W_1(y_1|x_1, s_1)W_2(y_2|x_2, s_2)\sigma_1(s_1|x_1')\sigma_2(s_2|x_2')$$
$$= \left(\sum_{s_1 \in \mathcal{S}_1} W_1(y_1|x_1, s_1)\sigma_1(s_1|x_1') \right)\left(\sum_{s_2 \in \mathcal{S}_2} W_2(y_2|x_2, s_2)\sigma_2(s_2|x_2') \right)$$
$$= \left(\sum_{s_1 \in \mathcal{S}_1} W_1(y_1|x_1', s_1)\sigma_1(s_1|x_1) \right)\left(\sum_{s_2 \in \mathcal{S}_2} W_2(y_2|x_2', s_2)\sigma_2(s_2|x_2) \right)$$
$$= \sum_{s_1 \in \mathcal{S}_1} \sum_{s_2 \in \mathcal{S}_2} W_1(y_1|x_1', s_1)W_2(y_2|x_2', s_2)\sigma_1(s_1|x_1)\sigma_2(s_2|x_2)$$

holds for all $x_i, x_i' \in \mathcal{X}_i$ and $y_i \in \mathcal{Y}_i, i = 1, 2$. This implies that $C(\mathfrak{W}_1 \otimes \mathfrak{W}_2) = 0$ as well which shows the additivity for this case as well as completing the proof. $\square$

These two results show that when the unassisted capacities are both positive or both zero, the overall unassisted capacity is additive. In addition, from Proposition 2 it follows immediately that super-activation is not possible for reliable message transmission over orthogonal AVCs.

Corollary 2. *Let* $\mathfrak{W}_1$ *and* $\mathfrak{W}_2$ *be two orthogonal AVCs. If the unassisted capacities satisfy* $C(\mathfrak{W}_1) = C(\mathfrak{W}_2) = 0$, *then super-activation is not possible for the combined AVC* $\mathfrak{W}_1 \otimes \mathfrak{W}_2$.

Finally, the following result solves the remaining case for which the unassisted capacity is actually super-additive.

Theorem 12. *Let* $\mathfrak{W}_1$ *and* $\mathfrak{W}_2$ *be two orthogonal AVCs. The unassisted capacity* $C(\mathfrak{W}_1 \otimes \mathfrak{W}_2)$ *is super-additive, i.e.,*

$$C(\mathfrak{W}_1 \otimes \mathfrak{W}_2) > C(\mathfrak{W}_1) + C(\mathfrak{W}_2), \tag{22}$$

if and only if either of $\mathfrak{W}_1$ *or* $\mathfrak{W}_2$ *is symmetrizable and has a positive CR-assisted capacity.*
Without loss of generality, let $\mathfrak{W}_1$ *be symmetrizable; then*

$$C(\mathfrak{W}_1 \otimes \mathfrak{W}_2) = C_{CR}(\mathfrak{W}_1) + C(\mathfrak{W}_2)$$
$$> C(\mathfrak{W}_1) + C(\mathfrak{W}_2) = C(\mathfrak{W}_2).$$

Proof. First we show that if $\mathfrak{W}_1$ is symmetrizable and $C_{CR}(\mathfrak{W}_1) > 0$, then the unassisted capacity $C(\mathfrak{W}_1 \otimes \mathfrak{W}_2)$ is super-additive. To do so, we use the idea of Ahlswede's de-randomization [13]. Although CR is not available, CR-assisted codes can still be used if the transmitter is able to inform the receiver prior to the actual message transmission about which realization of encoder and decoder has to be used. From [13] we know that the amount of information that needs to be transmitted prior to transmission for this task is polynomial in the block length and therewith negligible for increasing block length.

Since $\mathfrak{W}_2$ is non-symmetrizable, we have $C_{CR}(\mathfrak{W}_2) > 0$ and therefore also $C(\mathfrak{W}_2) > 0$. This allows us to use the second AVC to transmit information to the receiver to make CR available for the first AVC $\mathfrak{W}_1$. Then CR-assisted codes can be used for $\mathfrak{W}_1$ so that

$$C(\mathfrak{W}_1 \otimes \mathfrak{W}_2) \geq C_{CR}(\mathfrak{W}_1) + C(\mathfrak{W}_2)$$
$$= C_{CR}(\mathfrak{W}_1) + C_{CR}(\mathfrak{W}_2)$$
$$= C_{CR}(\mathfrak{W}_1 \otimes \mathfrak{W}_2)$$

is achievable. Since $C(\mathfrak{W}_1 \otimes \mathfrak{W}_2) \leq C_{CR}(\mathfrak{W}_1 \otimes \mathfrak{W}_2)$ is obviously true, we have equality which means that we actually achieve

$$C(\mathfrak{W}_1 \otimes \mathfrak{W}_2) = C_{CR}(\mathfrak{W}_1 \otimes \mathfrak{W}_2)$$

which shows the super-additivity of $C(\mathfrak{W}_1 \otimes \mathfrak{W}_2)$.

Next we show the other direction: If $C(\mathfrak{W}_1 \otimes \mathfrak{W}_2)$ is super-additive, i.e.,

$$C(\mathfrak{W}_1 \otimes \mathfrak{W}_2) > C(\mathfrak{W}_1) + C(\mathfrak{W}_2), \tag{23}$$

then either $\mathfrak{W}_1$ or $\mathfrak{W}_2$ must be symmetrizable so that $C(\mathfrak{W}_1) = 0$ or $C(\mathfrak{W}_2) = 0$.

Assume both unassisted capacities are strictly positive. Then from Theorem 10 it follows that $C(\mathfrak{W}_1) = C_{CR}(\mathfrak{W}_1)$ and $C(\mathfrak{W}_2) = C_{CR}(\mathfrak{W}_2)$ so that Equation (23) becomes

$$C(\mathfrak{W}_1 \otimes \mathfrak{W}_2) > C_{CR}(\mathfrak{W}_1) + C_{CR}(\mathfrak{W}_2)$$
$$= C_{CR}(\mathfrak{W}_1 \otimes \mathfrak{W}_2)$$

where the last step follows from the additivity of the CR-assisted capacity, cf. Theorem 11. This contradicts $C(\mathfrak{W}_1 \otimes \mathfrak{W}_2) \leq C_{CR}(\mathfrak{W}_1 \otimes \mathfrak{W}_2)$ which always holds. Accordingly, without loss of generality, we must have $C(\mathfrak{W}_1) = 0$. However, $C_{CR}(\mathfrak{W}_1) > 0$ must be true, since otherwise we would have

$$C(\mathfrak{W}_1 \otimes \mathfrak{W}_2) > 0 + C_{CR}(\mathfrak{W}_2) = C_{CR}(\mathfrak{W}_1 \otimes \mathfrak{W}_2)$$

which would be a contradiction. Thus, it must hold that $C_{CR}(\mathfrak{W}_1) > 0$ and $C(\mathfrak{W}_1) = 0$ so that $\mathfrak{W}_1$ is symmetrizable, proving the desired result. □

This result shows that the capacity of reliable message transmission over orthogonal AVCs is super-additive under certain circumstances. This breaks with the world view of classical additivity of resources.

Note that Example 1 discussed in Section 3.2 provides an AVC with $|\mathcal{S}| = 2$, which exactly displays the behavior characterized above. Interestingly, if the state set is reduced to $|\mathcal{S}| = 1$, such a behavior is not possible anymore.

5. Discussion

In this paper, we have studied communication under arbitrarily varying channel conditions. For the case of public message transmission over orthogonal AVCs we have completely characterized the behavior of the unassisted and CR-assisted capacity. While the CR-assisted capacity is additive, the unassisted capacity is super-additive, which means that there are orthogonal AVCs for which joint encoding and decoding results in a higher capacity than individual encoding and decoding.

If secrecy requirements are imposed on the message transmission, the capacity behavior for orthogonal AVWCs becomes even more involved. In this case, the phenomenon of super-activation occurs. A joint use of two completely useless AVWCs, i.e., with zero unassisted secrecy capacity, can result in a combined AVWC whose unassisted secrecy capacity is non-zero. From a practical point of view this has important consequences for medium access control and in particular for resource allocation.

The problem of reliable communication over AVCs is closely related to Shannon's zero error capacity problem, as the latter turns out to be a special case of the capacity of the AVC under the maximum error criterion. Shannon conjectured in 1956 that the zero error capacity is additive. Accordingly, the phenomena of super-additivity and super-activation for AVCs and AVWCs respectively are remarkable as these properties show the non-additivity of the capacity of the AVC.

The phenomenon of super-activation has substantial consequences for jamming strategies of potential adversaries. Let us assume that there are two orthogonal AVWCs that can be super-activated. Further assume that for each AVWC an adversary has a suitable jamming strategy to drive the unassisted secrecy capacity to zero. In more detail, for each AVWC the adversary can choose a corresponding state sequence that symmetrizes the legitimate AVC, prohibiting any reliable communication between transmitter and legitimate receiver. Now, joint encoding and decoding allows super-activation of the combined AVWC to make the communication robust: They can now transmit at a positive secrecy rate. This means that for the adversary there is no suitable jamming strategy for the combined AVWC although there is one for each AVWC individually. As there are no restrictions on the strategy space of the adversary, this includes even the case of a product strategy consisting of both individually working jamming strategies.

Super-activation is not an isolated phenomenon. We have shown that whenever orthogonal AVWCs can be super-activated, this is also true for all AVWCs in a certain neighborhood. As a consequence the overall system becomes stable as well. If a super-activated AVWC allows for secure communication with a positive rate, then this is true for all AVWCs sufficiently close to this super-activated AVWC.

Finally we want to note that this also has a game-theoretic interpretation of a *"game against nature"* [37]. The legitimate users (player) and the adversary (nature) play a two-player zero-sum game [38,39] with the secure communication rate as the payoff function. In this game, the set of state sequences corresponds to nature's action space, and nature's intention is to establish the worst possible communication conditions by selecting the state sequence such that the legitimate AVC becomes symmetrizable. The set of input distributions corresponds to the action space of the player and, clearly, the aim is to maximize the secure communication rate. Within this game against nature framework, the player and nature move simultaneously without knowing the other's choice which leads to the max min expressions in the corresponding secrecy capacity results.

Acknowledgments: Holger Boche would like to thank John F. Nash, Jr. for the discussions they had about game theory, equilibrium concepts, and the application of such concepts to communication systems. He would further like to thank Damian Dudek for the numerous discussions they had about physical layer security under practically relevant communication constraints and his insistence on elaborating the differences between public and secure message transmission. The authors would also like to thank Eduard A. Jorswieck and Carsten Janda for insightful discussions and suggestions. The work of H. Vincent Poor was supported in part by the U. S. National Science Foundation under Grant CMMI-1435778.

Author Contributions: All authors contributed equally to this work. All authors have read and approved the final manuscript.

Conflicts of Interest: The authors declare no conflict of interest.

References

1. Wyner, A.D. The wire-tap channel. *Bell Syst. Tech. J.* **1975**, *54*, 1355–1387.

2. Liang, Y.; Poor, H.V.; Shamai, S. Information theoretic security. *Found. Trends Commun. Inf. Theory* **2009**, *5*, 355–580.

3. Liu, R., Trappe, W., Eds. *Securing Wireless Communications at the Physical Layer*; Springer: New York, NY, USA, 2010.

4. Jorswieck, E.A.; Wolf, A.; Gerbracht, S. Secrecy on the physical layer in wireless networks. In *Trends in Telecommunications Technologies*; Intech: Rijeka, Croatia, 2010; pp. 413–435.

5. Bloch, M.; Barros, J. *Physical-Layer Security: From Information Theory to Security Engineering*; Cambridge University Press: Cambridge, UK, 2011.

6. Zhou, X., Song, L., Zhang, Y., Eds. *Physical Layer Security in Wireless Communications*; CRC Press: Boca Raton, FL, USA, 2013.

7. Schaefer, R.F.; Boche, H. Physical layer service integration in wireless networks—Signal processing challenges. *IEEE Signal Process. Mag.* **2014**, *31*, 147–156.

8. Deutsche Telekom AG Laboratories. Next generation mobile networks: (R)evolution in mobile communications. *Technology Radar Edition III/2010, Feature Paper*, 2010. Available online: http://www.lti.ei.tum.de/fileadmin/w00bgd/www/pdf/2010-III_Feature_Paper_Next-Generation-Mobile-Networks_final.pdf (accessed on 28 April 2016).

9. Helmbrecht, U.; Plaga, R. New challenges for IT-security research in ICT. In *World Federation of Scientists International Seminars on Planetary Emergencies*; World Scientific: Singapore, 2008; pp. 1–6.

10. Fettweis, G.; Boche, H.; Wiegand, T.; Zielinksi, E.; Schotten, H.; Merz, P.; Hirche, S.; Festag, A.; Häffner, W.; Meyer, M.; *et al. The Tactile Internet*; Technology Watch Report of ITU (International Telecommunication Union): Geneva, Switzerland, 2014.

11. Schaefer, R.F.; Boche, H.; Poor, H.V. Secure communication under channel uncertainty and adversarial attacks. *Proc. IEEE* **2015**, *102*, 1796–1813.

12. Blackwell, D.; Breiman, L.; Thomasian, A.J. The capacities of certain channel classes under random coding. *Ann. Math. Stat.* **1960**, *31*, 558–567.

13. Ahlswede, R. Elimination of correlation in random codes for arbitrarily varying channels. *Z. Wahrscheinlichkeitstheorie Verw. Gebiete* **1978**, *44*, 159–175.

14. Csiszár, I.; Narayan, P. The capacity of the arbitrarily varying channel revisited: Positivity, constraints. *IEEE Trans. Inf. Theory* **1988**, *34*, 181–193.

15. MolavianJazi, E.; Bloch, M.; Laneman, J.N. Arbitrary jamming can preclude secure communication. In Proceedings of the 47th Annual Allerton Conference on Communication, Control, and Computing, Monticello, IL, USA, 30 September–2 October 2009; pp. 1069–1075.

16. Bjelaković, I.; Boche, H.; Sommerfeld, J. Capacity results for arbitrarily varying wiretap channels. In *Information Theory, Combinatorics, and Search Theory*; Springer: Berlin/Heidelberg, Germany, 2013; pp. 123–144.

17. Boche, H.; Schaefer, R.F. Capacity results and super-activation for wiretap channels with active wiretappers. *IEEE Trans. Inf. Forensics Secur.* **2013**, *8*, 1482–1496.

18. Boche, H.; Schaefer, R.F.; Poor, H.V. On arbitrarily varying wiretap channels for different classes of secrecy measures. In Proceedings of the IEEE International Symposium on Information Theory, Honolulu, HI, USA, 29 June–4 July 2014; pp. 2376–2380.

19. Janda, C.R.; Scheunert, C.; Jorswieck, E.A. Wiretap-channels with constrained active attacks. In Proceedings of the Asilomar Conference on Signals, Systems, and Computers, Pacific Grove, CA, USA, 2–5 November 2014; pp. 1984–1988.

20. Wiese, M.; Nötzel, J.; Boche, H. A channel under simultaneous jamming and eavesdropping attack—Correlated random coding capacities under strong secrecy criteria. **2015**, arXiv:1410.8078.

21. Nötzel, J.; Wiese, M.; Boche, H. The arbitrarily varying wiretap channel—Secret randomness, stability and super-activation. In Proceedings of 2015 IEEE International Symposium on Information Theory, Hong Kong, China, 14–19 June 2015; pp. 2151–2155.

22. Boche, H.; Schaefer, R.F.; Poor, H.V. On the continuity of the secrecy capacity of compound and arbitrarily varying wiretap channels. *IEEE Trans. Inf. Forensics Secur.* **2015**, *12*, 2531–2546.

23. Shannon, C.E. The zero error capacity of a noisy channel. *IRE Trans. Inf. Theory* **1956**, *2*, 8–19.

24. Lovász, L. On the Shannon capacity of a graph. *IEEE Trans. Inf. Theory* **1979**, *25*, 1–7.

25. Ahlswede, A., Althöfer, I., Deppe, C., Tamm, U., Eds. *Rudolf Ahlswede's Lectures on Information Theory 3—Hiding Data: Selected Topics*; Springer: Cham, Switzerland, 2016.

26. Haemers, W. On some problems of Lovász concerning the Shannon capacity of a graph. *IEEE Trans. Inf. Theory* **1979**, *25*, 231–232.

27. Alon, N. The Shannon capacity of a union. *Combinatorica* **1998**, *18*, 301–310.

28. Ahlswede, R. A note on the existence of the weak capacity for channels with arbitrarily varying channel probability functions and its relation to Shannon's zero error capacity. *Ann. Math. Stat.* **1970**, *41*, 1027–1033.

29. Aigner, M.; Ziegler, G.M. *Proofs from THE BOOK*, 5th ed.; Springer: Berlin/Heidelberg, Germany, 2014.

30. Smith, G.; Smolin, J.A.; Yard, J. Quantum communication with Gaussian channels of zero quantum capacity. *Nat. Photonics* **2011**, *5*, 624–627.

31. Giedke, G.; Wolf, M.M. Quantum communication: Super-activated channels. *Nat. Photonics* **2011**, *5*, 578–580.

32. Csiszár, I. Almost independence and secrecy capacity. *Probl. Pered. Inform.* **1996**, *32*, 48–57.

33. Maurer, U.M.; Wolf, S. Information-theoretic key agreement: From weak to strong secrecy for free. In *Advances in Cryptology — EUROCRYPT 2000*; Springer: Berlin/Heidelberg, Germany, 2000; Volume 1807, pp. 351–368.

34. Liang, Y.; Kramer, G.; Poor, H.V.; Shamai, S. Compound wiretap channels. *EURASIP J. Wirel. Commun. Netw.* **2009**, doi:10.1155/2009/142374.

35. Bjelaković, I.; Boche, H.; Sommerfeld, J. Secrecy results for compound wiretap channels. *Probl. Inf. Transm.* **2013**, *49*, 73–98.

36. Schaefer, R.F.; Loyka, S. The secrecy capacity of compound MIMO Gaussian channels. *IEEE Trans. Inf. Theory* **2015**, *61*, 5535–5552.

37. Milnor, J. *Games against Nature*; RAND Corporation: Santa Monica, CA, USA, 1951; pp. 49–59.

38. Aumann, R.J.; Hart, S. *Handbook of Game Theory with Economic Applications*; Elsevier: Oxford, UK, 1994; Volume 2.

39. Basar, T.; Olsder, G.J. *Dynamic Noncooperative Game Theory*, 2nd ed.; SIAM: New York, NY, USA, 1999.

12

The Potential of Three Computer-Based Communication Activities for Supporting Older Adult Independent Living

Melinda Heinz [1,*], **Jinmyoung Cho** [2], **Norene Kelly** [3], **Peter Martin** [3], **Johnny Wong** [4], **Warren Franke** [5], **Wen-Hua Hsieh** [3] **and Joan Blaser** [3]

[1] Department of Psychology, Upper Iowa University, Fayette, IA 52142, USA
[2] Baylor Scott & White Health, Temple, TX 76508, USA; Jinmyoung.Cho@BSWHealth.org
[3] Department of Human Development and Family Studies, Iowa State University, Ames, IA 50011, USA; nbkelly@iastate.edu (N.K.); pxmartin@iastate.edu (P.M.); wenhua@gmail.com (W.-H.H.); jbaenzig55@gmail.com (J.B.)
[4] Department of Computer Science, Iowa State University, Ames, IA 50011, USA; wong@iastate.edu
[5] Department of Kinesiology, Iowa State University, Ames, IA 50011, USA; wfranke@iastate.edu
* Correspondence: heinzm@uiu.edu

Academic Editor: Anna Fensel

Abstract: Technology has become an increasingly integral part of life. For example, technology allows individuals to stay in touch with loved ones, obtain medical services through telehealthcare, and enjoy an overall higher quality of life. Particularly for older adults, using technology increases the likelihood that they will maintain their independence and autonomy. Long-distance caregiving has recently become a feasible option where caregivers for older adults can access reports and information about their loved one's patterns that day (e.g., food and medication intake). Technology may be able to offset age-related challenges (e.g., caregiving, accessing healthcare, decreased social networks) by applying technology to the needs of older adults. Solutions for meeting such challenges, however, have been less targeted. In addition, the healthcare system is evolving to focus on providing options and services in the home. This has direct implications for older adults, as the majority of healthcare services are utilized by older adults. Research is still at the beginning stages of developing successful technology tools that are compatible with older adult users. Therefore, the design, implementation, and outcome of such computer-based communication activities will be discussed in this paper in order to guide future endeavors in technology marketed for older adults.

Keywords: computer-based communication activities; technology; daily health diary; Skype; focus group

---

1. Introduction

1.1. Technology and Older Adults

As pointed out in [1], we are currently witnessing two remarkable trends: the rapid diffusion of technology and widespread population aging. Increasingly, technology has the potential to enhance older adults' abilities, relationships, and health. Compared to younger people, older people are less likely to adopt new technologies into their lives unless they see clear benefits to themselves [2]. Yet older adults are more willing to use technology than stereotypes suggest, and important predictors of adoption are attitude, nature of the experience, available support, and perceived utility [3]. Regardless of users' ages, existing research stresses the importance of a user-driven perspective in designing relevant, user-friendly technology [4–6]. Thus, the development and prototype of an innovation is aimed at older people needs to take into account all these factors.

A 2004 report from the National Research Council found that technology is typically developed by younger people for the use of younger people and marketed at younger target groups [7]. Similarly, it was noted in [8] that "[i]n the vast panoply of human-factors research that goes into design and marketing of modern technology, older users seldom make an appearance" (p. 68). Even when older adults are included in the development and design process, technology designers are still challenged to understand the sensory and cognitive effects that accompany aging [9]. In addition, the physical (e.g., arthritis) and cognitive changes (e.g., declining cognitive processing) of aging may affect ways in which older adults are able to use technology [10].

1.2. Technology and Safety

One example of opportunities presented by current technology is the ability of older adults to easily alert or check-in with professional staff or family. Older adults who do not check in may signal cause for concern and warrant further investigation from family or staff members. In particular, living alone is one of the greatest risk factors for older adults [11]. It was pointed out in [12] that falls posed societal and financial difficulties for individuals and the health care system at large. Technology applications may be able to alleviate some of the risk factors associated with living alone by simulating virtual contact through check-in measures.

It is also possible that older adults may feel more secure knowing that someone would check in with them if they failed to do so. This may also increase the likelihood that older adults would be able to remain independent in their own homes. For example, previous research has noted that older adult falls were linked to the loss of independence and autonomy [13]. If staff or family members were able to intervene more quickly, they may be able to render aid and assistance after a fall.

Although some devices allow users to indicate a current problem or emergency, other innovations can address the difficult-to-perceive yet critical effect of gradual decline. As pointed out in [14], *change* is a red flag in geriatric healthcare and is suggestive of the need for prompt investigation and action. They consequently called for research that helps determine which of today's technologies best support, motivate, and track healthy behaviors at home. Contemporary developments in science and technology are creating an evolutionary shift from clinic-centric to community-centric healthcare, placing health and wellness into the hands of an informed, proactive citizenry [14]. Healthy aging, therefore, "may evolve into a more holistic process through which optimal function and life quality are achieved using an array of health-related technologies that augment human interaction and support" ([14], p. 180). Thus, something like a daily health diary can play a vital role in this healthcare development. In terms of the design process, "small-scale outcomes studies of experiential prototypes" (p. 203) before larger studies with more thoroughly developed systems are contemplated have been recommended [14].

1.3. The Advent of Computer Tools

Tools such as a daily check-in or health diary, as well as currently available communication technologies such as Skype, have the potential to engender a broad positive impact in both individual lives and society. A daily check-in can ensure that older adult users will not be left incapacitated for a prolonged time; a health diary has the potential for early detection of serious problems; and Skype adds important visual information to traditional voice-only communication technology. Such advances support an older adult's ability to live independently, likely increasing both the quality of the person's life as well as the length of time the person can live outside the costly realm of professional care. Independence is a critical issue for many older adults, with their safety and health at risk as they try to cope with age-related issues [4,15]. Preventing or delaying the loss of independence should be a goal of people who care for older adults [15]. A Swedish study demonstrated considerable cost savings as well as benefits to older people and caregivers with the implementation of a home-based support system that used information and communication technology [5].

It was asserted in [4] that the diffusion of such innovations "begins with early adopters who are willing to explore new possibilities and risk trial use, and to lay the groundwork for others to follow" (p. 89). Meanwhile, the shortcomings of existing applied technologies lie in user compliance and effectiveness, cost and dependability, and sustainability and acceptance [4,16]. It was emphasized in [17] that one of the biggest research challenges of proactive health systems, especially for aging in place, was usability issues. Furthermore, three issues identified in [18] as impeding technology use by older adults are design factors, training issues, and users' awareness of potential benefits (or lack thereof). Given the previous findings, many technologies have supported older adults' independence, enhanced connection with family members or health care providers, and expanded their proactive roles in health systems; however, there are still challenges associated with older adults and healthcare professionals deriving benefits from technology tools. Thus, the purpose of the current study is to describe the set-up and installation of three computer-based communication tools for older adults and report on compliance and feedback related to such tools.

2. Method

2.1. Participants

After obtaining approval from the institutional review board at Iowa State University, participants were recruited from an independent living retirement community located in a university town. To be eligible for the study, participants had to be 70 years or older, possess a personal computer, have access to an Internet connection, and have basic computer skills. Eight older adults (three women and five men; Table 1) met the eligibility requirements and elected to participate in the study. Testing new computer tools is generally not feasible on a large scale because it requires significant hands-on time; we therefore included a relatively small sample of participants who would provide us with valuable information on the feasibility of the tools. Furthermore, previous research has indicated that sample sizes of four or five participants sufficiently yield information regarding usability and user experience concerns [19].

Table 1. Characteristics of participants (n = 8).

Category		Frequency	Percent
Age (M = 85.13, SD = 3.09)			
Gender	Male	5	62.5
	Female	3	37.5
	Total	8	100.0
Ethnicity	White	8	100.0
Marital Status	Married	6	75.0
	Widowed	2	25.0
	Total	8	100.0
Employment Status	Retired	8	100.0

2.2. Implementation of the Daily Diary and Skype

An interdisciplinary team of researchers including Gerontology, Human Development and Family Studies, Computer Science, and Kinesiology departments built a technology tool useful for tracking older adult health. After the Computer Science department completed the design process, research assistants tested the product for errors before implementing it in the independent living apartment complex.

2.3. Installation

Research assistants installed separate, easily accessible icons (*i.e.*, one icon for the check-in, a second icon for the daily diary, and a third icon for Skype (version 4.2) prominently on the desktop of the participants' computers to simplify the process. Therefore, unnecessary procedures and steps were eliminated, making the process more seamless and efficient. This was done to encourage compliance and reduce confusion or forgetfulness. Participants were also given written instructions on how to click on the separate icons in case they needed another reminder. In some cases, exchanging computers was necessary in order to make the computer-based activities fully functional. One participant had no additional disk space on his computer and thus needed to borrow a laptop, while another had a dial-up Internet connection, making the initial set-up cumbersome. In addition, several participants borrowed web cameras to participate in the Skype portion of the study since they did not possess their own. There were relatively few technical failures. In one instance, a participant had to attempt the Skype call again. However, no significant technical failures were reported.

2.4. Procedure and Compliance

Participants were assigned an ID and were asked to engage in a total of three computer-based communication activities during the ten-day period between the hours of 10 a.m. and 12 p.m.: (1) check-in with university researchers; (2) answer questions in a daily health diary; and (3) interact with research assistants via Skype. Task frequency, compliance, and answering questions for each participant were collected from all three tasks and entered into SPSS version 19 (IBM, Armonk, NY, USA). Following the ten-day period, a focus group session was conducted with participants. The purpose behind asking participants to engage in three tasks everyday was to assess how successful older adults were with following these instructions in order to simulate what it might be like to remotely monitor and interact with older adults from afar (*i.e.*, demonstrating what it might be like for older adults to call in with professional healthcare workers, caregivers, or family members).

2.4.1. Check-in

The check-in was the simplest task in which the older adults participated. Older adults simply had to click on the check-in icon and type in their ID. Participants knew they had been successful with this step after they received a cartoon and a message that stated "Thanks for visiting us, have a wonderful day and see you tomorrow".

2.4.2. Daily Health Diary

The daily health diary consisted of 21 questions across five domains (e.g., computer questions, overall perceived health, nutritional consumption, physical activity, and cognitive patterns). The complete list of 21 questions were chosen to simulate what it might be like for participants to complete electronic monitoring information to submit to healthcare professionals. The included questions were chosen and presented on a daily basis to provide a thorough view of participant health and to assess daily changes. Participants had the opportunity to review their answers before they officially submitted their answers. After submitting their answers, a new window opened that indicated their answers had been submitted successfully. Given that the focus of this paper is more about the implementation of computer-based communication activities, specific information regarding items and scoring in the daily diary is not included.

2.4.3. Skype Chat

The final task for participants to complete each day was a Skype chat with research assistants. Between the hours of 10 a.m. and 12 p.m. participants were asked to call in. This task served as another assignment to assess the success of a virtual face-to-face check-in device. It also served to simulate the benefits and challenges of virtual contact with older adults.

2.5. Focus Group Discussion

After the ten days were completed, participants were invited to participate in a focus group to discuss their thoughts and opinions regarding the interventions. The focus group was conducted at the independent living apartment complex. All individuals engaged in a focus group after the completion of the ten-day period. Table 2 presents a complete list of questions asked at the focus group. The focus group was open-ended in nature and lasted for approximately one hour. Discussion from the focus group was videotaped and later transcribed verbatim. The transcripts were coded and categorized by two different researchers. As is common with qualitative research, a peer review was completed when researchers shared their initial coding and categorization with the rest of the research team [20]. Detailed descriptions and examples of each theme are discussed in the results section.

Table 2. Focus group questions.

General Questions

1. What was your overall experience participating in this study? What did you like? What did you not like?
2. What was it like to have someone come to your home for software and equipment installation?

Check-In Task

3. What was your experience like with the "check in" assignment?
4. What difficulties did you encounter conducting this task?
5. How much time did it take every day to complete this task?
6. Would you be interested in using the check-in assignment every day, if doctors and nurses are available to review your information and provide you with recommendations?

Skype

7. What was your experience of using Skype?

    a   What do you like about using Skype?
    b   What do you dislike about using Skype?
    c   Did you encounter any difficulties?
    d   How did you feel about checking in with us on Skype every day?
    e   How much time did it take every day to complete this task?
    f   Do you think you might use Skype in the future? Why or why not?
    g   Would you be interested in using Skype every day, if doctors and nurses are available to review your information and provide you with recommendations?

Daily Health Diary

8. What was your experience of visiting the website with the health diary questions?

    a   What was it like answering the health diary questionnaire every day?
    b   Any recommendation on how we can improve the website? (e.g., appearance, questions)?
    c   What was the greatest difficulty you encountered conducting this task?
    d   How much time did it take every day to complete this task?
    e   Would you be interested in using the healthy diary every day, if doctors and nurses are available to review your information and provide you with recommendations?

9. What are the major factors that affect whether you want or don't want to use these applications?
10. How easy or difficult was it for you to remember to incorporate Skype and the daily diary into their regular routines?
11. How easy or difficult was it to navigate through the tasks? Did you use any type of "cheat sheet" or other written instructions to successfully complete the tasks?
12. Is there anything that you would like to let us know (e.g., suggestions for the future, clarification of any part of this study)?

2.6. Data Analysis

Both quantitative and qualitative information was obtained from participants in order to capture and analyze a broad range of data and feedback regarding the computer-based communication activities. This mixed methods design is known as the sequential transformative design approach where there are separate qualitative and quantitative data collection phases that are later integrated in order to understand the process [21] such as the user experience with the computer-based communication activities in this case. The qualitative data were analyzed using Track Changes and the highlighting function in Microsoft Word to organize codes and categories. Breaking down the qualitative data into smaller segments until larger themes arise was recommended in [22]. Examples of categories under each theme are shown in Table 3. Descriptive statistics (e.g., means and frequencies) were computed using SPSS version 19, whereas qualitative data were analyzed for content to supplement the quantitative data.

Table 3. Qualitative categories and themes.

Accessibility	Awareness	Safety and Intrusion
Finances	Eating	Privacy
Specificity	Routine	Security
Flexibility	Remembering	Emergency
Rural areas	Tech savvy	-
Timing	Socialization	-

3. Results

The results are reported in two sections. First, participants' performance and compliance rate in their usage for everyday health monitoring were examined in five domains (*i.e.*, general computer skills and usage, overall perceived health, nutritional consumption, physical activity, and cognitive fatigue). Second, themes that emerged from the focus group discussion are also presented.

3.1. Older Adults' Abilities and Compliance Rate in Health Monitoring

After the ten-day period, further statistical analysis was conducted to evaluate older adults' abilities and the compliance rate in their usage for everyday health monitoring. Participants of this study reported an average rating of 2.88 on a 5-point scale on their confidence in computer skills, meaning that participants were somewhat uncertain about their skills in using a computer (Table 4). However, about a third of the participants stated they were somewhat confident in computer skills. In terms of computer usage, participants reported their computer usage ranged from once a month to every day to several times a day. Half of the sample indicated they used computers every day.

Table 4. Baseline computer skills.

Category		Frequency	Percent
	Very Confident (= 5)	0	0.0
	Somewhat Confident (= 4)	3	37.5
General Computer Skill	Neutral (= 3)	2	25.0
	Somewhat Uncertain (= 2)	0	0.0
	Very Uncertain (= 1)	3	37.5
	Total	8	100.0
	Every day	2	25.0
	Several Times a Day	4	50.0
Computer Usage	Several Times a Week	1	12.5
	Once a Month	1	12.5
	Total	8	100.0

With regard to the compliance rate over the ten-day period, two users completed the 21 health diary questions every day (100% compliance rate) and two other users completed the health diary questions less than 50% over the 10-day period. Specifically, all users completed the health diary questions on Day 1 (100% compliance rate); however, the compliance rate dropped to 75% on Day 2, and the lowest compliance rate of 62.5% was reported on Day 3, 5, 6, and 10 (Figure 1). In addition, individual compliance rates can be found in Table 5.

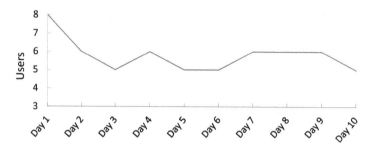

Figure 1. Number of users that completed the questionnaire each day.

Table 5. User compliance rates.

	User 1	User 2	User 3	User 4	User 5	User 6	User 7	User 8
Compliance Rates	90%	90%	40%	100%	80%	100%	70%	10%

Based on the compliance rate, two groups were created: a high compliance rate group (90% and above) and a low compliance rate group (below 90%). Mean differences in computer skills, computer usage, and health at baseline between the two groups were examined through t-tests. However, no significant differences in the three variables were noted: $t(6) = 0.27$, $p = 0.80$ for computer skills, $t(6) = 1.22$, $p = 0.27$ for computer usage, or $t(6) = 0.91$, $p = 0.40$ for health at baseline.

3.2. Three Themes from a Focus Group

The ten-day pilot test was successful in that all participants who started the pilot test completed the ten-day testing period. This study also yielded interesting findings regarding older adult user experience with computer-based communication activities. Three total themes emerged from the focus group transcript: accessibility, awareness, and safety and intrusion.

3.2.1. Accessibility

This theme dealt with the accessibility from a number of different perspectives including environmental inclusion (e.g., rural environments) and financial accessibility (e.g., inexpensive technology will be used by more individuals). Participants were intrigued that Skype was free and felt it offered an additional benefit over cell phones. One participant noted, "*A program that is free will be used.*" In addition, one participant suggested that a "*fee scale*" for healthcare services in which telehealth visits conducted using computer-based communication tools were cheaper than face-to-face visits could be advantageous. Another participant commented, "*If it's* [telehealth visits] *lower* [cost] *than the actual visit, that's convenient.*" However, one participant went on to mention, "*I thought professionals, if they wanted to use it for this type of thing* [for telehealthcare], *would need very good grade cameras.*"

Participants also felt that the check-in, daily diary, and Skype tasks were relatively easy to complete and use. A participant mentioned, "*I did find out that the computer doesn't bite … if you use it right.*" This sentiment seemed to illustrate the anxiety or hesitation that is sometimes associated with computers. Overall, after using computers over a ten-day period, participants seemed to possess more self-assurance. Although all participants did have their own computers, most individuals were only using their computers for basic tasks (e.g., playing games or checking email periodically). Only one participant had ever used Skype before. It was also apparent to the researchers that participants were much more at ease with the communication tools than they were at the beginning of the study. For example, researchers noted significant hesitancy and anxiety (e.g., concern that they might not complete the communication task successfully) on the day the programs were installed on participant computers. Participants also later stated how relatively easy the check-in task was to complete on the computer by indicating that it was *"very simple and easy."* Another participant stated, *"No, I didn't have any trouble with the check-in."*

Increased flexibility for check-in time periods was suggested by several participants. For example, one participant noted, *"Our problem is from 10 a.m.–12 p.m. . . . we didn't always get that* [check-in] *done."* Other participants noted conflicting appointments or schedules that interfered with the check-in time frame. Furthermore, some participants felt the daily health diary could be more tailored to individual needs. For example, one participant responded, *"I think that as the system would be refined . . . questions would vary over time."* Some participants seemed to note the importance of thinking about individual differences. The participant went on to explain:

> *"Not criticizing your question, but . . . if you carried this thing a step further and it was being used by professionals, your questions wouldn't be of such a general nature and ultimately the questions would have to be refined to the person."*

In regard to how detailed the daily health diary should be, one participant noted that some daily healthy diary questions may need to be more specific:

> *"Some will have quite the detailed questionnaire and others will have a relatively simple one. There is a lot of relativity as you move to one person to the other."*

Participants also appreciated that the computer-based communication activities were relatively easy and quick to complete. Participants commented that the daily health diary took the longest and ranged anywhere from three to ten minutes to complete.

Although participants in this study were not living in a rural area, several individuals discussed the benefits for rural populations. One participant noted, *"I think it would pertain more to people who are maybe more than maybe 100 miles away."* Another participant commented, *"And weather is important because in rural Iowa, winter weather snowy roads . . . this would be advantageous."*

3.2.2. Awareness

This theme was related to increased awareness of food and drink consumption, as well as increased awareness technology terms and opportunities for using technology. Participants appeared to be more aware of their own health when using the daily health diary as some questions asked about fruit and vegetable servings as well as liquid intake. For example, one participant noted, *"It just reminded us to eat a little better."* Similarly, an additional participant mentioned, *"Your two fruits, two vegetables and 3 to 5 glasses or cups of water reminded us."* Another participant noted, *" . . . It did make me very much aware of the fluid intake."*

One of the challenges associated with the computer-based communication activities were that *"you had to remember to do it every day."* For some, this requirement was challenging. Some participants reported difficulty remembering to complete the check-in, daily diary, and Skype tasks each day. Several participants noted they *"forgot."* However, one participant seemed to indicate that the tasks could soon become part of a routine. He stated, *"If I just did it when I got up in the morning, there are all those things that you do routinely."*

Participants also seemed to be more aware of available technology that might be useful to them and felt they became more knowledgeable about computer terms. One participant noted that *"She . . . our daughter . . . was Skyping her husband in Washington, D.C. If they had said we were 'Skyping,' we would have thought, 'what on earth are they doing?' But we knew the language . . . "* Participants reported feeling satisfied that they were more knowledgeable about computer terminology (such as Skype) and were more aware of how such technology functioned. Skype also offered increased opportunities for socialization. A participant noted *"I've made contact with relatives that I haven't seen for years. It's just like they're sitting across the table from you the way we sit and talk."*

3.2.3. Safety and Intrusion

This theme included discussion on increased safety due to technology tools as well as discussion on privacy and intrusion due to technology use. Participants mentioned that the computer-based communication tools would be helpful for safety reasons, particularly when professional staff members were away or unavailable. One participant mentioned that "[Staff members] *need to keep in contact with me so* [staff members] *don't find me at the bottom of the stairs in a mess.*" An additional participant seemed to echo similar points when he indicated that "*all the emergencies occur on weekends.*"

Participants seemed to acknowledge that check-in devices are important to ensuring the safety or older adults, especially those who reside alone or with little to no professional medical staff. One participant went on to further explain how useful check-in tasks are when he explained,

> "*But, uh, any kind of signal that we came up with [at the independent living apartment complex] ... either people didn't want us to be checking on them or they figured it wasn't a good enough plan and we've never done anything. And, generally speaking, we know what the next-door neighbor's doing or some person we are in touch with. But it failed once. I mean we lost somebody over a weekend ... *"

Another participant mentioned how beneficial a camera could be if one were to use Skype as part of telehealthcare. The participant said, "*It seemed to me that the Skype would add a lot to that ... just seeing the individual, more than the telephone.*"

Initially, participants were less eager to use Skype to communicate with research assistants at the University. However, at the end of the research project participants thoroughly enjoyed the added benefit of being able to see the person they were communicating with during conversation. One participant noted, "*I thought it was fun interacting with these students. I thought that was interesting.*" Another participant stated, "*They* [researcher assistants] *weren't being intrusive.*" At the conclusion of the study, participants were eager to have the Skype software left on their computers for continued use. One participant noted, "*You can take anything you want out of my computer, but leave Skype!*"

4. Discussion

The purpose of this research was to implement computer-based communication activities to test with an older adult population and to evaluate the user experience of such tools by conducting a focus group following the research study. Previous research has indicated that the acceptability of monitoring technology has been understudied [21]. This study helped fill that gap by obtaining further information leading to the understanding of older adult acceptance levels of computer-based communication tools. For example, participants appreciated Skype and noted the benefits of using similar technologies for telehealthcare purposes in the future, especially for rural older adults who may find it difficult to travel to appointments. This study also simulated what it is like to have virtual contact with older adults (including the oldest old) and adds to the existing literature in the field of technology and aging. For example, previous research has noted the importance of developing e-health interventions to assist older adults in managing their physical and mental needs [22]. The three different computer-based communication activities used in the study contribute to the literature on older adults managing their health both physically and mentally. For example, the daily health diary required participants to record and track various health behaviors over the ten-day period. Previous research has noted that tracking and reminding participants about health behaviors aids in managing and making changes to overall health [23]. This study is also unique in that the mean age of participants was approximately 85 years of age. Little research assessing computer-based communication activities has implemented technology tools with the oldest old although recent studies have shown more older adults aged 65 years and older have used Internet to obtain health-related information [24]. This study adds to the relatively unknown research about the user experience with computer-based communication activities among the oldest old.

Results from this study indicate that computer-based communication activities or health monitoring is a feasible option for older adults. Some participants were initially unsure about participating in the study and were concerned about the level of intrusiveness associated with the study. However, it was apparent during the focus group discussion that participants overcame their initial fears and relatively easily navigated the check-in, daily diary, and Skype tasks. This research also addresses previous concerns about older adult ability levels using technology for monitoring purposes [25]. Our findings indicate that older adults are able to successfully use computer-based communication activities despite initial concerns about monitoring and privacy.

4.1. Design Best Practices

In addition, it appears that part of the apparent success experienced by users may be due to researchers installing all software on participant computers, thereby providing one-click access. Offering support staff to install and demonstrate communication software also appears to be related to older adults finding the tools easy to use (*i.e.,* researchers were available to answer any questions participants had about using the software). In addition, it was advantageous for users to have written instructions about navigating the different communication tools. Many of these designs are based on best practices for designing content for older adults [23]. Future researchers would do well to incorporate these items as well as other suggestions about making computer applications and content user-friendly.

In addition, it is important to point out the relatively inexpensive technology used for the purposes of this study. Adopting free or inexpensive programs for health monitoring or communication with healthcare providers is also more inclusive than programs with higher financial price tags. Such programs exclude a proportion of the population unable to afford such options. Although relatively simple in nature, check-in devices can give family members peace of mind from far away. Healthcare professionals would also easily be able to phone an older adult if he or she had not "checked-in" that day. Such simple measures and applications can be beneficial and efficient for a wide range of individuals (e.g., older adults, family members, and healthcare professionals). Implementing computer-based communication activities with "real" healthcare staff involved may also prove useful in determining which design elements both older adults and healthcare professionals prefer.

4.2. Limitations

Limitations of this study are that only participants residing in one older adult independent apartment complex were included. It is possible that older adults residing in different types of communities and geographic locations may have had different experiences using the computer-based communication activities. It is interesting to note that the mean age of participants was approximately 85 years of age. Therefore, testing out technology tools with a younger sample of older adults may yield different perspectives. Additionally, this study was a pilot assessment; future opportunities exist in creating a randomized controlled study for comparisons with multiple conditions.

4.3. Implications and Future Research

Technology tools should continue to be tested with a geographically and demographically wider range of older adult populations in order to assess older adult preferences and overall effectiveness. The feasibility of using computer-based communication activities with older adults residing in other types of communities (e.g., assisted living) should also be conducted. Additionally, conducting studies assessing older adults using computer-based communication activities longer than a ten-day period should be conducted in the future. Compliance rates may vary with extended time intervals. Finally, compliance rates may also have been impacted by asking the same questions on the daily health diary each day. It is possible that if the individual were asked unique and tailored questions (based on previous answers), compliance rates may have been higher. Asking fewer questions each day may have also impacted compliance rates and made it easier for participants to complete each day. Several participants also noted that they were unable to call in during the Skype hours due to prior conflicts or forgetfulness. It is possible that, had the Skype phone call hours been extended, compliance rates would have been higher. If a longer study had been conducted, trends in decision-making could have been assessed (e.g., the extent to which participants changed their eating and exercise patterns) as a result of participating in the study and completing the daily health diary for a prolonged period of time. It is also likely that participants would have become even more adept at their computer skills with additional practice and a daily requirement in place. Lastly, a longer study would have been able to more accurately assess compliance (e.g., whether or not participants were more or less likely to complete tasks over an extended period of time).

As a result of this study, we believe using telehealthcare technology in the future with older adults can be a feasible option for monitoring and assessing the well-being of older adults. The older adults in this study enjoyed the computer-based communication activities and even reported that they were more aware of their health (e.g., aware of how many servings of fruits and vegetables to eat, how much fluid to drink) due to the daily diary tool. Participants also found the Skype tool to be useful when checking in with research assistants and seemed to enjoy the built-in socialization component. Overall, participants appeared comfortable and confident about technology use by the end of the study (e.g., eagerness to monitor their own health behaviors and enjoyment in using the computer prototypes). Finally, older participants became more informed and aware of what technology can do for them in terms of healthcare and social engagement.

While the telehealthcare field is a new area, this study advanced what is known by testing three computer-based communication activities and obtaining user feedback and metrics for each tool. Some older adults may be able to complete all three steps of the computer-based activities seamlessly, whereas others may experience more difficulty. As the medical community becomes more technologically advanced, older adults may need to have increased contact with technology to receive healthcare services. Therefore, continued studies need to address older adult technology use and compliance.

Acknowledgments: We would like to thank Hen-I Yang for his assistance setting up and assisting with data collection.

Author Contributions: Melinda Heinz assisted with collecting Skype and focus group data as well as data analysis and contributed to writing the paper. Jinmyoung Cho analyzed quantitative data and assisted with the writing of the paper. Norene Kelly assisted with data analysis and the writing of the paper. Wen-Hua Hsieh assisted with collecting Skype data and setting up data collection procedures. Joan Blaser assisted with collecting Skype data and focus group data analysis. Peter Martin conceived and designed the study, collected data, and oversaw data analysis. Johnny Wong conceived and designed the study and designed data collection tools. Warren Franke conceived and designed the study.

Conflicts of Interest: The authors declare no conflict of interest.

References

1. Burdick, D.C., Kwon, S., Eds.; *Gerontechnology: Research and Practice in Technology and Aging*; Springer: New York, NY, USA, 2004; pp. xxv–xxvii.
2. Rogers, E. *Diffusion of Innovations*, 5th ed.; Free Press: New York, NY, USA, 2003.
3. Czaja, S.J.; Lee, C. The impact of aging on access to technology. *Univers. Access Inf. Soc.* **2007**, *5*, 341–349. [CrossRef]
4. Demeris, G.; Rantz, M.J.; Aud, M.A.; Marek, K.D.; Tyrer, H.W.; Skubic, M.; Hussam, A.A. Older adults' attitudes towards and perceptions of "smart home" technologies: A pilot study. *Med. Inf. Internet Med.* **2004**, *29*, 87–94. [CrossRef] [PubMed]
5. Magnusson, L.; Hanson, E. Supporting frail older people and their family carers at home using information and communication technology: Cost analysis. *J. Adv. Nurs.* **2005**, *51*, 645–657. [CrossRef] [PubMed]
6. Wang, A.; Redington, L.; Steinmetz, V.; Lindeman, D. The ADOPT model: Accelerating diffusion of proven technologies for older adults. *Ageing Int.* **2011**, *36*, 39–45. [CrossRef]

7. Pew, R., Van Hemel, S., Eds.; *Technology for Adaptive Aging*; National Academy Press: Washington, DC, USA, 2004.

8. Cutler, S.J. Ageism and technology. *Generations* **2005**, *29*, 67–72.

9. Eisma, R.; Dickinson, A.; Goodman, J.; Syme, A.; Tiwari, L.; Newell, A.F. Early user involvement in the development of information technology-related products for older people. *Univers. Access Inf. Soc.* **2004**, *3*, 131–140. [CrossRef]

10. Charness, N.; Boot, W.R. Aging and information technology use: Potential and barriers. *Curr. Dir. Psychol. Sci.* **2009**, *18*, 253–258. [CrossRef]

11. de Moraes Barros, G.D.V. Falls in elderly people. *Lancet* **2006**, *367*, 729–730. [CrossRef]

12. Scanaill, C.N.; Garattini, C.; Greene, B.R.; McGrath, M.J. Technology innovation enabling falls risk assessment in a community setting. *Ageing Int.* **2011**, *36*, 217–231. [CrossRef] [PubMed]

13. Kannus, P.; Sievanen, H.; Palvanen, M.; Jarvinen, T.; Parkkari, J. Prevention of falls and consequent injuries in elderly people. *Lancet* **2005**, *366*, 1885–1893. [CrossRef]

14. Dishman, E.; Matthews, J.; Dunbar-Jacob, J. Everyday health: Technology for adaptive aging. In *Technology for Adaptive Aging*; Pew, R.W., Van Hemel, S.B., Eds.; National Academy Press: Washington, DC, USA, 2004; pp. 179–208.

15. Fallon, L.F., Jr.; Awosika-Olumo, A.; Fulks, J.S. Factors related to accidents and falls among older individuals. *Traumatology* **2002**, *8*, 205–210. [CrossRef]

16. Nehmer, J.; Becker, M.; Kleinberger, T.; Pruckner, S. Electronic emergency safeguards: Sensor-based detection and prevention of critical health conditions. *GeroPsych* **2010**, *23*, 91–98. [CrossRef]

17. Dishman, E. Inventing wellness systems for aging in place. *Computer* **2004**, *37*, 34–41. [CrossRef]

18. Rogers, W.A.; Mayhorn, C.B.; Fisk, A.D. Technology in everyday life for older adults. In *Gerontechnology: Research and Practice in Technology and Aging*; Burdick, D.C., Kwon, S., Eds.; Springer: New York, NY, USA, 2004; pp. 3–17.

19. Virzi, R.A. Refining the test phase of usability evaluation: How many subjects is enough? *J. Hum. Factors Ergon. Soc.* **1992**, *34*, 457–468.

20. Merriam, S.B. *Qualitative Research, a Guide to Design and Implementation*; Jossey-Bass: San Francisco, CA, USA, 2009.

21. Terrell, S. Mixed-methods research methodologies. *Qual. Rep.* **2012**, *17*, 254–280.

22. Creswell, J.W. *Research Design: Qualitative, Quantitative, and Mixed Methods Approaches*; Sage Publications Ltd.: Thousand Oaks, CA, USA, 2008.

23. Klasnja, P.; Consolvo, S.; McDonald, D.W.; Landay, J.A.; Pratt, W. Using mobile and personal sensing technologies to support health behavior change in everyday life: Lessons learned. *AMIA Annu. Symp. Proc.* **2009**, *2009*, 338–342. [PubMed]

24. Wright, P. The internet's potential for enhancing healthcare. *Gerontechnology* **2012**, *11*, 35–45. [CrossRef]

25. Preschl, B.; Wagner, B.; Forstmeier, S.; Maercker, A. E-health interventions for depression, anxiety disorder, dementia, and other disorders in adults: A review. *J. CyberTher. Rehabil.* **2011**, *4*, 371–385.

13

Computer-Aided Identification and Validation of Privacy Requirements

Rene Meis * and Maritta Heisel

paluno—The Ruhr Institute for Software Technology, University of Duisburg-Essen, Duisburg 47057, Germany; maritta.heisel@uni-due.de
* Correspondence: rene.meis@uni-due.

Academic Editor: Eduardo B. Fernandez

Abstract: Privacy is a software quality that is closely related to security. The main difference is that security properties aim at the protection of assets that are crucial for the considered system, and privacy aims at the protection of personal data that are processed by the system. The identification of privacy protection needs in complex systems is a hard and error prone task. Stakeholders whose personal data are processed might be overlooked, or the sensitivity and the need of protection of the personal data might be underestimated. The later personal data and the needs to protect them are identified during the development process, the more expensive it is to fix these issues, because the needed changes of the system-to-be often affect many functionalities. In this paper, we present a systematic method to identify the privacy needs of a software system based on a set of functional requirements by extending the problem-based privacy analysis (ProPAn) method. Our method is tool-supported and automated where possible to reduce the effort that has to be spent for the privacy analysis, which is especially important when considering complex systems. The contribution of this paper is a semi-automatic method to identify the relevant privacy requirements for a software-to-be based on its functional requirements. The considered privacy requirements address all dimensions of privacy that are relevant for software development. As our method is solely based on the functional requirements of the system to be, we enable users of our method to identify the privacy protection needs that have to be addressed by the software-to-be at an early stage of the development. As initial evaluation of our method, we show its applicability on a small electronic health system scenario.

Keywords: privacy; privacy requirements; privacy analysis; requirements engineering; computer-aided software engineering

---

1. Introduction

Privacy is a software quality that is closely related to security and that is gaining more and more attention in the public. Security is in general concerned with the protection of *assets* that are important in the context of the considered system against malicious attackers that want to get access to the assets, influence the content of the assets or affect the assets' availability. In contrast, privacy is concerned with the protection of *personal data*. We use the following definition of personal data from the European Commission [1]: *"'personal data' means any information relating to a data subject"*. Throughout the paper, we use the terms personal information and personal data synonymously. To address privacy, personal data shall be protected against malicious and also unintended processing, disclosure, or alternation. Such events may even be caused by the end-users themselves due to insufficient privacy awareness, or due to a lack of controls. Hence, privacy includes security properties that are limited to the protection of personal data as assets, but the protection needs of these contained security properties are not limited to attackers with malicious intentions. Additionally, privacy aims at increasing the awareness of users concerning how their personal data is processed by the considered system.

The need for security protection is more obvious to companies than the need for privacy protection, especially if the personal data are not the relevant assets. Additionally, companies do not see the benefit of increasing the awareness of end-users if end-users' personal data are the central asset in the system. This is, because increasing the awareness may lead to the situation that end-users provide less personal data. This leads to the situation that companies often underestimate the value of a thorough consideration of privacy during software development. But the costs caused by data breaches increased over the last years in all countries all over the world [2,3]. This entails that end-users lose trust in service providers that handle their data, and call for more transparency on how their data is processed [4]. A systematic privacy analysis of the *system-to-be* (software to be developed) can prevent the occurrence of data breaches and can provide means to identify how and about what kinds of data processing end-users have to be informed.

The above mentioned end-user concerns already show that the software quality privacy is not limited to the protection of data to prevent data breaches. Privacy also aims at increasing the awareness of end-users about how their data is handled and to empower them to keep the control over their data. Hansen *et al.* [5] propose six protection goals for privacy engineering. These are the three classical security goals confidentiality, integrity, and availability, as well as the protection goals unlinkability, transparency, and intervenability. In comparison to the classical security goals and unlinkability, transparency and intervenability got less attention in research as we found out during a systematic literature review [6]. Transparency is concerned with increasing the awareness of end-users by informing them about how their data is processed. Intervenability is about empowering end-users by providing means to them to control how their data is processed. In this paper, we consider all six protection goals for the identification of privacy requirements.

A privacy analysis especially for complex systems is a difficult and error prone task. The privacy analysis should be integrated into the development process as proposed by Cavoukian's privacy principles [7]. This integration shall lead to a reduction of the effort that has to be put into the privacy analysis. Additionally, it shall lead to the detection of privacy issues at the earliest stage possible. The existing methods for privacy requirements engineering provide only little support for the identification of privacy requirements and lack of tool support that automates the identification of privacy requirements (*cf.* Section 10). In order to handle complex systems, more guidance and automation is needed to systematically identify the privacy requirements that have to be satisfied by the system at hand.

In this paper, we present a method to systematically derive privacy requirements from a set of functional requirements represented as problem diagrams [8]. The proposed method is an extension of the Problem-based Privacy Analysis (ProPAn) method [9]. This extension adds the possibility to identify and validate privacy requirements in a systematic way, based on a set of functional requirements. To reduce the effort to perform our method, we extended the ProPAn tool [10] to provide as much automation as possible for the identification, generation, and validation of the privacy requirements. Based on our initial evaluation, we expect that our method supports its users to perform as complete and coherent privacy analyses as possible with a reasonable effort even for complex systems.

Our paper is structured as follows. Section 2 introduces an electronic health system scenario that we use as a running example throughout the paper. Section 3 discusses the relevant parts of the problem frames approach as background of this paper. Section 4 provides an overview of our method, and Sections 5–8 provide the details of the four steps of our method. Our tool support is described in Section 9. Section 10 discusses related work, and Section 11 concludes the paper and provides future directions.

2. Running Example

We use a subsystem of an electronic health system (EHS) scenario provided by the industrial partners of the EU project *Network of Excellence (NoE) on Engineering Secure Future Internet Software*

Services and Systems (NESSoS) [11] to illustrate our method. This scenario is based on the German health care system which uses health insurance schemes for the accounting of treatments.

The EHS is the software to be built. It has to manage electronic health records (EHR) which are created and modified by doctors (functional requirement R1) and can also be browsed by doctors (R2). Additionally, the EHS shall support doctors to perform the accounting of treatments patients received. The accounting is based on the treatments stored in the health records. Using an insurance application it is possible to perform the accounting with the respective insurance company of the patient. If the insurance company only partially covers the treatment a patient received, the EHS shall create an invoice (R3). The billing is then handled by a financial application (R4). Furthermore, mobile devices shall be supported by the EHS to send instructions and alarms to patients (R5) and to record vital signs of patients (R6). Finally, the EHS shall provide anonymized medical data to researchers for clinical research (R7).

3. Background

Problem frames are a requirements engineering approach proposed by Jackson [8]. The system-to-be (called *machine*) and its interfaces to the environment, which consists of *domains*, are represented in a *context diagram*. Jackson distinguishes the domain types *causal domains* that comply with some physical laws, *lexical domains* that are data representations, *biddable domains* that are usually people, and *connection domains* that mediate between two domains. Additionally, Jackson distinguishes between *given domains* that already exist in the environment of the machine and *designed domains* that are part of the system-to-be and whose behavior and structure can be defined by developers of the machine. The problem to be solved by the machine is decomposed until subproblems are reached which fit to problem frames. Problem frames are patterns for frequently occurring problems. An instantiated problem frame is represented as a *problem diagram*. A problem diagram visualizes the relation of a requirement to the environment of the machine and how the machine can influence these domains. A requirement can refer to and constrain phenomena of domains. Phenomena are events, commands, states, information, and the like. Both relations are expressed by dependencies from the requirement to the respective domain annotated with the referred to or constrained phenomena. Connections (associations) between domains describe the phenomena they share. Both domains can observe the shared phenomena, but only one domain has the control over a phenomenon (denoted by a "!").

We use the UML4PF-framework [12] to create problem frame models as UML class diagrams enriched with stereotypes. All diagrams are stored in *one* global UML model. Hence, we can perform analyses and consistency checks over multiple diagrams and artifacts. The context diagram (in UML notation) for the EHS is shown in Figure 1. The context diagram shows that the machine *EHS* (class with stereotype «machine») contains the designed domains *Invoice* and *EHR* (classes with stereotype «designedDomain»). All other domains in the context diagram are given domains. As given domains, we have the four causal connection domains *FinancialApplication*, *InsuranceApplication*, *MobileDevice*, and *ResearchDatabaseApplication* that represent devices or existing applications that are used by the EHS, and the three biddable domains *Patient*, *Doctor*, and *Researcher* that represent people that (indirectly) interact with the EHS. The *EHS* is directly or indirectly (through connection domains) connected to all domains of the context diagram (indicated by associations with stereotype «connection»). The problem diagram (in UML notation) for the functional requirement *R6* is shown in Figure 2. The problem diagram is about the problem to build the submachine *Record* that records the vital signs of *Patient*s sent to it via *MobileDevice*s in the corresponding *EHR*s. The functional requirement *R6* refers to the patient from whom the vital signs are recorded and to the mobile device which forwards the vital signs (indicated by a dependencies with stereotype «refersTo»), and the requirement constrains the EHR to store the recorded vital signs in the corresponding health record of the patient (indicated by dependencies with stereotype «constrains»).

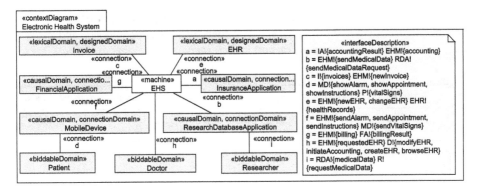

Figure 1. Context diagram for the EHS scenario.

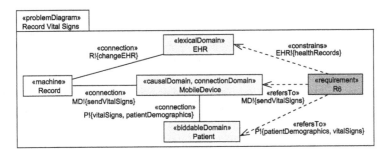

Figure 2. Problem diagram for functional requirement R6.

4. Overview of our Method

The UML2 activity diagram shown in Figure 3 visualizes our method to identify and validate privacy requirements based on a set of functional requirements. We will refer to the actions of the activity diagrams using the term *step*. Our method has to be carried out jointly by a requirements engineer, knowing the functional requirements, a privacy expert, knowing the privacy needs for the system under consideration, and an application domain expert, knowing the application domain of the system under consideration. In the following, we will refer to these persons using the term *user*.

Our method builds upon a central UML model, called *ProPAn Model*, which is used to provide the inputs and to store the outputs for all steps of our method. To be able to model all artifacts needed for our method, we extended the UML using profiles that define stereotypes.

In the following, we provide an overview of the four steps of our methods and briefly describe what is done in the steps and for which purpose, and how the steps are connected to each other. The details on how the steps are carried out are described in Sections 5–8.

The first step shown in Figure 3 (*Analyze Flow of Personal Data*) consists of several sub-steps that we presented in previous work. In this step, we identify privacy relevant domain knowledge as introduced in [13,14], we generate different kinds of graphs that visualize possible privacy issues implied by the functional requirements and the identified domain knowledge as introduced in [9,15], and we identify the personal data that are processed by the system under consideration, how it flows through the system and at which places (domains) the personal data are available and in which quality it is available there as introduced in [15]. These outputs produced during the first step form the foundation of the following steps.

The following steps form the main contribution of this paper.

In the second step of our method (*Generate Privacy Requirements Candidates*), we use the identified *flow of personal data* and the information about the *personal data at domains* to automatically generate the *privacy requirements* that are implied by the provided input. In this paper, we consider the generation of privacy requirements related to the protection goals for privacy engineering proposed by Hansen [5]. These protection goals include the classical security goals *confidentiality*, *integrity*, and *availability* and the privacy goals *unlinkability*, *transparency*, and *intervenability*.

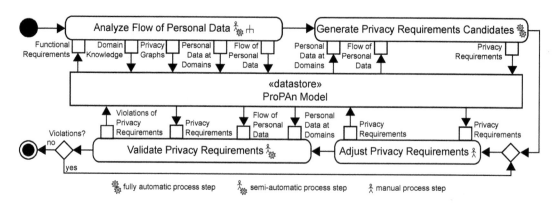

Figure 3. Overview of our proposed method.

In the third step *Adjust Privacy Requirements*, the user has to review, complete, and adjust the generated *privacy requirements*. This is needed, because the generated privacy requirements may lack of details that are not extractable from the ProPAn model or the generated requirements are considered to be incomplete, too strong, or too weak. As result of this step, we obtain a set of revised privacy requirements.

The revised privacy requirements are validated automatically in the fourth step of our method. It is, for example, checked whether the manually adjusted privacy requirements are still consistent with the flow of personal data and the availability of personal data at the different domains as documented in the ProPAn model. The tool support provides the user information about the kinds of violations of the consistency of the privacy requirements and the elicited information flows. Based on this information, the user has to decide, whether the privacy requirements have to be adjusted again, or whether the presented consistency violations are no violations or acceptable violations.

In the following, we will discuss all steps of our method in detail.

5. Analyze Flow of Personal Data

This step summarizes several sub-steps that we already published in previous work. The results of these sub-steps form the foundation of the steps that we introduce in this paper. Figure 4 shows the sub-steps of the step *Analyze Flow of Personal Data* from the overview of our method shown in Figure 3.

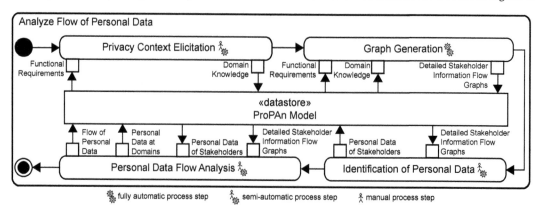

Figure 4. Refinement of the step Analyze Flow of Personal Data.

5.1. Privacy Context Elicitation

First, we elicit privacy-relevant domain knowledge based on questionnaires to identify (1) indirect stakeholders, *i.e.*, people of whom personal information is processed by the system under consideration, but who are not explicitly mentioned in the functional requirements; (2) indirect counterstakeholders, *i.e.*, people who possibly are able to access personal data processed by the system under consideration with or without malicious intentions; and (3) implicit information flows, *i.e.*, information flows that possibly occur between domains of the system under consideration, but that are not explicitly captured in the functional requirements as introduced in [13]. Additionally, we investigate whether interfaces between domains should be refined to identify connection domains which may cause privacy issues as introduced in [14] for the example of clouds as connection domains that possibly introduce privacy problems.

The identified domain knowledge is represented in so-called *domain knowledge diagrams*. These are similar to Jackson's problem diagrams, but they do not contain a machine and instead of a requirement they contain *facts* and *assumptions*. Facts and assumptions are both statements about domains that are indicative. Similar to requirements, facts and assumptions also refer to and constrain domains. The difference between facts and assumptions is, that a fact is a statement that is always true and an assumption is a statement that under certain circumstances may be violated. For example, most statements about the behavior of people (biddable domains) are assumptions, because people may show a different behavior than expected. In the following, we will use the term *statement* as a term that includes requirements, facts, and assumptions.

Application to Running Example

For the EHS scenario, we did not identify any privacy-relevant connection domains, but we identified additional indirect counterstakeholders and implicit information flows.

For example, we identified for the insurance application and the mobile device the domain knowledge shown in Figure 5. Assumption A4 documents that there is an information flow between the patient and the insurance application that is not covered by our requirements. A4 says that information about the patient's insurance contracts, including contact information, is available at the insurance application. Additionally, assumption A5 documents that employees of the insurances gain information about the patient's insurance contracts and their accounting requests from the insurance application. A5 documents the existence of the indirect counterstakeholder insurance employee and also the information this counterstakeholder may have access to.

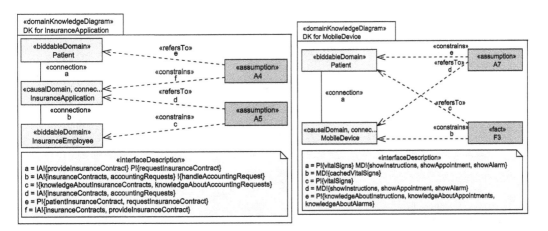

Figure 5. Domain Knowledge about the Insurance Application (**left**) and the Mobile Device (**right**).

Requirement R5 states that instructions, appointments, and alarms shall be sent to patients' mobile devices. What the requirement does not prescribe is that patients recognize the event that their mobile devices received instructions, appointments, and alarms and, e.g., that patients follow the instructions sent to them. Because this is out of the scope of the part of the environment the EHS machine can influence (*cf.* Figure 1). Hence, we document with assumption A7 that we assume that patients recognize and take care about the information sent to their mobile devices. This is another example for an implicit information flow. Fact F3 also documents an implicit information flow, namely that mobile devices will cache the vital signs which are recorded due to requirement R6, in their local memory.

5.2. Graph Generation

In the second sub-step, we automatically generate from the functional requirements and domain knowledge the so-called *detailed stakeholder information flow graphs*. These graphs are used in the following two steps to (1) identify the personal data processed by the system under consideration; (2) how these personal data flow through the system; and (3) at which domains these are available.

As the detailed stakeholder information flow graphs themselves are not relevant for this paper, we omit the details of their structure and generation. The details can be found in [15].

5.3. Identification of Personal Data

In the third sub-step, it is analyzed for every biddable domain in the ProPAn model which personal data of this human being are processed by the system and how these personal data are related to and collected from the owner. This information is documented in so-called *personal information diagrams* (see Figure 6). A personal information diagram is created for each biddable domain of the ProPAn model, and it relates phenomena that represent personal data of the considered biddable domain to that domain. This is realized by a dependency connecting the phenomenon and the domain with the stereotype «relatedTo». The stereotype «relatedTo» provides the possibility to document how the information was collected (attribute collection), from which statements the relation was identified (attribute origin), whether the personal information is sensitive information of the biddable domain (attribute sensitive), and whether the information itself allows one to identify the *single* individuals it is related to, a *group* of individual, or whether it provides no possibility to narrow down the set of individuals it is related to and is hence *anonymous* (attribute linkability). The details on collecting this information and generating the personal information diagrams can be found in [15].

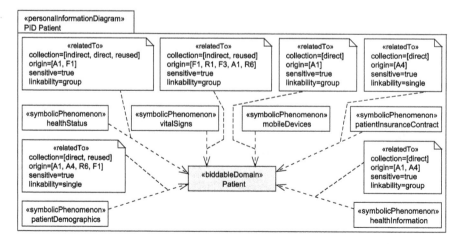

Figure 6. Personal information diagram for the stakeholder patient after the step Identification of Personal Data.

Application to Running Example

Figure 6 shows the personal information diagram for the stakeholder patient that is obtained as a result of the application of the step *Identification of Personal Data* to the EHS scenario. It shows that we identified as personal data for the *Patient* among others the following:

- The *healthStatus* that contains all data that is related to the patient's health and that is processed by the EHS. The health status is considered to be sensitive personal data and it can itself not directly be linked to the single individuals it belongs to, but due to the contained information, it can be linked to a group of individuals it possibly belongs to. The health status is collected in different ways from the patient, it is collected directly from the patient, e.g., during interviews with a doctor, it is indirectly collected by observation of his/her vital signs, and it is also reused from already existing data bases (*cf.* Figure 6).
- The *patientDemographics* summarize details of the patient such as contact information, insurance number, and billing contact. This information suffices to identify the single individual it belongs to, it is considered as sensitive information, and it is collected directly from the patient, e.g., during interviews with a doctor, and by reuse of already existing data sets (*cf.* Figure 6).

Additionally, the personal data *vitalSigns* that, e.g., represent records of patients' pulse and blood pressure, *mobileDevices* that represent information about patients' mobile devices, *patientInsuranceContract* that represent contracts that patients have with their insurances, and *healthInformation* that are used by insurance companies to select the patients' insurance contracts and tariffs are also considered as personal data of patients that are processed by the system-to-be.

5.4. Personal Data Flow Analysis

In the fourth sub-step, the user analyzes how the personal data that were identified in the previous step flow through the system due to the functional requirements and domain knowledge. The documentation of these data flows and the personal data identified in the previous sub-step form the foundation for the automatic generation and validation of privacy requirements.

To document which information is available at which domain, we use so-called *available information diagrams*. For each domain, an available information diagram (similar to a personal information diagram) is created, and for each personal information that is available at the domain, we document the relation between the corresponding symbolic phenomenon and the domain under consideration using a dependency with stereotype «availableAt». Similar to the stereotype «relatedTo», also the stereotype «availableAt» provides some attributes for documentation purposes. These attributes are set during the personal data flow analysis. For details on how the personal data flow analysis is performed and how the available information diagrams are generated see [15]. The attribute duration documents how long a specific information shall be available at the domain. The attribute origin documents from which statements it was identified that the personal data are available at the domain, and the attribute purpose documents because of which statements the personal information has to be available at the domain, *i.e.*, because of these statements the personal data flow to another domain. Figure 7 shows a view on an available information diagram that only contains the before mentioned relations.

In addition to the information which information is available at a domain, an available information diagram also contains the information whether and in which quality the available personal information is linkable to each other at the domain. To document this, we use associations with the stereotype «linkable» between the personal data in the available information diagrams. Again, this stereotype provides some attributes for documentation purposes. The attributes origin, purpose, and duration have the same meaning as for the «availableAt» relation. The additional attribute «linkability» documents with which certainty the data can be linked to each other.

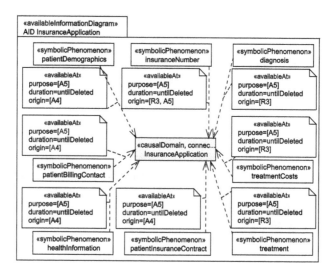

Figure 7. View on the available information diagram for the insurance application showing the which personal data of patients are available at the insurance application.

During the information flow analysis, we elicit two additional relations between the identified personal data. The relation *contains* documents that one personal information contains another personal information. We document this using an aggregation with stereotype «contains». The relation *derivedFrom* documents that a personal information can be derived from one or several other pieces of personal information. We document this using a dependency with stereotype «derivedFrom». The contains and derivedFrom relations are–in contrast to the linkable relation–globally valid relations, *i.e.*, the relations are not only available at specific domains, they are valid at all domains. Figures 8 and 9 present views on a personal information diagram and an available information diagram. These diagrams show how the contains, derivedFrom, and linkable relations are modeled.

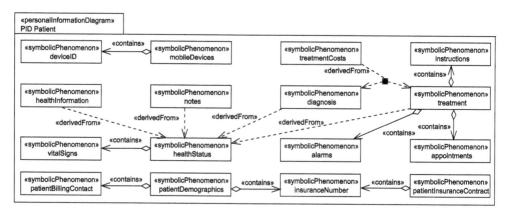

Figure 8. View on the final personal information diagram for the patient showing the personal information of the patient and the relations between this personal information.

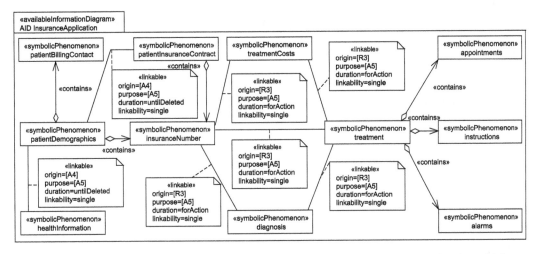

Figure 9. View on the available information diagram for the insurance application showing which links between the personal data of the patient are available at the insurance application.

Application to Running Example

Figure 8 shows all personal information that was identified for the patient. During the personal data flow analysis new personal information was identified based on the personal data that were identified during the step Identification of Personal Data (cf. Figure 6). All newly identified personal data can be derived from or is contained in the initially identified personal data and additionally, we identified contains and derivedFrom relations among the initially identified personal data. For example, we identified that the *healthInformation* of patients can be derived from the patient's *healthStatus*. Furthermore, it was identified that the *diagnosis*, which doctors create for patients, and the chosen *treatment* are derived from the patient's *healthStatus* by doctors. In addition, from the *diagnosis* and *treatment*, the costs for the performed treatment (*treatmentCosts*) can be derived.

Figure 7 shows which personal information of patients are available at the insurance application. For example, from requirement R3 (attribute origin) it was identified that for accounting, the patient's diagnosis, treatment, treatment costs, and insurance number are sent to the insurance application. This information is kept available there until there are no further legal obligations to keep it and it has to be deleted. It is documented that this information has to be available at the insurance application due to assumption A5 (attribute purpose) to ensure that insurance employees are able to perform the accounting.

Figure 9 shows which relations between the personal data of patients is available at the insurance application. For example, it is (globally) documented that the patient's billing contact and the patient's insurance number are contained in the patient's demographics (cf. Figure 8). Additionally, it is documented that from requirement R3 it was identified that for accounting the patient's diagnosis, treatment, treatment costs, and insurance number are linkable to each other at the insurance application. This linkability is obviously needed for the accounting to be able to check whether the treatment and the associated costs are covered by the patient's insurance contract.

6. Generate Privacy Requirements Candidates

To automatically generate privacy requirements candidates, we make use of the artifacts elicited in the previous step and documented in the ProPAn model. We assume that these artifacts reflect the intended information processing that is introduced by the system-to-be and that occur in its environment. This means, we generate the privacy requirements on the assumption that only the intended processing may be performed and the end-users shall be informed about this processing.

In this context, we aim at eliciting all relevant privacy requirements. The user can then decide in the next step of our method (see Section 7) to remove or change the generated privacy requirements if the assumptions made were too strong or too weak.

The ways how we identify the privacy requirements differs for the different kinds of privacy requirements. We consider the six protection goals for privacy engineering unlinkability, transparency, intervenability, confidentiality, integrity, and availability proposed by Hansen et al. [5]. Hansen et al. state that the protection goal of *unlinkability* includes further properties such as anonymity, pseudonymity, and undetectability. These properties aim at weakening or removing links between data and the persons they belong to. *Transparency* is about increasing the awareness of end-users on how their data is processed and for what purpose by providing them appropriate information about how their data is handled. By realizing the protection goal *intervenability*, end-users shall be able to have control over how and if their data is processed by the system-to-be. In this paper, we consider the security goals confidentiality, integrity, and availability from a privacy perspective and consider these as privacy requirements. This means that the assets to be protected by the security goals are limited to personal data, but the protection of these properties is not only limited to malicious attacks, but also to unintended disclosure, changes, or errors. In this sense, *confidentiality* aims at keeping personal data secret from specific entities. The protection goal *integrity* is concerned with protecting personal data from unwanted changes to keep the data consistent. Addressing the goal *availability* means to ensure that all entities can retrieve the personal data that they are allowed to access at any time. In the following, we describe for each protection goal the privacy requirements that are refinements of the protection goal, and how we automatically identify which of these privacy requirements have to be considered based on the information elicited in the previous step.

6.1. Unlinkability Requirements

To derive the privacy requirements related to the protection goal of unlinkability, we use the terminology introduced by Pfitzmann and Hansen [16]. Pfitzmann and Hansen define the privacy properties anonymity, unlinkability, undetectability, unobservability, and undetectability. Hansen et al. [5] summarize all these properties under the protection goal unlinkability. Based on this terminology, we created the UML profile shown in Figure 10. The top-level privacy requirement was originally introduced in [9] and specifies the core of every privacy requirement, namely the stakeholder who shall be protected, the counterstakeholders from whom the stakeholder shall be protected, and the personal data (expressed as phenomena) of the stakeholder that shall be protected. For the protection goal unlinkability, we derived the sub-requirements pseudonymity, unlinkability, and undetectability. The sub-requirement unlinkability is further refined into data unlinkability (requires that certain personal data shall not be linkable to each other) and anonymity (requires that certain personal data shall not be linkable to the corresponding individual). Note that the privacy property unobservability is not represented as a separate requirement, but it can be expressed by instantiating respective anonymity and undetectability requirements (*cf.* [16]). For the automatic generation, we only consider the following requirements that may be refined into pseudonymity requirements in the step *Adjust Privacy Requirements* (Section 7). In Section 7, also the meaning of a pseudonymity requirement is explained.

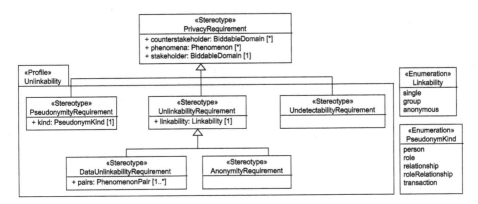

Figure 10. Used Taxonomy of Unlinkability Requirements.

UndetectabilityRequirement   Pfitzmann and Hansen define undetectability as: "Undetectability of an item of interest (IOI) from an attacker's perspective means that the attacker cannot sufficiently distinguish whether it exists or not."

AnonymityRequirement   Pfitzmann and Hansen define anonymity as: "Anonymity of a subject from an attacker's perspective means that the attacker cannot sufficiently identify the subject within a set of subjects, the anonymity set."

DataUnlinkabilityRequirement   Pfitzmann and Hansen define unlinkability as: "Unlinkability of two or more items of interest (IOIs, e.g., subjects, messages, actions, ...) from an attacker's perspective means that within the system (comprising these and possibly other items), the attacker cannot sufficiently distinguish whether these IOIs are related or not." Our data unlinkability requirements express the intended relations between messages, actions, and the like which a subject performs and do not concern the relations of these to the subject itself, as these are represented by anonymity requirements.

6.1.1. Undetectability

Based on the above given definition of Pfitzmann and Hansen, an undetectability requirement of our taxonomy (*cf.* Figure 10) has the following meaning:

> The <*counterstakeholder*>s shall not be able to sufficiently distinguish whether the personal information <*phenomena*> of the <*stakeholder*> exists or not.

If a personal information of a stakeholder is not available at a counterstakeholder and also not part of any personal information available at the counterstakeholder, then we assume that this personal information is undetectable for the counterstakeholder. Note that an undetectability requirement may be too strong for this case, because the counterstakeholder may be allowed to know that a specific personal information exists, but may not be allowed to know the content of it. Hence, the user may weaken an undetectability requirement in the next step of our method (Section 7) to a confidentiality requirement.

To keep the number of requirements that are generated small, we create for each pair of stakeholder and counterstakeholder only one undetectability requirement containing all personal information of the stakeholder that shall be undetectable for the counterstakeholder. A personal information p that shall be undetectable for the counterstakeholder c has to be related to the stakeholder s (represented by the existence of a relatedTo relation in s' personal information diagram that relates p to s) and must not be available to c (represented by the absence of an availableAt relation in c's available information diagram that relates p to c).

Application to Running Example

For the sake of simplicity, we only consider the stakeholder patient and the counterstakeholder insurance employee for the generation of the unlinkability requirements.

To the biddable domain insurance employee the same personal information of the patient is available as at the insurance application (*cf.* Figure 7). Hence, an undetectability requirement is generated for the counterstakeholder insurance employee and the stakeholder patient with all personal data of the patient (*cf.* Figure 8) that is *not* available at the insurance employee as value for the attribute phenomena. The undetectability requirement is represented in the first row in Table 1. When we instantiate the above template for the meaning of an undetectability requirement, then we get the following textual representation of it:

> The *insurance employee* shall not be able to sufficiently distinguish whether the personal information *healthStatus, mobileDevices, deviceId, vitalSigns, and notes* of the *patient* exist or not.

Table 1. Unlinkability requirements for the stakeholder patient and the counterstakeholder insurance employee.

UnlinkabilityRequirement	Phenomena / Pairs
Undetectability	healthStatus, mobileDevices, deviceID, vitalSigns, notes
Anonymity linkability=single	patientBillingContact, patientDemographics, healthInformation, insuranceNumber, patientInsuranceContact, treatmentCosts, treatment, diagnosis, appointments, instructions, alarms
Data Unlinkability linkability=single	(treatmentCosts,diagnosis), (treatmentCosts,patientDemographics), (treatmentCosts,healthInformation), (treatmentCosts,instructions), (treatmentCosts,alarms), (treatmentCosts,insuranceNumber), (treatmentCosts,patientBillingContact), (treatmentCosts,patientInsuranceContact), (treatmentCosts,treatment), (treatmentCosts,appointments),(diagnosis,patientDemographics), (diagnosis,healthInformation), (diagnosis,instructions), (diagnosis,alarms), (diagnosis,insuranceNumber), (diagnosis,patientBillingContact), (diagnosis,patientInsuranceContact), (diagnosis,treatment), (diagnosis,appointments), (patientDemographics,healthInformation), (patientDemographics,instructions), (patientDemographics,alarms), (patientDemographics,insuranceNumber), (patientDemographics,patientBillingContact), (patientDemographics,patientInsuranceContact), (patientDemographics,treatment), (patientDemographics,appointments), (healthInformation,instructions), (healthInformation,alarms), (healthInformation,insuranceNumber), (healthInformation,patientBillingContact), (healthInformation,patientInsuranceContact), (healthInformation,treatment), (healthInformation,appointments), (instructions,alarms), (instructions,insuranceNumber), (instructions,patientBillingContact), (instructions,patientInsuranceContact), (instructions,treatment), (instructions,appointments), (alarms,insuranceNumber), (alarms,patientBillingContact), (alarms,patientInsuranceContact), (alarms,treatment), (alarms,appointments), (insuranceNumber,patientBillingContact), (insuranceNumber,patientInsuranceContact), (insuranceNumber,treatment), (insuranceNumber,appointments), (treatment,appointments), (patientBillingContact,patientInsuranceContact), (patientBillingContact,treatment), (patientBillingContact,appointments), (patientInsuranceContact,treatment), (patientInsuranceContact,appointments)

6.1.2. Data Unlinkability Requirements

Based on the above given definition of Pfitzmann and Hansen, a data unlinkability requirement has the following meaning:

> For each pair of personal information *<pairs>* of the *<stakeholder>*, the *<counterstakeholder>*s shall at most be able to link instances of the two elements of the pair to each other with linkability *<linkability>*.

Note that a data unlinkability requirement with linkability *single* does not constrain the system-to-be to ensure that counterstakeholders are not able to link personal data of the stakeholder to each other, but nevertheless, we make this information explicit to document that this linkability is intended. We generate for each combination of stakeholder and counterstakeholder at most three data unlinkability requirements. Namely, one for each linkability (*single*, *group*, and *anonymous*) with which a counterstakeholder may be able to relate a personal information to the corresponding stakeholder. The information whether two pieces of personal information are linkable to each other by a counterstakeholder can be derived from his/her available information diagram using the linkable relation and the globally defined contains relation (*cf.* Section 5.4).

The linkable relation has a transitive nature. That is, if a personal information a is linkable to a personal information b and b linkable to a personal information c, then this introduces a link between a and c. These transitive relations do not have to be modeled by the user manually, they are automatically computed when needed by the provided tool. During this automatic computation, we consider all contains relations between personal information available at a domain also as linkable relations with linkability *single*. To decide which linkability a derived link between a and c has, we distinguish two cases. The cases are visualized in Figure 11. First (case (a)), if not yet a link between a and c is identified during the closure computation, then the linkability between a and c is the minimum of the existing linkability v between a and b, and the existing linkability w between b and c. Second (case (b)), if there is already a link between a and c, then we replace the existing linkability u only if the minimum of v and w has a greater linkability than u. Minimal and maximal linkability are defined by the total ordering *anonymous* < *group* < *single*. For example, if u = anonymous, v = single, and w = group, then $min(v, w)$ = group, and $max(u, min(v, w))$ = group. If no linkable relation is documented between a personal information a and a personal information b that both are available at a domain, then we consider a and b to be linkable to each other with linkability *anonymous* in the closure. That is, it is not known at the domain which personal information a is related to which personal information b.

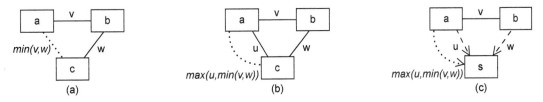

Figure 11. Cases describing how the linkability attribute of the linkable and related to relations are determined for the transitive closure of them. (a) Linkable relation exists between a and b, but not between a and c; (b) Linkable relations exist between a, b, and c; (c) a and b are related to S and a linkable relation between a and b exists.

Based on the computed closure of the linkable relation, the tool decides for each pair of the stakeholder s' personal information that is available at the counterstakeholder c with which linkability it is linkable to each other and to which of the three data unlinkability requirements for s and c it has to be added. In this way, we set the attribute pairs. The attribute phenomena is set to the set of all personal information that is contained in a pair of the attribute pairs of the same requirement.

Application to Running Example

To the biddable domain insurance employee not only the same personal information of the patient is available as at the insurance application, also the same personal information is linkable to each other for the insurance employee with the same linkability. Hence, we can see from Figure 7 that all personal information available to the insurance employee is connected to each other in the transitive closure of the linkable relation with linkability *single*. That is, an insurance employee is able to know which pieces of personal information that are available to him/her belong to each other. Thus, we only obtain one data unlinkability requirement, namely for the linkability *single*, because there is no pair of personal data available at the insurance employee that is not linkable with linkability *single*. This data unlinkability requirement is represented by the third row in Table 1 and contains all 55 pairs of the 11 pieces of personal information available to the insurance employee.

6.1.3. Anonymity Requirement

Based on the above given definition of Pfitzmann and Hansen, an anonymity requirement has the following meaning:

> The <*counterstakeholder*>s shall at most be able to link the personal information <*phenomena*> to the stakeholder with linkability <*linkability*>.

Note that an anonymity requirement with linkability *single* does not constrain the system-to-be to preserve the anonymity of the stakeholders personal data against counterstakeholders, but nevertheless, we make this information explicit to document that this linkability is intended. Similar to the data unlinkability requirements, we also instantiate three anonymity requirements for each pair of stakeholder and counterstakeholder, namely, one for each of the possible linkabilities.

We have now to decide which personal information a can be related to the stakeholder s by the counterstakeholder c with which linkability, to decide to which anonymity requirement's attribute phenomena a has to be added. For this, we use the relatedTo relation from s' personal information diagram and the previously discussed closure of the linkable relation from c's available information diagram. The relatedTo relation (*cf.* Section 5.3) describes for every personal information a of a stakeholder s with which linkability this personal information a can be related to s (by any domain). However, it is possible that we obtain at a domain a linkability of a to s that is greater than the linkability u documented in the relatedTo relation. This case is illustrated in Figure 11c. If a is linkable to a personal information b with linkability v at a domain and b can be related at that domain with linkability w to s, then this implies that at that domain a can be linked to s with at least the linkability $min(v, w)$. Similar as for the closure of the linkable relation, we only take into account the derived linkability $min(v, w)$ if it has a greater linkability than the existing linkability u. The described combination of the linkable and relatedTo relations introduces a new relation *linkableTo* that provides for a stakeholder, a counterstakeholder, and a personal information of the stakeholder that is available to the counterstakeholder the linkability with which the counterstakeholder can relate the personal information to the stakeholder. The linkableTo relation is generated on demand by the tool, and is used to instantiate anonymity requirements.

Application to Running Example

From the generation of the data unlinkability requirements, we know that all personal information of the patient that is available at the insurance employee is linkable to each other with linkability *single*. In addition, from Figure 6, we can see that, e.g., the personal information *patientDemographics* can be related to the single patient it belongs to. Hence, the computed linkableTo relation for the patient and the insurance employee returns for every personal information available at the insurance employee the linkability *single*. That is, for every personal information available to the insurance employee, he/she is able to know to which patient's demographics the personal information belongs. Hence, he/she is able to relate, e.g., the patient's *healthInformation*, which in isolation is only linkable to a group of possible patient's it might belong to, to the patient it belongs to. Thus, we only generate one anonymity requirement for the patient and the insurance employee. This anonymity requirement is shown in the second row of Table 1.

6.2. Transparency and Intervenability Requirements

Transparency and intervenability are protection goals that not yet got as much attention as unlinkability and the classical security goals. In [6], we developed a requirements taxonomy for the protection goal of transparency. In ongoing work, we are developing a similar taxonomy for the protection goal of intervenability. Preliminary results [17] show that we will obtain an analogous structure of intervenability requirements as we identified for transparency requirements. Hence, we assume that we will be able to apply the same strategies for the identification of intervenability requirements as we present for transparency requirements in this section.

The taxonomy of transparency requirements (shown in Figure 12) distinguishes three kinds of requirements. First, presentation requirements that are concerned about *how* the information has to be presented to the stakeholder, second, processing information requirements that inform the stakeholder how his/her data is processed by the system-to-be, and third, exceptional information requirements that state that in the case of exceptional cases, e.g., privacy breaches, the stakeholder and additional authorities have to be informed about these incidents. The first kind of requirements has to be set up manually, as we cannot derive from the output of the first step of our method how stakeholders have to be informed. Also the third kind of requirements cannot be derived from the previously elicited information, but it will be possible to derive them when threats to the unlinkability and security requirements are identified, which is part of our future work. For the second kind of transparency requirements, we show how we can identify about which collection, flow, and storage of personal data stakeholders have to be informed.

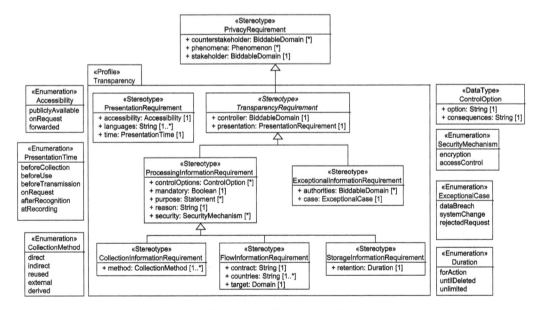

Figure 12. Used Taxonomy of Transparency Requirements.

Our basis to identify these transparency requirements is the data flow implied by the available information diagrams. If a personal information p is available at domain d_2 with origin st and at a domain d_1 with purpose st, then we know that due to statement st the personal information p flows from d_1 to d_2. Figure 13 shows an excerpt of a *stakeholder data flow graph* (SDFG) that visualizes which personal information of a stakeholder flows between which domains. For the sake of readability, the SDFG does not show due to which statements the data flow, but this information is be deduced from the available information diagrams when needed. For details on the generation of this graph see [15].

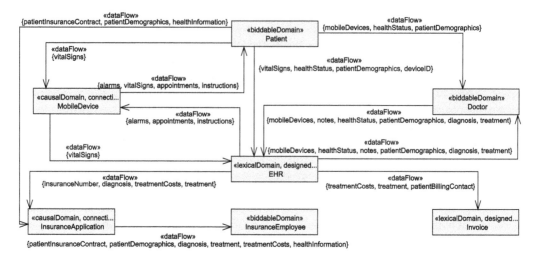

Figure 13. Excerpt of the Stakeholder Data Flow Graph for the stakeholder patient.

6.2.1. Collection Information Requirements

A collection information requirement has the following meaning:

The <*stakeholder*> shall be informed that his/her personal data <*phenomena*> are <*mandatory*>ly collected by the system-to-be that is run by the <*controller*>. The applied collection methods to obtain <*phenomena*> from the <*stakeholder*> are <*method*>. The <*stakeholder*>'s possibilities to control the collection of his/her data are <*controlOptions*>. <*phenomena*> are collected for the purpose of <*purpose*> because <*reason*>. The <*controller*> has selected the security mechanisms <*security*> to protect the personal data <*phenomena*>. The details on how the information has to be presented to the <*stakeholder*> are defined in the presentation requirement <*presentation*>.

Note that for all processing information requirements the attribute counterstakeholder is not relevant and hence, kept empty.

Data collection happens at those places in the system-to-be where personal information of a stakeholder flows from a given domain to a designed domain, which represent parts of the system-to-be (*cf.* Section 3). This is, because every information that is collected by the system-to-be has to flow from outside the system-to-be (a given domain) to a part of it (a designed domain).

For each personal information p and stakeholder s for whom p represents personal information, we instantiate a collection information requirement with the attributes stakeholder = s and phenomena = $\{p\}$ if p flows from a given domain to a designed domain. Additionally, we can automatically set the attributes purpose and method. As purpose, we set the statements due to which p flows to the designed domain(s) and due to which it (or contained personal information) flows from the designed domain further to other domains. The attribute method is instantiated using the documented collection methods from the relatedTo relations in the personal information diagram of s. All other attributes have to be adjusted by the user in next step of our method.

Application to Running Example

The data that is collected from patients can be derived from the in-going edges of the designed lexical domain EHR in Figure 13. In the EHS scenario, the electronic health records (EHR) are the central point of the system-to-be where all data about patients is collected. For example, the patient's *vitalSigns* are collected by the system-to-be from mobile devices, patients (indirectly through a possible reuse of already existing health records), and doctors (contained in the personal information *healthStatus*). Figure 14 shows the generated collection information requirement for the patient and the personal information vital signs. In Figure 14, only the instantiated attributes are shown, all other attributes have later to be set by the user. The collection methods for the vital signs were already collected during the Identification of Personal Data and documented in the relatedTo relation of the patient's personal information diagram (*cf.* Figure 6). It is documented that the vital signs are indirectly collected from the mobile devices and doctors that measure these, or may originate from already existing health records (reused). The vital signs as part of the health status of the patient are an information in the EHS from which other personal information of the patient is derived, such as diagnoses and treatments (*cf.* Figure 8). Hence, it is automatically derived that the vital signs are collected for the purpose of all functional requirements. Note that we also consider the statements due to which the information is collected (*i.e.*, R1 and R6) as purpose.

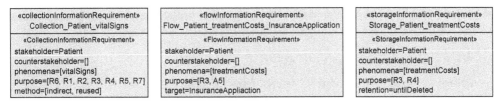

Figure 14. Examples of generated transparency requirements for the EHS scenario.

6.2.2. Flow Information Requirements

A flow information requirement has the following meaning:

The *<stakeholder>* shall be informed that his/her personal data *<phenomena>* flow *<mandatory>*ly to the *<target>* due to the system-to-be that is run by the *<controller>*. The *<target>* is located in *<countries>* and contractual obligations *<contract>* exist between the *<target>* and the *<controller>*. The *<stakeholder>*'s possibilities to control the flow of his/her data are *<controlOptions>*. *<phenomena>* flow to the *<target>* for the purpose of *<purpose>* because *<reason>*. The *<controller>* has selected the security mechanisms *<security>* to protect the personal data *<phenomena>*. The details on how the information has to be presented to the *<stakeholder>* are defined in the presentation requirement *<presentation>*.

Hence, stakeholders have to be informed about all data flows that are introduced by the system-to-be. Stakeholders do not have to be informed about the information flows inside the system-to-be, because they only have to be informed about the behavior of the system-to-be as a whole. Additionally, stakeholders do not have to be informed about information flows that happen independently of the system-to-be, because these flows are out of the scope of the system-to-be. Hence, we only consider the documented data flows to given domains that are caused by the system-to-be. We distinguish two kinds of data flows introduced by the system-to-be.

First, the system-to-be may introduce flows of personal information from designed domains to given domains. Second, there might be information flows between given domains that originate from a functional requirement. This can be the case if a part of the system-to-be is only responsible to forward personal information p of a stakeholder s from a given domain d_1 to another given domain d_2

without collecting or storing the data itself. We instantiate a flow information requirement for each combination of given domain d_2 and stakeholder s if a piece of personal information p of s is sent to d_2 from a designed domain and/or due to a functional requirement from a given domain.

In both cases of information flows, we generate a flow information requirement with stakeholder = s, phenomena = $\{p\}$, and target = d_2. Additionally, we can automatically set the attribute purpose to the set of statements for which it was documented that the personal information p has to be available at d_2 and due to which statements p flows to d_2. The other attributes have to be set manually by the user in the next step of our method.

Application to Running Example

In the EHS scenario, we have no example for a flow of personal information between two given domains that originates from a functional requirement, but the SDFG for the patient (*cf.* Figure 13) shows two information flows from the designed lexical domain EHR to the given domains insurance application and doctor. For the stakeholder patient, the target insurance application, and the phenomenon treatmentCosts, we generate the flow information requirement shown in Figure 14. The *purpose* for which this information flows from the system-to-be to the insurance application is deduced from the corresponding available information diagram shown in Figure 7. The availableAt relations documented in the available information diagram show that the personal information flows because of the functional requirement R3 and is needed at it due to assumption A5. Hence, both statements are documented as purpose for the flow of personal information.

6.2.3. Storage Information Requirements

A storage information requirement has the following meaning:

> The <*stakeholder*> shall be informed that his/her personal data <*phenomena*> are stored <*mandatory*>ly by the system-to-be that is run by the <*controller*>. The <*phenomena*>'s retention in the system-to-be is <*retention*>. The <*stakeholder*>'s possibilities to control the storage of his/her data are <*controlOptions*>. <*phenomena*> are stored for the purpose of <*purpose*> because <*reason*>. The <*controller*> has selected the security mechanisms <*security*> to protect the personal data <*phenomenon*>. The details on how the information has to be presented to the <*stakeholder*> are defined in the presentation requirement <*presentation*>.

Every personal information that is available at a designed domain, is stored by the system-to-be for at least the time that it is necessary to be there to satisfy the functional requirements. We instantiate for each pair of stakeholder s and personal information p of s a storage information requirement if p is available at a designed domain. For a storage information requirement with stakeholder = s and phenomena = $\{p\}$, we set retention to the maximal duration with which it is available at a designed domain. The maximal duration is determined by the total ordering *forAction* < *untilDeleted* < *unlimited*. Additionally, we can automatically derive the purposes for which p is stored by the system-to-be from the available information diagrams.

Application to Running Example

In the EHS scenario, all personal information that is collected by the EHS, is also stored by it. Hence, we obtain for each collection information requirement also a storage information requirement. For example, we get a storage information requirement for the patient and his/her vital signs similar to the collection information requirement shown in Figure 14, but instead of the attribute method it has the attribute retention with value *untilDeleted*. The value *untilDeleted* is selected because the vital signs may be retained longer as needed for the purpose, but they have to be deleted due to some regulations if the patient's health record becomes outdated. Additionally, the EHS stores personal information of the patient, that is derived from the collected personal information, e.g., the *treatmentCosts* are derived from the diagnosis and treatment performed by doctors (*cf.* Figure 8) and stored at the designed lexical domain *Invoice*. For the patient and his/her treatment costs, we generate the storage information requirement shown in Figure 14. The derived purpose for storing the treatment costs are the functional requirements R3 and R4, which are concerned with the accounting and billing of patients. Analogous to the storage information requirement for the patient and the vital signs, the attribute retention is set to *untilDeleted*.

6.3. Security Requirements

In this paper, we consider the basic security requirements confidentiality, integrity, and availability, which we interpret in the context of privacy. Figure 15 shows our UML profile to represent the three security requirements.

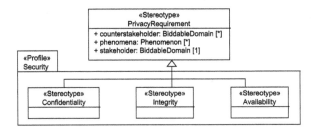

Figure 15. Used Taxonomy of Security Requirements.

A confidentiality requirement has the meaning:

The personal data *<phenomena>* of the *<stakeholder>* shall be kept confidential from *<counterstakeholder>*.

An integrity requirement has the meaning:

Random faults of the system and *<counterstakeholder>* shall not be able to negatively influence the consistency and correctness of the personal data *<phenomena>* of the *<stakeholder>*.

An availability requirement has the meaning:

Random faults of the system and *<counterstakeholder>* shall not be able to negatively influence the availability of the personal data *<phenomena>* to the corresponding *<stakeholder>*.

Note that if the set of counterstakeholders is left empty for an integrity or availability requirement, then the meaning is that the integrity and availability of the stakeholder's personal data shall be preserved against all possible counterstakeholders.

Our above definition of the security requirements also includes a dimension that is classically assigned to safety requirements, namely random faults that may cause harm to the system. For privacy, these random faults are also of relevance, because privacy issues may not only arise from attacks a counterstakeholder might perform or unwanted incidents he/she incidentally causes, but also because of random faults that do not allow access to information or that delete or change the content of the personal data of the stakeholder.

We do not generate confidentiality requirements during this step, but the user may refine an undetectability requirement to a confidentiality requirement as already mentioned above in Section 6.1.1.

The generation of our general integrity and availability requirements is straightforward. We instantiate for each stakeholder whose personal information is available at a designed domain one integrity requirement and one availability requirement with the attribute phenomena set to the set of all of the stakeholder's personal information that is available to the system-to-be, *i.e.*, available at a designed domain, and with an empty set counterstakeholder. During the next step of our method, the user may decide to refine the set of counterstakeholders.

Application to Running Example

For the patient all personal data shown in Figure 8 except *healthInformation* and *patientInsuranceContract* are available at designed domains and hence, we create corresponding availability and integrity requirements.

7. Adjust Privacy Requirements

In this step, the user manually inspects the automatically generated privacy requirements and has the possibility to complete and adjust these. In the following, we discuss the possibilities the user has to complete and adjust the generated requirements based on the different kinds of privacy requirements.

7.1. Unlinkability Requirements

The generated unlinkability requirements do not have to be completed, because all attributes of them are already automatically set. The user only has to decide whether the identified requirements really reflect the privacy protection needs.

7.1.1. Undetectability Requirements

For each undetectability requirement, the user may decide that not all of the personal information of the stakeholder s listed in the requirement has to be undetectable for the counterstakeholder c. That is, a counterstakeholder c may be allowed to know that a specific kind of information exists, but he/she shall not be able to know the exact content of the information. Hence, a user can decide to introduce a confidentiality requirement for s and c and move the personal information of s that only has to be kept confidential and not undetectable from the corresponding undetectability requirement to the new confidentiality requirement. It is possible that the user decides that all personal information shall only be kept confidential. Then the undetectability requirement is completely replaced by the introduced confidentiality requirement.

Application to the Running Example

For the stakeholder patient and the counterstakeholder insurance employee, the undetectability requirement shown in the first row of Table 1 was generated. As it is not possible and needed to hide the information that the EHS processes the patient's health status (including vital signs), mobile devices (including their IDs), and notes about patient's, we decide to relax the undetectability requirement to a confidentiality requirement.

7.1.2. Anonymity and Data Unlinkability Requirements

For each anonymity and data unlinkability requirement, the user has to consider whether the contained personal information or pairs of personal information belong to the correct requirement. That is, the user has to decide whether the linkability of the personal information to the stakeholder or the linkability between the pair of personal information was correctly derived from the ProPAn model. The user can decide to weaken or strengthen the requirements by increasing or reducing the linkability with which a personal information can be linked to the stakeholder or a pair of information can be linked to each other by the counterstakeholder, respectively. The user can even decide that a personal information shall be undetectable or confidential to the counterstakeholder.

Another possibility is that a user refines an anonymity requirement or a part of it to a pseudonymity requirement (*cf.* Table 1). The meaning of a pseudonymity requirement is:

For the personal information *<phenomena>* of the *<stakeholder>* the *<counterstakeholder>* shall only be able to relate it to a *<kind>* pseudonym and not to the *<stakeholder>* himself/herself.

An anonymity requirement with linkability *single* can be translated into a pseudonymity requirement with kind *person* or *role*. The pseudonym kind *person* means that for every individual only one pseudonym exists. Hence, all personal information can be linked to the single individual it belongs to if the relation between pseudonym and individual is known. A *role* pseudonym is used for specific roles. That is, an individual has a single pseudonym for each role. As we consider biddable domains as stakeholders and biddable domains normally represent roles of individuals, a *role* pseudonym allows the same level of linkability as a *person* pseudonym in our situation. This is, because we do not distinguish further roles that a biddable domain may have.

An anonymity requirement with linkability *group* may be translated into a pseudonymity requirement with kind *relationship* or *roleRelationship*. Due to the consideration of biddable domains as stakeholders, *relationship* and *roleRelationship* pseudonyms are also equivalent for our case. The pseudonym kind *relationship* means that for every communication partner another pseudonym is used. For example, only the messages sent to the same partner can be linked to each other using a *relationship* pseudonym and not all communication.

An anonymity requirement with linkability *anonymous* may be translated into a pseudonymity requirement with kind *transaction*. A *transaction* pseudonym is only used once for one action or information that is related to an individual. Hence, the pseudonyms themselves do not provide any link to the individual they belong to.

For more details on the kinds of pseudonyms see [16].

Application to the Running Example

We decide not to change or refine the anonymity and data unlinkability requirements for the patient and the insurance employee shown in the second and third row of Table 1. All this information has to be available to the insurance employee with the possibility to link it to the single patient it belongs to. In addition, the available information has to be linkable to each other with linkability *single*. This is, because insurance employees need all this information to perform the accounting of treatments patients received.

7.2. Transparency Requirements

Not all attributes of the transparency requirements were automatically filled during the generation of them. Hence, the user has to complete the generated transparency requirements manually. Normally, we do not expect further modifications on the generated transparency requirements, but the user can add, delete, or merge transparency requirements if needed.

Application to the Running Example

The completed versions of the transparency requirements of Figure 14 are shown in Figure 16. We added to all transparency requirements the same presentation requirement. This presentation requirement states:

The information contained in the related transparency requirements has to be presented *before* the data is collected from the stakeholder in *English* and made accessible to stakeholders by *forwarding* the information to them.

Additionally, all transparency requirements have the same controller that is the provider of the EHS. There are no options to control or intervene into the processing of personal information for the patient, and the processing is mandatory. The attribute security is not set, because yet no concrete security mechanisms where selected, but when such mechanisms have been selected, the attribute should be set. For each transparency requirement, we also provide a reason why the personal information is collected, stored, or flows to another domain.

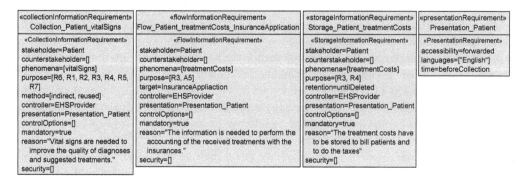

Figure 16. Examples of generated transparency requirements for the eHealth scenario.

7.3. Security Requirements

For the generated availability and integrity requirements, the user may decide for a specific personal information that its integrity does not have to be ensured by the system-to-be, or that it does not have to be made available to the corresponding stakeholder by the system-to-be. Furthermore, the user may limit the availability and integrity requirements to a number of counterstakeholders that shall not be able to negatively influence the availability or integrity of the stakeholders personal data.

Application to the Running Example

We decide not to change or refine the integrity and availability requirements for the patient.

8. Validate Privacy Requirements

In this step, we discuss how the privacy requirements adjusted by the user can be validated. We present validation conditions that indicate inconsistencies between the privacy requirements themselves, or between the privacy requirements and the elicited domain knowledge in the ProPAn model (from which the privacy requirements were originally generated). Our proposed tool is able to detect all inconsistencies discussed in the following and to inform the user about them. The user then has the possibility to correct the inconsistencies. Note that all privacy requirements that are automatically generated by our method do not cause any errors or warnings due to the validation conditions (except the validation conditions that check whether the user completed the attributes of the transparency requirements that cannot be derived from the ProPAn model). An inconsistency between the ProPAn model and the privacy requirements can only be introduced during the manual adjustment of the privacy requirements. Hence, the validation conditions check whether the adjusted privacy requirements are still consistent to each other and to the ProPAn model. We obtained these validation conditions by considering the possible inconsistencies that can be introduced by adjustments of the user between privacy requirements and the ProPAn model.

We distinguish two kinds of validation conditions. First, an adjustment of the user introduces an inconsistency between the privacy requirements or between a privacy requirement and the ProPAn model. In this case, the validation condition raises an error and the user has to remove this inconsistency. Second, an adjustment can be consistent to the ProPAn model, but represent a weaker property than the one that we derived from the ProPAn method during the step *Generate Privacy Requirements Candidates* (*cf.* Section 6). In this case, we present a warning to the user because he/she possibly incidentally weakened the privacy requirements.

8.1. Privacy Requirements

For every privacy requirement, the tool checks whether every phenomenon documented in the requirement is personal information of the privacy requirement's stakeholder. If this is not the case, the user has to correct the privacy requirement or the documented personal information of the stakeholder in the ProPAn model. We formulate this using following validation condition.

VP1 Raise an error for every privacy requirement if the following condition is not satisfied. Every p in *phenomena* has to be personal information of the *stakeholder*.

Application to the Running Example

In this paper, we only consider the privacy requirements for patients. Hence, it has to be checked for these privacy requirements whether the attribute phenomena only contains the personal information presented in Figure 8 for validation condition **VP1**. The privacy requirements shown in Table 1 and Figure 14 satisfy this condition and hence, **VP1** does not raise an error for the discussed privacy requirements.

8.2. Unlinkability Requirements

For each combination of stakeholder s and counterstakeholder c, the corresponding undetectability, anonymity (one for each linkability), and confidentiality requirements have to be consistent to each other. That is, a personal information p of the stakeholder s may only occur in one of the requirements. Otherwise, we have contradictory requirements. This is checked by the following validation condition.

VU1 Raise an error for every undetectability, anonymity, and confidentiality if the following condition is not satisfied. Every p in *phenomena* must not be contained in another undetectability, anonymity (with a different linkability), or confidentiality requirement for the same *stakeholder* and *counterstakeholder*.

In the previous step, the user may have introduced inconsistencies between the unlinkability requirements and the ProPAn model.

In the case that the user strengthened an anonymity requirement (and analogously for data unlinkability requirements), then this introduces an inconsistency to the documented linkability in the ProPAn model. The user may have strengthened an anonymity requirement in one of the following ways:

1. By deciding that the counterstakeholder shall only be able to link the personal information with a weaker linkability to the stakeholder.
2. By changing an anonymity requirement (or a part of it) to an undetectability requirement.
3. By changing an anonymity requirement (or a part of it) to a confidentiality requirement.

Based on the available information diagram of the counterstakeholder, the user has to decide whether his/her adjustments introduce too strong privacy requirements, or whether the functional requirements are not restrictive enough concerning the implied information flows. The following validation conditions check the described inconsistencies.

VU2 For every undetectability and confidentiality requirement do the following. Raise an error if a phenomenon exists in *phenomena* that is available to the *counterstakeholder*.
VU3 For every anonymity requirement do the following. Raise an error if personal information exists in *phenomena* that is linkable to the stakeholder with a greater linkability than *linkability* for the *counterstakeholder*.
VU4 For every data unlinkability requirement do the following. Raise an error if a pair of personal information exists in *pairs* that is linkable to each other with a greater linkability than *linkability* for the *counterstakeholder*.

Weakening unlinkability requirements does not introduce inconsistencies. For example, if counterstakeholder c is able to link personal information p with linkability *group* to the stakeholder s and the related anonymity requirement allows that c is able to link p to s with linkability *single*, then the system-to-be satisfies this anonymity requirement.

If the user deleted an unlinkability or confidentiality requirement that belonged to stakeholder s and counterstakeholder c, then it might be the case that a personal information p (or a pair of personal information) of s does not occur in any of the other unlinkability or confidentiality requirements that belong to s and c. In this case, we have no statement how p has to be protected against c. This might be intended by the user, but nevertheless, the tool will warn the user about this situation.

VU5 For every combination of stakeholder s and counterstakeholder c, warn the user when a personal information of s exists that does not occur in the *phenomena* of any of the undetectability, anonymity, or confidentiality requirements for s and c.

VU6 For every combination of stakeholder s and counterstakeholder c, warn the user when a pair of personal information of s exists for which both elements are available at c, but that does not occur in the *pairs* of any of the data unlinkability requirements for s and c.

Application to the Running Example

During the adjustment of the unlinkability requirements, we only decided to turn the undetectability requirement shown in Table 1 into a confidentiality requirement. Hence, all personal information of the patient occurs either in the confidentiality requirement, or in the anonymity requirement with linkability *single* (*cf.* Table 1). Hence, **VU1** does not raise an error for any discussed undetectability, anonymity, and confidentiality requirements. The validation condition **VU2** does not raise an error for our confidentiality requirement that was created from the undetectability requirement shown in Table 1, because the phenomena referenced by the requirement are all not available at the counterstakeholder insurance employee (*cf.* Figure 7). **VU3** and **VU4** do not raise errors, because we did not strengthen the generated anonymity and data unlinkability requirements and hence, the linkability attribute of these requirements is still consistent to the linkability documented in the ProPAn model. The conditions **VU5** and **VU6** do not cause warnings, because all personal data of patients occur in an undetectability, anonymity, or confidentiality requirement for the stakeholder patient and the counterstakeholder insurance employee, and also each pair of personal data of the patient occurs in a respective data unlinkability requirement.

8.3. Transparency Requirements

For the transparency requirements, it has to be checked whether the user completed all generated transparency requirements. The user is informed which transparency requirements have unset attributes and have to be completed.

VT1 Raise an error for every transparency requirement where an attribute is unset.

VT2 For every transparency requirement, warn the user if an attribute with a multiplicity greater than 1 (except counterstakeholder) is empty.

A user might have changed the transparency requirements inconsistently by adding phenomena to transparency requirements that are not collected or stored by the system-to-be, or do not flow to the specified domain. These inconsistencies have to be corrected by the user.

VT3 Raise an error for every collection and storage information requirement if a p in *phenomena* exists that is not available at a designed domain.

VT4 Raise an error for every flow information requirement if a p in *phenomena* exists that is not available at the *target*.

The user could have deleted transparency requirements or removed phenomena from them. This would lead to an inconsistency between the transparency requirements and the transparency needs that can be derived from the ProPAn model as described in Section 6.2. However, these inconsistencies might be intended by the user, e.g., if there is no need to inform the stakeholder about a specific processing of his/her personal information.

VT5 Warn the user if a personal information flows from a given domain to a designed domain, but no corresponding collection information requirement exists.

VT6 Warn the user if a personal information is available at a designed domain, but no corresponding storage information requirement exists.

VT7 Warn the user if a personal information flows from a designed domain to a given domain, or between two given domains due to a functional requirement, but no corresponding flow information requirement exists.

Application to the Running Example

For the completed transparency requirements shown in Figure 16, the tool notifies us due to validation condition **VT2** that the attributes controlOptions and security are empty, which might indicate that the requirements are incomplete. As we left these attributes empty on purpose, we can ignore this warning. All other validation conditions for transparency requirements are satisfied. **VT1** does not raise an error, because no attribute is unset (*null*). All phenomena contained in the considered collection and storage information requirement are available at a designed domain. Hence, **VT3** does not raise an error. The phenomena contained in the flow information requirement are all available at the insurance application (*cf.* Figure 7) and hence, **VT4** does not raise an error. The validation conditions **VT5**, **VT6**, and **VT7** do not cause any warnings, because there exist no personal information flows from given to designed domains that are not covered by a collection information requirement, there is no personal information available at a designed domain for which no corresponding storage information requirement exists, and there are no personal information flows from designed to given domains, or between given domains due to a functional requirement for which no corresponding flow information requirement exists.

8.4. Security Requirements

Users may remove or add phenomena from availability and integrity requirements during the previous step. To ensure that the user did not incidentally remove a personal information of a stakeholder that is available at a designed domain, we have the following validation condition.

VS1 Warn the user if a personal information of a stakeholder that is available at a designed domain is not contained in the corresponding availability and integrity requirements.

Furthermore, we check whether the user added personal information of a stakeholder to a corresponding availability or integrity requirement that is not available at a designed domain. The system-to-be cannot assure the integrity or availability of personal information that is not processed by it. Hence, we have the following validation condition.

VS2 Raise an error if not all phenomena contained in an availability or integrity requirement are available at a designed domain.

Application to the Running Example

As we did not modify the generated availability and integrity requirements, both validation conditions for security requirements do not cause errors or warnings. **VS1** does not cause an warning because all personal data of patients that are available at a designed domain are contained in the availability and integrity requirements. Furthermore, **VS2** does not raise an error, because only the personal data of patients that is available at a designed domain is contained in the integrity and availability requirements.

The evaluation of all proposed validation conditions can be performed efficiently by the ProPAn tool, because the needed information, e.g., personal data of stakeholder, information flows, designed domains, and given domains, is added to the ProPAn model during the first step of our method. The asymptotic complexity of the evaluation of all validation conditions is limited by $\langle$number of phenomena$\rangle^2 \times \langle$number of domains$\rangle^2$, because for each validation condition (finitely many), we have to intersect two sets of phenomena and in the worst case, this has to be done for all pairs of domains.

9. Tool Support

In this section, we discuss the tool support that we developed to realize the automatic generation and validation of privacy requirements.

9.1. Technical Realization

We integrated the tool support for our proposed method into the ProPAn tool [10]. The ProPAn tool itself is based on the [18]. The UML4PF tool provides UML profiles that allow users to model Jackson's problem frame models as UML diagrams enriched with stereotypes from the UML profiles. Examples for these diagrams are given in Figures 1, 2 and 5. The ProPAn tool provides additional profiles that make it possible to capture and document privacy-relevant knowledge in UML diagrams. Figures 6–9 and Figure 13 show diagrams that are created using the UML profiles that are already provided by the ProPAn tool. For this paper, we added additional profiles to the ProPAn tool that allow users to represent privacy requirements in UML diagrams. These profiles are shown in Figures 10, 12 and 15. For the transparency requirements, we show in Figures 14 and 16 UML diagrams that use the newly introduced UML profiles.

To edit the UML diagrams, we use Papyrus [19] in the Eclipse IDE [20], but in general every UML tool that creates a UML-conform model can be used.

For the automatic and semi-automatic steps of our method, we use the Epsilon platform [21]. Epsilon offers a variety of languages for, e.g., manipulating, transforming, and validating EMF-based [22] models. Additionally, Epsilon provides a language to specify wizards that can easily be integrated into GMF-based ([23]) editors, such as Papyrus. We use these languages for the (semi-)automatic generation of the ProPAn model and the validation of it.

Hence, the ProPAn tool consists of two parts. First, a collection of UML profiles that allow users to model the needed elements for the method in a single UML model. Second, a collection of Epsilon programs that can be called from the Papyrus user interface using the wizard and validation languages provided by Epsilon.

9.2. Using the ProPAn Tool

The UML profiles provided by the ProPAn tool can be used in the same way as all UML profiles using the built-in features of Papyrus. The (semi-)automatic support for the steps of the ProPAn method can be called by a right-click on the biddable domain that shall be considered as a stakeholder and selecting in the context menu the Entry "Wizards->ProPAn: Wizards for selected element" as shown in Figure 17. Then the user can select the step that he/she wants to perform for the selected stakeholder. The steps correspond to the method steps that we introduced in this paper.

From Figure 17, we can see that our tool supports all sub-steps of the first step of our method *Analyze Flow of Personal Data* that was discussed in Section 5. Furthermore, our tool supports the second step of our method, namely the generation of privacy requirements (see Section 6). The sub-steps of the first step of our method are semi-automatic steps that require further user interaction, while the second step of our method is fully automatic and requires no further user interaction.

A part of the automatically generated privacy requirements for patients is shown as a tree view on the UML model in Figure 17. This tree view also shows that we structure the generated privacy requirements using packages to avoid that users get lost in the number of generated privacy requirements. We generate for each stakeholder for whom privacy requirements are generated a package. In this package we add sub-packages for the protection goals unlinkability, security, and transparency. The sub-package for unlinkability contains for each biddable domain that is considered as a counterstakeholder in a privacy requirement belonging to the stakeholder a sub-package that contains all unlinkability related privacy requirements. The sub-package for security contains the stakeholder's confidentiality, integrity, and availability requirements. The transparency sub-package includes for each personal information of the stakeholder for which a transparency requirement exists a sub-package. These sub-packages contain the transparency requirements that are concerned about the respective personal information.

The third step of our method is the adjustment of the automatically generated privacy requirements (see Section 7). The adjustments of the privacy requirements can be performed manually using the standard user interface of Papyrus. Only for turning an undetectability requirement into a confidentiality requirement, we provide a wizard that can be called using a right-click on an undetectability requirement (similar to Figure 17). We added this wizard because attribute values cannot easily be copied from one stereotype instance to another.

Figure 17. Generation and validation of privacy requirements with the ProPAn tool.

The validation of the adjustments of the privacy requirements, which is the fourth and last step of our method (see Section 8), is also supported by the tool support (see Figure 17). After the validation an overview of all errors and warnings detected during it is presented to the user (*cf.* Figure 17). Additionally, the corresponding privacy requirement is annotated with the symbol ⊗ in the case that an error was raised for it during the validation or with the symbol ⚠ if a was warning produced for it. In both cases a tooltip provides the information which validation condition was violated and why.

10. Related Work

The LINDDUN-framework proposed by Deng *et al.* [24] is an extension of Microsoft's security analysis framework STRIDE [25]. The basis for the privacy analysis is a data flow diagram (DFD) which is then analyzed on the basis of the high-level threats Linkability, Identifiabilitiy, Non-repudiation, Detectability, information Disclosure, content Unawareness, and policy/consent Noncompliance.

The PriS method introduced by Kalloniatis *et al.* [26] considers privacy requirements as organizational goals. The impact of the privacy requirements on the other organizational goals and their related business processes is analyzed. The authors use privacy process patterns to suggest a set of privacy enhancing technologies (PETs) to realize the privacy requirements.

Liu *et al.* [27] propose a security and privacy requirements analysis based on the goal and agent-based requirements engineering approach i^* [28]. The authors integrate the security and privacy analysis into the elicitation process of i^*. Already elicited actors from i^* are considered as attackers. Additional skills and malicious intent of the attackers are combined with the capabilities and interests of the actors. Then the vulnerabilities implied by the identified attackers and their malicious intentions are investigated in the i^* model.

The above mentioned methods all support the identification of high-level privacy threats or vulnerabilities and the selection of privacy enhancing technologies (PETs) to address the privacy threats or vulnerabilities. These steps are not yet supported by the ProPAn method. But in contrast to a problem frame model, DFDs, goal models, and business processes, as they are used by the above methods, contain not as detailed information as problem frame models. These details help to identify personal data that is processed by the system and how the personal data flow through the system in a systematic way. Hence, our method provides more support for the elicitation of the information that is essential for a valuable privacy analysis than the methods proposed by Deng *et al.*, Kalloniatis *et al.*, and Liu *et al.*. In addition, the above mentioned methods do not consider all six protection goals for privacy engineering. Hence, our method provides a more complete consideration of privacy. Additionally, we provide a tool-supported method to systematically identify flows of personal data and the implied privacy requirements. Thus, there exist approaches to model the refinement of privacy and security goals to requirements in the literature, but to the best of our knowledge there is a lack of systematic and automated methods that assist the refinement process. Our proposed method aims at closing this gap.

Omoronyia *et al.* [29] present an adaptive privacy framework. Formal models are used to describe the behavioral and context models, and users' privacy requirements regarding the system. The behavioral and context model are then checked against the privacy requirements using model checking techniques. This approach is complementary to ours, because the knowledge and privacy requirements identified by our method can be used to set up adequate models, which is crucial to obtain valuable results.

Oetzel and Spiekermann [30] describe a methodology to support a complete process for a Privacy Impact Assessment (PIA). Their methodology describes which steps have to be performed in which order to perform a PIA. The results of our work can be used to concretize the steps and to generate the artifacts proposed by Oetzel and Spiekermann.

Antón and Earp [31] derived from around 50 website privacy policies in the e-commerce and health domain a privacy goal and a vulnerability taxonomy. These taxonomies shall help consumers to compare different website privacy policies and to decide which website provides the privacy protection fitting to their needs. All privacy goals considered by Antón and Earp are also reflected by the privacy requirements that we consider. For a more detailed comparison of our work to Antón and Earps's concerning transparency requirements see [6].

Hoepman [32] proposes eight so called privacy design strategies. These privacy design strategies describe fundamental approaches to achieve privacy goals. The considered privacy goals are purpose limitation, data minimisation, data quality, transparency, data subject rights, the right to be forgotten, adequate protection, data portability, data breach notifications, and accountability. The goal data quality is covered in our work by the requirement integrity. The protection goal transparency covers Hoepman's goals transparency and data breach notification. Hoepman's goals data subjects rights, the right to be forgotten, and data portability are covered by the protection goal intervenability. The goal adequate protection is covered by the security goals and the goal unlinkability. The goals purpose limitation, data minimisation, and accountability are directed towards the implementation of specific mechanisms to realize or contribute to the other privacy goals. At this point, we are not interested in selecting possible solutions for the identified privacy goals, but we plan to consider the goals purpose limitation, data minimization, and accountability in a further extension of our method.

11. Conclusions

In this paper, we presented a method to systematically derive high-level privacy requirements for a system-to-be based on its functional requirements. Our proposed method is an extension of the Problem-based Privacy Analysis (ProPAn) method and is integrated into the [10]. We showed how the existing elements of the ProPAn method can be used to elicit (1) the personal data that the system-to-be processes; and (2) the flows of these personal data that the system-to-be introduces. We described how the developed tool generates privacy requirement candidates from this information. For the generation of privacy requirements, we presented refinements of the protection goals for privacy engineering unlinkability, transparency, intervenability, confidentiality, integrity, and availability [5] by means of UML profiles and textual descriptions of each refined requirement. We discussed how a user of our method may adjust and complete the generated privacy requirements. Finally, we presented how our tool is able to validate the consistency of the resulting privacy requirements.

Due to the systematic nature of our method and the high degree of automation, we expect that our method empowers requirements engineers to identify an as complete and coherent set of privacy requirements as possible, especially for complex systems. The results of the application of our method on the electronic health system (EHS) scenario are promising, but we have to further validate our method based on industrial-size case studies and empirical experiments as part of our future work.

The main limitation of our approach to generate privacy requirements is that the completeness and correctness of the generated privacy requirements highly depends on how complete and correct the first step of our method was performed by the user. Otherwise the assumptions on which the generation and validation of the privacy requirements are based (cf. Sections 6 and 8) are not valid. That is, if personal data or data flows were not correctly identified and documented, then also incorrect privacy requirements are generated. Hence, the first step of our method should be carried out jointly by a requirements engineer, knowing the functional requirements, a privacy expert, knowing the privacy needs for the system under consideration, and an application domain expert, knowing the application domain of the system under consideration. Another limitation that we have to cope with is that the user of the methods has to be familiar with the problem frames approach and is willing to create problem diagrams for the functional requirements of the system-to-be.

As future work, we want to further extend the ProPAn method to identify privacy threats that could lead to violations of the defined privacy requirements. The elicited information about the flows of personal data will be useful to identify the parts of the system were the identified threats may manifest. Then we want to suggest privacy enhancing technologies (PETs) that can be used to mitigate the identified privacy threats. Finally, we want to elaborate how these PETs have to be integrated into the requirements model in order to mitigate the privacy threats and to satisfy the privacy requirements.

Acknowledgments: This work was partially supported by the Deutsche Forschungsgemeinschaft (DFG) under grant No. GRK 2167, Research Training Group "User-Centred Social Media".

Author Contributions: Rene Meis wrote the paper and Maritta Heisel provided substantial feedback that improved the paper.

Conflicts of Interest: The authors declare no conflict of interest.

Abbreviations

The following abbreviations are used in this manuscript:

EHR	Electronic Health Record
EHS	Electronic Health System
PET	Privacy Enhancing Technology
ProPAn	Problem-based Privacy Analysis
SDFG	Stakeholder Data Flow Graph

References

1. European Commission. Proposal for a Regulation of the European Parliament and of the Council on the Protection of Individuals with Regard to the Processing of Personal Data and on the Free Movement of Such Data (General Data Protection Regulation), 2012. Available online: http://ec.europa.eu/justice/data-protection/document/review2012/com_2012_11_en.pdf (accessed on 24 May 2016).

2. Verizon. 2016 Data Breach Investigations Report. Available online: http://www.verizonenterprise.com/verizon-insights-lab/dbir/2016/ (accessed on 24 May 2016).

3. Ponemon Institute. 2015 Cost of Data Breach Study: Global Analysis. Available online: http://www-03.ibm.com/security/data-breach/ (accessed on 24 May 2016).

4. GSMA. MOBILE PRIVACY: Consumer Research Insights and Considerations for Policymakers, 2014. Available online: http://www.gsma.com/publicpolicy/wp-content/uploads/2014/02/MOBILE_PRIVACY_Consumer_research_insights_and_considerations_for_policymakers-Final.pdf (accessed on 24 May 2016).

5. Hansen, M.; Jensen, M.; Rost, M. Protection Goals for Privacy Engineering. In Proceedings of the 2015 IEEE Symposium on Security and Privacy Workshops, SPW 2015, San Jose, CA, USA, 21–22 May 2015.

6. Meis, R.; Heisel, M.; Wirtz, R. A Taxonomy of Requirements for the Privacy Goal Transparency. In *Trust, Privacy, and Security in Digital Business*; Springer: Cham, Switzerland, 2015; pp. 195–209.

7. Cavoukian, A. The 7 Foundational Principles, 2011. Available online: https://www.ipc.on.ca/images/resources/7foundationalprinciples.pdf (accessed on 24 May 2016).

8. Jackson, M. *Problem Frames: Analyzing and Structuring Software Development Problems*; Addison-Wesley: Boston, MA, USA, 2001.

9. Beckers, K.; Faßbender, S.; Heisel, M.; Meis, R. *A Problem-based Approach for Computer Aided Privacy Threat Identification*; Springer: Berlin/Heidelberg, Germany, 2014; pp. 1–16.

10. ProPAn: A UML4PF Extension. Available online: http://www.uml4pf.org/ext-propan/index.html (accessed on 24 May 2016).

11. Network of Excellence (NoE) on Engineering Secure Future Internet Software Services and Systems. Available online: http://www.nessos-project.eu (accessed on 24 May 2016).

12. Côté, I.; Hatebur, D.; Heisel, M.; Schmidt, H. UML4PF—A Tool for Problem-Oriented Requirements Analysis. In Proceedings of the 2011 IEEE 19th International Requirements Engineering Conference, Trento, Italy, 29 August–2 September 2011; pp. 349–350.

13. Meis, R. Problem-Based Consideration of Privacy-Relevant Domain Knowledge. In *Privacy and Identity Management for Emerging Services and Technologies*; Springer: Berlin/Heidelberg, Germany, 2014.

14. Beckers, K.; Faßbender, S.; Gritzalis, S.; Heisel, M.; Kalloniatis, C.; Meis, R. Privacy-Aware Cloud Deployment Scenario Selection. In *Trust, Privacy, and Security in Digital Business*; Springer: Cham, Switzerland, 2014; pp. 94–105.

15. Meis, R.; Heisel, M. Supporting Privacy Impact Assessments Using Problem-Based Privacy Analysis. In *Software Technologies*, Proceedings of the 10th International Joint Conference, ICSOFT 2015, Colmar, France, 20–22 July 2015; Lorenz, P., Cardoso, J., Maciaszek, L.A., van Sinderen, M., Eds.; Communications in Computer and Information Science; Springer: Cham, Switzerland, 2016; pp. 79–98.

16. Pfitzmann, A.; Hansen, M. A Terminology for Talking About Privacy by Data Minimization: Anonymity, Unlinkability, Undetectability, Unobservability, Pseudonymity, and Identity Management, 2010. Available online: http://www.maroki.de/pub/dphistory/2010_Anon_Terminology_v0.34.pdf (accessed on 23 May 2016).

17. Sabit, S. Consideration of Intervenability Requirements in Software Development. Master's Thesis, University of Duisburg-Essen, Duisburg, Germany, 2015.

18. UML4PF Tool. Available online: http://www.uml4pf.org (accessed on 24 May 2016).

19. Papyrus. Available online: https://eclipse.org/papyrus/ (accessed on 24 May 2016).

20. Eclipse IDE. Available online: http://www.eclipse.org (accessed on 24 May 2016).

21. Epsilon Platform. Available online: http://www.eclipse.org/epsilon (accessed on 24 May 2016).

22. EMF-Based Models. Available online: http://www.eclipse.org/modeling/emf/ (accessed on 24 May 2016).

23. GMF-Based Models. Available online: http://www.eclipse.org/modeling/gmp/ (accessed on 24 May 2016).

24. Deng, M.; Wuyts, K.; Scandariato, R.; Preneel, B.; Joosen, W. A privacy threat analysis framework: Supporting the elicitation and fulfillment of privacy requirements. *Requir. Eng.* **2011**, *16*, 3–32.

25. Howard, M.; Lipner, S. *The Security Development Lifecycle*; Microsoft Press: Redmond, WA, USA, 2006.

26. Kalloniatis, C.; Kavakli, E.; Gritzalis, S. Addressing privacy requirements in system design: The PriS method. *Requir. Eng.* **2008**, *13*, 241–255.

27. Liu, L.; Yu, E.; Mylopoulos, J. Security and Privacy Requirements Analysis within a Social Setting. In Proceedings of the 11th IEEE International Conference on Requirements Engineering, Monterey Bay, CA, USA, 8–12 September 2003; pp. 151–161.

28. Yu, E. Towards Modeling and Reasoning Support for Early-Phase Requirements Engineering. In Proceedings of the 3rd IEEE International Symposium on Requirements Engineering, Annapolis, MD, USA, 6–10 January 1997.

29. Omoronyia, I.; Cavallaro, L.; Salehie, M.; Pasquale, L.; Nuseibeh, B. Engineering Adaptive Privacy: On the Role of Privacy Awareness Requirements. In Proceedings of the 2013 International Conference on Software Engineering, ICSE '13, San Francisco, CA, USA, 18–26 May 2013.

30. Oetzel, M.; Spiekermann, S. A systematic methodology for privacy impact assessments: A design science approach. *Eur. J. Inf. Syst.* **2014**, *23*, 126–150.

31. Antón, A.I.; Earp, J.B. A requirements taxonomy for reducing Web site privacy vulnerabilities. *Requir. Eng.* **2004**, *9*, 169–185.

32. Hoepman, J. Privacy Design Strategies (Extended Abstract). In Proceedings of the 29th IFIP TC 11 International Conference on ICT Systems Security and Privacy Protection, Marrakech, Morocco, 2–4 June 2014.

Permissions

All chapters in this book were first published in Information, by MDPI; hereby published with permission under the Creative Commons Attribution License or equivalent. Every chapter published in this book has been scrutinized by our experts. Their significance has been extensively debated. The topics covered herein carry significant findings which will fuel the growth of the discipline. They may even be implemented as practical applications or may be referred to as a beginning point for another development.

The contributors of this book come from diverse backgrounds, making this book a truly international effort. This book will bring forth new frontiers with its revolutionizing research information and detailed analysis of the nascent developments around the world.

We would like to thank all the contributing authors for lending their expertise to make the book truly unique. They have played a crucial role in the development of this book. Without their invaluable contributions this book wouldn't have been possible. They have made vital efforts to compile up to date information on the varied aspects of this subject to make this book a valuable addition to the collection of many professionals and students.

This book was conceptualized with the vision of imparting up-to-date information and advanced data in this field. To ensure the same, a matchless editorial board was set up. Every individual on the board went through rigorous rounds of assessment to prove their worth. After which they invested a large part of their time researching and compiling the most relevant data for our readers.

The editorial board has been involved in producing this book since its inception. They have spent rigorous hours researching and exploring the diverse topics which have resulted in the successful publishing of this book. They have passed on their knowledge of decades through this book. To expedite this challenging task, the publisher supported the team at every step. A small team of assistant editors was also appointed to further simplify the editing procedure and attain best results for the readers.

Apart from the editorial board, the designing team has also invested a significant amount of their time in understanding the subject and creating the most relevant covers. They scrutinized every image to scout for the most suitable representation of the subject and create an appropriate cover for the book.

The publishing team has been an ardent support to the editorial, designing and production team. Their endless efforts to recruit the best for this project, has resulted in the accomplishment of this book. They are a veteran in the field of academics and their pool of knowledge is as vast as their experience in printing. Their expertise and guidance has proved useful at every step. Their uncompromising quality standards have made this book an exceptional effort. Their encouragement from time to time has been an inspiration for everyone.

The publisher and the editorial board hope that this book will prove to be a valuable piece of knowledge for researchers, students, practitioners and scholars across the globe.

List of Contributors

Ron Cottam and Roger Vounckx
The Living Systems Project, Department of Electronics and Informatics, Vrije Universiteit Brussel (VUB), Pleinlaan 2, Brussels B-1050, Belgium

Willy Ranson
Interuniversity Micro Electronics Center (IMEC) vzw, Kapeldreef 75, Leuven B-8001, Belgium

Jie Liu and Jinglei Liu
School of Computer and Control Engineering, Yantai University, Yantai 264005, China

Yuebo Zha, Wei Pu, Gao Chen, Yulin Huang and Jianyu Yang
School of Electronic Engineering, University of Electronic Science and Technology of China, 2006 Xiyuan Road, GaoxinWestern District, Chengdu 611731, China

Marcin J. Schroeder
Akita International University, Akita, Japan/193-2 Okutsubakidai, Yuwa, Akita-shi, 010-1211 Akita, Japan

Jiaxi Wang
School of Traffic and Transportation, Beijing Jiaotong University, Beijing 100044, China

Yan Sun and Maoxiang Lang
School of Traffic and Transportation, Beijing Jiaotong University, Beijing 100044, China
MOE Key Laboratory for Urban Transportation Complex Systems Theory and Technology, Beijing Jiaotong University, Beijing 100044, China

Shahab Asoodeh, Mario Diaz, Fady Alajaji and Tamás Linder
Department of Mathematics and Statistics, Queen's University, Kingston, Canada

Qiuming Liu, Yong Luo and Yun Ling
Jiangxi University of Science and Technology, 1180 Shuanggang Road, Nanchang 330013, China

Jun Zheng
School of Science, Zhejiang A&F University, 88 Huancheng Road, Lin'An City, Hangzhou 311300, China

Marko Angjelichinoski, Čedomir Stefanović and Petar Popovski
Department of Electronic Systems, Aalborg University, Aalborg 9220, Denmark

Frede Blaabjerg
Department of Energy Technology, Aalborg University, Aalborg 9220, Denmark

Xiaoling Tao
Key Laboratory of Cognitive Radio and Information Processing, Guilin University of Electronic Technology, Guilin 541004, China
Guangxi Colleges and Universities Key Laboratory of Cloud Computing and Complex Systems, Guilin University of Electronic Technology, Guilin 541004, China

Deyan Kong
Key Laboratory of Cognitive Radio and Information Processing, Guilin University of Electronic Technology, Guilin 541004, China

Yi Wei
Guangxi Colleges and Universities Key Laboratory of Cloud Computing and Complex Systems, Guilin University of Electronic Technology, Guilin 541004, China

Yong Wang
Guangxi Colleges and Universities Key Laboratory of Cloud Computing and Complex Systems, Guilin University of Electronic Technology, Guilin 541004, China

Guangxi Key Laboratory of Trusted Software, Guilin University of Electronic Technology, Guilin 541004, China

Ming Li and Mengyue Yuan
School of Business Administration, China University of Petroleum, Beijing 102249, China

Rafael F. Schaefer
Information Theory and Applications Chair, Technische Universität Berlin, 10587 Berlin, Germany

Holger Boche
Institute of Theoretical Information Technology, Technische Universität München, 80333 Munich, Germany

H. Vincent Poor
Department of Electrical Engineering, Princeton University, Princeton, NJ 08544, USA

Melinda Heinz
Department of Psychology, Upper Iowa University, Fayette, IA 52142, USA

Jinmyoung Cho
Baylor Scott & White Health, Temple, TX 76508, USA

Norene Kelly, Peter Martin, Wen-Hua Hsieh and Joan Blaser
Department of Human Development and Family Studies, Iowa State University, Ames, IA 50011, USA

Johnny Wong
Department of Computer Science, Iowa State University, Ames, IA 50011, USA

Warren Franke
Department of Kinesiology, Iowa State University, Ames, IA 50011, USA

Rene Meis and Maritta Heisel
paluno—The Ruhr Institute for Software Technology, University of Duisburg-Essen, Duisburg 47057, Germany

Index

Printed in the USA
CPSIA information can be obtained
at www.ICGtesting.com
JSHW051358221024
72173JS00006B/1312